ENGLISH ANCESTRAL NAMES

J. R. Dolan

ENGLISH ANCESTRAL NAMES

The Evolution of the Surname
from Medieval Occupations

Clarkson N. Potter, Inc./Publisher   NEW YORK
DISTRIBUTED BY CROWN PUBLISHERS, INC.

With deepfelt gratitude to my wife
Betty
For her great patience
And much practical help
In the preparation of this book.

Printed in the United States of America
Library of Congress Catalog Card Number: 73–139349
Published simultaneously in Canada by
General Publishing Company Limited.
Inquiries should be addressed to Clarkson N. Potter, Inc.,
419 Park Avenue South, New York, N. Y., 10016.
First Edition.

Designed by Margery Kronengold

Acknowledgments

To put together a study as complicated as this has had to be requires a really vast amount of help from friends, associates, and institutions. This work extended over a period of more than three years, and I feel enormously grateful to all of them, for their patience has never wavered; their enthusiasm has never dampened. I particularly want to thank the following:

Smithsonian Institution in the person of Doctor P. W. Bishop, Curator, Division of Manufacturing, and his staff; the Metropolitan Museum of Art, particularly Mr. Nickel, Curator of Arms and Armor; the British Museum; the Sheffield City Museum; the National Geographic Society; the Public Libraries of Daytona Beach, Florida, whose staffs have been very helpful and whose Interlibrary Lending Service has been of much practical help; my close personal friends Win Shiras and Phil Shulins for the almost continuous use of their personal libraries; and finally the authors of all the books listed in the bibliography, whose help has been prodigious.

Contents

Foreword

This book serves a double purpose, for when you have looked up your name among the 5,000 or so that Mr. Dolan has investigated, you may spend many a happy hour browsing among the ancient craftsmen. In fact, I am not sure that, as a library tool or as a means of settling arguments, the book's usefulness will not lie in the fact that it classifies most of the activities of the pre-industrial era in the English scene. Not many of those trades flourish today except in a form that would not be recognizable by those who first acquired the name, but those who are the present-day representatives of the early economies may well be proud of their ancestry—prouder, possibly, than those whose genealogy, however accurately assembled, leaves them with a minimum of information about the occupations of their forebears. Few genealogists, indeed, can take you back to the first bearer of your family name.

Mr. Dolan's research has been a formidable achievement. If he has been obliged, from time to time, to indulge in speculation, his thinking has been sound and his solutions reasonable. He is to be envied, too, for the fun he must have had in following his clues, and congratulated for the extent of his collection. He should be thanked, too, for the surprises he will give many unsuspecting "craftsmen."

P. W. Bishop, Curator
Division of Manufacturing
National Museum of History
and Technology
Washington, D.C.

Introduction

Until quite recently tracing the origin of family names seems to
have been largely a scholarly pursuit if we can judge by the number of
excellent studies published over the past century. More and more, however,
the man in the street is showing an increasingly active interest in surnames—and not just his own. It is in the hope of contributing something
to his quest that I have directed my efforts.

Very recently excellent studies have been published dealing with the
numerical and geographical distribution of English surnames. These are
very interesting and useful to anyone with even a passing interest in the
subject, but they necessarily have to cover the whole broad field of names
—a very big order indeed.

I felt that if somehow I could draw a circle around just one of the
recognized classifications I might be able to treat it in some depth and
still avoid both the excessive use of foreign words unfamiliar to the
average man as well as the hundreds of abbreviations more scholarly
writers are compelled to use.

All this pointed directly at the surnames that clearly originated in the
occupations of our medieval ancestors. Occupational names were inclined
to be automatic and spontaneous—a man was called a baker or a miller
or a weaver because it was plainly evident that he followed that trade.
Also they were more apt to survive in a family longer than those originating from other sources—a place name would lose its meaning if the
man moved his home, and a nickname might not fit the son of the man it

was first given to, but the man with a shop had a tangible thing to leave to his son. If I could collect today's occupational surnames and determine just which medieval trade the original bearer of the name must have followed, I might have something useful. This would mean listing such different-sounding names as Bowles, Potts, Crocker, Mugger, Beakerman, and Cupper together because they were all Potters. This might be of immediate and lasting interest to many people throughout the English-speaking world.

CHAPTER 1

The Rise of the Surname

Just when and in what circumstances did we acquire the family names we have today? We haven't always had them.

In biblical times it was Peter, James, and John—there was no mention of any family name. Joseph of Arimathea had no last name; Arimathea was just the name of the city from which he came. It was the same with Saul of Tarsus, who later changed his name to Paul. Similarly the writers of the gospels, Matthew, Mark, Luke, and John, are known only by their first names.

Yet today, nearly two thousand years later, civilized people in most parts of the world have family names, names they were born with (or, for married women, names their husbands were born with) and that will automatically pass from father to child. When did this change take place? And, more importantly, *how* and *why* did the change come about?

Most of us know something about our immediate ancestors, perhaps as far back as three or four generations, but if we try to follow the ancestral trail much farther, we run into a dead end. The family name disappears from the records, and one finds only first names.

If, for example, your name is COOPER, William COOPER, you can trace the COOPER family back to the time when the first of that name arrived on our shores. And you may be able to trace that name COOPER back many more generations, if your patience and your bankroll hold out, because the English, as a people, have always been such painstaking record-keepers. It will take a lot of doing, to be sure, but as long as there is that name COOPER to look for in the musty old tax rolls, you can keep on digging till you find yourself far back in the Middle Ages.

But sooner or later something happens—the name COOPER disappears. You can thumb through every record in England without finding any more COOPERS. Just where you think you should be able to locate more of them, there may be a CUVER, a KITTWRIGHT, a HOOPER, or even a PAYLOR, but not one more COOPER. All is not lost, however, because each and every one of these names (and many more) were Coopers. The names have become disguised over the centuries and one may not be able to recognize their ancient medieval origin. The earliest record of the name is Robert Le Cupere in 1176 but, over several generations, the name went through numerous changes in different parts of the island. Some of these variations survived, others did not. COWPER is an example of one that is still with us.

The question of *when* our ancestors began to feel that having merely a first name was not enough is just a matter of dates, but unless we know something of the conditions and circumstances, the *hows* and the *whys* that brought this about, we are going to miss most of the fun. And to call it fun is no exaggeration, because our names grew naturally out of the daily lives of our forebears; they tell us how a man earned his living, what kind of food he ate, what he did for amusement, what kind of clothes he wore, and frequently even his address in the village.

Our names were not acquired through a law. No parliament or royal edict ever ordered the people of medieval England to assume a name, yet they did just that in such overwhelming numbers that by about 1350 nearly everyone in Great Britain had one. An individual might change his name once or twice, but he had a family name, as did all of his friends, and he meant to hold on to it.

THE ANGLO-SAXON WAY

Previous to the eleventh century, when the Normans were to pour into Britain and change just about everything, the island was dominated by a mixture of Germanic stock—the Anglo-Saxons from the Continent and the Danes or Norsemen from Scandinavia.

For long centuries they considered a man's name to be his very personal property, something that should belong to him as exclusively as his head or his hands. When a child arrived in an Anglo-Saxon family, a detailed search for a name was begun almost immediately. It had to be absolutely original, a name completely different from any other in the village, and furthermore, a name that no ancestor had ever used. (This is, of course, the exact opposite of what is often done today, when the given name of either a living relative or an ancestor is deliberately selected for the precise purpose of keeping the name in the family.) An Anglo-Saxon family would dig back into the old sagas of the family and the tribe to make sure that the name being considered had not been preempted by some long-gone ancestor, and once satisfied on this point, there was still another criterion. The name selected should be one that would inspire the child in his growing-up years. The name of a weapon, for example, might serve to make him become expert in its use. Hence, the name *Sweord* might be chosen—that meant "sword"—and if it had been used before, the word for "good" or "sharp" or any other acceptable adjective could be added to it. If nobility of character was more important to the parents than the more common warlike attributes, *aethel,* Anglo-Saxon for "noble," and *sunu,* the word for "son," might be combined. It could be *Sunuaethel* or *Aethelsunu*—each one meant "Noble-son."

Sooner or later, a name satisfactory to the parents would be decided upon and the uncomprehending youngster would be so named. Needless to say, modern students of Old English (as the Anglo-Saxon language is also called) almost give up in despair at the infinite variety of names this system produced. And not a single one of them could possibly be classified as a family name.

THE NORMAN INVASION

Late in the eleventh century, a radical change was about to take place. It would not be immediate; far from it, a full two hundred and fifty years would be needed before having a family name ceased to be a novelty. It would come about by a succession of political and economic events that could hardly have had any other result.

Just why it took two hundred and fifty years to bring about a change that was so obviously advantageous and yet could be effected without cost to anyone is hard to understand today, when people are accustomed to overnight changes almost as radical.

If we consider twenty-five years a generation, about ten generations had to come and go before the change was complete—a very long time for a whole people to be in a state of flux. But consider the almost total lack of communications of the period. One was born in a tiny village consisting of two or three dozen families, and one lived one's entire life right there. Politically, economically, and even socially, a man was tied as firmly to that village as though he were chained to a post. No one even had a desire to go to the village only ten miles away, because it could not offer anything new or interesting, and the people there were all foreigners anyway.

Try to imagine it—absolutely no media of any kind as we know them. It's almost impossible to realize what life must have been like. But, with conditions like this everywhere, it is at least possible to begin to understand how for many generations a man could live a whole lifetime without even hearing about a new idea.

Of course, in the big city of London, with its more than ten thousand people, things would be a bit different. Shopkeepers and skilled craftsmen might move around town now and then and, London being a seaport, one would undoubtedly hear something of what was going on in the rest of the world.

If we have to pick out one historical personage responsible for the onset of surnames, it would have to be Duke William of Normandy. However, I am sure the duke went to his grave without having the slightest idea that future generations would credit him as an innovator, particularly in the matter of surnames.

William had a shadowy claim to the throne of England and, in 1066, organized an army of his fellow Normans, sailed across the channel to England, and conquered the Anglo-Saxons under King Harold. In the course of the next few years, his forces subdued the whole of England. The English had a weak and poorly organized form of feudalism at the time. William instituted many reforms, and they were rigid and so well enforced that modern England is still strongly influenced by them.

At the time of the Norman Conquest in 1066, England was a land of scattered villages and hamlets, with London its largest city. In area about the size of Michigan, it was divided into shires more or less corresponding to modern counties. An earl who was appointed directly by the king presided over each shire or over a group of shires. In his own shire, an earl's power was practically absolute. He collected the taxes, dispensed what he considered justice, and appointed his assistants.

The shire was subdivided into a great many units varying in size from a few acres to many square miles. Each unit was known as a manor, and the lord of the manor lived in a more or less fortified wooden house on the property. The manor house of that period usually consisted of one big room, or hall, in which the lord and his family ate their meals on a dais at one end, while the servants ate at ground-level at the other; the lord and his lady had a small room for sleeping while the servants rolled up in blankets on the floor. Meals were cooked on a great flat slab of stone somewhere in the large dining hall. The smoke from the open fire escaped as best it could through the many cracks and accidental openings throughout the structure.

The lord of the manor was known by various titles in different sections of Anglo-Saxon England: sometimes he was called the constable, while in other areas he would be the bailey, or the stewart, and again he would have the title of sheriff, although this was frequently reserved for the official immediately under the earl.

William the Conqueror was a practical man and he realized very quickly that merely wearing the crown of England wouldn't mean very much if he did not have definite control over the shires and their subdivisions. Consequently, just as soon as the coronation was over, he split up his army into several powerful units and began a systematic working over of the whole island. Descending on one of the great Saxon earls, the king would order the earl to swear fealty to him. If the Saxon acceded to the demand, he and his family might be allowed to pack a few things of a personal nature before they were turned loose on the countryside to wander about hopelessly and eventually to fall in the feudal scale far below what they had been accustomed to.

If the Saxon refused submission to William, he was banished, or worse, with scant ceremony, but in either event the entire estate, large or small, was handed over to one of the king's loyal followers. But this did not mean a transfer of ownership—the king was far too canny for that; the new holder simply became a proprietor. Under Norman feudalism, the king owned everything, and he could therefore parcel it out as he pleased. The new Norman lord had to obey each and every command of the king without question. He had to supply the king with a definite number of fully equipped soldiers any time the king snapped his royal fingers. And, needless to say, the new lord would also have the privilege of contributing frequently to the royal treasury.

If the manor house happened to have a strategic position on top of a hill or alongside a river, the new lord would be ordered to tear down the old place and build anew with stone. This meant a castle, and many of the castles built at this time were to give future kings a lot of trouble; they were built so strongly that the barons were able to defy even the king's forces.

The men who came over with William were naturally given the choicest pieces of real estate as a suitable reward for their superior contributions to the Conquest. And understandably, these favored Normans were not averse to letting their new neighbors know where they stood with King William. An obvious way to do this, and in a permanent fashion, was to tie one's old Norman given name to the name of the castle one had held in Normandy. Thus, one might have been known as John or Robert or Gilbert in Normandy, but now, with the name of one's Norman castle added, one became John de Montague or Robert de Sackville. The preposition *de* might be dropped, or not, but the real point is that here at last was a name made up of an honest-to-goodness first and last element. The records are not clear enough to identify precisely the earliest surnames, but like circumstances undoubtedly did bring similar names about.

Not all of William's noble followers had castles back in Normandy; some of them were a step or two lower in the feudal scale, but they were faced with the same problem of establishing themselves in their new English possessions. With no great castle in Normandy whose name they could appropriate, they usually assumed the name of the village from which they came. This served very well, for after all, how many people in the England of that period knew whether Neuville or Neville was an important place in France or just a wide place in the road? It sounded Norman, and that was all that counted at the time.

This should not give the impression that all of William's followers were large landholders—this was not true at all. The great majority were more or less penniless young men open to any venture that held promise of substantial return. Each had a horse and a makeshift suit of armor and a burning ambition. The king had plenty of land with which to reward everybody and he passed it out as fast as he took it in. The landless adventurer of 1066 might well find himself a baron in England before the year was out. Adopt the name of the manor given, and he was all set. Sir Hugh de Melville, or Robert de Summerfield or Carrington or Morton—who cared? He was one of the landed gentry.

THE ENGLISH ECONOMY

Long before all the nobles and near-nobles were settled in their new lands, King William started something that clearly proved his farseeing good judgment. He seems to have realized that England's whole economy was badly in need of drastic reform. All too frequently, he found whole areas of England where everybody was in the same business: raising food.

And these people were raising just enough to fill their own needs, with nothing left over that could be exchanged for the simple tools and equipment that even a peasant needed to live.

At least one modern economist has expressed it by saying, "No use having your neighbor do your washing if you have to pay him by doing his." Somebody had to manufacture needed goods that could be readily exchanged for the food he needed. Although there were some craftsmen at the time William took over, generally a peasant had to make his own tools as well as his own clothing. It was a hopeless task, particularly when the peasant had to spend up to three days out of every week taking care of his lord's crops.

So the word went back to Normandy, offering inducements to skilled craftsmen to migrate across the channel. The records show that many thousands of them did just that. With all respect to the Anglo-Saxons of that period, the Norman craftsmen were more advanced than the English in a number of areas. Norman weavers could turn out a dozen types of fine fabrics as compared to the rough burl of the English. Norman smiths had developed the skill of making arms and armor as well as a large variety of tools and appliances: a skill that was beyond the ability of the English at that early date.

So in poured the Norman craftsmen—potters, coopers, tanners, weavers, and dyers, and the whole tribe of smiths. The craft of smithing became so large that, at this very time, it was already breaking up into groups of specialists. In England, they spread out all over the land. There was hardly a town that did not have shops set up along a village street where before only the cottage of a farmer existed. These men turned out goods and exchanged them for the food the farmer raised, producing a balance of economy that is still the backbone of any prosperity. While food production continued to be the principal occupation, it is estimated that within a couple of generations after the Conquest, about 40 percent of the population was engaged in some trade or occupation other than farming. This phenomenal rise in skilled labor was to have a drastic effect on the development of surnames.

The systematic taking over of manors and even whole shires by the Norman nobles went on, year after year, from 1066 until 1086, when the aging king began to wonder just where he stood. How much had he given away and exactly to whom? What was the actual value of each of the manors he had passed out so generously, and was he collecting all the taxes to which he was entitled? What he wanted was an inventory, or better yet, a census.

DOMESDAY BOOK

A small army of clerks (meaning anybody who could write) was organized and sent throughout the land to call on every manor-holder or
member of the gentry, reappraise the property, and set this appraisal in
the big book. Two huge volumes, hand-lettered on vellum, resulted and
are still preserved in England. They are faded and worn and thumb-
marked and torn by the thousands of researchers who have scanned their
pages through the nine centuries that have elapsed since they were written. Some of the pages are still readable, however, if one has plenty of
patience and good eyesight.

This ancient record is unique in the whole field of record-keeping. Not
only was it the first of its kind, but the most thorough census by far that
was to be taken by any nation until the opening of the nineteenth century in the United States.[1]

Virtually all the names in Domesday are clearly Norman and just as
clearly refer to nobles or at least gentry, who were the only people at the
time with any taxable property. Here are a few names from this old
record:

One was Geoffrey de Mandeville, who came from Mandeville in France,
of course. In modern times, the name changed to MANVILL. There
were many more names of this type, but one that is different and very interesting is Henry de Ferrers. *Ferrers* is not the name of a community in
Normandy at all; it is the old French word meaning "iron," and could refer to an ironworker or, for that matter, a smith. What would an ironworker be doing in the Domesday Book? We shall never know, but it is
safe to assume that he must have done something outstanding in the way
of his trade to have had to pay a tax in 1086.

Other names in Domesday are Ralph de Courci and Robert de Montfort. Simon de Montfort, undoubtedly a descendant of Robert, later made
a place in history. He was the earl of Leicester and the brother-in-law
of Henry III, who led a revolt of the barons in 1258, now considered one

---

[1] Robert S. Hoyt in his *Europe in the Middle Ages* reproduces an entry from Domesday Book. I'll put it into modern English to make it easier to read.

Land of the King   In Woking Hundred
In Guildford King William has seventy-five houses in which one hundred and
seventy-five dwell. In the time of King Edward it rendered eighteen pounds and three
pence. Now it is valued at thirty pounds and nevertheless it renders *thirty-two
pounds.*
The hike in the tax rate indicated does not need modernizing—it is still common
practice.

of the first steps toward the formation of a parliament. Hugh de Monceaux is unusual because records a century later show the name changed to HURSTMONCEAUX. *Hurst* is an Anglo-Saxon word meaning "woods" or "forest," so this may indicate that the Monceaux family integrated with the lowly Saxons. At any rate, the Hurstmonceaux family built a very solid castle close to where the Normans landed and won their battle, and the family retained possession of it until 1708—more than six hundred years. According to L. Valentine in his *Picturesque England,* the family remodeled the place in 1440.

The names *Neville* and *Neuville* appear several times in Domesday and became famous in the years following the Conquest. In the fifteenth century Richard Neville was earl of Warwick and known as "the Kingmaker." He was killed in 1471, when the Lancastrian cause finally collapsed. Since both names simply meant "new town" and soon became NEWTON, we can see the effect that time has on many words. Another such is *Beauchamp,* which in modern times is usually BEECHAM. *D'Aubigny* appears in Domesday; before long, it became DAUBENY, and then DABNEY and even DOBNEY. The old Norman name *Mortain* became plain MORTON, and so on.

Domesday gave us many of our modern names, but unless one happens to be something of a linguist, one may not be able to recognize the relationship to their modern forms. Indeed, your name may have come over with the Normans, and L. C. Lloyd's *Anglo-Norman Families* is a good place to check.

Most of the names in Domesday did eventually become surnames, but one should bear in mind that the necessity of having a family name at all was still very new at that time; it would take two or three generations of continuous use before such names were generally accepted as family names.

CHAPTER 2

Classification of Surnames

Modern scholars classify everything these days. Nothing seems to escape the attention of the researchers; even our family names that have been such a vital part of our civilization for nearly a thousand years are picked up and examined in the minutest detail and finally placed, at least tentatively, in categories. While this is a definite help to anyone interested in the subject, it should not be taken too seriously, as many names seem to fit into two and even three classifications and there are a few that are hard to fit into any. But for what it is worth, the accepted classifications are as follows: Names that refer to a place or locality—I prefer calling them *address* names; names that show *relationship*; names that came from *nicknames*; names from the *occupation* or the *status* of the individual.

ADDRESS NAMES

The Norman dukes and barons living on their newly acquired estates in England had names belonging in the *address* classification, whether it was the name of the castle they came from in Normandy, the Norman village they had lived in, or the Anglo-Saxon manor house that had been given them.

But for each one of these nobles, there were hundreds of lowly peasants, farmers, tradesmen, and mechanics who were about to acquire family names as well. In any small village, there might be two or three Johns and almost certainly five or six Williams—what better way to please the new king than to adopt his name? This created new problems. The old Anglo-Saxon custom on names was to give a child an absolutely new name, without a duplicate anywhere. This resulted in thousands of almost unpronounceable names, but it did distinguish every individual. With a growing number of Johns and Williams, Roberts and Walters, another way of distinguishing them had to be devised.

No one pretends to know exactly when or precisely in what village it may have started, but on some rare occasion when one of the inhabitants had to be singled out for a moment, it may have been remembered that he lived near one of the town gates and he was referred to as "William atta gate." The word *atta* was an Anglo-Saxon word meaning "at" or "near." And so this man's accidental proximity to the gate served to distinguish him from all the other Williams in town. "William atta gate" might continue to be applied to that man for months or even years, particularly if he had little or no occasion to make use of it. But in the course of time and as the name was used more, the preposition might be dropped entirely, making it William GATE or GATES, or a part of the atta might be retained, making it William ATGATE or ADGATE.

In other villages, the identical situation would occur, only this time the name might come out GATESBY ("by the gate") or GATELY or maybe another GATES. Now and then an unsuspecting but hardworking peasant might have his humble cottage not only close by a gate but also near enough to an apple tree so that either the tree or the gate could be made to describe where he lived. In this case, the result might be the delightful name of APPLEGATE.

If nearness to a gate proved to be convenient in distinguishing one Walter from another, other prominent landmarks could do the same for others, and there might be POND and MARSH, HILL and HILL-MANN, BROOKS, FORD, and RIVERS. And surely the man living near the village well would be quickly associated with it by being called WELLS or WELLMAN or even ATWATER. The village church was always a prominent landmark, and any man living close by could expect to be called CHURCH or GRAVES or even TOWER.

Sooner or later a man living near the castle, at least near enough so that if you located the castle you would see his cottage, would be tagged CASTLE or maybe CASTLEBY. If he was employed in the castle in some minor capacity, he might become known as CASTLEMAN. The manor house was a castle if it was built of stone, but if it was one of the older Saxon structures built of wood, it was a hall; that became a name, too.

Not one of these names, however, was immediately accepted as a name by anyone. They were simply convenient ways of distinguishing one man from another by indicating where he lived. One day's Walter Castleman might be called Walter le Cook or Walter le Kitchener another day, if someone heard that he was employed in the kitchen of the castle. A name had to stick for a long period and frequently be accepted by a man's children before it could be considered a real surname.

Of the more than one hundred thousand family names of English origin in use around the world today, almost half were originally applied to describe where a man lived. They became genuine surnames only when time and circumstances permitted a descriptive word to stick.

RELATIONSHIP NAMES

All during the period when address names were being applied to men, other names were being created by an entirely different process. I refer, of course, to the names that clearly indicate relationship.

Numerically, this class is much smaller than that of address names, but it contains a very great many of the most popular names in the English-speaking world today.

Just as in the address class, the relationship names originally served the convenience of the moment without the slightest thought of permanence. It is easy to visualize a situation such as must have occurred thousands of times during the two hundred and fifty years in which our family names were being formed. Two men meet casually and stop to chat for a moment. One of them wants to inquire about the health of the son of a mutual friend, John. At the moment he can't recall the name of the boy, so he calls him "John's son." A repetition of this scene might be enough to fix the name Johnson upon the boy for life. Indeed, this must have been an everyday and every-village occurrence because the name JOHN-SON, according to C. M. Matthews in her *English Surnames* (1966), is today the third most popular name in New York, while in Atlanta it is second, and in Chicago, first.

The oldest written record of this name is in 1287, but it was surely a conversational commonplace long before then. And a name that has been used by so many people over so many years has had to stand some rough and, at times, downright careless treatment. If this needs any proof, look at a few of the ways the name is spelled around the world: JONSON, JOINSON, JOHNSTON, JOYNSON, JOHNSTONE, and many others. The names JOHNSON and JONES have the same original meaning. As we have seen, the name JOHNSON was at first just a conversational convenience when one wanted to refer to the son of a man named John. JONES was originally just plain John (a first name), but in the course of time, the *h* was dropped because it served no purpose, and apostrophe-*s* was added at the end of the word to take the place of the word *son*. Putting in the apostrophe was too much trouble and so it was dropped, leaving JONES. And the very same thing happened to a large number of other names, for the same reason. The first name Andrew gave ANDREWSON. Soon after, the *-son* was dropped, leaving in its place what was, in effect, an apostrophe-*s*, and, sure enough, the apostrophe disappeared and the name became what it is now, ANDREWS. Phillip became PHILLIPS by the same process and Hugh became HUGHES. The *-son* ending on a name supposedly indicates it is of Scandinavian origin. And that type of name is indeed more common in the northern part of England where in the early centuries Scandinavian influence was greatest, but today's experts are inclined to doubt that it gave us any really large number of *son* names. The reason they give is the John-Johnson-Jones process just described. William, Edward, Walter, and many similar names are not considered Scandinavian at all, and when one adds *s* to any of them to take the place of *son*, the name is no more Scandinavian than it was before.

Many historians are rough on William the Conqueror, and not without cause, but we have to thank him for at least one good thing he did for all of us—he buried most of those almost unpronounceable Saxon names and gave us the name William. The Anglo-Saxon and Celtic races had dominated the island for many years before the arrival of the Conqueror and had been Christian for several centuries. As such they were thoroughly familiar with the Bible and all the biblical names in it, through the painstaking work of the monks in the monasteries, *but they did not name their children after the saints*—probably out of an exaggerated respect for the saints—until the arrival of William the Conqueror. Then, not only were saints' names more prevalent but the name of William itself became the most popular given name in every town and village in the land. And from this came WILLIAMSON, soon shortened to WILLIAMS, then WILSON, shortened to WILLS and WILLIS, then WILKINSON and WILKINS, WILKIE, WILLETT, and many others, all of them probably meant to curry favor with the king, but each and every one of them relationship names.

The modern nickname for William is, of course, Bill, but this did not become popular until long after people had forgotten why they were still naming their children William. Less than a century after the Conqueror had died, the name John, together with a host of derivatives, had become just about as popular as William. Since no king named John was to reign until the end of the twelfth century, these Johns probably have to be credited to the well-known saint.

NICKNAMES

Most people think the custom of giving nicknames is strictly a modern occurrence, but this is not true at all. Nicknames have been used for centuries and the records that have come down to us are quite numerous and very convincing that nicknames were even more popular in the Middle Ages than they are now. They are of special interest here because, more than any other type of name, they give us a real glimpse into the lives of the common people at a time when the daily grind of any man, excepting the nobility, must have been dreary and monotonous indeed.

His workday was long and arduous; his food would be considered unpalatable today; he had absolutely nothing to read (even if he were able to); and he seldom traveled more than a day's walk from the village in which he was born. Yet the nicknames he produced indicate he must have had an abundance of good humor. Nicknames were never the product of serious thought or long consideration—they were spontaneous exclamations on the spur of the moment.

Take, for example, the name STANLEY, well known today in the fields of African exploration and, in this country, tool manufacturing. It's easy to imagine how it might have come about. In some nameless village in the thirteenth century, two peasants are enjoying a pint of ale in the tavern when a mutual friend walks in. The newcomer walks with just a bit more natural dignity than the usual man of his class; noting this, one of his friends remarks, "Well, here comes old *stan-lea*. Wouldn't you think he was lord of the manor?" *Stan* was the old Anglo-Saxon word for "stone" and *lea* meant "field" or "meadow," so the friends were simply having a laugh out of this newcomer's misfortune; he owned a stony field where it was more than ordinarily difficult to raise any kind of crops. Stanley is not a nickname today, but it definitely was back in the days of its origin.

Or take the name KING, easily one of the more common names wherever English is spoken. Today's families with that name are not descended from royalty, however. It's true enough that in the naming period many kings did have far more children than can legitimately be accounted for, but it is beyond imagining that any reigning king would allow illegitimate children to grow up as potential claimants for the crown. No, the name KING was definitely a nickname that in all probability came from the numerous pageants and amateur theatrical performances the peasants of that day loved to take part in all over England. A man might play the role of a king so well that he would be asked again and again to repeat his performance. Soon he would be dubbed "King" by his friends and it might stick. Exactly the same thing could happen with all the titles of royalty and nobility—queen, prince, duke, baron, lord (in Scotland it would be laird), and all the rest.

The clergy of the Middle Ages, such as the pope, bishop, rector, and deacon, were also frequently represented in the pageants of the peasants and craftsmen over a period of centuries. The clergy did not marry and therefore did not have families, so the old names from their titles probably came from the simple play-acting of medieval entertainers. There are, however, some additional possible origins of these clerical names that will be discussed in chapter 24.

There are many nicknames that must have been applied initially because of some physical characteristic of an individual. If a peasant had a friend who was unusually large, he might call him SMALL or SMALLEY, or if he were bald, might say, "Hello, CURLEY." If a young fellow could run unusually fast, sooner or later he would be dubbed SWIFT or LIGHTFOOTE or even HARE or TROTTER, while another who was notably slow of foot would be called POKEY or OXON or maybe AMBLER or HOBBLE.

Even the Conqueror's own son William, who inherited the throne, was far better known in his day by the nickname Rufus, from his red hair. The name may not have been mentioned in the presence of the king, but it was his everyday name among the people.

Thousands of our most respected names today had their origin in the momentary effort of some long-forgotten peasant or mechanic to brighten up his day with a bit of rustic humor.

CHAPTER **3**

Occupational Surnames

Occupational names, names either assumed by or bestowed on our ancestors because of the work that they did, are generally names that stayed with the individual to a much greater extent than the three previous classes discussed. A tanner or a cooper had to have a high degree of skill as well as a shop stocked with special tools, both of which he would hope to pass on to his son.

To classify the entire five thousand names that follow as "occupational" may not be strictly accurate, as so many of them could also be classified as place names, relationship names, or nicknames. KNIGHT certainly was not an occupational name in the sense that a man so named earned his living by being one, but his status and therefore his movements and actions were determined by it, and so all such names will be treated as though they were truly occupational.

It is difficult for me now to look back through the years and recall when I first became interested in the origin of names, but I do remember reading in some now forgotten book that a man who wove cloth on a loom in the England of the twelfth century was called a webber. In the same paragraph the same man was called a weaver, and before I had turned the page, he was called a draper and still later a webster. Was it possible that one trade could have so many different names? It was easy enough to imagine a man being addressed by the name of his trade in circumstances where his real name was unknown at the moment, but how does one explain so many different names for the same trade? How can a man operating one single loom be referred to interchangeably as a weaver, a webster, a webber, or a draper? When I began to try to find the answer to this question, I found that I had not touched bottom yet; there were actually eight more names applied indiscriminately to this type of worker—a total of twelve different names, and maybe more if I kept on digging.

Was there something different about the weaving trade, something peculiar about that operation that I would not find in the other highly skilled crafts of the same period? A brief study of the building trades in the same period brought to light the astonishing fact that the roofers alone were referred to by no less than forty-six different terms, every one of which meant putting roofs on buildings.

Still not satisfied, I dug back into the old records to see what names our medieval English ancestors used for a tradesman in the business of selling meat. I found BUTCHER easily, but I also found HOGG and BACON and FLESHER and SLAUGHTER and KELLOGG (meaning "kill-hog"), and twenty or so more, all of which referred to the same trade. Today you can find them in any phone book; only now they are family names. Mr. BACON may be in the insurance business, and Mr. KELLOGG may be a lawyer, and Mr. SLAUGHTER a merchant, but at least one of their nominal ancestors must have been in the meat business.

THE TAX COLLECTOR

In the twelfth century, the power to tax belonged primarily to the king; he not only owned everything, but he had no such thing as a parliament to curb or question his judgment. He could levy as many taxes as he wanted.

Then the lord of each shire could, and frequently did, collect his own taxes whenever he pleased. And the lord of each individual manor had the power to tax as well, and he exercised that power with an iron hand. Furthermore, taxes could be imposed and collected several times a year. The individual was helpless. The power to tax was indeed the power to confiscate.

The taxing authorities were practical men. Coin or cash of any kind was little used, so hard-nosed, no-nonsense collectors were sent from house to house, accompanied by a clerk and usually a fully armed soldier, with a wagon suitable for collecting movable property in lieu of cash, if necessary. Over a period of time, this high-handed procedure did produce some practical standards of value: a man was taxed one shilling for a cow, twopence for a young pig, and fourpence for a grown pig, while a chicken was something less, and so on.

The important thing was that some honest effort was made actually to credit a farmer or shopkeeper with having paid his taxes, and this made some kind of distinguishing name necessary.

Thus it was that the practice arose among collectors of having a scribe write down the taxpayer's first name and a surname; if he had no surname (a condition that was still very common), the collector would give him one. It might be a word that described where the man lived, like GATESBY or WELLMAN, or it might be a relationship name, such as ROBERTSON or WILLIAMSON. A third possibility was that the man might have a nickname, like STRONG or TALLMAN or OXMAN, which could be recorded.

Neither the collector nor the clerk cared the least bit whether the taxpayer liked his new name or not, and they most certainly had no idea that they were creating something new. Their sole thought was to record something on the tax roll that would satisfy their superiors when they turned it in for the day. And the recipient of the new name probably shrugged it off as just another nuisance; given a choice, he would surely have exchanged it for one of the fat pigs that the collector had extracted from one of his neighbors earlier in the day.

SHOPKEEPERS, TRADESMEN, AND MECHANICS

We have already spoken of William's effort to encourage Norman mechanics to set up their shops and carry on their multiskilled labors in England, and we know that a steady stream of them migrated to England for more than a century. William's successors seem to have carried on this policy. No accurate figures are available, but we are certain that by the time of Henry II (1154–1189), the towns and villages of the English countryside had taken on a different appearance. Whereas before a village had consisted of a wooden manor house, a church and sometimes a monastery, and hovels scattered about the landscape, now some of the cottages were a little larger and better built. Some had a lean-to in back, and now and then a whole separate structure behind the main house. In a few of the villages, some cottages would appear to have been built more or less to conform in position to their neighbors, although the idea of such things as streets was still in the future.

Interestingly, one could go from one end of England to another, from the largest castle to the most wretched cottage, and not find a single fireplace at this period. Cooking was done on an open fire near each cottage in dry weather; in bad weather, the fire was kindled inside, and the smoke escaped through the open door or one of the slits in the wall that served as a window.

If a man had a trade that required having a shop, that shop was invariably right in his house. Usually, it would occupy most of the space in his cottage; he and his family would live in the lean-to in the rear. The shop was also his showroom, as at that time everything was sold by the producer directly to the consumer.

THE TAX COLLECTOR ARRIVES

Let us create a hypothetical situation. The dreaded collector stops his cart before the door of a man called Robert. Robert was his only name and, he felt, all the name he needed. Friends now and then called him LONG or LANG because he was on the long side and at least once someone called him DALE because his shop was in a little hollow near the outskirts of the village, but what did it matter—did it help him earn a living?

So when the collector in his best Norman French demanded his name, he said simply, "Robert." To the officious collector, it was not enough; there were at least three other Roberts in that village, and if this fellow were to receive credit for the tax he paid, he needed a name that would distinguish him from any and all other Roberts in the town.

The situation was a common one for the collector—it came up several times a day—and in cases like this, where the occupation of the taxpayer was obvious from his shop, there was an easy and permanent solution. He had noticed that the man was making bowls: there was a whole row of them that he had just taken out of the kiln. So since Robert makes bowls and the tax collector hadn't seen anybody else making bowls, Robert is named BOWLMAN or BOWLER or maybe just BOWLS. The heretofore nameless Robert has become Robert Bowls, and a genuine surname has been created.

Since there was no right or wrong way to spell then, the tax collector, pleased himself and he might very well put it down as BOALS or even BOALES. It made no difference—Robert would be credited with having paid his taxes and the manor house would be satisfied.

A similar situation occurs in a village a few miles away—but this town has a different collector. He calls at the shop of a man who insists his name is William. William is making pots out of reddish-looking clay.

The collector has seen the clay before but the pots are different in shape and size than others he has seen, so he calls him William POTTS or POTTMAN or POTTER or, if none of these come to mind at the moment, he might enter the name in Norman French as William le Pottier. Similar situations happened all over England during that naming period. Names were invented by hundreds of petty collectors who cared not one whit about the reactions of the taxpayer—satisfying their superiors back at the manor house and, more importantly, collecting all the traffic would bear were their only concerns.

Let us follow these hypothetical collectors around for a few hours. The one who has just finished with Mr. Bowls goes on to the next cottage, but this place looks different: this man has a second small building in back of where he lives and smoke is pouring out of a hole in the roof. When the wind is right, the collector catches the delightful. odor of baking bread.

Stepping into the shop, the collector introduces himself to the occupant, states his unpleasant business, and listens to the arguments of the taxpayer, but only for a moment—it is pay or else, and the occupant knows it. What is his name? "Hugh" is what he is called and he bakes the best bread in the whole shire. "Yes, that's fine, but what is your last name? I've got to give you a name of some kind if you don't already have one." The collector then puts him down on the record as Hugh PANNER or he might choose to spell it the Norman way, Hugh le Pannier. Both words meant "bread baker," although the Middle English term would be BACKER or BACKMAN (a *c* was usually put before the *k* in that name until the seventeenth century). On the other hand, he might name the baker BACKHOUSE (meaning "bake-house"). And if it was BACKHOUSE, it would soon become either BACKUS or BACCHUS. Another interesting possibility—if the baker's wife seemed to be a little more authoritative than normal—was the name BACKESTER, which would change in the course of years to BAXTER.

The lady in the house seems to have influenced a sizable list of occupational names from this period—always in the same way. BREWER was masculine while BREWSTER was feminine. If the housewife seemed to be in charge of brewing the beer, the collector might very well write down BREWSTER. And if a family wove cloth, chances are the collector would give the name WEBBER unless he favored the distaff side, in which case he might select WEBSTER. During the latter part of the naming period, this custom died out so that by the 1300s no distinction was made on the basis of sex. The collector used feminine or masculine endings indiscriminately.

Now let us take a look at another collector in the next village. He, too, ties his horse in front of the shop of a baker, but this fellow is obviously not baking bread; he's baking pies. (Even back in those days the English were fond of pies, particularly those made with meat.) What does he call this baker? It would be PYE or PYBAKER or even PASTER, you can be sure.

Obviously, any taxpayer would try to pay his taxes in the goods he produced. This would surely be preferable to having the collector take any livestock. There must have been heated arguments between the collector and the taxpayer in this regard, the collector being obliged to make a quick calculation on just how acceptable a dozen steaming meat pies might be to the lord of the manor.

In this case the taxpayer (now Mr. Pybaker) wins the argument and the collector rolls along to the next stop. This fellow was obviously making some kind of wagon or two-wheeled cart. The collector knew something about carts because he drove one of them every day, so he would give this man the name of CARTWRIGHT or possibly WAIN-WRIGHT (not CARTER—that would be for a man that drove a cart).

Let's go back to the first collector for a moment. He too stops at the shop of a man making wagons, but the only name he can think of to describe the man's labor is WAINMAN and he might put it down as WENMAN or even WEYMAN. He could hardly care less, as long as the name meant a man who made wagons of some kind.

Chances are that next to the shop of Mr. Cartwright or Mr. Wainman would be the shop of a man who made wheels for carts. Making good solid wheels that were perfectly round and able to carry a lot of weight was a very highly skilled accomplishment, and not a common one. Let's see what each of our collectors might do with such a man. One collector might call him a WHELSMYTH or a WHELSTER, while the other one might call him a WHEELRIGHT or a WHEELER, maybe even a WHEELMONGER. The English of the Middle Ages loved the word *monger* and applied it to a great many different tradesmen. In modern times, it has become restricted to only fishmonger, ironmonger, and cheesemonger.

In the following chapters, categories of occupations, with the names deriving from them, are discussed. At the end of each chapter, the names are listed alphabetically by stem. The names have been taken from every available source—telephone books, city directories, dictionaries of surnames, magazines, newspapers, television, and, of course, from volumes on medieval history.

Every name on each list indicates to me either by its obvious literal meaning, its derivation, or its spelling, or, frequently, by a careful weighing of all three, that it comes directly or indirectly from the status or occupational source indicated in medieval England. No claim whatever is made that any of these lists is complete. This would be impossible; the changes that have been brought about by something like thirty to forty generations of human frailty make it out of the question.

CHAPTER 4

The Potters

If one of your nominal ancestors was in the pottery business in the England of the twelfth, thirteenth, or fourteenth centuries, a possibility indicated by finding your family name on the list at the end of this chapter, you may find it interesting to take a look at some of the conditions he had to contend with in his quest for a living.

His was a very ancient trade even back in those times. Men had been making pottery long before written history. In fact, the first things a modern archaeologist expects to find when making systematic excavations are pieces of broken pottery. The original vessel may have long since been broken in a thousand pieces, but the pieces themselves remain very much as they were when the original maker took the vessel out of the fire. Prehistoric races in widely separated parts of the world seem to have had such reverence for even very crude pottery that they buried it with their dead. Many of these vessels may have contained food for the use of the spirit of the departed in the afterlife, while others had holes in their bottom, apparently put there deliberately.

The English people of the medieval centuries, however, had no religious feeling about their pottery. To them, the making of pottery was strictly utilitarian, something that made life a little easier. The vast majority of them were illiterate and lived under conditions that hardly would be tolerated in our modern slums, but they were far from being unintelligent. They desperately wanted all the conveniences known to them.

Vessels to hold milk, butter, water, wine, and ale were considered necessities even in the tiny house of the lowliest peasant. Ale was the every-day drink of all classes of people from royalty to peasant in the early part of the naming period; beer came in a bit later, but both were brewed in the home, which required barrels, as well as earthenware beakers to drink out of. There was much demand, therefore, for the product of those who had the skill to turn clay into practical vessels for holding liquids.

Before the arrival of William in 1066, the native Anglo-Saxons were turning out quantities of practical earthenware, in shades of red from the iron-rich clays that were available throughout England. In the early part of the period, the pieces were almost entirely unglazed, which meant they would be porous and not a great deal more durable than one of to-day's flowerpots. But the influx of Norman potters in the 1200s made some improvements; apparently the Normans taught the English how to glaze pottery and definitely introduced additives of copper that made a green-colored piece instead of the common reds.

GROUP 1

The Potters

Turning a cartload of clay just fresh from the earth into a cartload of finished pottery was a slow process involving at least two weeks of hard work for one man and his helper. Usually, one shop developed skill in making one item and concentrated on this; thus the man who made crocks did not make pots or bowls, jugs or pitchers.

The shop of the potter was usually a little one-room affair with a lean-to in the rear, where he lived. The shop contained his kiln, which, when loaded with freshly made pieces, was fired up and kept hot for twenty-four to thirty hours. It also held the potter's wheel on which he shaped lumps of prepared clay into any form he wanted. No one seems to know who invented the potter's wheel or even where or when, but we do know that it was in common use throughout England in this period.

If the potter's own little piece of land held by agreement with the lord of the manor did not have suitable clay for pottery, he would make an arrangement with someone who did; this would be his CLAYMAN or, if suitable clay was to be found under the bed of a stream or pond, the supplier might be called CLAYBROOK or CLAYPOOL or CLAY-BURN. The supplier would not be a potter himself but would surely be included in the industry.

The raw clay would contain pebbles and considerable extraneous material that had to be eliminated, so after it dried out, it was broken into small pieces, which were put through a sieve. But the sifted clay still contained a lot of small pieces of foreign material, so the whole batch would be put in a mixing vat, and water added. The potter then stirred this with a paddle, with his strong right arm, till it had the consistency of thick soup. This would enable the heavier materials to sink to the bottom and the lighter stuff to float to the top, where it could be skimmed off from time to time. He would let it settle overnight and then decant off the clear water through a hole in the side of the vat to get rid of the soluble material in the clay. By this time, several days had passed. There was still much to be done.

Once a potter decided that his material was fairly clean, he was ready to add the other materials necessary for the mixture to bake out satisfactorily. Here he had to draw heavily on his experience with that clay and the very small variety of hardening agents available. Nearly always he would have to add some fine white sand and some finely ground flint. Pieces of flint had to be heated as hot as possible and then plunged into cold water, which would crack them into small bits. Then these had to be ground into a powder with a mortar and pestle. Once the mixture was complete, the potter allowed it to settle, drawing off as much water as possible and slowly drying out the whole mass of clay. When dried out enough so that it could be handled in great soft lumps, it was kneaded thoroughly to get the air bubbles out of it and then set aside for a couple of days to season.

Finally, it was ready to be shaped on the wheel into a jar, a crock, a bowl, or a dish of any kind. This was called "throwing," and the man who did this was often called THROWER or TROWER. After this, handles would be put on, if needed, and after another night of seasoning it was ready for firing. The fire would be built up under the kiln and then the pieces would be put in the kiln on a long wooden or metal peel (from which came the name PEEL), where they would slowly vitrify for twenty-four hours or more. Once the pieces were done, the fire was allowed to die out slowly. The pottery had to cool gradually or it would crack. At this point, the pieces were porous, and if they were to be glazed on the outside or inside or both, a creamy mixture of some lead or copper compound would be applied. If they were to be decorated, a design would be scratched through the thin coating of glazing material, and they would be refired in the kiln for another twenty-four hours. A vast amount of work for a few pieces of crockery! And a potter could normally expect about half of his production to crack or break up somewhere in the process.

At some point during the medieval period, a way was discovered to reduce this loss. Instead of the flames in the kiln being allowed to come into direct contact with the pottery, the pieces were placed in bowl-shaped pieces of rough pottery pierced with tiny holes. These rough bowls were called seggers, and the man who made them, SEGGERMAN.

Most of the twenty names beginning with *pot* are the result of scribal variations; that is, spelling errors either by careless tax men or by individuals through the centuries. It is easy to understand how a tax man in one village might put down POTTMAN while in another POTMAKER was used. Perhaps one collector might be impressed by the smallness of one man's pots and call him POTKIN. POTTLE and its variant POT-TELL referred to a measure that still means one-half an imperial gallon. POTTINGER may come from the pottery shop by way of the kitchen, as its derivation is "the maker of potage in a pot." The earliest recorded name from the pottery business appeared in the tax roll of 1197 (now referred to as the Pipe Roll): John le Potier.

All this applies to the twenty BOWL names as well. And the same may be said of the six CROCK names. In Middle English,* CROCKER was often spelled CROKER.

There are only one JARMAN and only four JUG names because jugs were not in common use in England in the Middle Ages. They were used for vinegar and wine, but at that time England did not have a great deal of either, and had to import it from abroad.

The CUPP names might as well appear on a list of names deriving from the medical profession. They were made by potters but used by doctors for cupping, a process of drawing blood to the surface of the body for bloodletting.

The STEYN names have been very much mutilated over the centuries. All of them started as *stan*, the Anglo-Saxon word for stone, but became mixed up with the old German word *stein*, or the old Norse *steinn* meaning the same thing. STAINER may also derive from the late Middle English word *steynen* meaning "to paint" (see chapter 10, Group 43).

BEAKER, MUGG, and TANKARD names need no explanation, and the CLAY names have been discussed. The CHALK names were given to suppliers of certain hardening agents used by the potter.

URNER is perfectly straightforward, though it is a rare name. HAMPER is also rare, but referred to a maker or seller of goblets. VESSELER indicates a potter who displayed many different kinds of pottery or a

---

* Middle English is the term used for the English language of the period approximately A.D. 1150–1500.

GROUP 1

The Potters

Beaker	Clayburn	Mug	Staine
Beakerman	Claycomb	Mugg	Stainer
Beakers	Clayer	Muggar	Staines
Beekerman	Clayman	Mugger	Stainmaker
•	Claymore	Mugman	Stainman
Boaler	Claypool	•	Steyn
Boales	Claysmith	Peel	Steyne
Bohler	Claysmyth	•	•
Bole	Clayton	Pitcher	Tankard
Boler	•	Pitcherman	Tankardmaker
Boles	Crock	•	Tankerd
Boll	Crockard	Potamkin	Tankers
Boller	Crocker	Potee	•
Bolles	Crockman	Potier	Thrower
Bolley	Crocks	Potisman	Trower
Bollman	Croker	Potkins	•
Boule	•	Potmaker	Turner
Bouller	Cupman	Pott	•
Boulware	Cupp	Pottell	Urner
Bowell	Cuppe	Potter	•
Bowl	Cupper	Potteridge	Vesseler
Bowle	Cupperman	Potterton	
Bowler	Cupps	Pottharst	
Bowles	•	Pottier	
Bowlman	Discher	Pottinger	
•	Disher	Pottle	
Chalk	Dishman	Pottman	
Chalke	•	Potton	
Chalker	Hamper	Pottruff	
Chalkman	•	Potts	
Chaulk	Jarman	Potwine	
•	•	•	
Chalmers	Jugg	Segger	
Chambers	Juggar	Seggerman	
•	Jugger	Seggers	
Clay	Jugman	•	
Claybrook	•	Stain	

tax man who didn't know the specific name of what he saw and used a general catch-all term.

There were few DISH names for the simple reason that our ancestors rarely used them. A slice of bread served as a plate and was either eaten at the end of the meal or thrown to the dogs. PITCHER and PITCHER-MAN are also rare names because few pitchers were made.

The name CHAMBERS (or CHALMERS) was common in Scotland and most certainly belongs in the pottery category—the man referred to made chamber pots!

The earliest potter recorded in America is Philip DRINKER. His kiln was turning out crockery in Massachusetts as far back as 1635.

CHAPTER 5

The Smiths

No reader of these pages needs to be told that the family name of SMITH is more numerous and widespread than any other name in the English-speaking world. There are twice as many Smiths in London as the nearest rivals—Taylor, Miller, and Baker—and about the same ratio holds in New York, Denver, or San Francisco. And in Australia, Canada, or New Zealand—almost anywhere English is the dominant language, the name Smith is by far the most common.

The word *smith* is a very old Anglo-Saxon term meaning simply "one who smites," but in medieval England its use seems to have been largely restricted to smiting or striking with something in the hand, such as a hammer. And since striking with a hammer must have been an all-day, everyday occurrence for a vast proportion of Englishmen of that period, the noun form of the word must have been in common use throughout the land.

P. H. Reaney in his scholarly *Dictionary of British Surnames* lists one Ecceard-smith far back in the written records in the year 975. This was nearly a century before the Conqueror took over England. We know that Ecceard was the only real name this man ever had. The "smith" was added to distinguish him from any other Ecceard that might be in the same area.

Matthews, in her study of English surnames, gives us some details about the very same Ecceard-smith. He appeared as a witness in a charter application at a time in English history when to be called as a witness in such serious matters invariably meant that one must be an important citizen. Such confidence was usually reserved for a bishop or an earl or lord of the manor, and consequently we can believe this humble crafts- man must have been a very exceptional citizen.

The next incident we know of in which a smith distinguished himself occurred at the actual landing of the Conqueror on the beach near Hast- ings in that fateful year of 1066. It is very easy to visualize the scene. Duke William would be dressed in his most impressive suit of armor, with the ducal crown on his head; and his manner would be dignified and pompous as would become a monarch about to establish his fancied rights to a foreign land. His noble charger, caparisoned in the richest materials obtainable, would already be on the beach, being held by an attendant, ready for the duke to mount and lead the attack. Undoubtedly a large group of his noble followers had selected the moment he would step out of the boat onto the shore of England as the most appropriate to acclaim the duke as the mighty conqueror, the righter of wrongs and the bringer of justice. But some whimsical fate stepped in and almost changed the whole course of English history.

In stepping from the boat to the sand, the duke's foot slipped and he fell on his face on the pebbly beach, his nose spreading blood all around him. Nothing so serious, you might think, but to those Norman nobles, it came as a real shock (this was no way for a conquest to begin) and boded nothing but ill for the whole expedition.

But at that moment, out from the crowd of Normans gathered around the duke, presumably helping him to wipe the blood off his face, stepped a man of very humble birth. He had a very different idea—far from read- ing failure at the sight of the duke's blood on the beach, he argued that it was a definite omen of success. The duke was destined to take posses- sion of that land by first sprinkling some of *his own blood* on it. Unfortu- nately, history doesn't give us anything further on the career of this resourceful man, but surely he must have gone on to greater things. After all, the duke rejected the counsel of his nobles and followed the advice of this commoner and went on to conquer all England.

We know the essential facts in the above incident from an account of the whole conquest written shortly after, known as the *Chronicle of Bat- tle Abbey*. It was written in Latin and at least parts of it are still intelli- gible today.

The fast-thinking man is definitely mentioned in the old chronicle but, written in Latin, his name shows up as Williemus-faber. That word, *fa- ber,* after his first name, William, tells us just how that man earned his living when he was not serving in the army. FABER meant a man who worked with iron, a smith.

Of course, this man's Norman companions, speaking French, called him le ferrer or le Farrar, French for the Latin word for iron, *ferrum*.

If you happen to feel this detail is not important, please look at Group 2 in the list of family names on page 46. There are twenty-eight modern surnames on it, every one of which has come down to us from the efforts of the eleventh-century Norman invaders to identify men who worked with iron, the smiths. They, and the several hundred other names in this chapter, all derive from last names of smiths back in the naming period, making allowances for the changes that centuries of human pride, bad spelling, and lack of communication have brought about.

At that time, Smith in any language meant about the same thing as our word *mechanic* does today. We have already suggested that the reason the surname Smith is so widespread today is that in the medieval naming period a vast proportion of all men doing almost any kind of work that required the use of a hammer were given some form of the name. In fact, as early as the twelfth century, the simple name Smith began to lose its power to distinguish and identify one man from another. Some variations were necessary, and as we have seen, the tax collectors inadvertently supplied some of the variants. Instead of calling a man smith, the tax man might note that this particular person seemed to be making such things as stirrups and bridles for horses, so he would give him the French name le loremier, whose spelling was soon simplified to LORIMER or LORRIMAR or LORINER, as it is today.

Today a blacksmith shop is a genuine rarity in any of our towns and cities—our ironwork is made in huge factories and becomes available to us through hardware retailers. But up to a century or so ago the blacksmith made all our ironwork to order—the knob and latch for our doors, the equipment for our fireplaces, and our cooking utensils. Just how modern the hardware store of today really is can be judged by a Philadelphia census taken in 1800: the population was about 40,000 and there were 120 blacksmith shops.

GROUP 2

Names Based on French and Latin

All twenty-eight names on this list (page 46) mean *smith* beyond any doubt, but none of them gives us any inkling as to what kind of smith the original bearer of the name might have been. He may have made garden tools; he may have shoed horses; he may have made nails, or he may well have spent his working life making and repairing arms and armor.

I am sure this list does not exhaust all the variations that could be found by patient scanning of modern directories, but it tells us with a certainty not always possible in things stemming from so far back in the past that each original bearer of one of these names made things out of iron. The words FABER or FERRUM may be hard to recognize in some of their modern renditions, but frequently enough of the original root remains to point to the origin.

The final three names in Group 2 might look as if they came from Egypt—perhaps a translation of some ancient hieroglyphic on one of the tombs along the Nile—but this is definitely not so. Somebody with one of the FARO names may have thought that a change in spelling might possibly increase his status—after all, Pharo does sound exactly like Farro when you hear it spoken.

GROUP 3

Names Based on English

The names in Group 3 (page 46) differ from those in Group 2 in that they are all essentially English in origin as opposed to French and Latin, and some of them give us a little more information about the original bearer.

The last twenty-one are plain variations of the basic name. SMITHY might originally have been applied to a smith as a friendly nickname or could have been used just as easily to refer to the smith's shop itself and indirectly to the man who owned it. Those names ending with -*son* are obvious, while those ending with -*man* could have been given to the smith's helper. Others of these are probably scribal errors that occurred at the time and have been retained, although it is just as likely that they represent later variations.

But the names ANGOVE, GOFF, and GOFFE are different, as they are colloquial and tell us with a fair degree of certainty what part of England they came from. GOFF, with or without the final *e,* comes from Lincolnshire, while ANGOVE definitely originated in Cornwall. All three derive from the Galic word *gobha,* meaning "smith."

FORGE, FORGER, and FORGMAN are names given to smiths to identify them with their forge, but BLAKESMITH looks quite modern. It is in fact the same world *blacksmith* that we use today, except for the old Middle English spelling. Little is known about CAIRD except that its origin is probably Irish and it has been used in England since the

1600s. ATHERSMITH indicates a man who lived at the smithy, probably the smith, but WATERSMYTH is something different. Since it was probably a tax man who created this name, it is interesting to imagine the scene that prompted it.

From the outside, the smithy probably looked like any other one but inside there was one noticeable difference. The usual forge at that time was provided with a large bellows operated by either the smith himself or his assistant. This was done by pulling a rope hanging down from a wooden beam and attached to the bellows. Each pull on the rope caused the bellows to force a stream of air into the fire. In this case, however, the smith had rigged a paddle wheel in the fast-running stream under his shop and connected it by a couple of wooden gears to his bellows. To operate the bellows, he would pull a lever that would mesh the gears and cause the wheel to work the bellows, thus freeing both hands for the work he was doing. As early as the twelfth century, the waterwheel had been used in connection with mills for grinding grain, but applying this force to a bellows was still somewhat new and undoubtedly impressed the tax collector. The records also indicate that some smiths managed to gear the waterwheel to a hammer, which must have been a real saver of time and muscle. There is a John Watersmyth in tax records of 1333.

The remaining names of Group 3 are obviously names applied to smiths because they were using a bellows of some kind. There is no indication why these were singled out for that distinction, since hand-operated bellows were the rule rather than the exception.

Finally, the name IRONCUTTER does not appear in any record that I know of, but can anyone doubt what his occupation was?

GROUP 4

Horseshoers

At last we come to a list of smiths who were clearly named for the exact type of work they did; they shoed horses and oxen and, like all shoeing smiths of that time, they knew enough about the ordinary ills of farm animals to prescribe remedies when they were called upon to do so. This may sound strange to some, but it will be found that at this same period in our history barbers not only shaved men and cut their hair but performed at least minor surgery as well.

Shoeing a horse, even in the Middle Ages, required a lot of know-how. Each shoe had to be fitted snugly to the hoof of the horse and fastened so it would stay there till it was worn out. This meant that either each hoof had to be filed off flat or the shoe had to be curved to follow the contour of the hoof. This was—and still is—frequently accomplished by applying a moderately hot shoe to each hoof for a few seconds until it has burned a place for itself in the horny substance of the hoof. This horny substance is very much like our fingernails in that it grows fast and continuously throughout life. The outer and lower portion of the hoof can be trimmed and nails driven through it without discomfort to the animal.

No figures are available on the number of shoeing smiths in medieval England, but we can be sure that every castle and manor house would have a shoeing smith along with one or two more smiths skilled in making and repairing tools and armor. The lord of the manor would certainly maintain a very sizable stable of horses for hunting, because hunting was about the most important amusement he had. It was the way he entertained his own family and guests, and it necessitated a lot of horses. There would be the lighter breeds, something like the modern hunters, although the sport of fox hunting was still in the future, and there would be "great horses" that the lord and his knights used for tournaments or real war. These tremendous animals had been bred in the Low Countries and imported during the naming period, specifically to carry a knight encumbered with armor and weapons. Aside from a daily exercise workout by a trainer, they were never used except in tournaments or, of course, in actual war. They were magnificent creatures somewhat resembling the modern Clydesdale and Percheron.

National Geographic magazine's colorful volume *This England* gives us a story that certainly indicates the almost reverential respect the British people had for the hardworking smiths of Group 4. Once a year in modern London a robed and bewigged delegation walks into the Royal Court of Justice in search of Queen Elizabeth's Remembrancer (a protocol officer of great dignity). When he is located, the delegation bows respectfully to him and presents him with six horseshoes ". . . suitable for the forefeet of a great Flemish warhorse, sixty-one horseshoe nails, one hatchet and a billhook." The Remembrancer accepts the items in a suitably dignified manner and bows the delegation out of the chamber. What has happened is that the City of London—about a square mile of the costliest real estate in the world—has paid its rent for a year to the sovereign, and this little ceremony has been going on without a single interruption for more than five hundred years! Incidentally, the horseshoes and nails find their way back to the city for representation, but the hatchet and the billhook are new each year.

The last five names in Group 4 hardly need explanation, although

SHOUGER is not so well known. It comes from a very old Anglo-Saxon word, *scogan,* meaning simply a shoer of horses.

The MARSHALL names on the list are highly interesting because today the term *marshal* calls up a picture of dignity, authority, and high honors. In the United States, it is a highly respected title frequently given to the officer in each judicial district empowered to execute the process of the courts and perform various other duties similar to those of a sheriff. In many American cities, the head of the fire department and the police department carries the title of marshal. In Europe now the title is usually reserved for the very highest office in the army or the air corps, such as field marshal.

But look how it has changed over the years. In the sixteenth century, England had a marshal of the king's hall. His duties were to place the king's household servants and strangers at table according to their quality. At about the same time, England had a marshal of the exchequer. His duties seem to have been largely confined to putting anyone unable to meet his financial obligations to the king in jail. Then there was a marshal of the king's bench. He seems to resemble our American sheriff more closely, as he was obliged to take into custody all persons so committed by the King's Bench Court. In the eleventh, twelfth, and thirteenth centuries, however, the term *marshal* (regardless of how it was spelled, and the list indicates eight variants) was the man in charge of the horses. He was a shoeing smith who fed the horses under his care, bedded them down for the night, saw to it that they were given proper exercise, and treated their ills when he could. The root of the word is probably the old French word *mareschal* meaning "one who tends horses."

MARSHALL is only one of the respected modern names that over the course of many centuries has ascended the social scale to heights that were never dreamed of when the name was first applied to some trusted servant. Let us look back into the medieval period to see what explanation we can find for such a drastic change.

By the end of the thirteenth century, horses were becoming vastly more important to the feudal society of England. From the lowly peasant to the highest noble, the ownership of horses tended to fix the status of the individual. The peasant found them capable of plowing almost twice as much in a day as a team of oxen, so the peasant who could boast of even one broken-down old horse suddenly found himself the recipient of a respect he had never known before. But it was with the great barons, dukes, and earls, who could maintain a huge stable of horses, that they really began to count. Keeping up with the Joneses is not a modern weakness—it is as old as human nature.

You are visited by Baron de Courci with a great retinue of retainers, including some horses that are far better than you have ever seen before. The baron may have been unable to hide his disdain completely for your modest string of horseflesh. So as soon as he goes on his way, you call on every horse dealer in the area, determined to equal, if not outdo, your friend the baron. This was a common situation in that period, and one of the results was that the stable and its contents began to assume greater importance. One needed a man who really knew horses, a man who could go to a horse fair and come back with some animals that you would be anxious to show off to your friends. When you found such a man, you treated him with a respect that was reserved for servants much higher in the feudal social scale than a mere shoer of horses. And so it went—as one noble tried to outdo the other in the matter of horseflesh, the worthy caretaker was pushed up the social ladder. But for some reason that is hard to account for now, the descriptive name that was applied to him a thousand years ago never changed.

ARSNELL and HORSENAIL, along with the six that follow on the list, come from nothing more than a horseshoe nail. Perhaps there were smiths who specialized in making nails suitable for shoeing, or perhaps these were merely friendly nicknames indicating just another shoeing smith.

FARRIER has almost passed out of the language both as an occupational name and as a surname, but in medieval times it indicated a good shoer of horses.

GROUP 5
Smiths Named for the Items They Made

In this group are arbitrarily put together the smiths who apparently were originally named for some item they may have been making at the moment that the tax man visited. It is difficult to think that Mr. SPURRIER, for example, made nothing but spurs, although this cannot be ruled out.

The eleven SPUR names in Group 5 (page 47) all derive from the old Anglo-Saxon word *spura* or *spora,* meaning simply a more or less pointed instrument that a horseman fastened to his heels, to be used when he wanted to speed up the gait of his animal. Such things were in common use in the naming period and it is possible that here and there all over

England certain smiths may have acquired particular skill in making a type of spur that gave them a reputation and hence the surname.

We have already touched on the LORIMER type of name; they were spurriers all right, but some of them made bridles and stirrups too, so they properly belong in that group.

SHEATHER and its variant SHETHER refer to the smiths who made sheaths for knives. They may have made them entirely out of iron at first, but iron was not plentiful and it was heavy, so undoubtedly some agreement was made with leatherworkers to supply leather for a sheath made from a combination of both materials. There seems reason to believe that a smith who bought his leather from that industry and thus was able to turn out a superior sheath became known as a CHAPEMAKER. This was particularly true in London, where the looks and style of a gentleman's accouterments counted so much more than in the rural districts.

The BRIDLE names are obvious, and what we have suggested on the SPUR names applies equally to the STIRRUP names, too. BOKELERE and BOTONER are just the old way of spelling Buckler and Buttoner, all used in connection with horses and their equipment.

GROUP 6

Smelters and Charcoal Makers

In modern times, no one would think of associating a blacksmith with a steel mill; they are as far apart in their functions as horseshoes are from boiler plates. But far back in the centuries, even before the naming period, the man who dug iron ore from the ground near his forge, carried it into his shop, smelted it in his tiny blast furnace, hammered some of of the slag out of it, and then proceeded to make something useful with it, was one and the same individual—a smith.

It seems incredible today that one man, with a couple of helpers, could perform all the basic functions of miners and the workers in a whole complicated modern steel mill and finally could make some tool or weapon out of the metal, but for a long period in medieval England this definitely happened. No figures are available on the volume either an individual or all the smiths in England could produce. We know it must have been pitifully small, and the quality far below today's standard, but it was iron, a metal so valuable that at times it was used as a medium of exchange instead of gold.

Large heaps of iron *scoira*, or half-smelted iron ore, are still uncovered in various parts of England. In the Weald of Kent and Sussex, in the hills of Somerset, in the Forest of Dean in Gloucester, and in many other spots, this unmistakable evidence of the work of early smiths can still be found. Frequently the age of an old slag heap can be roughly determined by the discovery of Roman coins and other items of unquestionable origin in them.

No less than seventy-five separate deposits of such remains have been located in the Forest of Dean alone, indicating clearly the location of early smithies. The smiths used charcoal to smelt the ore, so the supply of wood had to be plentiful and nearby.

Today, iron ore is smelted with either coke or limestone, depending on the type of ore at hand, but in the period we are talking about, coal and, of course, the coke made from it were unknown.

The Egyptians had some success in smelting the nonferrous metals and the Romans and Greeks were able to produce small amounts of iron but, until well into the medieval period, bronze would continue to be the basic metal for armor, weapons, and tools. To extract pure iron from its ore requires a very hot fire that can be maintained for many hours or even days. For this purpose, fast-burning wood is entirely impractical. But someone discovered that while a piece of wood would quickly burn up and leave nothing but a small amount of ashes, a similar piece of wood covered with damp soil, wet leaves, and similar material to exclude nearly all the air, burned slowly and resulted in a piece of black material that not only retained the original shape of the wood but would burn in the open air with an intense heat and very little smoke, and for a long time.

This was charcoal, a material that was to be of major importance in the development of modern living. It would serve this purpose clear into the nineteenth century before another form of carbon called coal was put generally to use.

But these old-time smiths had their troubles. To get all the iron out of the ore, the mixture has to be cooked, actually made to boil for some hours. This necessitates a high temperature, which must be maintained for long hours. Today this is accomplished by blowing a constant stream of very hot air into the furnace (hence the name "blast furnace"), but in Anglo-Saxon England preheated air was unheard of and the blast had to be whatever nature provided. The tiny furnace would be built on the top of a hill at a spot where the nearby hills would provide a sort of chimney facing the source of the prevailing winds. This would tend to funnel the wind into the furnace. Imagine the doleful look on the smith's face when the day was calm or the wind was blowing from the wrong direction.

By the time of the Middle Ages, the bellows had been developed. This was of great help, as it enabled the smith to carry on regardless of the weather. At first the bellows was operated by hand, but before long somebody found a way to rig a bellows to a paddle wheel in the nearby stream, and the day of power had arrived.

Even with a continuously operated bellows, however, those smiths were never able to liquefy the mass in the furnace completely. As a consequence, they were never able to extract more than half of the pure iron in the ore. In the nineteenth century, when men began to unearth the great heaps of partially smelted ore left by the medieval smiths, they found much of it rich enough in good iron to make it worth smelting all over again.

The Anglo-Saxon monks were as interested in the manufacture of iron as they were in the development of agriculture. One of them, Saint Dunstan, who lived in the tenth century, is said to have maintained a forge in his monastery where he made himself a skilled blacksmith and metallurgist.

Interestingly, one of the last Anglo-Saxon kings was called Edmund Ironside, a name that could indicate an unusual interest in the making of iron, though more probably a fondness for armor.

It may seem strange that such a small number of names would have come down to us from an occupation so vital to the advancement of civilization as iron-making certainly was. The only reasonable explanation seems to be that many of the men in that industry were known to friends and associates as smiths. The individual thought of himself as a smith because he followed the same type of work that other smiths did.

He certainly would not be conscious of the fact that in smelting iron ore he was doing something that centuries later would be considered an entirely separate industry. The individual considered his real business to be making shovels, or ploughs, or weapons for the soldiers. The fact that he had to dig his raw material from the earth and spend days getting it ready before he could begin to hammer it into rakes and hoes and axes would not strike him as being the least bit odd or unusual. He would have smithy friends who followed much the same procedure, and he might have a friend who was a carpenter accustomed to cutting down a few trees as the first step in building a house.

So as a natural consequence, the tax man would enter him as another smith. Why not? Didn't he know several others like him? Of course, we many suppose that now and then a collector might call on a smith just at the moment the smith was reheating the pitifully small ingot of iron he had been heating over and over and hammering the daylights out of to remove enough slag to start making something out of the iron. If the tax man happened to be a native Briton instead of the usual French-speaking Norman, he might be so impressed by the looks of that white-hot ingot that he would use the old Anglo-Saxon word for ingot, which was *bloma,* and in the course of many years this word would change to BLOOM, or BLOOMER, BLOMER, or BLUMER. They all meant "blooms." Another word that meant the same thing was *ancony.* It is rarely seen today and when it is, it is spelled either ANCONY or AN-KENY.

I find two names in the tax records that must have been given by somebody to whom French came easier than English, most likely a Norman tax collector. They were Willimus Blomere in 1202 and Robertus Blomere in 1279. I have not been able to find Blomere in any modern directory as a family name, but it may have fallen by the wayside in the course of so many generations. If it were to be found, we would know at once that its original bearer had to be a husky blacksmith.

The last three names in Group 6, STEEL, STEELE, and STEELS are problems to the nominologist. All three are fairly well known family names. The old Anglo-Saxons used a word spelled variously as *stel, steli,* and *style*—all pronounced as though spelled with a double *ee*—and when they used it, they were trying to express the thought that something, or somebody was hard in the sense of being tough and unbreakable or even sharp. These are the very qualities that we look for in a piece of steel today. So did some long-forgotten tax man apply this word to some man because of the man's personal characteristics, or could it have been taken from the enthusiastic remarks of some experimental smith trying to harden some of his iron so that a knife would keep its edge? We may never know, but I am inclined to think the latter is very near the truth.

At some point, there was a very interesting development: a new group of names developed around charcoal, indicating that some of the smiths' work was now being taken over by a separate group of workers. The Old English word for charcoal was *col,* and when one finds a Robertus Cole entered in the Domesday Book in 1086, one is clearly entitled to believe he must have been associated with charcoal. He was probably a maker of the item, although he may have bought charcoal from other men and sold it to the SMITHS. The records of the eleventh century are well supplied with other COLES as more and more men went into the business of making charcoal for the smiths. By the early part of the twelfth century, the name was firmly established all over England and Wales. Richard

Coleman came along in 1166 and John Colkin just a little later (the *kin-*ending usually indicated that the man was either smaller than average or meant it was a pet name for a charcoal maker).

The COLLIER names sprang up in the same period and they come from the same word *col.* A Bernard le Coliere is recorded in 1172 and a Ranulf Colier in 1151.

BERNER, BOURNER, and BRENNER also go back to charcoal. They come from the Old English word *beornan,* meaning "to burn." Robert le Berner appears in 1190 and Nicholas Brenner in 1213.

GROUP 7

Nail Makers

Centuries before the naming period, men were making nails. In Assyria as far back as 1700 B.C., they were making them out of copper, and in Egypt too we know they were making copper nails at least 700 years before the Christian era. The Romans must have been highly skilled at nail-making because in modern times a huge store of their nails was discovered in Inchtuthil in Perthshire, Scotland. No fewer than seven tons of perfectly good iron nails were unearthed, all unquestionably of Roman manufacture.

English smiths in the naming period were making nails from iron by strictly hand methods, a procedure that was to last until the nineteenth century, when machines were developed to take over much of the labor. The process was a simple one and did not require great skill.

First, iron would be beaten and shaped into rods, which might be either roughly round or square and of the desired diameter. The end of a rod would be heated to white-hot in the forge and yanked out of the fire, and the end hammered to a point. Then the rod was cut off, and the short piece quickly inserted in a piece of iron with a hole through it. The "bolster," as this piece came to be called, allowed the upcoming nail to stick out about a quarter of an inch; a few sharp blows with a hammer flattened this projection into a head and the nail was finished. All this could be done with one heat by a practiced nailer, and as he thrust one rod back into the fire, he pulled another one out and repeated the same routine. This produced the wrought nail; some time later, the cut nail appeared. It is different in that the nail maker started with a sheet of iron of the desired thickness, put the sheet through a slitting mill, cutting the sheet into long strips the width of the desired nail, and carried on from there.

All twelve of the names in Group 7 (page 48) are descended directly from smiths who made nails. The nail names tell us nothing beyond that fact, but SPIKER obviously indicates a man who made extra-large nails. CLOUTER and CLOWER refer to nail makers, all right, but these names have been confused with Anglo-Saxon words that meant a maker of patches. TINGLE and TINGLER were smiths who made small nails.

GROUP 8

Shear Makers

In spite of all our technology today, we still find hand-operated shears a virtual necessity; the tailor, the dressmaker, the barber, and many other modern tradesmen would be very hard pressed to stay in business if they had to throw away their scissors. In medieval England a pair of sharp shears was vital to the entire textile industry. They were essential to the men who sheared the sheep, and without the sheep and its fleece of wool there would have been almost no textiles and we might still be wearing skins. Though silk and linen were in use at that period, they too depended somewhat on shears for their manufacture.

One can imagine then the importance of a smith with the ability to make a pair of shears and the almost equal importance of a man who owned a pair of them. Making a pair of shears capable of doing a good job of cutting is more complicated than the ordinary user might imagine. It is not enough that both blades be sharpened at exactly the correct angle. They must also be very slightly curved toward each other so that only one tiny point on each blade meets the corresponding point on the other blade at the same instant. Scientific machinery takes care of this today, but in medieval England it must have taken a great deal of skill developed by years of practice.

We can learn something about this by studying the names in Group 8 (page 48). Most of the names probably came from smiths who made shears. It is not unreasonable to think that the smith who managed to make a good pair would be called upon to make another, thereby establishing a reputation that would identify him with shears. If and when this happened, we might expect a prying tax man to seize upon this for the man's name—it certainly would distinguish him from all the other smiths in the area. The earliest written record of the name that I have found was on a tax roll in the year 1231. And as one might expect, it was written in Norman French as Robertus le Sherer.

SHEARSMITH and SERSMITH are obviously makers of shears, but

SHEARMAN, SHARMAN, and SHERMAN may or may not be shear-making smiths—they may have been men skilled in the use of shears. There were certainly far more people willing and anxious to get their hands on a pair of good shears than there were shears, and surely some of them acquired a reputation for their use. SHEARER is another name that leaves us in doubt whether it came from a maker of shears or a user of them.

GROUP 9

Locksmiths

The history of locks and keys must go far back into prehistoric times, because the desire and need for the security of the individual and his valuables is something basic in human nature. The oldest existing lock that we know of was discovered in Khorsabad Palace near Nineveh. It is said to be about four thousand years old. It is made of wood throughout and is enormous compared to anything modern. This type of lock had to have a key correspondingly large—so large, in fact, that the key was ordinarily carried on the shoulder. This fact explains the passage in the Bible, Isaiah 22: 22—"And I will place on his shoulder the key of the house of David."

A particularly interesting point about this old lock and key is not either its size or the fact that it was made entirely of wood, but that its loose-locking pin construction was to be adopted a great many centuries later, in 1848, by Linus Yale in Connecticut. Mr. Yale and his son may or may not have ever actually seen a picture of that old lock at Nineveh, but they did use the basic idea of it and completely revolutionized the making of locks in the nineteenth century.

Romans made the first all-metal locks, around the time of Caesar. They either knew nothing about the Nineveh lock or, if they did, ignored it. They produced at least crude examples of the type of lock that was to be used all over the world until Yale came along.

The locksmiths of England in the Middle Ages, like the rest of Europe, used a system of interposing wards, which may be described briefly as follows: When a key is put into a keyhole and turned, the blade of the key engages the bolt so the bolt can be flipped backward to unlock or forward to lock. This is the way it works with the *right key,* the one that was made for that particular lock and no other. With the wrong key, the blade will strike solidly against one or more obstacles deliberately put there by the smith who designed the lock and key. These obstacles are called *wards,* and over the centuries a lot of locksmiths' brains have gone into the type and arrangement of these obstacles. All the little grooves and slots and odd-looking cuts you see on the blade of these old keys have been painstakingly put there to allow that key to get past all the wards and operate the bolt.

It is on this simple but effective principle that nearly all locks were made between the time of the Romans and the arrival of Linus Yale in the 1840s. Medieval locksmiths used additional means as well, to make it impossible to open a lock without the proper key, such as making the keyhole hard to find and putting wards just inside the keyhole that would prevent the wrong key from entering the hole at all. Both these ideas are still in use.

Generally, the English locks made during the naming period were considerably larger than anything we have today—the key alone was quite a chunk of hardware. About eight inches long, it was made from an iron rod almost as thick as a finger and might easily weigh over a pound. One certainly would not carry such keys around in a pocket. A jailer or some official who had to carry a few of them about would have them on a ring suspended from his belt.

The LOCK names on this list need no explanation—they obviously refer to men who either made locks or were in some way associated with them. The earliest name of this type I have found is Henry le Lokier in 1221.

Another Old French word for locksmith was *serrurier.* This was simplified to SERRUR. Names derived from KEY are not quite as simple. Often such a name was applied to a smith who made keys, and since the man who made a key had to make the lock that went with it, he could have been given any name on the entire list. However, the name might be used now and then as a nickname for a man who frequently appeared with a bunch of keys dangling from his belt. He may have been a petty official in charge of the castle's food supply or even a jailer—although jailers were more apt to be called KEEP or KEEPER. The earliest written record of the name I have found is Robertus le Keyere, on the tax rolls of Kent in 1275.

GROUP 10

Anchor Makers

The anchor makers' names are a small group because the ships of that time were made almost entirely from wood. Since the craft of the smith was confined to iron, he could contribute little to the shipbuilders except the anchor and an occasional iron pin. Pins were employed to fasten wooden beams together in circumstances that today would call for a bolt with a washer and nut on it. While the idea of a bolt with a thread was known in the Middle Ages, the ability to make the thread was not, so bolts were put through the beams red-hot, and a washer was slipped over the end and riveted down tight.

Medieval smiths knew almost nothing about cast iron. When a bloom in the forge turned out brittle because of too much carbon, it was considered a failure and thrown back to be treated over again. So when called upon to make an anchor for a ship, the smith began the long process of smelting batch after batch of ore until he had enough more or less pure wrought or malleable iron to be welded together and hammered into the shape of the desired anchor.

Specifically, the first eight names in Group 10 (page 49) more or less are self-explanatory and even BOTSMITH clearly indicates a smith equipped to make any kind of iron part a shipbuilder might demand.

GROUP 11

Makers of Iron Tires

This group is very small for a rather obvious reason: the number of carts and wagons on the road in the naming period was exceedingly small. It is said that absolutely no one traveled in a wheeled conveyance at that time except the condemned criminal on his way to execution. In medieval England, all travel that was not on foot was on horseback, but unless one belonged to the wealthy nobility or was one of the occasional wealthy merchants, one didn't have a riding horse. Goods were transported by packhorses.

Wheeled vehicles of any kind were not very practical in the eleventh century, for no one knew how to hitch a horse to a wagon. This may sound strange, but until such a simple thing as the horse collar was developed in the late eleventh century, people commonly put a rope or strap around a horse's neck and wondered why the horse objected to pulling a cartload of stone.

By the early twelfth century, however, carts and wagons began to be a little more practical, and consequently more of them were to be seen, particularly in the city of London. To get good use out of a cart, the rim of the wheels had to be protected from the rocky roads. Even the great skill of wheel makers could not enable a wooden wheel to stay together very long with the road conditions of that period. We shall probably never know who first developed the idea of putting a strip of iron around the rim of a wagon wheel, but it might very well have been a smith, particularly one who was conscious of the habit iron has of shrinking when a piece of it, heated to red, is allowed to cool off. Whoever the originator of the idea was, he must be numbered among the great benefactors of humanity. Iron tires were heated and shrunk onto cart and wagon wheels and still are in this century.

The four names that have come down to us from the smiths who did this type of work are few in number, but their contribution to civilization cannot be measured.

GROUP 2

Names of Smiths Based on French and Latin

Faro	Feavers	Feuer	Le Fever
Farra	Feaviour	Fever	Lefevre
Farrah	Feron	Fevers	Le Fevre
Farrar	Ferrar	•	•
Farrey	Ferrer	Le Feaver	Pharaoh
Farrow	Ferrers	Lefeaver	Pharo
Fearon	Ferrour	Le Feure	Pharoah
Feaver	Ferun	Le Feuvre	

GROUP 3

Names Based on English

Angove	Blower	•	Smithy
Goff	•	Smeeth	Smithyes
Goffe	Blakesmith	Smidman	Smithyman
•	•	Smisson	Smyth
Athersmith	Caird	Smith	Smythe
•	•	Smithe	Smythiman
Balismith	Forge	Smither	Smythson
Bellow	Forger	Smitherman	Smythyes
Bellows	Forgman	Smithers	Smythyman
Beloe	•	Smithies	Smye
Billows	Ironcutter	Smithson	Watersmyth

GROUP 4

Horseshoers

Arsnell	Horsnell	Marskell	Shoesmyth
Horsenail	•	Mascall	Shoosmith
Horsenell	Farrier	Maskall	Shosmyth
Horsnail	•	Maskell	Shouger
Horsnaill	Mareschal	Maskill	
Horsnall	Marschall	•	
Horsnel	Marshall	Shoesmith	

GROUP 5

Smiths Named for the Items They Made

Bokelere	•	Sperrin	Spurring
Botoner	Lorimer	Sperring	•
•	Loriner	Spoor	Stirrop
Bridel	Lorrimar	Spore	Stirrup
Bridell	•	Sporier	Sturrup
Bridle	Sheather	Sporiere	
Bridleman	Shether	Spurr	
•	•	Spurren	
Chapemaker	Spearon	Spurrier	

GROUP 6

Smelters and Charcoal Makers

Ancony	Bloomer	Collar	Colman
Ankeny	Blumer	Colleer	Colyer
•	•	Coller	Coulman
Berner	Coales	Colliar	•
Bourner	Cole	Colliard	Steel
Brenner	Coleman	Collier	Steele
•	Coles	Collman	Steels
Blomer	Colkin	Collyear	
Bloom	Colla	Collyer	

GROUP 7

Nail Makers

Clouter	Nailor	Naylor	Tingler
Clower	Nails	•	
•	Naylar	Spiker	
Nail	Nayler	•	
Nailer	Nayles	Tingle	

GROUP 8

Shear Makers

Sersmith	Shearman	Sheeres	Sherr
Sharman	Shears	Sheers	Shurman
Shear	Shearsmith	Sher	
Sheara	Sheer	Shere	
Shearer	Sheere	Sherman	

GROUP 9

Locksmiths

Care	Keays	Locker	Locksmyth
Kay	Keer	Lockersmyth	Lockyer
Kayes	Keeys	Lockeyear	Lokyer
Kays	Key	Lockier	Lokyster
Kear	Keys	Lockman	•
Keay	•	Locksmith	Serrur

GROUP 10

Anchor Makers

Anchor	Ankersmith	Annercan	Botsmith
Anker	Ankier	Annercaw	
Ankers	Annacker	•	

GROUP 11

Makers of Iron Tires

Weldsmith	Whilesmith	Wildsmith	Wilesmith

CHAPTER 6

Smiths Who Made Weapons

In the previous chapter we considered some of the various types of work performed by the medieval smiths from which many of today's family names derive. In this chapter, we shall confine ourselves to the smiths who made weapons for both war and hunting. Such smiths were very numerous; museums all over the world display their handiwork, and their skill is further attested to by the long list of names that have come down to us.

When the Normans landed in England in the second half of the eleventh century, they brought weapons with them that were not very different from those the Roman legions had used nearly a thousand years before. The Normans, however, did have better iron and more of it, and· they had developed a metal that, while it might not pass for steel today, was definitely superior to the best the Romans ever had.

Norman foot soldiers carried two-edged swords, battle-axes, and daggers, and were accompanied by bowmen and arbalesters (crossbowmen). The knights were mounted and carried the usual sword, dagger, and ax, but in addition were provided with a lance. This was a fifteen-foot-long weapon carried in the right hand of the knight and designed to unseat an opposing knight, not by the force of his arm but by the power of his onrushing horse.

Anglo-Saxon troops under Harold had essentially the same weapons as the invaders, but were not quite as well off in the matter of protective armor. While the Normans made some use of spear-carrying foot soldiers, the English seem to have been more dependent on them.

Whatever they were, these weapons were the product of hardworking smiths in both countries, who specialized in the field. The smith who developed skill in making weapons found the demand for his handiwork so great that he would leave the rakes and hoes and shovels to other smiths.

In general, the techniques and know-how of the Norman smiths were greater than those of the native English in the eleventh century. They seem to have known better how to apply the power of wind and water to the working of forges. At least some of the time, they were able to make an edged weapon that would keep its edge, and blades that would not bend backward when used to strike a heavy blow.

As the English weapon makers improved the quality and quantity of products, greater prosperity could be noted in the London streets of this period. Many of the shops now had two floors, the second one extending out over the street, and were built out of sawed timber instead of the old wattle and daub construction with its thatched roof. They were shops in the real meaning of that word—goods were made there, displayed, and sold directly to the consumer.

The shops of various kinds of smiths were by far the most numerous in any town. They were easily distinguishable by the black smoke pouring out, the sound of hammers, and the flying sparks. London smiths made most of England's weapons in the twelfth century. London was the biggest city, and the king and his enormous troop of followers were headquartered there. Thus it offered the craftsman the best market for his skill and the customer the best selection.

GROUP 12
Knife Makers

This group contains those names that have come down to us from the smiths who made knives. Some of them may have made cutlery of all types, but if we can judge by the family names, these hardworking craftsmen were all knife makers. We can be reasonably sure that none of them made swords or spears or lances to any extent, because each of these weapons produced their own names.

The all-purpose cutlery that these men made must have been a very sizable portion of the medieval market. Their trade was not restricted to nobles and gentry in the castles and manor houses—not at all; the masculine habit of carrying a knife of some kind was universal and went back to the Stone Age when knives had to be chipped out of flint.

In describing one of his pilgrims, Chaucer said, "A Sheffield thwitel baar he in his hose." In the Middle English of Chaucer, "thwitel" was pronounced "Whittle" and it meant just about any kind of knife a man of that period would carry about his person for any number of uses. He would certainly use it to cut his food into bite-size pieces, and since forks were virtually unknown at that time, we can easily guess at another use he would have had for it.

The modern pocketknife with blades that fold conveniently back into the handle was still far in the future in Chaucer's time. A knife consisted of a single blade hammered out of the best iron a smith could produce. It would be pointed at one end so that things could be easily speared, and the other end would be drawn out into a tang and covered with bone or wood to serve as a handle. It would not, however, have a guard at the top of the blade to protect the hand; this would not come for some years yet.

For centuries, smiths, not only in London but all over the world, had been trying to make a blade hard enough to keep an edge but not brittle enough to break in normal use. What they were trying to make was, of course, steel—and now and then a fairly good blade would result. One method was to heat the blade till red-hot, cover it with fine charcoal, and try to hammer as much of the charcoal into the metal as possible. Repeated over and over again, this method did seem to help a little, but modern metallurgists believe that the repeated hammering was the real cause of the improvement. Another way was to surround the blade with charcoal in the forge and maintain heat for several hours, then plunge the blade into some cold liquid.

At any rate, a man bought his knife from the smith he had the most faith in and went on his way. It might be thrust into whatever type of leg covering was favored, as Chaucer's pilgrim did, or it could be stuck loosely into one's belt. The affluent would carry it in a scabbard made in part by the smith and in part by the leatherworker. Making scabbards from metal and leather became popular enough to produce at least one family name still with us—CHAPEMAKER (see Group 5, page 47).

BLADES, BLADER, BLAYDES, and BLADE are Anglo-Saxon in origin, although the word was spelled *blaed* in the old records. I find one entry in 1305 as Andrew le Blader.

The three COTTELL and five CUTLER names came directly from the Norman word *coutelier* meaning, of course, "a maker of knives and similar cutting utensils." It does not seem to have been applied, or at least not accepted, as a name for a knife maker until about 1400. By that date, most family names were fairly well set, but CUTLER managed to stick, nevertheless.

COTTEL and its variations are from the Old French word for a short knife and in practice probably meant a cutler.

All five of the DAG names come from the old French word *dague,* but whether it meant a man who made knives or a man who carried one is unclear. The word was probably used to distinguish a maker of knives, for surely such smiths were far less numerous than men who carried knives.

KNIFESMITH and KNYFSMITH simply combine the words *knife* and *smith.* In Old English, *knife* was spelled *cnif.* Somewhere along the way, the *c* was changed to *k* and an *e* added.

The last four names might seem hard to explain but since the *k* in *knife* has been dropped in pronunciation it is not difficult to imagine some tax man putting it down the way it sounded, giving us NAE-SMITH, NAISMITH, NASMYTH, and NASMITH. The name NA-SMYTH first appears in London records early in the thirteenth century and is still fairly widespread today, particularly in England.[1]

---

[1] The name Nasmith brings up an interesting question. Is it possible that an individual might quite unconsciously inherit an innate talent from one of his ancestors; something he might not be even aware of unless and until he happened to be thrown into circumstances that brought it to light? Possible examples of this are known.

James Nasmyth was born in Scotland in 1800 and died in London in 1890, a highly successful ironmaster. The nineteenth-century British applied that term to anyone in the trade who had his own shop. C. L. Mateaux, in his *Wonderland of Work,* written in the 1880s, says of Nasmyth as a boy: "When Nasmyth was a little lad, the youngest of a family of ten, nothing delighted him more than to spend his half-holidays and spare moments in a neighboring forge that belonged to the father of one of his school fellows. The boy did not merely go staring and wandering aimlessly here and there, but was always intently watching and trying to understand the different processes through which the metal passed, learning all the details of the moulding, casting, forging and smithing work going on about him, so that after long years of hard work and self-denial, he became exceedingly prosperous, he was glad to remember how much he had learned in those days and often declared that the time spent in the different shops connected with that foundry was the true and only apprenticeship of his life."

The real point of the story of James Nasmyth for us is that he seems to have been born with a love of the whole business of ironworking. At an age when most children have little or no interest in work of any kind, there he was spending most of his playtime watching every movement of the smiths.

Many years later he was to become the inventor of the steam hammer. Up to the year 1943 when he introduced the steam hammer to an astonished world, the old helve hammer was the best power-driven hammer known. It worked by either water or wind power, but its blows were relatively light because it depended entirely on gravity; the heavy hammer was lifted by power but struck its blow when the load was released.

Nasmyth's steam hammer could strike very much harder and far more rapidly. Because power not only lifted the hammer but propelled it downward. It is still the basic hammer in any forging shop today. It is said that a skilled operator can so

GROUP 13

Swordmakers

And now we come to the sword, one of the oldest and most widely
used weapons man has ever made. Long before written history, men were
fighting with swords of every size and shape, made in a variety of materials. A sword was the weapon a commanding general handed to his opponent as a token of surrender; it was the weapon a young squire placed
on the altar the evening before he was to be knighted.

Today, of course, its use is confined to ceremonial affairs, both military
and civilian, but in England from 1100 to 1350, it was the distinguishing
mark of the knight.

Before the arrival of the Normans, the Anglo-Saxons used a straight
two-edged sword that had been brought into England by the Vikings. It
was usually a twenty-inch blade with a handle but no guard or hilt whatever. When the Norman smiths began spreading over England in the
twelfth and thirteenth centuries, they brought new ideas, such as a guard
dividing the handle from the blade. Today we call that guard a hilt but
the Norman name for it was *quillon*. It was not merely ornamental—it
protected the hand from the blade of an opponent. One fellow's blade
might strike the other's and slide right down into his hand if something
were not there to stop it. The Saxons had always used a metal-covered
glove for this purpose, but such bulky gloves must have been terribly awkward in getting a firm grip on the handle. The quillon was far superior
and it became popular very quickly. Over the years, the quillon developed into quite a complicated arrangement with rings for the index
finger and finally a wire cage covering the hand. This made the sword a
defensive weapon as well as an offensive one. With such a sword, a man
could get along with a smaller shield on his left arm. This small shield
came to be called a buckler.

London had its share of smiths who specialized in making swords, like

---

completely control its power blows that a common pin can be driven into a board
up to the head without bending the pin.

Was it inherited talent that made the young Nasmyth want to hang around
the shops watching the smiths instead of playing with the children of his age? As
he watched those brawny workmen sweat and toil, was some ancestral voice within
him whispering that there must be a better way?

Nasmyth never became specifically a knifesmith; he covered nearly the whole field
including knives.

Robert Suerd in 1185, Peter Sword in 1297, and Richard Swordere in 1354, but only the last name seems to have survived as a family name.

Competition among the swordmaking smiths must have been terrific, and it was not confined to London. Smiths from many parts of Europe developed reputations for the quality of their blades. Toledo in Spain, Passau on the Danube, and Solingen in what is now West Germany became so famous that English noblemen who could afford it vied with each other to buy swords from there. Willingly they placed orders for Toledo blades, knowing that they would have to wait years for delivery.

Exactly how these smiths managed to make such good steel is gradually becoming known to modern metallurgists. It is known that some of these blades were strip-welded; that is, bundles of iron cut in long strips were heated and hammered together. The bar that resulted would be reheated, bent double, and hammered together again. This would be repeated many times, and perhaps between these treatments the piece would be roasted in a bed of charcoal for a long period. Today, these swords, labeled with the name of the smith and the town he came from, are museum pieces.

The first nine names, beginning with BRAND, are of somewhat uncertain derivation. Some of them look as though they might have become mixed up with German at some point. *Brand* was Old French for sword and *brandr* is Old Danish, so BRANDER and BRANDMAN have to mean makers of swords.

CLAYMORE was the name of an extra-large two-edged sword developed in Scotland by the Highlanders. It was designed to be held by both hands at once and consequently its handle was twice as long as that of an ordinary sword. The name comes from the old Gaelic word *claidheamh*.

HANSARD is from the Old French word for sword, particularly one that featured a long sharp point for thrusting as opposed to one designed for cutting. It appears in the old tax records of 1200 as Roger Hansard and has survived unchanged in spelling.

LANGSPEE means long sword. It could have been applied as a nickname to some man carrying a sword of greater length than usual or it could also have been given to the smith who specialized in making such things.

The old Anglo-Saxon word for sword was *sweord*. From it come the last seven names in this group.

GROUP 14

Spear, Bill, and Lance Makers

Group 14 (page 59) consists of surnames that came directly or indirectly from three of the commonly used weapons of medieval England. We know beyond a doubt that some of them originated with the smith who made one or more of them, but it is impossible now to single out each one of them with complete certainty. SPEARMAN could certainly be applied to a man who carried a spear, but it could just as easily be applied to a man who made them. I am inclined to think the latter more likely—a certain smith was a SPEARMAN rather than a NAISMITH or a BLADER.

The spear is an extremely ancient weapon. Spearheads have been found in prehistoric excavations throughout the world. In ancient times, the spear was a hunting weapon, but by the time of the Romans it had become recognized as a weapon useful in war too. In the Middle Ages, it was definitely used for both purposes. It varied in length from about four feet to as long as eight feet. The spearhead would be hammered out of the best metal the smith could obtain and a tang welded to it that would be as long as desired. Wooden strips were welded to the tang to form the handle.

The spear could be thrown at an enemy or, if one were close enough, thrust at him—either way, it was a wicked weapon. If one were lucky enough to have a spear made from reasonably good steel, one could drive it through the chain mail of an enemy but as frequently happened, the point would be so soft that on impact it would bend backward and be useless until it could be straightened out. In the early part of the naming period, the smith would hammer out a spearhead in the form of an elongated diamond, but before long some smith started adding fancy touches, like barbs near where the head became the tang, or useless but ornamental holes in the blade.

The bill was simply a long spear with a sizable hook sticking out at the base of the head. It resembled a bird's bill, whence the name. Once again, it is not known for sure whether a BILLMAN or a BILLER was so named because he carried the weapon or made it. The bill was used in war just as any other spear, but it had an advantage—the hook on it enabled the carrier to hook into the armor of a mounted knight and drag him off his horse. A knight on foot loaded down with heavy armor couldn't move around nearly so fast as the BILLMAN.

Out of the bill developed the halberd. This was simply a very elaborate and fancy combination of the spear and the bill. It was altogether too fancy and expensive to have ever become a practical weapon of war. For the most part, halberds became museum pieces and are still used in ceremonial affairs. The halberd does not seem to have given us any family names, probably because it did not reach full development until the fifteenth century, when the naming period was over.

The lance, in medieval times, was that fifteen-foot-long spear carried by a mounted knight. Usually it was seated in a pocket provided for the purpose on the saddle. The point was controlled by the right hand of the knight while his left arm manipulated his shield to ward off his opponent's lance. For some reason, no surnames originating with the lance seem to have come down to us.

The PIKE names in all their spelling variations have a mixed origin. The Old English word for any sharp point was *pic,* and in the course of years that little word was used rather carelessly to mean almost anything. The weapon known as a pike was longer than a spear but usually not as long as a lance. It was used mostly by foot soldiers. LEPICK and PICKER have moved so far in their spelling that they may be hard to recognize, but they both refer to either a man who carried this weapon or the smith who made it.

GROUP 15

Cleaver Makers

A CLEAVER was a wicked combination of an ax and a knife. It was very heavy and very sharp. One blow at a man's head could cut through almost any metal helmet and, if the blow was struck directly downward, the cleaver would split a man's head as well.

The last nine names in this group come from the same root, *taille fer,* which literally means "something or somebody who could cut through iron." Undoubtedly, some version of the name was given to or assumed by a fairly sizable number of people back in those days—to the man who was strong enough to cut through a piece of iron (perhaps with his cleaver) or possibly to the smith who could make such a weapon.

GROUP 16

Caltrop Makers

A CALTROP was a little star-shaped piece of iron, something like the jacks children play with, except that they have six arms. The caltrop, however, was not a toy: it had only four arms and all were razor-sharp. Handfuls of these would be scattered over the path enemy horsemen would be expected to take, three of the arms resting on the ground and the fourth one sticking up an inch to an inch and a half. Chances were a horse who stepped on one of these would be made permanently lame.

GROUP 17

Ax and Hammer Makers

An ax is familiar to us as a tool used to chop down trees and split wood for the fireplace, but back in the naming period an ax had an additional use. Axes were made with short handles or long handles; either type could easily cave in the whole side of a man's rib cage or his head, with one blow. Armor offered no real protection from the deadly weapon because an ax's weight was so concentrated in one spot that it tended to crush anything with it.

The names AX, AXER, and AXMAN are obvious, while EXSMITH comes from the Old English word for ax, *aex*.

GROUP 18

Makers of Clubs

I suspect that CLUBS were not made by smiths, since they were entirely of wood, but they were nevertheless something that could not be overlooked by the men of the period. Under the Assize of Arms, every adult man was bound to be provided with at least a *Coutel* (a knife) and a *Baculus* (a staff or club). The names beginning with *K* in this list are probably from the source of our word *cudgel*. TROUNCER came from Old French, meaning simply a club or a cudgel. The Old French word was *tronche*. The earliest record of any form of the word as a name was Henry Truncer in 1315.

GROUP 19

Mace Makers

A MACE was just a glorified club. It might be made of wood but its upper half would be studded with spikes and knobs of all kinds. It was a powerful persuader, but like the knight's sword it is now relegated to ceremonial use. In some of the older universities, a member of the faculty still carries a decorative mace in any academic procession. It supposedly symbolizes the authority of the university.

GROUP 12

Knife Makers

Blade	Cottle	Dagg	Knyfsmith
Blader	Cutler	Daggar	Naesmith
Blades	Cuttell	Dagger	Naismith
Blaydes	Cuttill	Daggers	Nasmyth
•	Cuttler	Daggett	Naysmith
Cottel	Cuttles	•	
Cottell	•	Knifesmith	

GROUP 13

Swordmakers

Brand	Braund	Hansard	Soords
Brander	Brauns	•	Sword
Brandman	Bront	Langspee	Sworder
Brandt	•	•	Swordere
Brant	Claymore	Soards	Swords
Braun	•	Soord	

GROUP 14

Spear, Bill, and Lance Makers

Bill	Le Pick	Pikeman	Spears
Biller	Le Pyke	Pyke	Speer
Billes	Pick	•	Speers
Billman	Picker	Spear	Speir
Bills	Pickers	Speare	
•	Pickman	Speares	
Lepick	Pike	Spearman	

GROUP 15

Cleaver Makers

Claver	Taillefer	Tilford	Tulliver
Cleaver	Talfourd	Tilfourd	
Cleever	Telfer	Tolliver	
.	Telford	Tolver	

GROUP 16

Caltrop Makers

Calthorp	Caltrap	Caltrop

GROUP 17

Ax and Hammer Makers

Ax	Axer	Axman	Exsmith

GROUP 18

Makers of Clubs

Club	Keable	Keeble	.
Clubb	Kebbell	Kibbel	Trouncer
Clubber	Kebell	Kibble	
.	Keble	Kibel	

GROUP 19

Mace Makers

Mace

CHAPTER 7

Smiths Who Made Armor

The idea of either wearing or carrying some kind of protective armor to ward off an enemy bent on one's destruction is as ancient as fighting itself. Probably a protective shield that could be worn on the left arm and manipulated as needed, leaving the right arm free to attack, was the first development. Without exception, every time explorers discover some previously unknown primitive tribe, they report shields already being used as established equipment.

The Greeks, in Homeric times, and later the Romans not only used shields but developed protective armor for the body that was far ahead of the Assyrian or Persian, and later, the Egyptian. They used bronze, mostly because iron was very scarce and steel almost nonexistent.

In England between 1100 and 1350, when our family names were slowly growing out of the daily occupations of our ancestors, the smiths that gave their time and thought to the production and development of armor contributed a large share of these names.

Virtually all the armor used in England in that period has to be classified as chain mail. I don't suppose the people of that time called it chain mail: it was the only kind they knew, so to them it was just armor. It was made by welding hundreds of tiny iron rings together into a chain and then welding each ring to the rings of another chain. The result would be a very supple piece of material that could be made into a coat, a jacket, a leg covering, or whatever the customer wanted.

Museums have very little chain armor because during the greater part of the period in which it was made and worn it was also being buried with its owner. Besides, being made of iron, it was subject to rust. Five hundred years of exposure to air and moisture is enough to destroy completely anything made of iron unless it is exceedingly thick. Nevertheless, we still know a great deal about medieval armor. There are a few actual samples of chain mail and some reasonably clear drawings in old manuscripts. Now and then, these drawings give surprising details. Then, of course, the work of the medieval sculptors tells us a great deal. Their work often appears in wall niches of cathedrals and on sarcophagi. Possibly, the richest source of information is the wonderful Bayeux Tapestry.

Just as the Normans had better weapons than the English, so also they had better armor. A well-equipped Norman would be provided with a coat or shirt of mail that would reach down to his knees. It would be slit a few inches both in front and back so he could ride his horse with at least some degree of comfort. The Norman word for this chain-mail garment was *hauberk*. On his head, he would wear a close-fitting cap that was cone-shaped and made of heavy leather reenforced with iron bands radiating from the point. The front band would extend down over the wearer's nose and was called a *nasal*. His legs would be wrapped with folds of chain mail that extended from his ankles well up under his hauberk.

A duke or a marquis would almost certainly be proudly wearing one of the newest improvements in armor, called a *gorgette*. It was a mail cover for all of the head except the face and it hung down in graceful folds to the shoulders, covering all of the neck. The shield varied in size, shape, and material, depending on whether the soldier were mounted or on foot.

The English under Harold were still wearing the older mail covering called a *byrnie*. This was shaped very much like a modern T-shirt. It had a low neck and short sleeves and was as long as the wearer desired, usually not much below the waistline. A byrnie had the advantage of being much lighter in weight and handier to move around in than the hauberk, but it did not give as much protection.

This description of a Norman and an Anglo-Saxon fighter is not typical of the great majority of fighters on either side. At that time, and for many years after, there was no such thing as a national army with organized and uniform equipment. In that period, a monarch would do his best to enlist the support of all the nobles in his area. He might be lucky enough to win over most of them, but some saw no personal advantage in supporting the monarch at all. Those who did come to the king's aid brought their own retainers and fought as independent units, and therefore the equipment of the rank and file varied tremendously. Each man wore the best equipment he had. This might mean a very scanty suit of ancient armor or it might mean no armor at all, with perhaps only a club or scythe or pitchfork for weapon.

It is reasonable to think that every normal able-bodied man wanted to own good weapons and a complete set of armor, but those things were costly. For any man who could pay the price, however, London was well provided with smiths able and willing to outfit him, smiths who specialized in armor.

GROUP 20

Makers of Chain Armor

All of the names in Group 20 (page 69) clearly refer to smiths of this type. Certainly a smith who made tools or hardware or shoed horses would never be called *le armurer* or, in Old French, *armurier*. So, the first eight names derive from the word *Armor*, and the next seven from *byrnie*. GORCH, GORDGE, and GORDGETT derive from the combination mail cover mentioned earlier in this chapter. The HAUBERK names derive from the Old French word *le hauberge*, frequently spelled *haubergier*, and through the centuries, spelled in an astonishing variety of ways. They all indicated a man who made things out of chain mail.

The remaining names in this group, ERNEST and HARNESS, at first glance don't seem to belong here at all, but they definitely do. The Old French origin is *erneis* or *hernais* meaning "a suit of armor." They both refer to a man who made suits of mail.

GROUP 21

Shield Makers

The SHIELD names, with their variations, come from the most ancient piece of defensive armor ever made, as indicated earlier in this chapter. Shields could not be made out of mail, as they had to be carried on the arm and readily moved in all directions to ward off a blow from a sword, a spear, an ax, or a lance. This meant they had to be stiff and to prevent penetration by any of the weapons that would be aimed at the bearer. This was a big order.

Primitive tribes made their shields by stretching animal hides over a crude wooden frame. They knew little or nothing about tanning, which would have increased the toughness of the hide, but these early shields were undoubtedly effective against the crude weapons of other savages.

In the Greek and Roman eras, shields were usually made of bronze. Fairly thin bronze sheets were fastened to wooden frames. The Romans experimented with many different shapes—round, oval, rectangular but flat, or rectangular but somewhat cylindrical to fit the body of the bearer.

The Normans seem to have favored what might be described as an egg-shaped shield, with the smaller end of the egg pointing down. This would give great protection to the upper parts of the body where most of the blows of an enemy struck. This shape would also make the shield lighter, and the pointed end down would keep one's feet free.

The typical Anglo-Saxon shield seems to have been either perfectly round or rectangular with rounded corners. Frequently the Englishman of the medieval period sharpened the boss or central point of the shield facing the enemy to a point. Thus, at close quarters with the enemy, the shield could be made to serve as a weapon of attack as well as defense.

In the early part of the naming period in England, most of the shields were made of the hardest and toughest wood obtainable. While such shields offered some protection, if they were made thick enough to be truly effective they were too heavy and cumbersome to be worthwhile. Quite possibly the next material tried was horn and boiled leather, called by the Normans *cuir bouilli*. This was not too heavy a shield, and a spear, even thrown from some distance, would go through it. Bronze was tried and it was a big improvement over anything previous because it was metal. But if bronze was good, iron would be even better, and so the hardworking smiths were called in to make shields out of iron and steel.

Not many of these medieval iron shields are to be found in the museums. They were hammered out as thinly as seemed practical, to keep them as light as possible. None of them could stop an arrow from a longbow unless it struck at a glancing angle. And while the shield might be effective against a sword, a spear, or a pike, it was hopeless against an ax. Therefore when the knights prepared for a tournament, they carried a shield of extra thickness. If they could prevent the other knight's lance from penetrating their shield, the lance might glance harmlessly off to the side, or even break.

The first name in Group 21 (page 70) is BUCKLER and comes from the Old French word *boucler,* indicating a shield with a spear point in the middle or simply a small shield. FORTESQUE (and FOSKEW, which was probably the way the name sounded to the man who first had to enter it into a record) was simply a combination of two Old French words, *fort* and *escu,* meaning strong shield. FORTESQUIEU merely gilded the lily.

SHIELD, SHIELDMAKER, SHIELDMAN, and SHIELDS are obvious, but I cannot finish the story of the armor-making smiths without some words about a nineteenth-century occurrence that involved this name. In 1803, President Jefferson authorized Lewis and Clark to explore from the Mississippi River west through hundreds of miles of territory which, to a great extent, had never been seen by a white man. This was an enormous undertaking. It meant many weary months of travel over the trackless plains, finding a pass through the Rocky Mountains, living off what game they could shoot, and avoiding trouble with the Indians. A party of forty-seven men reached the Pacific Ocean and then returned to its starting point in 1806, spending fully three years completely out of touch with civlization and all normal sources of supply. A thousand different kinds of accidents to their equipment could, and did, happen on their historic trek—weapons and tools were lost and stolen, guns were broken, and parts lost that made the guns useless. In spite of all the difficulties, the expedition succeeded. Captain Lewis and all the many researchers and writers on the expedition since are in enthusiastic agreement that the man who contributed most to the expedition's ultimate success was the smith they had carefully selected. Referred to as a smith, blacksmith, and frequently as a gunsmith, we know that somehow he managed to carry with him not only the tools of his trade but also a portable forge with a bellows. He made new parts for guns and even new stocks when, as happened more than once, one of the party had to use his gun as a club to beat off the attack of a bear. Writings describing the resourcefulness and skill of this smith are many. His name was John SHIELDS.

Nothing is known of either the ancestors or descendants of John Shields, but a genealogical study of his forebears would almost certainly reveal at least a few highly skilled smiths on the rungs of a ladder leading back to 1206 and the first record of the name—Robert Scild, maker of shields.

GROUP 22

Makers of Armored Head-Coverings

Of the smiths who made armor, some went on to concentrate on armored head-coverings. At first the head-covering consisted of a leather cap, which was well padded underneath and protected on the outside with a few metal strips. A blow from an enemy sword downward on the head, however, could hardly fail to guide the sword down the metal strips to lop off an ear. The gorgette, already described, was one solution to this problem since it covered the ears and the neck with mail. But another solution soon appeared. The inventor must have been painfully aware of the number of ears being sliced off owing to the cone-shaped helmet because he designed a cylindrical metal can that would come down over the entire head, neck and ears included. It must have looked like a metal wastebasket turned upside down, with holes in the front to allow the wearer to both breathe and see. It was perfectly flat on top, just as a wastebasket is flat on the bottom. It did protect the ears, and its flap top provided a convenient place for a gay-looking plume or some type of crest, but if an enemy were to hit the top of it with a downward blow, the whole helmet would be jammed down on the wearer's shoulders, and he couldn't see or hear until he removed it. And an enemy would hardly stand by idle.

This sorry bit of gear did not last long, as may be imagined, but so-called improvements on it were, for some time, not improvements at all. Making the top semispherical offered almost as tempting a target as the old flat top, and none of these devices offered any real protection to the face. Bowmen and crossbowmen were becoming so expert that they could take deliberate aim at an enemy's fully exposed face and frequently hit it at more than a hundred yards. Something that would protect the face as well as the entire head was necessary.

No existing record gives credit to any one smith for the development that followed. It was probably the work of a great many smiths, not in England alone but all over Europe. At any rate, something called a *bas-inet* was developed, and it seemed to solve the problem. Made entirely of iron, it started with a cone that pointed slightly to the rear. The section that would have covered the face was cut away entirely and over this opening was another iron cone pointing forward. This forward cone was hinged to the upright cone just above the ears, and its front was pierced with small holes for breathing and slits for seeing. When no battle was to be expected, the forward cone, or *visor,* could be tilted back on its hinges, but it could be flipped down into position in seconds. Made of heavy iron, thick enough to turn aside most blows, it must have been very uncomfortable to the wearer since it might weigh several pounds. It was said that the English longbowmen with a range of two hundred to three hundred yards used to look for enemy knights careless enough to ride along with the visor up.

The BASINET names in this group clearly derive from the head-protecting device so named, but the next five names beginning with HELM originally meant a covering for a small building. With the development of a new piece of head armor, variations of the word were applied to it.

HOMER and HOMERE came from the Old French word *heaumier* or *heumier,* meaning simply "a smith who made helmets." HEUMER was merely a spelling variation of the same.

GROUP 23

Makers of Plate Armor

The names in Group 23 (page 70) appeared in the fourteenth century with the development of plate armor. Since most surnames were fairly well set by the middle of the fourteenth century, there are few which emerged from this profession. Also plate armor took a couple of centuries of very painstaking work on the part of the smiths before it came into general use. In fact, by the time it was obtainable everywhere, it had begun to pass out of use, because of the development of firearms, against which it was practically useless. Nevertheless, it is a fact that the very finest armor ever made was produced more than a century after the introduction of firearms. Vienna's fine Kunsthistorisches Museum has a truly magnificent collection of plate armor, but almost every piece in it was made in the sixteenth and even seventeenth centuries. Frequently inlaid with gold, they are beautiful works of art and fine tributes to the skill of the smiths who made them. Almost every individual piece of metal in them has a name, but none of them has come down to us as a family name, for they were made too late.

The few PLAT names in this group undoubtedly were given to those progressive smiths who were quick to see the market for plate armor and began making it while chain mail was still in use.

GROUP 24

Makers of Leg Armor

The names in this group refer to the earliest type of plate armor made —GREAVES or leg-covering armor. Some armor-making smith must have conceived the idea of hammering out an iron plate that could be bent to fit around a man's shins. Certainly it was easier to make than chain mail, and strapping it on was no problem. The Old French word for shin was *greve;* hence the term *greaves* and the resulting variations of surnames.

GROUP 25

The Cleaners, Polishers, and Sharpeners

Throughout chapters 6 and 7, the subject has been weapons and armor. These were objects that were to be used and worn frequently, objects that friends would see on a man whenever they met. A sword or dagger would be worn whenever one appeared on the street, and on the occasion of a tournament one would bring out one's very best suit of armor and one or two spare outfits if available. It was possible to lose a suit of armor in a tournament during the greater part of the naming period; if an opposing knight knocked one off one's horse with a lance in the approved fashion, it was his privilege to strip the vanquished of his whole outfit. If it was too large, it would mean a trip to his favorite smith for some alterations.

Back in those days, armor was made of iron and had the same weakness it has today: it would rust. Exposed to air and the frequent wet weather that plagues England still, a suit of chain mail would be red with rust in a couple of weeks. There was no such thing as stainless steel at that time, and the blue or browned steel from which modern gun barrels are made was not even dreamed of in medieval England. It was rust, rust, and more rust without surcease.

That situation gave rise to an occupation from which developed many well-known names like FORBER, FURBER, and FURBISHER. Since the Normans dominated everything at that time, whenever a slightly new situation would arise, some Norman would dig into his vocabulary of what we now call Old French and come up with a word to describe the situation. That word would suffice from then on, or at least until some other Norman changed it arbitrarily or, as more frequently happened, because spelling then was not standardized.

These men corresponded more or less to today's dry cleaner: they were the people to whom one sent one's rusty old suit of armor when it needed a cleaning. Cleaning and polishing armor must have been a sizable industry in the Middle Ages. Ample proof of that exists in the family names that have come down to us. RUBBAR was one of them, coming from a Norman word that meant "to rub." The only way a suit of mail could be cleaned was to rub it with sharp sand and keep on rubbing. Then there was DUBBER, which referred to a man who could not only clean one's armor but could make at least minor repairs as well.

GRATER is a little uncommon today, but in the old records of 1333 will be found William le Grator, *grateor* being Old French for "furbisher."

The name SLYKER is a little uncommon today, but it is interesting because it has an English origin. There was a Middle English word *sliken,* meaning "to polish something" (don't we still speak of slicking up something?). Anyway, it was given to a man in the business of polishing armor in 1333 instead of the usual French word. We can't be sure now whether this indicates that the man himself was English or that the tax collector was.

The next five FURBISHER names might well be placed in a separate list, as their original owners' primary skill was to sharpen weapons. But having sharpened a man's sword, it was natural for a conscientious tradesman to hand it back to his customer all polished and shining as well as sharp. Certainly the owner of the sword would like his sword polished and sharpened in one stop, so the sword-sharpener functioned also as a FURBER. SWERDSLIPER is probably of Scandinavian origin, and so too are SLIPPER, HONER, FILER, and WHETTER. All of them point to local tradesmen with the mechanical skill and equipment to sharpen weapons or tools of any kind and polish them as well.

GROUP 20

Makers of Chain Armor

Armar	Berney	•	Habershon
Armer	Bernie	Gorch	Habeshan
Armor	Bierney	Gordge	Habishaw
Armurer	Burney	Gordgett	Hauberger
Larmer	Burnie	•	Hauberk
Larmor	Burnier	Habberjam	Hauberks
Larmour	Byrnie	Habbeshaw	•
Le Armour	•	Habbijam	Harness
•	Ernest	Habergham	

GROUP 21

Shield Makers

Buckler	Fortesquieu	Shield	Shields
•	Foskew	Shieldmaker	
Fortesque	•	Shieldman	

GROUP 22

Makers of Armored Head-Coverings

Bascinet	•	Helmer	Heumer
Basinet	Helm	Helmers	Homer
Basinett	Helme	Helms	Homere

GROUP 23

Makers of Plate Armor

Plater	Platten	Playter
Platner	Platter	Playtner

GROUP 24

Makers of Leg Armor

Greaver	Greavey	Greve
Greaves	Greeves	Greves

GROUP 25

The Cleaners, Polishers, and Sharpeners

Dubber	Furber	Honer	•
•	Furbisher	•	Slyker
Filer	Furbrisher	Rubbar	•
•	•	•	Whetter
Forber	Grater	Slipper	
Frobisher	•	Swerdsliper	

CHAPTER **8**

The Bow and Arrow

The bow and arrow are associated with primitive races and tribes in all parts of the world. They formed a dependable weapon in the hands of early man, and with it he could kill small game for food and defend himself against his enemies. Enormous collections of flint arrowheads from all over America attest its popularity here before the white man and his firearms arrived.

It was in medieval England, however, that the weapon reached the apex of its development. In thirteenth-century England and until long after the first crude firearms appeared, the English longbow dominated the battlefields of western Europe. Since it was a superior weapon, those who developed great skill in its use found themselves the beneficiaries of unprecedented social change. No longer was a man just another rude peasant fighting at the beck and call of the lord of the manor, with whatever farm tool was at hand; he was now a highly respected soldier, a member of an organized company, and well paid for his skill and time. He was a YEOMAN, a FRANKLIN, a FREEMAN: titles glorious to have in a time when society was composed almost entirely of but two classes, nobles and peasantry.

No one seems to know exactly where or when the longbow first appeared. Wales is usually thought to be the area from which it came, but in any case the last quarter of the thirteenth century saw the longbow in general use all over the island of Great Britain. Undoubtedly it was the product of many experimenters seeking to improve the ancient weapon that had been used by the Britons before the coming of the Romans.

72

The peasants took to the longbow quite naturally—it was cheap and it could be obtained almost anywhere. Mechanics able to turn out reasonably good longbows appeared in every town and village. However, real skill was required to turn a stave of selected wood into a bow that would bend without breaking under the pull of a powerful arm and send an arrow at a target with accuracy.

Knights, and the nobility in general, looked with undisguised scorn on the new weapon. They had been trained from childhood to fight an opponent in individual combat, either toe to toe with swords or mounted on war-horses with lances. The very thought of killing a foe two hundred yards away, perhaps under circumstances where he could not even be seen, was inconceivable to them. It was undignified. But the popularity of the longbow swept like an avalanche over England. Edward I (1272–1307) seems to have had more common sense than his noble vassals. Instead of scorning use of the weapon, he encouraged it by making practice in its use compulsory on Sundays and holy days after mass. It is said that many a stone church throughout England still bears the marks made by countless archers sharpening their arrows on it preparatory to butts practice. A later king ruled that anyone injured during a practice session could not bring charges against another archer.

Kings had to ensure that their subjects were not distracted from archery practice by idle pastimes. Golf was forbidden in 1363 in an order to the sheriffs of England so that man "shall in his sports use bows and arrows, pellets and bolts." But golf was so popular in the fifteenth century that the fourteenth parliament of James II of Scotland decreed in 1457 that "fute-ball and golfe be utterly cryed downe and not to be used" because they interfered with the practice of archery.

Not a single complete longbow has come down to us today, though the British Museum has portions of several and some iron arrowheads as well. Made entirely of wood with a linen cord, the longbow was perishable. Nevertheless we know fairly well how they were made.

The preferred wood was yew, but ash, hazel, and even elm could be used. A small tree was cut down and split into staves six to seven feet long. (Sawing a stave out was supposed to produce an inferior bow because it disregarded the natural grain of the wood and the bow would not be as strong.) The stave would then be tapered gently from a central point to each end, leaving the central portion an inch and a half to two inches thick. The stave selected would be free of knots if one were in luck, but such staves were rare, so allowances had to be made in the tapering. A notch was then cut near each end for the cord and only then the really fine work began. The side of the stick away from the shooter had to be flat, while the nearer side was rounded off until it was semicircular. Furthermore, the flat outside of the stick had to be largely sap wood, while the inside rounded portion was to be heart wood. The sap wood on the outside would stretch under pressure, while the inside heart wood resisted stretching.

The cord was usually pure linen, either woven or braided to the required thickness, and looped at each end so it could be readily slipped into the notch prepared for it. The arrow shafts were made from any straight-grained wood available, and the iron head was the work of a smith. The head might be two inches long and provided with either a socket into which the shaft would fit or a tang to be slipped into the shaft and reinforced with thread. Sometimes the head would purposely be left sufficiently loose so that it would come loose from the shaft to remain in the flesh of the man or animal hit.

An arrow was generally described as a "clothyard shaft." Many of the arrows used with the longbow were undoubtedly a yard long, and some even longer than that, but we also know that many were no longer than twenty-eight inches. The advantage of the longbow was in being long, so as to cover more ground and the longer the bow was, the longer the arrow had to be. The length of the bow depended on the height of the man for whom it was made. A six-foot man would want a bow six and a half feet long; if he was much taller, he would want it to be a full seven feet in length.

It took a powerful arm and a great deal of practice to pull a longbow back until the fingers of the hand on the cord touched the jaw and then to let it loose without flinching. The experienced bowman of that day could match the rifleman of today in accuracy at a range of around two hundred yards, if we are to believe the stories of marksmanship that have come down to us. One such tale concerns a lord out observing his bowmen at the butts one Sunday after mass. Noticing one great brawny fellow who by his manner seemed to hold nothing but contempt for the marksmanship of the other yeomen, the lord of the manor approached him and said, "See that man away out there—can you hit him in the eye?" Quickly came the reply, "Certainly, m'lord—which eye?"

A weapon that could shoot so accurately and yet be accessible to almost anyone presented a problem. By no means was every man able to develop the skill necessary to qualify for a spot in the organized troop of the baron or duke. He could, however, be a poacher; he could kill one of his lordship's deer to give his family fresh meat. The English nobility of that time seem to have had more love for the game animals in their private forests than they had for their children. While this may seem an exaggeration, the fact is that for something like three centuries when a poacher was caught red-handed, he was punished immediately by the PARKER (the appointee of his lordship for that purpose), and his punishment was strangulation with his own bowstring. He was then left on the spot as an example to others.

The popularity of the longbow steadily increased through the 1300s. It was the longbow that first brought immortal fame to the common soldier; without it, he might never have even been mentioned in English history. The longbowmen at Crécy, Poitiers, and Agincourt were the deciding factors in winning those battles. Without that weapon and the men who carried it into battle, the Black Prince and Henry V would scarcely be remembered in history.

But trouble was on the way—so many bows were being made, and so many broken in normal use, that the supply of suitable wood was disappearing. Something had to be done or England's ranks of expert BOW-RIGHTS would be unable to maintain their production. And something was done. Correctly credited or not, it is reported that Richard III came up with a very clever solution to the problem of more staves.

It was known that much suitable wood for making bows grew in Italy and in Spain, but neither of these nations was at all anxious to sell any of it to the English. However, Italy and Spain made vast quantities of good wine, a great deal of which was exported to England (who made very little that was worth drinking), so a deal was made: every cask of wine imported into England had to incorporate four good yew staves. It worked so well that over a few years a ratio of ten staves to every tun of wine was achieved.[1]

An ARCHER in a company prepared to enter battle was usually equipped as follows: he wore a small steel helmet shaped something like an old-fashioned chocolate drop, or one made of leather with iron straps. Frequently he wore an iron breastplate over a short leather tunic. Not much in the way of armor, since he wanted mobility. In his belt he would carry a small sword or a battle-ax and dagger. In his quiver he would carry at least twenty-four arrows, the head of each arrow being about two inches long and ground to razor sharpness. In addition, he would carry about a half dozen arrows that were very much shorter than the others. Arriving at his battle station, he commonly removed all the ar-

---

[1] A tun equaled 252 wine gallons.

rows from his quiver, sticking each one into the soft soil immediately in front of him, where he could take them up one at a time without looking.

The short arrows had a strategic use. Because they were so much shorter than the regular arrows, the bow could not be drawn back nearly as far and consequently the arrow's flight would cover much less distance than that of the normal ones. If the craggy old veteran in command of the troops had reason to feel that the enemy might not have had much experience with the longbowmen, he would pass the word along the line to load with the short arrows and shoot them at the enemy. The normal range of regular arrows might be two hundred and fifty yards, but the short shafts would fall far short of that—maybe less than one hundred yards. The enemy, seeing the short distance covered and not knowing it was a trick, would promptly move in much closer, only to meet inevitable disaster.

No mention has as yet been made of the men who made the longbow. Who were they? What trade did they follow before demand for the longbow created a full-time business? What about the feathers that were always attached to the shaft of an arrow? And how about the sharp iron head on the arrow?

GROUP 26

Bowmakers

Unfortunately, not a great deal is known about the BOWMAKERS. They must have been first-class craftsmen with experience in working with wood. They had to be able to judge the suitability of a given stave —whether or not it would finish up straight and true—before expending any serious time on it. The finished bow had to bend into a perfect half circle when the string was fully drawn, without a twist to either side. And allowing for the knots in the stave certainly called for long experience.

About the only record we have of these fine woodworkers is through their names. They, like the smiths, managed to get along with only first names until an occasion would arise where an individual had to be singled out and given some second name that seemed appropriate. The tax collector was usually responsible, but there were other occasions as well.

From the many names that undoubtedly started in the early days of the longbow, I have selected ten that, in all probability, were the first to designate men who made bows. In this group, BOWEWRIGHT, BOWMAKER, BOWRICK, and BOWYER are perfectly straightforward. The others are probably spelling variations, while the last name, GOOD-

BOWE, sounds like one that was given to a bowmaker as a friendly compliment.

All during the fourteenth and fifteenth centuries, England probably had a force of at least fifty thousand longbowmen at any one time able to take the field. In terms of equipment, think what that must have meant: since every bowman carried at least one spare bow, there had to be one hundred thousand longbows in working order!

GROUP 27

Arrowmakers

A bowman usually carried a standard supply of large-size arrows. Arrows were definitely expendable in huge quantities, so millions of them must have either been in stock, or in preparation, during the whole period of the longbow.

Providing arrows called for a whole additional group of skilled workmen. The superior work of the bowmakers would be wasted if the bowman's arrows were not made with the same care as the bow. Here again, the only record we have of the arrow is the list of names that indicates beyond any reasonable doubt that the original bearers of these names were in the business of making arrows. Unfortunately, these names cannot be separated into the woodworkers who made the shafts and the smiths who must have made the iron heads. I strongly suspect that in the early days of the industry these men were all ironworking smiths, and that with the phenomenal growth of the bow business, many smiths developed the skill of making the wooden shafts too.

This would certainly explain the name ARROWSMITH and its variations. (ARUWEMAKER meant an arrowmaker too, but it came from the Old English word *arwe* meaning "arrow.") FLECHER is a name we can be sure about. There was a Robertus le Flecher in 1203 and a Peter le Flechier in 1227. Both of them were arrowmakers. The name comes from the Old French word *flechier,* meaning maker of arrows.

FLOWER and FLOWERS may not look like names from the arrowmaking industry, but they are. In Old English, the word for arrow was *fla,* which became *flo* and later *floer* in Middle English.

TIPPER goes back to 1176, when William Tipere appears in the tax rolls. The year of 1176 is early in terms of the longbow, but probably Mr. Tipere was an ironworking smith who developed such skill and speed in hammering out arrowheads that somebody called him TIPPER and it stayed with him.

GROUP 28

Wood Suppliers

This group of names needs little explanation. It is obvious that as the business of making bows and arrows grew into a big industry, suppliers of raw materials sprang up naturally.

GROUP 29

String Suppliers

Bowstrings were made of linen, and bowmakers had to buy them from the linen spinners. Probably some linen spinners began to specialize in bowstrings and became known as STRINGERS or STRENGERS.

GROUP 30

Goose-feather Suppliers

At first glance, the size of Group 30 (page 82) seems to be out of all proportion to its importance. Certainly, in the very early part of the naming period, raising geese was just another backyard occupation designed to supplement the food supplies of a peasant-farmer and perhaps provide soft feathers for a mattress. But today there are at least thirty-six modern family names that unquestionably were originally given to peasants because raising geese was part of their way of life. From the vantage point of time, the answer is easy: another, and far more important, use for the big birds was found.

It was discovered that if three of the tail feathers of a goose were fastened to the tail of an arrow, that arrow would be greatly steadied in its flight. Without this complement of feathers, the arrow would wobble in flight and almost surely land some distance away from the intended target.

As we have seen, the twelfth century saw the development of the longbow from just another weapon to the major weapon of the later Middle Ages, at least as far as England is concerned. Millions of arrows were needed and many more millions of goose feathers. In many cases, a peasant was able to pay his rent just by selling feathers to the arrowmakers —and he would still have all the goose meat left to feed his family.

The names in this group are quite straightforward. *Gos* meant "goose" in Middle English, and over the years letters were added, and then omitted, and the spelling changed from the original.

GROUP 31

Men in Charge of the Butts

Every able-bodied man had to practice shooting with the longbow, and usually this practice was supervised by veterans and occurred at places established in every village for the purpose. Such places were called BUTTS, and the man in charge would be named accordingly.

GROUP 32

Skilled Bowmen

All twenty-three of the names in Group 32 (page 83) definitely stem back to BOWMAN in meaning and almost certainly were first used in a complimentary sense. Can there be any doubt of a man who was called BOWMASTER? BENDBOW with its variations refers to the powerful arm needed to bend one of these mighty bows. BENDER surely is another expression of admiration for a man's ability to bend a longbow. The SHUT names would be easier to understand if they were spelled with a double *oo,* as in the word *shoot.* ARCHER with its variations means a BOWMAN and differs very little from its Old French source *archier.*

I have found a Hugh le Archer far back, in 1199. His descendants have probably long since dropped the article *le.* Even a few years before him (1166), I find a Robert Larchier. In this case, he, or some of his early descendants, dropped part of the *le* and made LARCHER out of it.

GROUP 33

Crossbow Makers

We have talked about the English longbow and the family names that originated from it. Its long-time rival, the crossbow, also created a number of well-known names that are still with us.

The crossbow can be briefly described as a very short bow and string (about eighteen inches long) mounted on the front end of a wooden stock about the shape and size of a modern shoulder gun. The string is pulled far back until it engages a triggerlike arrangement. The short eight- to ten-inch arrow is placed in the slot provided, with its notch engaging the string. When the trigger is pulled, the arrow is released.

The crossbow seems to have developed first in Italy. Gradually it spread all over Europe, but in the earlier years the Italians were so much more expert with it that large contingents were hired as mercenaries by monarchs of other European countries.

In the more powerful examples of the weapon, the bow was so strong that it could not be pulled back without the use of a winchlike contraption that the soldier had to carry with him. He put his foot in a stirrup on the front end of the arm and turned the crank of the winch until the string would catch onto the trigger. This meant that the crossbowman had to use a good part of a minute to reload and get off a second shot.

Opinions differ today on the comparative value of the crossbow and the longbow. The crossbow probably had more power and its projectile would travel farther, but an experienced archer handling a longbow could get off at least four shots while the crossbowman was firing one. It would be like comparing a single-shot breach-loading rifle with a light-caliber repeating rifle.

In the crossbow, the bow determined its power. Through the eleventh century, bows were made of hickory and other woods glued together; then horn was added and even animal sinews. Only when it was made out of steel, however, or at least something approaching steel, did the weapon reach its apex. Steel had spring in it and this meant power. It also made the bow impervious to dampness. Steel did not, however, speed up its fire power.

The names in this group were probably given to men associated with the making of crossbows. Some of them may have been given to men trained in using the crossbow—it is impossible to be sure from the evidence.

BOLT is from Old English and, strange to say, it has not changed at all over the centuries—it still means a short, heavy piece of metal. The simple word *bolt* was applied to the projectile used in the crossbow and thence to the man who made it. BOLTSMITH and the names that follow mean the same thing.

QUARRELL, QUARRELLE, and QUARRELS come directly from the Old French word *quarel,* meaning a short, heavy, square-headed arrow. They were smiths because the quarel was usually made from iron.

GROUP 34

Crossbowmen

The first ten names all derive from the Anglo-French word *arbalestier* meaning a man armed with a crossbow. This word, like so many others in medieval England, is both English and French, for when the official language was French and the language of the people was English, commonly used terms were in danger of getting mixed up in daily use.

The remaining five names come from the Old French *carnel,* meaning a place on the wall of a castle where a man with a crossbow might be expected to be stationed. Any man ordinarily placed in that strategic position found himself so named.

GROUP 26

Bowmakers

Boayer	Bowrick	Boyar	Goodbowe
Bowewright	Bowyer	Boyer	
Bowmaker	Bowyers	Boyers	

GROUP 27

Arrowmakers

Arrasmith	Harrismith	Fletcher	•
Arrowsmith	Harrowsmith	•	Tipper
Arsmith	•	Flower	
Aruwemaker	Flecher	Flowers	

GROUP 28

Wood Suppliers

Arrowood	Bowstock	Stavely	Staves
•	•	Staver	

GROUP 29

String Suppliers

Strengers	Stringer	Stringers

GROUP 30

Goose-Feather Suppliers

Goose	Gosse	Joce	Josling
Gooseman	Gosselin	Jocelyn	Josolyne
Goseling	Gosset	Joscelyn	Joss
Gosere	Gossett	Joscelyne	Josse
Gosland	Gossling	Jose	Josselyn
Goslin	Gostling	Joseland	Jossett
Gosling	Gozzard	Joselin	
Gosmanger	Gozzett	Josland	
Goss	•	Joslen	
Gossard	Joass	Joslin	

GROUP 31

Men in Charge of the Butts

Butt	Buttman	Butts

GROUP 32

Skilled Bowmen

Archer	•	Bendbow	Beauman
Larcher	Benbough	Bender	Boman
Le Archer	Benbow	•	Bower

Bowers	Boyman	Shut	Shutter
Bowman	•	Shuter	Shutts
Bowmaster	Shooter	Shutt	
Bowyer	Shotter	Shutte	

GROUP 33

Crossbow Makers

Bolt	Boltman	Boulter	Quarrels
Bolte	Boltsmith	•	
Bolter	Boltwright	Quarrell	
Boltmaker	Boult	Quarrelle	

GROUP 34

Crossbowmen

Alabastar	Arblastar	Ballister	Carnell
Alabaster	Arblaster	Balster	Carnelley
Albisser	Ballaster	•	Crenel
Arbelaster	Ballester	Carnall	Crennell

CHAPTER 9

Smiths Who Worked with Nonferrous Metals

Isn't it strange about gold? We can't eat it, we can't make clothing with it, and we can't build shelter for ourselves with it, yet we can get all three of these necessities in abundance in exchange for gold.

Gold has always been coveted by men. Long before there were written records of events, gold was man's most valued material asset.

The Assyrians craved gold; the Egyptians made ornaments for their deities out of it; the Etruscans seem to have worshiped the metal itself, and the Greeks, along with the Romans, often placed a higher value on gold than on life itself. Today the total amount of gold in the world must be vastly greater than at any period in history, but in spite of this it grows more valuable with each generation. No surplus of the metal has ever been reported anywhere.

Medieval England, along with the rest of Europe, tried for centuries to create a surplus of gold. A scattering of chemically ignorant but probably mainly sincere alchemists tried their best to change basic metals like iron into the precious metal. Frequently they were encouraged and even subsidized by the socially and politically powerful and, as might be expected, this led to widespread quackery.

For example, there was the fellow who could produce a lump of pure gold by merely stirring a beaker of water (or any other liquid) over a fire. He stirred with a rod about the size of a lead pencil and, after he had spoken the proper incantations and made prescribed motions to make it look as difficult as possible, he would thrust the rod into the hot liquid, stir it for a moment, and say, "There you are, sir—only a small piece, but it is the purest gold. Here, feel it, see how heavy it is, hammer it out on an anvil, test it any way you care to—all right before your eyes, gentlemen." All eyes would be on the little pea-sized piece of perfectly good gold, and no one would notice the hollow metal stirring rod. The bit of gold was *inside* the stirring rod, held there by a bit of wax that would quickly melt when the rod was thrust into the hot liquid, causing the gold to tumble out into the liquid. Old records of medieval alchemists are full of similar trickery.

The art of working with gold is probably about the most ancient of all the metallurgical crafts. Because gold is soft and capable of being readily shaped into an unending variety of ornamental forms that retain their lustrous beauty apparently forever, it has always had a strong appeal to those smiths with an artistic bent.

Unfortunately, very few samples of the work of the goldsmiths of the eleventh and twelfth centuries have survived the ravages of time and human cupidity. In that period, much of the goldsmiths' work was devoted to making ecclesiastical vessels for the church. However, during the religious revolution of the sixteenth century and the dissolution of the monasteries that followed, anything made of gold or silver was melted for personal gain, just as whole libraries of priceless manuscripts were burned or used for wrapping paper.

Nevertheless, we have been able to visualize and reconstruct many of the techniques used by the early medieval workers in gold and silver. The term *goldsmith* in that period was used interchangeably with *silversmith*. While the methods used in working with each of these precious metals was necessarily different, there were enough similarities to make the skilled worker in one fairly capable in the other. Silver was always much more plentiful, so, in effect, a smith tended to have much more practical experience with silver than with gold.

With the possible exception of an experiment made in the reign of Edward III (1327–1377), who had some coins made from pure gold and others from pure silver, these metals were never used in their pure states to make any item designed for either practical or ornamental use. Both are far too soft. Some other metal such as copper must be added to the gold or silver while in a molten condition to produce a satisfactory alloy.

This was no problem for the honest smith—a small uniform addition of copper produced a much better piece of metal—but not all smiths were content with a fair profit for their labors. Human nature being what it is, one smith might add more copper than needed to a melt, and if the result still looked satisfactory, he would add still more the next time. A neighboring smith would hear about this and would try the same thing. Copper was, of course, vastly cheaper than either silver or gold, so the more added to a melt, the lower the costs, and yet the diluted product could be sold for the same price that a more honest mixture brought.

Something had to be done about this—and something was, something so eminently sensible that, including improvements made in the regulations from time to time since, the measures taken in the 1300s are still protecting the buyer of gold and silver. In 1180, the goldsmiths were loosely associated with an organized group of craftsmen from other trades. Henry II (1154–1189) saw fit to fine this group because they were operating without a license from him. We can't be sure that these craftsmen even knew they were supposed to have a license, but regardless of this, it may have given them an idea. The honest smiths were seething with anger and frustration at the trickery of their unfair competitors. Henry III, undoubtedly goaded into action by the long-suffering smiths, made a ruling in 1238, commanding the mayor and aldermen of London to appoint a group of six "discreet goldsmiths" to superintend the work of all the goldsmiths in London. Similar regulations were soon made operative in some of the smaller cities. They were carried out and seem to have worked fairly well because in 1300, sixty-two years later, successors of the original six were still actively on the job. Now they were known as *gardiens* with the chief goldsmith being called a warden. The word *warden* simply indicated the "head man," and it was applied to men in charge of many different things during this period. One of the primary functions of the gardiens was actually to test the percentage of alloy in every piece of work before it left the shop of the maker. If the piece met the accepted standard of the time, it was stamped with a mark called the "leopard's head." (Actually, it looks more like the head of a lion but it is still known as a leopard's head.) This mark was to undergo numerous changes over the centuries. Most of them would be improvements, and all of them would be more complicated, but this was the beginning of what we now call the hallmark.

In 1327, the gardiens were given a royal charter under the resounding title of "The Wardens and Commonality of the Mystery of Goldsmiths of the City of London." This made it a full-fledged guild with very real powers. One of the earliest acts of the guild was to make every member provide himself with his own distinctive mark, to be stamped into every piece of his work. His mark was registered at the guildhall, and consequently the appearance of that mark on a piece of silver or gold was the personal guarantee of the maker that the item met all existing standards.

One more step in the long process is worth a moment's attention. In 1378, somebody suggested that in spite of all worthy efforts to maintain honest standards in both gold and silver, nevertheless "the goldsmiths were their own judges." Action was taken to correct this situation at once. Instead of the warden of the guild taking all the responsibility, a rule was made that when a goldsmith had completed an item and duly put his personal mark on it, he must then take it to the mayor or governor of the city, who would add his own mark to it. The word *hallmark* derives from Goldsmiths' Hall, London, where gold and silver articles were assayed and stamped.

Out of all this grew the standards that are used today. Sterling silver is 92.5 percent pure silver; the balance is usually copper. With gold, the troy ounce by which it was weighed was divided into twenty-four parts; each part is a karat, so a piece marked eighteen karats must contain eighteen parts of pure gold and six parts of alloy.

GROUPS 35 AND 36

Goldsmiths and Silversmiths

Although there are separate lists for the goldsmiths and the silver-smiths, they are discussed together here, for, as mentioned earlier in this chapter, the worker in one of the metals was invariably capable of working with the other. A man might spend virtually all his time working in gold, for example, but if he happened to be working in silver at the moment fate imposed a name on him, he would be so tagged on the records and the name might easily stay with him and be passed down to his son along with his tools.

The first five names in Group 35 (page 94)—BATER, BATOUR, BETER, GOLDBEATER, and ORBATOUR—almost certainly belonged to goldsmiths but they derive from a particular operation in the trade. A lump of pure gold, when placed between two pieces of selected animal skin and beaten with a hammer for a long period, will flatten out to an astonishing thinness. Experts say it can be beaten so thin that a quarter of a million sheets will not measure more than an inch in thickness. Today this is called gold leaf.

The next three names—FINAR, FINER, FINUR—indicate a man who refined gold or silver as it came from the earth. FINESILVER, listed in Group 36, specifies that the man worked with silver.

Then come twelve names meaning "goldsmith." GOLDSMITH appeared first as Thomas Goldsmith in the London records of 1255. GILD-

ERS is interesting because it was probably first given to the son of a goldsmith and developed similarly to the examples cited in chapter 2, such as PHILLIP, PHILLIPSON, PHILLIP'S, and finally, PHILLIPS.

GOLDHOPER and the RING names indicate men who made gold rings. *Hoper* is easier to understand if thought of as *hooper,* which means "ring-maker." GRAVER and ORGRAVER immediately indicate that these men were engravers, another phase of goldsmithing. Finally, the JEWELL names obviously refer to a man who made jewelry.

In Group 36, the last five names are perfectly straightforward and mean men who worked in silver. The earliest record I can find of the SILVER names is Robert Silverhewer. It appears in the Yorkshire records of 1212. The English were fond of the word *hewer,* and used it for anyone who hewed a substance in order to shape it.

As a group, the medieval goldsmiths and silversmiths must have been men of character as well as ability. Working with precious metals exclusively, the temptation to cheat must have been enormous, yet they constantly invented self-regulatory restrictions that would protect the public as well as the honest workman.

In the eleventh century the medieval cabinetmaker provided the goldsmith and silversmith with strong oaken chests bound with iron in which he could pack his entire stock of gold and silver at the close of each working day and bury it beneath his shop. Nothing resembling a police force existed and wholesale thievery was a nightly occurrence. Fires, too, were unbelievably common. The chests used originally by the goldsmiths were called COFFERS and the men who made them were distinguished by some variation of the word. As time went on, however, the wooden chest was supplanted by a permanent masonry vault built well below the level of the goldsmith's shop.

GROUP 37

Coppersmiths

Gold and silver are weighed in ounces and fractions, while copper may be weighed in tons, but don't discount the value it had in medieval times. Even in prehistoric centuries, copper was important, particulary when it was discovered that if a little tin was mixed with it, one had an alloy that was much harder than any other metal commonly known at that time. It was bronze—a vast improvement over the flint and stone implements of the Stone Age.

In the England of the Middle Ages, copper was in wide demand. The ore from which it came, however, contained a great many impurities that took a lot of know-how to eliminate. Both lead and silver are commonly present in ore in which copper is the major part, so a smith had to try to extract all the copper without destroying the lead and silver. The arsenic and sulfur in the ore could be burned off and allowed to escape.

In order to extract the metal, the ore had to be crushed into as small pieces as possible, and this must have been a backbreaking job at a time when no such thing as a stamping mill existed. When the ore was reduced about as far as it could be, a lot of salt was added and the mixture roasted over open fires for hours without end. This drove off the sulfur and arsenic. Next, the crushed ore was mixed with water to dissolve any soluble material; the mixture was allowed to settle and then the liquid was decanted. Now the metal was ready to be worked on.

In a furnace that did not allow the flame to pass through the crushed ore (as in a blast furnace) but rather to pass over it, a very hot fire was made and kept going for several days. A bellows run by either wind or waterpower could be used for the draft, but not through the mass of ore.

Gradually the copper in the ore would liquefy—along with any other metals that might be in that batch of ore—and run down through the slag into a clay crucible prepared for it. From there it was drained into small pigs in the sand. At this point it still had far too many foreign substances in it to be of much use, so the pigs were melted and the slag skimmed off two or three times. Now the metal was fairly pure copper.

Several things could be done with the few hundred pounds of basic copper this method produced. It could be sold to someone who made brass or bronze: they could never get enough copper, particularly the bronze-makers, since bronze called for more copper than anything else. Of course, one could make either brass or bronze oneself if one cared to. It could also be sold to the fellow down the street who made church bells— bell metal was nearly all copper, and if a batch did have some silver in it, so much the better, as every bell maker knew that a little silver in a bell always made it sound better. A master coppersmith could decide to hammer the whole batch into sheets of any thickness and make the sheets up into kettles or caldrons. These could be made in a variety of sizes and easily sold.

All the names in Group 37 (page 94) go back to the early part of the thirteenth century. The six names beginning with COPERSMITH are definitely from smiths who could refine the ore to a fairly pure state and then make alloys of copper or just sell their pure copper. The two BROWN names come from the Old English *brun smid*.

GREENSMITH and GREENSMYTH mean coppersmith too: GREENSMITH comes from the green flames commonly seen in a copper shop. ORSMITH and ORSMYTH simply mean "a worker in copper" but may well have been given to a smith who just smelted the ore.

The CALDERON names and the KETTLE names mean exactly the same thing: men who had kettles to sell.

GROUP 38

Brassworkers

Brass is an alloy of copper and zinc, while bronze is an alloy of copper and tin; back in biblical times and in fact well into the Middle Ages, there was much confusion between the two. The trouble resulted from the smiths' inability during much of that long era to distinguish clearly between the different ores as they were taken from the earth. A zinc ore was frequently mistaken for tin and vice versa, with the result that what should have been called brass was really bronze. We know that real brass, by today's definition, was often produced by accident—unavoidable if you added a zinc ore to a melt of copper. It was an age of a mangled metallurgy that may be confusing to the nontechnical reader but, in any case, does not greatly matter in our search for family names.

The Low Countries seem to have mastered the art of making brass at least two centuries before the English, as indicated by several different things.

With rare exception, to see much Old English brass, one has to visit the cathedrals and churches in East Anglia. They were much nearer to the Low Countries, as travel went at that time, and consequently the men who made early brass visited or settled there.

Sheets of brass hammered to desired thinness were given the name *latten,* from the Norman word *laiton.* From these sheets some remarkable, almost life-sized, statues of religious and secular heroes were painstakingly hammered out. Many of them are still proudly displayed. A brass worker who could do this kind of work would certainly be called a LATNER or a LATONER.

Some years later, English brass workers began to experiment with casting brass. This really opened up the industry and produced most of the family names that are still with us. ORSMITH and ORSMYTH were probably smiths who smelted the ores, as indicated in Group 38, but the ten names beginning with BATER originated helter-skelter in the mind of some petty tax man.

GROUP 39

Leadworkers

Lead was not too plentiful in the England of the medieval period, but it could be imported and this, together with the domestic supply, made a lead-working industry of some size and importance. Smelting lead from its ores was much easier than smelting any of the other metals. A low melting point and the fact that sulfur was the principal impurity made it possible to get a fairly pure product by simply roasting the crushed ore in a furnace. Molten lead ran down into a prepared container. This simple process seems to have been known to many of the earliest civilizations, as items made of lead have been discovered in all of the Mediterranean countries. The principal use for lead at this time was in the form of sheets used for roofs of churches and cathedrals. The sheets were made by pouring a ladle of molten lead onto a smooth slab of stone that had been leveled and provided with a fence around the edges to limit the flow to the required thickness. The resulting sheet could then be conveniently rolled up and brought to the cathedral, where it could be easily remelted around the edges with others to form a weather- and time-proof roof.

Casting lead in prepared molds for statuary became a business too. A beautiful example of a lead casting is still to be seen in the baptismal font of Lady Saint Mary's Church in Wareham. It must weigh at least two tons and was cast in the twelfth century.

A worker in lead was destined to be given one of two types of names: one based on the Latin-French source or one from Old English. Latin was still the language of the scholars, so a tax collector might name a lead worker *Rogerus Plumarius*. There is such a name recorded in 1176, but it did not stick. The Latin word for lead was *plumbum*, but the Norman variation might be *plomb* or even *plummier*. If, as sometimes happened, Old English influenced the creation of the family name, it would be based on the word *lead*.

In this group, the first names come from the Old English source and all the rest from Latin-French.[1] Those names ending in *-beater* were

---

[1] Some confusion in the origin of these names is unavoidable: the Latin-French word for the metal was *plumbum*, while the Latin word for feather was *pluma*. Variations in spelling and consequently in origin make it virtually impossible to distinguish them today. There is as well a third possibilty. The records show a Thomas de Plummer in 1272. This was an address name, indicating that this man lived near a plum tree.

an attempt to differentiate between one type of leadworker and another but can't be taken too seriously, as hammering lead was a practice common to all workers with the metal.

GROUP 40
Pewter Makers

Somewhere far back in antiquity, probably in the Bronze Age, some unknown metallurgist in the process of making bronze may have mistakenly reversed the amount of copper and tin and produced pewter. Pewter is made by alloying a little bit of copper into a great deal of tin— exactly the opposite of bronze. Pure tin is too soft for many practical uses, but when small amounts of copper are added, a metal is produced that is practical, cheap, and handsome as well. Today, a little lead and antimony or bismuth is added to the copper and tin, depending on what is going to be made from the pewter.

In medieval England, pewter filled a fast-growing social gap. The nobles and the very wealthy had their silver and gold table services while the great mass of people ate from wooden trenchers or, in the absence of even a trencher, from a huge slice of bread. The arrival of pewter came to the relief of the growing middle class of people. They could have dishes on the table. Pewter dishes would not have the glamour of silver, but they did add greatly to the dignity of a meal, and we can suppose that for many years a few pewter dishes on the table improved the owner's status too.

For some unknown reason, making pewterware did not leave us many family names. I do have one record, however, going back to 1311, showing the name Lambert le Peutrer.

The first five names in this group are obviously variations of the Norman spelling, while the last three have an Old English source. All of them were originally applied to a man who either made pewter or sold it —and as middlemen were scarce, the man who made an item usually did the selling himself.

GROUP 41
Hornsmiths

Hornsmiths were the men who made a variety of small but highly useful things from the horns of cattle.

Quite properly, this list could be placed further along in the book because the hornsmith does not work in metal and up to this point we have confined ourselves to smiths who did. The men of medieval England, however, chose to call the worker in horn a smith, so we shall too.

Not many things are made from horn today, but for many centuries, in fact into the early part of the twentieth century, the work of the hornsmith was in steady demand. He was the one who made combs for the ladies in a day when hair was long and might require a number of them. And the men of those years also wore their hair down to the shoulders and must have needed the handiwork of the horn maker.

The hornsmith also turned out spoons of all kinds and sizes, as well as ladles. But probably the most important single item the hornsmith made was the reed or shuttle for the weaver.

Briefly, a hornsmith sawed off both ends of the horn to get rid of the solid portion around the point of the horn and the gristly part where it joined the head. He soaked the horn in water for several days, then boiled it until it became soft. When it was soft, he slit it from end to end and flattened it out. This was best accomplished by putting the piece of horn between two heated plates of iron and clamping them tightly together. He usually followed this with a tempering process: the piece was heated as hot as he dared, then plunged into cold water and put between the clamps again for a few hours. After this, it was ready to cut and shape into any item desired.

In this group, the HORN names are obvious—except the first four were sometimes applied to men who blew musical horns. COMBES, SPONERE, SPOONER, and SPOONS simply meant men who made those particular items, and LADELER was probably tagged with this name because he made large, deep spoons that were to be used for spooning stew out of a pot. CUILLERER meant the same thing, but its origin was Old French. TURNOUR was applied to a man who ran a lathe. He might turn several different materials on his lathe, but horn was one of the most common. A PENIUR was a combmaker.

SLAYARE and SLAYWRIGHT go back to the textile industry. The old English derivation is *slege* meaning "slay, stroke" and the term was used to describe an instrument used in weaving. The shuttle on a loom was of great importance, since the whole operation of weaving largely depended on its smoothness. Making shuttles out of horn became a specialty of some hornsmiths and quite naturally, they would be given a name that indicated this.

GROUP 35

Goldsmiths

Bater	•	Gouldsmith	•
Batour	Gelder	Offer	Graver
Beter	Gilder	Orfeuere	Orgraver
Goldbeater	Gilders	Orfeur	•
Orbatour	Gildsmith		Jewell
•	Golder	•	Jewels
Finar	Goldman	Goldhoper	
Finer	Goldsmith	Ring	
Finur	Goldsmyth	Ringe	
		Rings	

GROUP 36

Silversmiths

Finar	Finur	Silverhewer	Silversmyth
Finer	•	Silvermaker	
Finesilver	Silver	Silversmith	

GROUP 37

Coppersmiths

Brownsmith	•	Greensmith	Kettless
Brownsmyth	Copersmith	Greensmyth	Kittle
•	Copper	•	•
Calderon	Copperman	Ketial	Orsmith
Caldroner	Coppersmith	Kettel	Orsmyth
Cauldron	Coppersmyth	Kettell	
Cawdron	Cowpersmyth	Kettle	
Coldron	•	Kettles	

GROUP 38

Brassworkers

Bater	Brass	Brasy-Eter	Latoner
Braizier	Brasseur	Brazier	•
Brasher	Brassey	•	Orsmith
Brasier	Brasswell	Latner	Orsmyth

GROUP 39

Leadworkers

Leadbeater	Ledbetter	Lidbetter	Plumbe
Leadbeatter	Ledder	•	Plumber
Leadbetter	Leder	Plimmer	Plumer
Leadbitter	Ledsmith	Plomer	Plummer
Leadman	Ledsmyth	Plum	
Ledbeter	Ledyeter	Plumb	

GROUP 40

Pewter Makers

Peutherer	Pewtress	Tinker
Peutrer	Powter	Tynkeler
Pewter	•	Tynkere

GROUP 41

Hornsmiths

Combes	Horner	•	Sponere
•	Hornor	Peniur	Spooner
Cuillerer	Hornsmith	•	Spoons
•	Hornsmyth	Slayare	•
Horn	•	Slaywright	Turnour
Horne	Ladeler	•	

CHAPTER **10**

The Building Trades

At least three hundred family names come directly from the building trades of England: such names as MASON, STONE, CARPENTER, and SAWYER.

To understand how and why such a large number of names came from the business of building, it is necessary to know something about the kind of buildings people lived in at the beginning of the naming period and what happened to the house-building trade in the two hundred and fifty years that followed.

What happened was not just a building boom; it was something far more fundamental: the gradual appearance of the middle class. In all the preceding centuries, society had consisted almost entirely of two classes—the nobility and the peasants. The nobles lived in barns and everybody else lived in wretched hovels. The nobles didn't think of their dwellings as barns—far from it. Their residences were referred to as the hall or the manor house, but though they might vary in size, they would hardly measure up to a farmer's barn today. Imagine a one-story frame house made of the roughest kind of wood—some of it sawed out but most of it green saplings roughly adzed on opposite sides to eliminate the space between. There were no windows—glass was rare—and no chimney, and it had a thatched roof that was expected to catch fire every so often.

Inside, there was one large room. In the middle of the room was a slab of flat stone with a wood fire blazing on it; the smoke would have to find its own way out through cracks in roof and walls. The lord and his family and guests dined at a table made out of boards laid over trestles, and perhaps on a raised dais. The floor of the hall was hard clay, more or less smoothed out by the pressure of many feet and covered with rushes about an inch or so deep that protected the feet from the accumulated filth. Somewhere in the room would be another rough table of temporary construction where the servants would eat, together with any guests of low degree who happened to be there.

At one side of the room would be a bench where the cook and his assistants prepared great pieces of meat by sticking an iron spit through them and then bringing them to the fire. Up near the roof the cook might hang a number of hams and slabs of bacon to take advantage of the ever-present smoke.

When the meal was over and the remains given to the dogs, it was bedtime. The lord and his lady might have a small space in one corner of the room that could be curtained off where they could sleep on one or two large burlap sacks filled with straw. The straw might have a bit of some fragrant herb mixed with it to offset the normal odors. They might even have slightly better sleeping quarters, such as a tiny penlike partition built out of wooden slabs running vertically partway up to the roof. They could keep their bed bags permanently there. The servants and any lowly guests, however, rolled up in blankets, if they owned any, and picked a spot on the floor. The manor house described so briefly was typical of the better living accommodations in eleventh-century England. The hovels that the great mass of people lived in were almost beyond description. They were made of saplings more or less woven together with reeds and vines and kept freshly covered with mud or clay as the rain washed the mud away; the roof was a makeshift thatch. The fire for cooking was on a stone slab outside the door.

The people of England at this period, both high and low, never dreamed of spending an afternoon or evening at home unless severe weather gave them no choice. Their houses had little heat, almost no light, and not much furniture. With the exceptions of wintertime and a miserable inn here and there where ale could be bought and where impromptu entertainment by the guests was allowed, nothing went on indoors because the insides of houses from the manor of a great noble to the hovel of a peasant were decidedly unpleasant places to be. Even events such as meetings of a lord and his vassals and of the courts were commonly held outdoors. The only exception was the monasteries. These were great institutions in both size and in accomplishments and will be discussed more fully later on. They were, however, only slightly better than the manor houses.

There were many churches—about one to a village—but there were practically no castles. This may sound strange since we associate castles with the English countryside, but in the eleventh century, they did not yet exist. The oldest building in England that can properly be called a castle is the White Tower of the Tower of London. This was built by William after the Conquest late in the eleventh century. Going back to churches, they were built of wood at the time, though there were a few cathedrals built of stone.

Therefore, it can be said that at the very time that families were beginning to take on names, England was a nation of inadequate and quite crude houses and other buildings.

All this was about to change. It would not happen suddenly, but over a period of two to three centuries, and England would never be the same.

Briefly, this is what happened. In an earlier chapter, we mentioned William's insistence, at the time of the Domesday survey, that many old manor houses be torn down and replaced with solid stone structures. Knowing that the English builders of that period had little experience with stone, he offered inducements to the stoneworkers of France and Italy to come to England, and they came by the hundreds. They were followed by plasterers from the Continent who would add that finishing touch to hundreds of buildings that otherwise would have remained with rough board interior walls. Plastering was an ancient craft dating to the Egyptians, and there still exist examples of Roman and Greek plastering, yet the Anglo-Saxons previous to the eleventh century were almost unacquainted with it.

Along with the plasterers came many joiners from the Low Countries to offer their skill in making interiors more livable. Then came the glaziers and tilers and men who knew how to make various kinds of roofing considerably more fire-resistant than thatched straw.

This meant, of course, a large influx of skilled mechanics, many of whom were freemen or franklins under no obligation to work the customary three days a week for the lord of the manor. With the payment of a slight sum to his lordship, they were free to sell their expert services to anyone and collect all that the traffic would bear. Such men were not going to be content to live in hovels; they wanted decent houses for themselves and were determined to get them.

Unfortunately, no figures are available on the number of new houses built during this period, but there is a statistic that is informative. During the reign of Henry 11 (1154–1189), 157 entirely new abbeys or major additions to old ones were built. It is estimated that fully double that many castles were built during the twelfth century. The number of churches and cathedrals commenced during this period was almost certainly far greater. In a nation that heretofore had been almost purely agricultural, this meant that the whole appearance of an English village was changing. From a village with a few dozen mud-encrusted one-room huts, a frame church, and an antiquated manor house, there now was a fine stone castle, a solid stone church, and a dozen or more two-story houses built out of sawed timber, smoothly plastered inside, and with a stone chimney.

The rise of the merchant class simply cannot be underestimated as a reason why so many family names came from the building trades. Of course, peddlers who carried goods on their backs had always been part of the scene, and there had been merchants who imported goods from foreign lands and sold them to the public from established places of business. But now there were many more, and the numbers were constantly increasing.

There were also fairs. These grew to be great sources of profit to the merchants who ran them and, incidentally, to the nearby landlord too. He could and did extract a toll from the merchants in return for what he called protection.

Lastly, there were the crusades—those gigantic expeditions of thousands of English and Norman men. To go on a crusade meant that a man would leave his home and family for a long and highly indefinite period to fight in the Near East. Thousands never returned but on the other hand, a great many did. They brought back things that were entirely new to both the English and the Normans: silk, satin, and velvet, soft morocco leather, perfumes, rugs, and carpets. These goods provided inspiration to the English to learn how to duplicate them.

The total effect on medieval life in England was enormous. No longer did a man feel that because he was born a peasant he must forever keep that status. A young man could become an apprentice to any skilled craft and, with industry and good luck, he could become a master of his craft, open a shop of his own, join the craft guild, and build a respectable house for himself and his family. During this period, at least two men born in very lowly circumstances became not only very wealthy but lord mayors of London.

GROUP 42

Stonemasons

The earliest written record of the name I have been able to find is John Macun, circa 1130. This was one way the Normans spelled the word, but it does not seem to have survived. There are nine names on the list on page 111 derived from it, however, that are still with us—from MACHEN through MAYSON. The MEACHAM names seemingly did not appear until after the naming period, in the 1600s, but they also were masons.

CARRIER and CARRYER, while sometimes used to designate a carrier of messages, were more apt to designate the husky young fellow who carried the mortar and other materials the mason would use. Today we call these young men hod carriers.

CARVER does not indicate whether the man carved in stone or wood, but undoubtedly he was an artist with the mallet and chisel.

The HEWER names refer to the act of hewing, or cutting. As with the name CARVER, we can't be sure that a hewer was cutting stone—it might have been wood. Of course, STONEHEWER settles any doubt as to the material. Wood carving was a highly developed art at the same time that stone carving was. Almost any fine old cathedral contains examples of both stone and wood carvings unequaled today.

LAYER and LEIR give a glimpse of the working methods of masons of the Middle Ages. The stones going into a section of straight wall would have to be hewn to perfectly uniform lines before being cemented into place. This would require an experienced man to inspect each stone carefully before it was laid in proper order to be put into the wall.

MARBERER refers to a mason who worked with marble. Somewhere there must be a man named Marbler, but I have not been able to find one.

Men with the STONE names may or may not have been full-fledged masons at the time they acquired their names—they may have been journeymen or possibly apprentices. A journeyman was a man who had served as an apprentice for many years and was about to become a master mason. An apprentice was apt to be called PRENTICE, but since this applied to any of the crafts, the name is not included with the stoneworkers. The STONE names all come from the Anglo-Saxon word *stan,* meaning "stone." In the name STONWRIGHT, *wright* is derived from another Old English word, implying a skilled worker in a certain material, in this case stone. It is my opinion that the STONE names applied to masons accustomed to working with stone of more than ordinary hardness. This would require tools with good steel in them and experience that other masons might not have.

The WALL names are almost certainly those of masons. Men who developed both speed and skill in laying up straight wall structures as opposed to more complicated portions would be singled out with a name to so indicate.

MASONS AS ARTISTS

The medieval masons and stone carvers must have been extraordinary men to have created the monuments to their genius that the cathedrals, the remains of monasteries, and even the village churches of England represent today.

There is a story of a man who stopped to question some masons chipping away at their benches in the shadow of the cathedral where they were working. The first one he asked, "What are *you* doing?" The reply came, "Can't you see? I'm chipping this piece of stone into shape." The second mason questioned replied, "I'm shaping the arch over the doorway." The same question to the third man brought the answer, "You ask what *I* am doing? I am building a cathedral."

Surely that last man had the vision of the artist. He must have combined the mechanical skill of the stonecutter, the artist's eye for beauty, and the overall vision and imagination of the architect. For a reason that is hard to understand today, few if any of the names of these extraordinary men have come down to us. We honor and preserve the names of the builders of the fifteenth and sixteenth centuries, but those of the men who labored in earlier centuries seem to have become lost. Usually it is the bishops of medieval dioceses who are credited with building England's many beautiful village churches as well as her grand cathedrals. Undoubtedly a saintly bishop did supply the inspiration and leadership that such an undertaking would require, but without the faithful day-in and day-out workmanship of the masons, the inspiration might have come to naught.

The Sculptors

We know that England's towns and villages almost invariably contain an ancient church dating back to the twelfth, thirteenth, or fourteenth century. Some of their original beauty has been spoiled by the religious vandals of the sixteenth and seventeenth centuries, but enough remains to give one a good idea of their original glory.

Intricate carved detail abounded in these ancient churches, not just in the now too often empty niches of the interior but over much of the outside too. Over and around the entrances would frequently be dozens of figures illustrating stories from the Bible. These must have been highly effective at a time when almost no one knew how to read. And all this highly skilled carving on a great number of widely scattered churches and cathedrals must have been the work of a large number of sculptors. No other conclusion is possible; there must have been hundreds of men with very unusual artistic ability. I have been unable to locate even one family name that comes down to us from the sculptors. Clearly, this would seem to indicate that in the naming period, sculptors were called by some other name, and that name must have been MASON, or one of the other variations listed. The tax man simply wrote down John MASON, or whatever other variant suited his fancy at the moment, and he never dreamed of differentiating between one type of mason and another.

This conclusion is further supported by the fact that most of the fine carving on churches was done as an integral part of the whole structure, indeed, out of the same stone as the rest of the structure. Marble and alabaster were used a bit later, but statues carved from these materials were probably made in London and shipped to the church when it was finished. This practice did not become general until late in the fourteenth and early in the fifteenth centuries, when such work was largely taken over by the craft guilds. By that time, surnames had become settled and quite permanent.

Time was not the factor in building in the Middle Ages that it is now. The workmen simply kept at their tasks until they had finished or until old age brought an end to their labors. If the building was a castle or cathedral, to finish it in twenty-five years would be miraculous, fifty years extraordinary, and two hundred years, normal.

As a result, it was the universal custom of the masons to build houses for their families right alongside the foundation of the building. They expected to spend the rest of their lives on that spot and they commonly did so. The masons tended to form a community of their own fellow craftsmen, ruling out those of other trades—not, as we may suppose, from any snobbish reason, but because they would be on the job continuously for generations while the tilers, the glaziers, and all the rest would not be needed for many years to come. Some writers have called these communities of stone carvers "lodges." And it is known that some lodges provided these families with the mutual benefits that would later be adopted by many of the craft guilds.

GROUP 43

Plasterers

Modern man is inclined to take plastering for granted. A man looking at a house with the possible intention of buying it examines the baths and the kitchen in great detail, measures the size of the living room, and counts the bedrooms, but if someone were to ask him the next day if the house was plastered, he would probably look at that person in blank amazement.

This was not true back in the naming period of English history. The art of plastering the inner walls of a building was virtually unknown in England or anywhere else in western Europe before the twelfth century. In ancient Athens and Rome, all buildings, except the most humble, were plastered beautifully but, like bathtubs, running water, and central heating, the knowledge of this convenience was lost in Britain when the Romans left in the fifth century.

The Normans brought some knowledge of plaster over with them, and during the eleventh and twelfth centuries, men from the Low Countries came in who had some experience with it, but probably it was the returning crusaders who should be credited with introducing its use to the English people as a whole. Of course, for some years plaster was used only by the rich nobles, but as it became better known and cheaper, its use became fairly general in the houses of the rapidly increasing middle class. By the late thirteenth century, skill in making and applying plaster must have become fairly common, because many names came from the new occupation.

DABER, DAUBER, DAWBER, DOBER, DOBERER, and DOBERMAN sound suspiciously like our word *dabber* and probably with good reason. They were all carelessly applied to any man who worked in either real plaster or in some more or less amateur mixture of whitewash and gypsum.

GYSSER meant a plasterer, only it came from the Old French word *gissier.*

PARGETER and its two variations come from the Middle French word *pargeter,* whose origin is not too clear. They were definitely plasterers, but probably did more elaborate, possibly decorative, work.

Finally, PLAISTER, PLASTER, and PLASTRER were the obvious names given to a man in this business.

GROUP 44

Carpenters

Medieval England was covered in many areas with vast forests of oak, beech, and many other trees. While large areas were restricted to hunting by the nobility, the supply of wood for building must have seemed inexhaustible. In those days a peasant who needed a new house for his family built it himself by cutting down young saplings, dragging them to the building site, setting them into the ground, weaving them together with anything he could find, and then plastering mud or clay 'over the saplings. A thatched roof was added, and he was ready to move in. Occasionally some whitewash was put over the mud, as it helped keep the mud from being washed away by the rain. "Wattle and daub" is the highly appropriate name given to the cottage of a peasant before about 1100.

The kind of house a Saxon noble lived in has been described earlier in this chapter. He was the lord of the manor and his word was the law in his own domain, but though his manor house was a great deal larger than the cottage of a peasant, in the matter of refinements and accommodations, it was not much better. It would be surrounded with a palisade of some kind, and inside the palisade would be a row of rude structures to accommodate his horses, cattle, poultry, and, of course, the servants who took care of his livestock.

Every village had a church, and scattered widely over the whole land were monasteries, abbeys, and priories—veritable islands of learning and progress at a time when such things were hard to find in England.

This, then, was the face of England when the great middle class began to emerge. Either by virtue of their personal accomplishments or by outright purchase from a landlord, certain individuals became free of their feudal obligations. Such a man's financial obligations to his lord became nominal. He could grow whatever crops he wished and sell them wherever he could. He might raise beef cattle or poultry on a large scale or, if a skilled mechanic, he could build a shop for his craft and hire certain fellow workers to carry on the work while he handled the business end of the venture.

As he prospered, this man would want a better house for his family—something considerably better than he could build himself. This meant he would have to deal with an experienced builder of houses. This builder might be called a CARPENTER or possibly CARPENTIER or even CHARPENTIER. If the builder happened to be English, he might be given any one of the WRIGHT names listed.

The name JOINER, with its four variations, is very interesting. A joiner was then as he is now a woodworker experienced in doing more accurate work than the carpenter. The carpenter would cut the beams, the sills, the gables—that is, the whole frame of the house. Then, for interior woodwork—maybe some paneling, a bench to sit on, and a bedstead—one called in a joiner. The interesting point as far as name origins is that as far back as the late twelfth century it was considered necessary to distinguish the joiner from the carpenter. They were two different workmen and not to be confused with each other.

Another highly significant point is that the joiner has always been the woodworker who built stairs. In fact, it is the joiner who developed the whole idea of a stairway in the house. As it happens, two- and three-story buildings were first built in this period.

BINNER and BINNS, and for that matter COTTEMAKER too, must have been either joiners or simply all-around handymen. It took some know-how to make a bin for the housewife to keep flour in and as for a dovecote—well, some doves are more particular what kind of house they live in than are the people who own them.

The BOARD names refer to the man who smoothed off the boards sawed out of a log. A plain board was too rough to be used in any house; it would have to be planed off on one side anyway. This could have been done very nicely by the joiner, but since there are at least nine names in this group, it would seem that certain joiners made a business of making boards for the other joiners. BOARDMAN, BORD-WRIGHT, and such certainly suggest this.

BORER is a strange name. It must have been given to a man boring a hole in a board by some clerk who knew little or nothing about woodwork. It was something a woodworker must have had to do every day and so it was not much of an identification.

The CAPSTACK names are a bit unusual in that they came from both Old French and Old English. In Old French, the word *couper* meant "to cut," and in Old English, the word *staca* meant "a stake." From these two sources came all four names. In practice, they simply meant a woodworker.

LATTER and LATTEWRIGHT were the woodworkers who made lath to which the plaster was applied.

The three PALLISER names were applied to men who build palisades or fences.

The fourteen names beginning with SAER come from the action of sawing wood. A tree would be cut down, and if one wanted to make boards out of it, one had to saw it up. This would take some doing. A pit would be dug five or six feet deep and the log to be sawed carefully placed across the pit. The SAWYER would stand on top of the log holding one handle of the saw and his assistant would be down in the pit at the other end of the saw. Of course, he would be called PITMAN or one of the variations listed. Sawing wood was not always done over a pit. Boards had to be sawed right on the building site and, since new and better houses were being built everywhere, a lot of carpenters and joiners may well have been given any one of the SAWYER names.

The TALLBOY names came from the Old French word meaning "cut wood." They could be applied to anyone seen doing such an act.

The TIMBER names were applied to men in the business of selling wood. We can hardly suppose that they carried a full selection of two-by-fours, but they definitely did sell lumber.

The WARWICKER names have an aristocratic sound to many ears, but they were first applied to men who built scaffolds. This would seem to bear out the earlier statement that two- and three-story houses were something of a novelty in this period—enough so that a scaffold would be unusual enough to attract attention.

The derivation of the WOOD names, including the HACK names, is not as clear as many others, but in all probability they were just names casually given to woodworkers unwilling or unable at the moment to be more specific.

GROUP 45

Stone Quarriers

Medieval England was blessed by nature with plenty of fine building stone; large outcroppings of it could be found in a vast number of widely scattered areas. Huge veins of rough stone in the ground, however, presented some real problems to medieval quarriers. They had no blasting powder of any kind and no power-driven drills to make holes for the dynamite if they had had any.

It must have been backbreaking labor to manually drive iron wedges deep enough into a ledge and in just the right places to cause a slab of manageable size to split off. Wooden rollers placed under it and human muscle behind it would eventually get the stone to where it could be rolled slowly onto a sledge and be pulled away by several teams of oxen.

Here it would be taken over by the masons, who would cut and chip away at the slab until it was reduced to a number of practical-sized building blocks.

Considering the length of time it must have taken to get that one slab out of the quarry and into the hands of the masons and the pitifully few cut stones it would produce, can we wonder why it took centuries to build a great monastery or cathedral?

For a full five centuries, this went on, until the advent of the religious revolution of the sixteenth century, which brought with it what is known today as the "dissolution of the monasteries." This is a soft-spoken reference to one of the most regrettable periods in all English history; I shall not go into it here, except to say that the patient labors of thousands of medieval builders were torn down and scattered over the countryside. A leisurely day's trip through almost any shire in England today reveals a dozen old monastic ruins. Some of them still retain a touch of their ancient beauty in the remains of an archway or a stained-glass window.

One thing that is apt to strike today's sightseer is the almost complete absence of loose building stones scattered about the ruins. All that remains now is an occasional bit of wall with a broken column or two still showing a fragment of its carved capital. The answer is not far away: the thousands of carefully cut stones painfully carved out by the masons of the Middle Ages are still in use—as foundations for the relatively modern buildings surrounding these sites.

Looking at the names in this group, the first eight, beginning with MARBER, indicate quarriers who worked with marble. In 1230 there is listed a Ricardus le Marbrer. The Normans called any hewer of marble a *marbrier*. This could mean he was a carver of marble, a mason who worked with marble, or a quarrier.

The next five names, beginning with PEROUR, identify definitely with the occupation of quarrier. *Perriur* is Old French for "quarrier." The earliest record of it I have found is Robertus Perier, in 1194.

The last four names are of Norman origin. In the records can be found Henry de la Quarrere in 1279, and another Henry le Quarreur in Yorkshire in 1275, and a William atte Quarere in 1332. That little Anglo-Saxon word *atta* was mentioned in an earlier chapter. It meant the same thing as our word *at,* so this particular Mr. Quarere may not have been a stoneworker of any kind, but rather just an interested onlooker at the moment the tax man happened along. This is unlikely, however, as when he left the vicinity of the quarry, he would probably forget ever having had the name.

GROUP 46

Floor and Pavement Layers

In the naming period, pavements and floors made from anything more durable than mud were few and far between. In the cathedrals and the more important churches, tile floors were to be expected, and during the latter part of the period an occasional manor house might have some ceramic flooring.

Tile was still largely foreign to the English in the Middle Ages. The Dutch, the French, and particularly the Italians were far ahead of the Britons. There is evidence, however, that the skilled worker in tile was held in great esteem by the people of England, and particularly in London. In 1398, two *paviours* from London were invited to dine with the Fellows of New College, Oxford, an extraordinary honor at that time.

In 1308, one Peter le Pavier was employed to lay a tile floor for Saint Stephen's Chapel, Westminster. The earliest written record of the name is Walter Pavier in 1212.

The names in this group need little explanation. The first six, beginning with PAVER, indicate a man who laid floors or paving, but it is uncertain what material he used. The rest of the list, from TILEMAN on, must have made and laid tile of their own making. The tile-makers did not organize into a craft guild until well into the 1400s.

GROUP 47

Painters

Painting from the standpoint of the building trades in the Middle Ages had little or no place in the life of the times. When a cathedral or church was built, artists might be employed to put murals on the walls or to lend color to the work of the woodcarvers, but that was about all.

We know that a painter named Hugh le Peyntour was employed on Saint Stephen's Chapel, Westminster, in 1308, but we have no record of what he did. It must have been considered important at the time to have given him the name.

The six PAINTER names are of men who must have done some kind of painting; otherwise, why the name? And, with the further exception of STAINER and STAYNOR, from the Middle English word *steyner* meaning "to paint," the rest of the names on this list have to be classified as whitewashers. This is not to call their skill into question, but we have to suppose they did not work with paints made from lead and oil to any extent or they would have had one of the PAINTER names on the list. Covering a building with whitewash was very common in that period— even the mud-and-thatch cottage of the humblest peasant would be whitened if the owner could manage it. The White Tower in the Tower of London was given that name because of the whitewash applied to it regularly.

GROUP 48

Roofers

It seems incredible that there should be twenty different ways of spelling one name (and there may be several more). The twenty names beginning with TACKARA started far back in Anglo-Saxon England as *pacian,* meaning "to cover." But by the 1300s it had developed into the astonishing variety listed. Some variations did not survive; for example, Roger le Thacchere, 1339; Anabilla Thekker, 1327, and John Thackerowe, as late as 1548.

The confusion is only compounded when we look at the nine names beginning with READER. Allowing for normal changes over the intervening years, these names were given to roofers who used reed of some kind to do their thatching. They could just as well have been called by any one of the THATCHER names, although the REED names are just as ancient. (The Old English word *redyn* meant "to thatch with reeds.") This name with all its variations is still common in Norfolk. Symon le Redere in 1279 is the earliest written record I have found.

RISHER and RUSHER were names given to people who supplied rushes to the roofers, but since rushes were also used for floor-covering, it is not certain that these names belong with the roofers. There was a John le Russere back in 1296 and an Alen le Rusmangor in 1210. The ending *mangor* is a variation of *monger* and indicates that this man was a dealer in rushes.

The name COUEROUR is unusual. It is a combination of Old French words meaning "a man who covers roofs." Perhaps the tax man who used that name didn't know any of the THATCHER or READ names.

COVER is an obvious name, but this man's material may have been straw, reeds, or rushes.

The nine names beginning with HELLIAR all mean a roofer, but there is a suggestion in the Old English word these names came from, *helian,* that might indicate that these men did their roofing with either slate or tile.

The LEADBEATER names including LEDTHEKER have been included in with the roofers because they beat lead into sheets for the roofers to use.

PITCHER and PITCHERS come from roofers who used pitch on a roof job.

PLUM and PLUMB mean "lead," as has been indicated earlier. So do PLUMBE, PLUMER, and PLOMER. These men worked with the heavy metal, and surely they put roofs on churches, castles, and such. Lead was not for the peasant cottage.

The SLATE names indicate material used for certain roof jobs. It may not have been as picturesque as thatch but it would last a lot longer. SHINGLER and SHINGLES tell their own story.

STREULEGGER is Old English for "straw layer" so not only was he a roofer but straw was the material he used.

The last two names, TIULUR and TYGHELER, originate from an old word meaning tile, and it may be supposed that their owners used tile for their roofing contracts. Tile was not commonly used for this purpose until the 1500s. Far more frequent use was made of it for floors and pavement (see Group 46, page 113).

GROUP 49

Glassworkers

The art of making glass goes back as early as 2500 B.C. in Egypt, but the first record of its introduction into England was in A.D. 680 when Benedict, bishop of Wearmouth and Jarrow, had glaziers brought in from Gaul to put glass in the windows of the churches he was building. Only a generation later, Saint Wilfred followed his example at his new minster at York.

These windows are regrettably long since gone, but there seems reason to believe that they consisted of many small pieces of colored glass leaded together for color effect with no design attempted.

Not until late in the twelfth century would there be design, and fortunately we have samples of this work remaining at Canterbury and York cathedrals. The figure work of this period leaves something to be desired, but the color effects produced—mostly ruby, green, blue, and dark red—are surprisingly beautiful.

As far as is known, no serious attempts were made in England to do anything with glass other than church windows until well after the naming period, in the 1400s. Consequently, any name on this list probably belonged to a glazier-artist in stained-glass windows. *Glaes* was the Old English word for "glass," while the Old French word was *verrieur*. Thus there is a Thomas le Glasyer in 1297 and Robert le Glasiere in 1327—undoubtedly from a French tax man's efforts to make an English word look French. All the names on this list come from either the English or the French word for glass and, allowing for the inevitable changes over time, all appeared before 1400.

GROUP 42

Stonemasons

Carrier	Machent	•	Stones
Carryer	Machin	Marberer	Stonhard
•	Machon	•	Stonier
Carver	Macon	Stanier	Stonwright
•	Mason	Stannard	•
Hewar	Massen	Stannet	Wall
Hewer (*see*	Masson	Stanyer	Walle
Stonehewer)	Mayson	Stonard	Wallers
•	Meacham	Stone	Walls
Layer	Meachem	Stoneman	Walmaker
Leir	Meachim	Stonehewer	Walman
•	Meachin	(*see* Hewer)	Woll
Machen	Meecham	Stoner	Woller

GROUP 43

Plasterers

Daber	Doberer	•	•
Dauber	Doberman	Pargeter	Plaister
Dawber	•	Pargetter	Plaster
Dober	Gysser	Pargiter	Plastrer

GROUP 44

Carpenters

Binner	•	•	•
Binns	Hackamore	Saer	Waraker
•	Hacker	Sare	Warrack
Board	Hackwood	Sawyer	Warricker
Boarder	•	Sawyers	Warwicker
Boardman	Housewright	Sayer	Woracker
Boord	(*see* Wraight)	Sayers	Woraker
Border	•	Sayre	Woricker
Borders	Joiner	Sear	•
Bordhewer	Joyner	Seares	Wooder
Bordier	Joyngur	Sears	Woodger
Bordwright	Joynter	Seear	Woodier
•	Joyntur	Seers	Woodyear
Borer	•	Seyers	Woodyer
•	Latter	Syur	
Capstack	Lattewright	•	Wraight (*see*
Capstick	•	Tabois	Housewright)
Copestake	Palliser	Ta Bois	Wraighte
Copestick	Pallister	Talboys	Wrate
•	Palser	Tallboy	Wreight
Carpenter	•	Tallboys	Wright
Carpentier	Pitman	•	Wrighte
Charpentier	Pitt	Timberman	
•	Pittman	Timmerman	
Cottemaker	Pitts	Tymbermonger	

GROUP 45

Stone Quarriers

Marber	Marlehewer	Perrier	Quarreur
Marberer	Marler	Perryer	Quarrie
Marble	Marlor	Purrier	Quarrier
Marbler	•	Puryer	Quarry
Marbrow	Perour	•	

GROUP 46

Floor and Pavement Layers

Paver	Pavour	Tiler	Tyghler
Pavier	Pavyer	Tilur	Tyleman
Pavior	•	Tiulur	Tyler
Paviour	Tileman	Tygheler	Tylor

GROUP 47

Painters

Chalker	Painter	Peyntour	Wheater
•	Painters	•	Whiter
Limer	Paynter	Stainer	Whitter
Lymer	Peinter	Staynor	Whyter
•	Peynter	•	

GROUP 48

Roofers

Couerour	Leadbeatter	Plumer	•
Cover	Leadbetter	•	Sclater
•	Leadbitter	Reader	Sclatter
Helliar	Ledbetter	Readers	Sklatemanger
Hellier	Ledtheker	Readman	Slate
Hellyer	Lidbetter	Reder	Slater
Helyer	•	Redman	Slator
Hilliar	Pitcher	Reed	Slatter
Hillier	Pitchers	Reeder	•
Hillyar	•	Reeders	Shingler
Hillyer	Plomer	Reedman	Shingles
Hilyer	Plum	•	•
•	Plumb	Risher	Streulegger
Leadbeater	Plumbe	Rusher	•

Tackara	Thackray	Thakester	Theecher
Thackara	Thackway	Thakor	Theker
Thacker	Thackwell	Thakrey	.
Thackeray	Thackwray	Thatcher	Tiulur
Thackra	Thakera	Thaxter	Tygheler
Thackrah	Thakers	Theaker	

GROUP 49

Glassworkers

Glaisher	Glassman	Glayzer	.
Glasenwright	Glaswright	Glazer	Verrer
Glasman	Glasyer	Glazier	Verrier
Glass	Glaysher	Glazyer	Verriour

CHAPTER **11**

The Wool Industry

One might expect the textile trades of medieval England to be the source of a very sizable proportion of the family names we know today, and indeed it could hardly be otherwise. During the entire period our names were forming, the business of changing raw wool, flax, and silk into usable materials was the biggest industry on the island. It has been estimated that at one time almost every other adult in England was engaged in some part of the textile industry, and that meant frequent personal contact between individuals, making identification a matter of daily necessity.

CLOTHMAKING

No one knows just when or where the first man or woman decided that something more convenient and desirable than the raw skins of animals could be produced and made into clothing.

At least as far back as five thousand years ago the Egyptians were weaving linen of a very good quality. In India they were making cloth out of cotton before the birth of Christianity, and in China they made silk. The Greeks were making fairly respectable woolen goods before the age of Pericles, and the Romans, as might be expected, seem to have mastered the art of weaving very early. But with the fall of Roman civilization in the fifth century in most of western Europe, more or less all their accomplishments in the art of good living disappeared. Without that typical Roman drive and appreciation for the countless little things that collectively add up to modern comfort, the people in what is now western Europe slipped back many centuries. The Romans had warmed their luxurious houses with central heating, had taken daily hot baths in exquisitely carved marble pools, and sat down to elaborate dinners of excellent quality while the people of Europe outside the empire in general lived in wretched houses devoid of any heat, ate the roughest kind of food, and didn't know what bathing was.

By the eleventh century, western Europeans slowly began to emerge from this lethargy. It didn't happen suddenly but rather through a series of events and situations such as the return of the crusaders. When streams of these fighting men returned to England with tales of the luxuries they had seen in the Near East, local artisans were stimulated to produce the same things. A man who had once seen a window with glass in it was not going to be satisfied with windows that were more or less closed with rough slabs of wood.

Then too, there was the rise of the merchants in England. Buying and selling merchandise was becoming respectable; the merchant could import luxuries and offer them for sale at his place of business. The merchant now belonged to a guild formed to regulate conditions in his trade, and the larger market towns were beginning to be chartered by the king.

Trade fairs were becoming an important factor in the distribution of both new ideas and new materials. A fair at that time consisted of a large group of merchants who by prearrangement with the local powerful lord were allowed to set up booths in a designated area of the town and sell their goods to all who could pay for them. A fair usually lasted one week before going on to the next town.

Much earlier in this book, I mentioned the influx of Norman craftsmen into England at the bidding of the Norman kings. It is estimated that as many as one hundred thousand of them came over in the thirteenth century. They brought their skills with them and frequently some of their equipment too. Many of them were highly skilled textile workers —far advanced over the native English and Britons of that early period. Previous to this, the Anglo-Saxons turned out a lot of what was called burel. This was a rough piece of material that must have resembled our modern burlap, although modern burlap is made from hemp or jute fibers while burel was made from wool. It served very well for the clothing of the peasants, but the noble and the well-to-do merchant imported the materials for their clothing.

Before one can talk about the WEAVERS and the WEBBERS, the TUCKERS and the WALKERS, something must be said about the

SHEPHERDS. After all, the wool business has to start with sheep, and to raise sheep in that faraway time required shepherds. Wolves attacking sheep have been the subject of many old nursery stories but in this period it was a serious matter. England at that time had a large wolf population that roamed the country at will. A sheep was helpless before a wolf, and if a shepherd was not on the job, there would have been few sheep. Thus shepherds were everywhere. Every peasant-farmer and craftsman wanted to own at least a few sheep. The farmer would take care of his own, and for a share in the profits he would include the sheep of one or several village craftsmen not in a position to do their own shepherding. Of course, the lord of the manor would have an enormous flock—five thousand sheep would not be unusual. He would have to employ a crew of caretakers around the clock, who would also work on a profit-sharing basis.

The Cistercian monks, with monasteries scattered all over England and Scotland, were leaders in the development of sheep breeding to improve both the quality and the yield of wool. They competed with each other, often in a none too friendly way, but over the years they accomplished much in the way of improvements.

At that time, wool was not classified by the breeds of sheep but rather by the county from which the sheep came. Shropshire, Herefordshire, and the Cotswolds produced the best fiber, while Lincolnshire, Hampshire, Kent, Essex, and Surrey produced a fiber of somewhat lesser quality. Naturally, efforts were constantly being made to produce a breed that would be superior in the quality of its mutton as well as its wool.

It's easy to see the economics of sheep-raising at that time. A single sheep might produce five to six pounds of wool per year; if one were lucky, the yield might go as high as fifteen pounds. The cost of maintaining the animal was negligible when distributed over a large flock. Good grass was about all that was required, and at that time it was plentiful. An increase of 500 percent in the flock in a period of five years was not uncommon.

In the early part of the period under consideration, English wool was one of the best in all Europe, but up to the middle of the thirteenth century, England's spinning and weaving facilities were not sufficient to match her wool production. Consequently, the excess was exported to the Continent, mostly to Flanders, which at that time was the leading manufacturing area in the industry. This situation soon changed and the English sheep breeders were forbidden to export any part of their production.

GROUP 50

Shepherds and Overseers

BARKER is a name with two meanings: either the bearer of this name was a tanner who used bark in the process of tanning leather, or if his name came from a Norman source like *berchier* or *barcher,* he was a shepherd.

CALL and CAULES don't seem to belong in this list at all, but in Middle English, there was a word *calle,* meaning a place where sheep are kept. In the usual carefree manner of the period the word was sometimes applied to a shepherd.

FEMISTER and its four variants meant a shepherd, but usually the names were applied to the man in charge of several flocks—an overseer over other shepherds. Its origin is somewhat cloudy but we know it meant "Fee master," literally. We can assume that a man given this name must have been a trustworthy individual.

MOTTON and MUTTON refer to the meat of the sheep.

PASTOR, as a name, has at times meant a pastry cook, a shepherd, and in late medieval times, a priest. The name comes from an Old French word, *pastur.*

The SHEEP names are just different ways of spelling shepherd. In Anglo-Saxon, it was *sceap-weard* or *sheep ward.* That word *ward* always meant a guard or watchman of some kind. Variations of the name with SON tacked on at the end (SHEPHERDSON) were given to sons of shepherds who were to be identified as such.

WEATHER and WEATHERS also mean shepherd. The name comes from a still older Anglo-Saxon word *wether,* meaning "sheep." I find an Almer Wether back in the twelfth century.

I have purposedly put SHEPSMERER and SMERER, SHEEPWASH and SHIPWASH in with the shepherds even though they were not necessarily shepherds. Any readers who lived through the American Prohibition will remember stories about drinking genuine old sheepdip. This term was generally used by a host who was rather proud of the quality of the liquor he was serving. The first two names can be taken as fairly positive proof that the medieval shepherd did have some kind of medicine that was to be smeared on sheep who became wounded or cut in some manner. The names SHEEPWASH and SHIPWASH come even closer to modern sheepdip and tell us that those old-timers actually did have ponds or even wooden troughs filled with water to which some mixture was added to cure or kill whatever ills the sheep had.

GROUP 51

Shearers

It takes a full year for a sheep to grow a crop of wool and, for obvious reasons, he is not relieved of his winter growth until the approach of summer. Shearing a sheep is a highly skilled job, and back in medieval times it must have been a lot harder. Besides skill and experience, it takes a good pair of shears, and as we have seen in an earlier chapter, these were not easy to come by. Good steel that could be brought to a sharp edge was more or less an accident in the Middle Ages.

A man lucky enough to have acquired a good pair of shears must have been in great demand; he would be called in to do all kinds of shearing and, as a consequence, he might well acquire the needed skill. This brings up an interesting point. Back in chapter 5 we gave a list of names that apparently refer to the smiths who made shears (see Group 8, page 48). Some of these like SHEARSMITH and SERSMITH definitely did come from the maker, but the others leave us in some doubt as to whether they *made* shears or used them skillfully. A SHEARMAN could be either one. A man able to make a pair or professionally use them might very understandably be given any of the names either in Group 8 or here.

CRAPPER and CROPPER were applied to men who sheared sheep. The origin is the Middle English word *cropper,* meaning to crop or cut.

FORCER is an Old French word and means to clip or sheer sheep, and POLLARD or POLLER was a Middle English nickname for a man who cut or clipped something.

TONSOR and TUNDER lean toward a sheep-shearing origin, but it is my belief that most of the names in both groups are a little too indefinite to be pinned down. The Latin word is *tonsorius,* meaning "to shear," which the Normans changed to *tonsor.* As will be seen a little later, there is still another group of craftsmen who were expert in the use of scissors. They did a highly skilled job on the almost finished roll of cloth with a pair of those precious shears. They were SHEARMEN too. I suspect that the man who sheared sheep for a month or two each spring had another pair of shears, very different in shape and size, with which he could do a very important job in the final finishing of the web of woolen cloth.

GROUP 52
Sorters

At first glance, this might seem to be a rather minor and unimportant job, but in fact it was crucial. As soon as the wool was removed from the sheep, it went to the WOOLSORTER. It was up to his sharp eyes and trained sense of touch to pick out the coarse fibers from the soft and fine, and both these in turn from the medium. The price the industry paid for the wool depended on accurate and honest grading. All grades were good, but soft, fine fibers, particularly if they were long, were worth considerably more than the other grades. Also, if the sheep had been butchered for meat before he was sheared, that wool could not be mixed with wool taken from the live animal. It was up to the SORTER to put such wool in separate bags.

GROUP 53
Washers

After the wool is clipped from the sheep and sorted and bagged into grades, it must be washed. Before raw wool can be spun into yarn, it has to be cleaned to remove any dirt or foreign material and then placed in an alkaline solution to remove the natural grease and oil that nature put in it. Then it is rinsed with clean water and spread out in the sun to dry. When dry and still spread out on a large flat surface, it is beaten with sticks to separate the fibers.

The names this part of the process has given to us are perfectly straightforward. STEEPER and its variant STEPER simply mean somebody who steeped something in a liquid. (That's what we do when we soak clothes before washing them.) BOUKER meant the same thing, only it was more specific. It tells us that the soaking was being done in lye (probably wood ashes). *Bouken* is an Old English word that meant just that.

The LAUNDRY, LAVENDER, and WASCHER names simply mean to wash. The LAVER names derive from the Old French word *lavandier,* meaning "anyone who washes something" and the LAUNDRY names also come from that. WASCHER has an Anglo-Saxon origin.

GROUP 54
Carders

Once the wool is clean and free from foreign matter, it may still be badly tangled. Before it can be spun into yarn, it must be untangled— not an easy task. There were three different ways of doing this, and each way left family names that are still with us.

Carding is not only one of the very oldest ways to process wool at this stage, but it is still used in many odd parts of the world. A card was a piece of wood measuring something like nine inches by six inches. It had a handle on it and was covered with leather on one side. Through this leather, several hundred fine wires projected out about a quarter of an inch. There were two of these cards exactly alike. A handful of wool was put onto the wires of one of them and the other card rubbed against the first over and over again. Each rub took a little of the wool off the other. When it was all off the first card and all on the second one, then one rub was given in the reverse direction and the whole bunch of wool changed over to the other card. It was now in a spongy roll and ready for spinning into yarn.

It should be noted right here that a fiber of wool is not a smooth hair-like thread, but rather a hair studded with a great many tiny hooks that stick out in every direction. They can and do catch onto each other when given half a chance, which is the reason why wool shrinks when washed in hot water. But, as it is taken off the card in a soft fluffy roll ready to spin into yarn, its fibers are crossed in every direction and consequently, when it is twisted into yarn, the yarn is soft and fluffy.

All the names contain the word *card* and so are easily recognizable.

GROUP 55
Combers

I mentioned that there were three different methods by which a man could handle his wool: he could card it, as we have just described, or he could comb it or "bow" it if he wanted to.

Combing wool is a very ancient practice, and it is still used in the twentieth century, although machinery does the work that used to be done by hand. In the Middle Ages, the process was simply this: the wool was slightly dampened with water and sprayed with oil, and the combs were heated to make them easier to pull through the wool. After a lot of combing, the wool would have its fibers more or less parallel to each other instead of all crossed up, as with carding.

When this combed wool was spun into thread and woven into cloth, it would be known as worsted, a material with a hard, smooth finish and little or no nap.

Of course, the people who used this method were just as numerous and important as those who carded their wool. The comb names are perfectly obvious, though the KEMBER names might be confusing. They come from Old English.

TESER and TOSER are slightly different. These men obtained the same result as the COMBERS did, but they used a fuller's teasel instead of a comb. The teasel is a thistlelike weed that can still be seen in many places. *Dipsacus fullonum* is the botanical name for it. This weed has a great many sharp little thorns on it, and when one of these is allowed to dry out and harden, it is capable of doing just as fine a job of combing as a man-made comb. The same weed would be used further on in the process and would give us still more names.

GROUP 56

Bowers

The process of bowing seems to have originated in Italy but became quite common in England in the thirteenth century. A bow, similar to that used by an archer but without any arrows, did the job. With the wool spread out, all clean and dry, on a table or bench, the string of the bow was plucked by the operator, and while it was vibrating, it was worked into the wool. The very rapid vibrations of the string in contact with the wool had the almost magical effect of separating the tangles in the fibers. When continued for a time, the total effect was indistinguishable from the carding separation. The fibers would be untangled, but they would still be sufficiently crisscrossed to produce a fine, soft yarn when spun.

This group indicates the few names that have come down to us from the bowing method of preparing wool for spinning. Unfortunately, the name BOWMAN does not distinguish between the man who used a bow as a weapon (see chapter 8) and the man who used a bow in the preparation of wool.

GROUP 57

Spinners

Wool fibers, when untangled by any one of the three methods described, were finally ready to be spun into yarn. For untold centuries, spinning was the task of women, so much so that the word *spinster* became synonymous with *woman,* and particularly with *unmarried woman.* And the distaff, one of the traditional tools used in spinning, came to stand for the entire feminine side of a family.

Those of us not particularly familiar with the history of textiles, especially spinning, are apt to think of the spinning wheel that we see in museums and antique shops as the original type of equipment used by the spinners. This is not so. The spinning wheel is a relatively modern invention, developed during the 1600s and thus well after the naming period.

The Egyptians, the Greeks, the Romans, and all of the other races before and after did their spinning with two wooden sticks. One stick would be about three feet long with either a knob or a notch at the top of it to which a bundle of wool fibers could be attached. This was the distaff, and it was usually held under the left arm of the spinner (leaving the left hand free). The right hand held the other stick of wood. This was the spindle; it was smooth and tapered slightly toward the top of its twelve inches or so of length. Frequently it would have a notch cut into the upper end of it to hold a wisp of fiber temporarily, or sometimes the partially spun fiber would be temporarily tied to the spindle. Near the lower end of the spindle was a weight called the whorl; it was round and made of bone, stone, or even wood. It was slipped over the spindle and held there by the taper. Its sole purpose was to act as a flywheel—the spindle was going to have to do a lot of turning and that weight near the bottom of the stick made it a lot easier.

The spinning process would start by using a yard or so of finished yarn as a sort of bait. One end was fastened to the spindle in the right hand the other draped over the wool on top of the distaff in the left hand. Then the right hand would turn the spindle clockwise: it would dangle in the air supported by the finished yarn fastened to it and grasped by the spinner's right hand. The whole piece of finished yarn would twist with it. Then the spinner would pull a few fibers of wool off the distaff with her left hand and allow them to wrap around the length of finished yarn, while she stopped the spin of the yarn with the fingers of her left hand for a few seconds. Then the right hand moved up to the left hand,

and the pressure on the left-hand fingers was released while at the same time a few more wisps of wool were pulled out and allowed to twist themselves onto the yarn. Soon the short length of finished yarn used for bait would be finished, but as the spinner continued turning that spindle and releasing more and more wool, brand-new yarn would be formed. The yarn that was produced would then be wound up on the spindle at frequent intervals, and when the spindle was almost full, it would be unwound onto a reel, leaving a short length on the spindle with which to start the next round. The spinning wheel performs exactly the same movements that human hands aided by two wooden sticks and ten wonderful human fingers did for thousands of years. The wheel is a little faster, of course, and the huge, complicated modern spinning machine operated by power is a great deal faster, but the movements and motions are simply reproductions of those of the ancient distaff and spindle.

Since it took no fewer than four skilled spinners to keep one weaver in yarn and we know that spinning was done in the housewife's spare time, actually one good weaver would require the spinning output of eight or ten spinners. This gives us some idea of the very large number of women who must have been spinners in this period. The name SPINNER was applied to individuals now and then, but there were so many of them in every city, town, and village that it must have failed completely in distinguishing any one of them.

This list shows how very small the number of names is that came from the spinning operation. WINDER may have been a name given to a spinner because at the moment the lady may have been winding her yarn on the reel, but since every spinner had to do this off and on all day long, it must represent a desperate effort on the part of a tax man to avoid having another SPYNNER on his list. And TWINER sprang from the same situation.

GROUP 58

Weavers

I often wonder how we ever developed the word *homespun*. It is always applied to a piece of woven material that by its look indicates that it was made in somebody's house—but why homespun and not homewoven? It's in the weaving that the work of a professional shows up that of the amateur. Today, of course, weaving is done on great, complicated, power-driven machinery, but up to the latter part of the eighteenth century it was a highly skilled handcraft.

Like spinning, weaving goes so far back in human history that we have no idea where or when it originated. Probably the first looms were little more than two wooden slats nailed between two trees. Nails would be studded as close together as possible along each slat and yarn strung up and down between these slats like the strings on a harp. Then another length of yarn would be woven crosswise, going under and over each vertical thread. If these cross-threads were frequently pushed together tightly, a fairly practical piece of cloth would result. By the Middle Ages, some improvements on the loom had been made. Now heavy, square-sawn, well-seasoned boards fastened together with tight joints were used. A loom that was not stiff and square was useless, as it would produce cloth that was out of square. If one thinks of an old-fashioned wooden four-poster bed (circa 1800), it is easier to visualize a medieval loom. The bed of the loom would now be horizontal and at a convenient height above the floor. At the back of the bed would be a wooden roller, and at the foot of the bed, where the weaver sat, a nice smooth rounded-off board. This was the breast beam. Underneath would be another wooden roller to hold the finished cloth. The warp yarn would be wound around the roller at the head of the bed and each and every thread in it strung forward to the breast beam. The threads passed through a comb-like device to keep them exactly the same distance apart. In one's hand would be the shuttle. This was a boat-shaped piece of wood or horn holding a small reel of yarn that would run off when the shuttle was passed between alternate warp threads and then reversed.

Once this point had been reached, real improvements on the loom started. If one passed the shuttle over and under alternate threads, one would produce the simplest weave possible. Today it is called tabby, but in the Middle Ages it was called burel. For centuries most of our ancestors made all their clothing from this weave. It was a little rough to look at and probably fairly stiff, but it was warm. The nobility in the period bought the fancy materials that were being made in France and Flanders. In any case, better cloth was on the way for everyone. The discovery that the simple over-and-under weave could be changed meant that an almost infinite variety of weaves could be produced.

THE AGE OF HEDDLES AND TREADLES

Such a term may never be applied to the Middle Ages by historians but it might well be, because at least partly as a result of greatly improved weaving techniques in England, clothmaking became the leading industry. This resulted in the formation of craft and merchant guilds and the consequent rise of a large middle class of citizenry.

Getting back to the mechanics of weaving, it was found that if, for instance, the shuttle passed over two warp threads and under four, a very different kind of material would result. And this could be done rather easily by means of small pieces of strong cord with an eye in each one. These cords were attached to a stick over the warp threads in front of the weaver, and the warp threads passed through the eyes and down below to another stick. The cords were called heddles, and the whole arrangement came to be known as a harness.

It worked this way: the weaver pressed his foot on the treadle; this raised and depressed the warp threads in the prearranged combination he wanted; then he passed the shuttle through the shed of warp threads thus formed and, with a comblike device called a reed, pushed the thread he had just passed through the shed tightly up against the previous one in the finished cloth.

Combinations of these heddles are still used today. They operate automatically now and much faster, and as many as a dozen harnesses may be used on one loom at one time. In the Middle Ages, two harnesses were probably the limit.

The development of the heddle and treadle seems to have first come about late in the twelfth century, and it so revolutionized the textile industry that this industry was singled out in the Magna Carta in 1215. Even today, the Lord Chancellor, who presides over the British House of Lords, takes his official seat on the woolsack, derived from the medieval sack of wool.

The crown at that time (1215) was just as alert to new sources of revenue as today's politicians are, and a tax was placed on every loom in England. The export of raw wool was forbidden, but not that of finished cloth. Of course, a slight charge at dockside would have to be paid to the king, and no raw wool could be imported.

ALL WOOL AND A YARD WIDE

Just where this old saying comes from or even when it became current is unknown but it does have the ring of antiquity to it. Actually, a webb of cloth (called a "whole cloth") was supposed to measure twenty-four yards long, but its width would vary from time to time and in different places. Cloth one yard wide was not as economical as greater widths, but the width of a cloth depended on the width of a man's loom. If one's loom was built for thirty-six-inch cloth, it could not possibly turn out anything wider.

Old records show that cloth was measured in quarters. One yard wide was four quarters, and soon five-, six-, and even seven-quarter widths were being made.

Earlier in the chapter was discussed the rough English burel that the Anglo-Saxon weavers had been turning out for many years before the age of heddles and treadles arrived. Burel continued to be woven for a great many years after much nicer cloth was available. It was much cheaper than the fancy flannels of the new age in weaving, and it continued to be the material from which was made the clothing of the common people. Now and then, great quantities of it were ordered by a king to give to the poor.

As a consequence of this, a sizable number of weavers who could not make any of the new materials stuck to their old looms. They were eventually named from the goods they made—BOREL, BURLER, and the other four variations.

CLOTHER, CLOTHIER, and CLOTHMAN, along with WOLLER, WOLLESTER, WOOLER, and WOOLLER will be treated later on in this chapter. They were all probably WEAVERS who later became wool merchants. There is some confusion with WOLL names, as some of them probably come from the Middle English word for wolf. There are more variations of the name than listed here, but these four are almost certainly from the wool business. LANER belonged to this group too.

The four DRAPER names are a little different in that their Norman origin indicates that Walter le Drapier back in 1148 and Robert le Drapier in 1181 were almost certainly weavers to start with but later became merchants who sold the output of other weavers. This was quite common all during this fast-growing period.

SAKWEBB indicates a man who was a weaver of material suitable for making bags or sacks.

THREADER and its variant THREDDER seem to have been first applied to one Thomas Thredere in 1365. He may have been an assistant or apprentice to the weaver because, judging by the obscure Old English word from which the name derives, he was engaged in keeping the weaver supplied with shuttles filled with thread.

The next seven names beginning with TISSER come from an Old French word, *tisseur*, meaning "weaver."

WEAVER itself, along with its variants, is distinctly English in origin, coming from another Old English word, *wefan*.

The WEB names on the list are fairly obvious. They all stem back to the original Old English word *webbe,* which meant "weaver." Probably the first time somebody had occasion to refer to a particular weaver, he might have been spoken of as a webbe and his product as a web of cloth. WEBBE became WEBBER or WEBER, or with the feminine ending, WEBSTER. The earliest record I have found is Elyas le Webbe in a tax roll of 1255.

WINDERS, WINDES, WINDOWS, and WINDUS come from another Anglo-Saxon word, *windan.* The word was applied only to men who wound wool, so such a man worked alongside a loom. An apprentice was usually either given the name PRENTICE or simply assumed the name of the master weaver in charge.

GROUP 59

Fullers

When the weaver had finished his task with the loom, he would have a roll of material, but it would be far from ready for the market. It still had to go through several treatments. This was recognized fully in the trade, and as the volume in woven material doubled and tripled, many new specialized skills were developed. Langland in at least one of the versions of *Piers Plowman* in the fourteenth century recognized this when he wrote:

> Cloth that cometh from the weaving is not comely to wear
> Till it be fulled under foot or in fulling stocks
> Washen well with water, and with teasels cratched,
> Towked and teynted and under tailor's hands.

Many weavers preferred to sell each roll of their product "as is" to a fuller, walker, tucker, or some other variation. This would enable the man who wove the goods to gain speed in weaving and the fuller more skill with his specialty.

Raw cloth definitely needed several treatments before it was ready to be made into garments. It had to be fulled, which meant it had to be thoroughly washed in water, scoured, cleaned, and thickened by beating it in water to which a quantity of what became known as fuller's earth was added. This particular earth was not generally plentiful in England, but large deposits were found around Nutfield and Reigate.

In the early part of the naming period the fuller worked in a particular way. The cloth was spread on a wooden or stone floor sprinkled liberally with fuller's earth and plenty of water and then the real work started. Hour after hour for several days, that cloth had to be tramped on by the bare feet of the fuller. The cloth had to be frequently turned. This must have taken some doing, as a piece of wet woolen cloth twenty-four yards long and a yard or more in width must have been hard to handle. Up and down he would walk, and then crosswise, and then all over again before the cloth had to be turned over and the process repeated on the other side.

Obviously a man with big feet had a clear advantage over a man not so well provided; he could do the job in less time or at least more thoroughly. In the northern counties and well down into the Midlands, the FULLER became better known as a WALKER, while in some of the southern shires, particularly in the Southwest, the same man would be called a TUCKER. The Old English word *tucian* meant to torment something.

VOLLER and BETER meant exactly the same as the above but, as names, were far less common. VOLLER was probably a southwestern dialect form of FULLER.

GROUP 60

Washers, Stretchers, and Dryers

The next step must have been far from easy, too. The cloth had to be washed again, and all that fuller's earth that had been so patiently beaten into and through every inch of the cloth had to be washed out.

This developed into a skilled specialty that gave us a dozen names. LAVER and LAVENDER came from the Latin word for "wash" and over the years in Normandy and medieval England settled down into the dozen forms listed in this group.

The next step provided an opportunity for the cheater, and there must have been quite a few. The cloth, having been cleaned, had to be dried and stretched. This was done on an adjustable wooden frame called a TENTER. (The same thing exists in modern laundries where they dry and stretch lace curtains.) A limited amount of stretching was perfectly legitimate and even necessary, but what happened when a TENTER applied a powerful set of winches and racks and levers? The cloth was stretched so far beyond its limits and was so weakened by hundreds of tiny broken warp threads that it fell apart almost immediately. There is an old legal case from Reading dealing with a web of cloth that came from the weaver a fair thirty yards in length but when it left the hands of the TENTER, after being treated by "a gyn and a leaver with a vice and a roape," measured thirty-five yards long. This became a real problem in that period. "Guildford cloths," known for their quality, and made in Surrey, Sussex, and Hampshire, completely lost their good reputation. For a time, the whole process of drying and stretching had to be supervised and inspected by officials appointed either by the crown or by the guilds.

BURLER, in this list, is hard to pin down because it had more than one meaning. It meant a weaver of burel cloth, as mentioned earlier, but was also applied to a man who became a specialist in going over a piece of finished cloth with a pair of tweezers. He would pick out of the cloth any bits of foreign material that had found their way into the goods. The DRESSER performed about the same duties as the BURLER. The DREYER names come from the Old English word *drygean* meaning "to dry." Roger le Dreyere appears on the tax rolls in 1318.

WASHER needs no explanation.

GROUP 61

Bleachers

Bleaching cloth, like dyeing, could be done at optional intervals in the process. Both depended on the character of the cloth one was working with and just how much of the whole process one intended doing oneself. With the cheaper materials, no bleaching at all might be done and the goods might be sold in the natural shades that the yarn had taken on after the various washings. But the people of the Middle Ages were, on the whole, probably a little fonder of bright colors than we are today, and so the cloth would be put into a bleaching solution and then spread out on the grass for several days in the bright sun. This would usually result in the whole piece becoming several shades lighter, and, more importantly, of a more uniform shade.

BLATCHER, BLAXTER, BLEACHER, BLECHER, BLETCHER, and BLEXTER all come from the Old English *blaecan,* meaning "to bleach." BLACKER and BLAKER may have sprung from the same word, but chances are they come from another Old English term meaning "to blacken," in which case these two should be listed with the dyers (Group 62).

GROUP 62

Dyers

The list of names in Group 62 (page 139) contains forty-three family names, most of which are well known today. All stem back to a dyer of cloth.

The six BLACK names tell their own story: they were dyers who handled black dyes.

The five names beginning with CORK may sound as though they belong on a different list, but they were dyers too. A certain lichen that grew in Scotland produced a fine reddish-purple dye that was different from any other available at that time. The Middle English name for the plant was *cork* (in Gaelic it was *corcur* and may have been instrumental in naming the Irish city of Cork). When properly prepared and applied to a piece of material, cork gave it a color that came to be known as royal purple. Five names are still with us today that derived from this Scottish weed.

The Old English word *deagere* meant DYER, but with the flexibility in spelling of the Middle Ages, the names came out in the five variations noted. One variation, Henry le Deghar in 1260, did not last, and neither did another, Robert le Deyare in 1275. Next came Alexander Dyghere in 1296; this too failed to catch hold, but Henry le Dyer in 1327 was simple and easy, and survived. DEYER, DEXTER, DEYSTER, and DYSTER are probably just a bit later than DYER.

HEUSTER is interesting in that it could have come from the Old English word for a man who hews wood, but the feminine ending on it tells us that it was given to a woman. This would seem to indicate that it must have come down to us not from the Old English word for woodchopper but from the word *hiew,* meaning "hue" or "color."

There are seven LISTER names. They were given to dyers too, but they seem to have all come from East Anglia. The people in East Anglia had a word *litte,* which they applied to a dyer. Ralph Litster in 1286 is the earliest name on the old lists.

The MADD names hardly need an explanation, as madder is still a fairly well known, brilliant red dye.

TEYNTUR and TEYNTURER would have a hard time convincing anyone that they were not dyers. The names even sound like tinter. Of course, these were undoubtedly the invention of some Norman who must have had the Old French word *teintur* in mind.

Finally come the names WADEMAN through WODESTER. Every one of the original owners made his living dyeing cloth. However, they must have specialized to the extent of using one type of dye, and that was blue. The Anglo-Saxon word for the herb that produced this blue dye was *wad*. Blue must have been a color greatly favored by our English ancestors to have produced so many names that have lasted so long. Robert le Wader in 1296 and Barth le Wodere in 1337 are two of the numerous old recordings of the name.

GROUP 63

Cloth Finishers

The web of fine cloth, though dyed in the desired color by now and allowed to dry for a time, was still not quite ready for the cloth market. The people who bought cloths like this were experts on textiles (many of them used to be weavers themselves) and knew every trick in the trade. They could detect the slightest blemish, and if any showed up in a web, they might still buy it, but they would insist on a discount.

The question was should a man do the important job of finishing the cloth himself or would he be smarter to hire an expert finisher? An outside finisher would cost money and his fee would reduce the already small profits but, on the other hand, those men could pick out blemishes that the weaver might not see and they were really expert in fixing most of them so they would not be noticed by the buyer.

If the weaver decided to bring in an outside finisher, he could be warping the loom for the next web while the finisher was doing his job. The finisher went by several different names, depending on the part of England. In the southern shires, he would probably be called a TEASLER or any of the ten variations. In other areas, he might be a DRAWER or a ROWER, but his job was to work with the teasel weed (see Group 55). When these plants were dried out, the hooks of the teasel could be used by an experienced TEASLER to raise the nap on a cloth with a thoroughness that could not be equaled by anything else.

A TEASLER must have had good eyesight. He would roll up the cloth on the table under the best light possible and go painstakingly over every square inch of that web with his teasels, drawing up all of the nap along with any loose fibers. If he found a place where either the warp or the weft threads were knotted or too loose, he was usually able to fix them so they would not be detected.

The TEASLER might sometimes be a SHEARMAN or CROPPER

also, although the final shearing operation was usually left for another man. This called for a very long-bladed pair of very sharp shears, and such a man's job was to go over every inch of the cloth with that scissors and cut off every trace of nap that the TEASLER had pulled up to the surface.

One more process was developed in finishing cloth, but it came almost too late to give us any names. It is known as calendering and was essentially a matter of applying a hot iron to the dampened cloth. Five CALENDAR names are listed, but the earliest appearance of the name— Walter le Kalendoer—was in 1495. Its origin is the Old French word *calendrier*.

GROUP 64
Makers of Loom Equipment

The loom was, of course, the most important piece of equipment in the whole wool trade in medieval times. The ordinary carpenter of that period would hardly undertake making a loom. The joiner or cabinetmaker might, but to make a loom, some exacting work had to be done. Instead of mortise-and-tenon joints with a pin driven through, the joints were usually wedged. This allowed the loom to be taken apart for moving or even to be enlarged. Understandably, loom-making became a specialty for some woodworkers. LOOM, LOOMER, LOOMIS, and LOOMWRIGHT are still with us.

There was also the sley or reed, a comblike piece of equipment that the weaver pulled back during each cycle of the operation. It served to push the weft thread that had just been laid across the warp tightly against the thread of the preceding pass of the shuttle.

The SLEY was an important part of the loom because it had to fit the material with which one was working. A weaver might have quite a selection of them. Making them became a specialty, as can easily be seen from the no less than nineteen variations listed.

The SPINDLER names hardly need explanation. The spindle must have been a very simple thing to make.

ROCKER, ROKKER, ROOKER, and RUCKER were given to men who made distaffs for the spinners, the Middle English word for "distaff" being *roc*. Richard le Roker is recorded in 1279.

CARDMAKER is easy. Earlier in this chapter is explained the construction and uses of cards.

SHEARSMITH and SERSMITH were definitely shearmakers.

The SACH and BADGER names refer to the men who made the sacks and bags in which raw wool had to be packed.

GROUP 65

Wool Merchants

Both from an economic and a social standpoint, the original holders of these names were of truly great importance to England. They were the men with the courage and foresight and the organizing ability that changed the cloth-making business of Britain from a haphazard, household occupation to the leading industry of the island.

At the beginning of this chapter, we talked about the thousands of shepherds scattered over the whole length and breadth of the island and the countless thousands of sheep they took care of. Each sheep produced five to fifteen pounds of wool each year. What became of this wool? Did the owner of each flock pack his wool into a few bags and then, in competition with every other flock owner, shop around to find a wool comber or carder who would buy his wool? It was hardly this primitive, because every bag had to be sorted and graded before it could be priced. This required knowledge and experience, and out of this situation arose the woolsorter. After a shearing, he would end up with a warehouse full of wool, all sorted and graded, and the flock owners could return to their sheep.

The woolsorter would have lined up a sufficient number of carders and combers to whom he could sell his whole stock of staple (as they called it). The carders and combers were not spinners, yet no cloth could possibly be made out of the wool until it had been spun into yarn. As discussed earlier, spinning the prepared wool into yarn at that time (and for centuries after) was the part-time job of the housewife; and she had to have wool that was thoroughly prepared to be made into yarn. There had to be some kind of merchant who would carry a stock of carded or combed wool. This might be Mr. WOOLSORTER, if he had broadened his operations to include prepared as well as raw wool. But it might just as well be any of the other fourteen WOOL names in this group.

There is still another question: what did the individual housewife do with the three or four small reels of yarn she might turn out on one of her better days? She had to collect cash or some equivalent for them and obtain some more prepared wool, and Mr. WOOLMAN filled this need. He knew that if he were to stay in business, he would have to have contacts and understandings with a great many spinners, for on the average it took the output of eight to ten spinners to keep one single weaver busy.

Mr. WEAVER, Mr. WEBER, or Mr. WEBSTER were skilled weavers. If luck was with them and they did not run out of the proper kind of yarn, any of them could turn out a sizable web of cloth in a week or so. But this could not be done if they had to close up shop every few days and chase all over the area trying to find enough yarn of the kind they needed to complete the webs on which they were working. Obviously, the weaver would have to have some kind of merchant who would buy his cloth (and even finance him on his next cloth, if necessary).

This merchant might be Mr. WOLMONGER, Mr. DRAPER, or Mr. LANER, and he had to know where he could sell every web of cloth he bought. Some of these merchants became exporters. British cloth developed a fine reputation on the Continent. British cheviots, tweeds, and worsteds became justly famous in all parts of Europe. International banking probably started in Venice, but it has been said that a Venetian banker at that time cared almost as much for his British tweeds as he did for his moneybags.

PACKARD and PACKER were definitely in the wool trade. Probably they were associated with a wool merchant and later became merchants in their own right. I find a John le Pakkere in 1254 and a Henry Packard in London in 1327.

STORAH and its variations come from the Old French word *estorer* meaning "to build," "to establish," or "to stock a place of business." The wool trade being much the largest business in England at that time, one of these names would be given to a man in the wool business.

By no means did all the weavers who were tempted to greatly broaden their operations realize their ambitions, but the record indicates that a great many of them did very well and at least a few of them became very wealthy. Some of them became bankers, either local or international, and a long line of English kings was happy to be able to borrow sizable sums from the woolmen. At least one of these cloth merchants became lord mayor of London. He was the famous Dick Whittington (d. 1432). We read the stories about Dick Whittington and his cat when we were children. The stories about the cat and the fortune the cat was supposed to have brought him are just fables, but the stories about Mr. Whittington being a highly successful cloth merchant are completely factual. He left an enormous fortune for that day to a long list of charities in London, some of which are still active.

Mr. Whittington does not have one of the occupational names on the list because a short time before he was born, very nearly all of our names were fixed.

GROUP 50

Shepherds and Overseers

Barker	•	Sheperd	Shepperson
•	Motton	Sheperdson	Sheppherd
Call	Mutton	Shephard	Shepsmerer
Caules	•	Shepheard	Shippard
•	Pastor	Shepherd	Shipperdson
Femister	•	Shepherdson	Shipwash
Fimister	Sheep	Sheppard	Smerer
Phemister	Sheeper	Sheppardson	•
Phimester	Sheepwash	Shepperd	Weather
Phimister	Shepard	Shepperdson	Weathers

GROUP 51

Shearers

Crapper	Sharer	Sheere	Sherman
Cropper	Sharman	Sheeres	Sherr
•	Shear	Sheers	Shirer
Forcer	Sheara	Sher	Shurman
•	Shearer	Sherar	•
Pollard	Shearman	Shere	Tonsur
Poller	Shears	Sherer	Tundur
•	Sheer	Sherere	

GROUP 52

Sorters

Sortar	•
Sorter	Woolsorter
Sorters	

GROUP 53

Washers

Bouker	Landrey	Laver	•
•	Landry	Lavender	Wascher
Lander	Launder	•	Washer
Landers	Laundrey	Steeper	
Landray	Laundry	Steper	

GROUP 54

Carders

Card	Carden	Carding	Cardoner
Carde	Carder	Cardon	Cardster

GROUP 55

Combers

Comber	Kember	Kempster	Teser
Combster	Kembester	•	Toser

GROUP 56

Bowers

Boayer	Bowman	Boyer
Bower	Bowyer	

GROUP 57

Spinners

Spinester	Spinster	•	•
Spinner	Spynner	Twiner	Winder

GROUP 58

Weavers

Borel	Drapper	Tyssur	Webbster
Borrell	•	Tystour	Weber
Burler	Laner	•	Webster
Burrel	•	Weafer	•
Burrell	Sakwebb	Weaver	Winders
Burrells	•	Weavers	Windes
•	Threader	Wheaver	Windows
Clother	Thredder	•	Windus
Clothier	•	Web	•
Clothman	Tisser	Webb	Woller
•	Tisserand	Webbe	Wollester
Draiper	Tissier	Webber	Wooler
Drape	Tister	Webbere	Wooller
Draper	Tisterer	Webbester	

GROUP 59

Fullers

Batour	Fullere	Touker	Voller
Beter	Fullester	Toukere	Vollers
•	Fulloon	Tucker	•
Fulister	Fulun	Tuckerman	Walker
Fullen	Fulur	Tuckermann	Walkere
Fuller	•	•	Walkerman

GROUP 60

Washers, Stretchers, and Dryers

Burler	Dryer	Launder	Tenter
•	•	Laundrey	Tenterman
Dresser	Lander	Laundry	Tenters
•	Landers	Laver	•
Dreyer	Landray	Lavender	Washer
Dreyster	Landrey	•	
Drier	Landry	Tentar	

GROUP 61

Bleachers

Blacker	Blatcher	Bleacher	Bletcher
Blaker	Blaxter	Blecher	Blexter

GROUP 62

Dyers

Blacchere	Dexter	Litster	Wader
Blacchester	Deyer	Lyster	Wadere
Blacker	Deyster	•	Wadester
Blackster	Dyer	Madder	Wadman
Blexter	Dyster	Madders	Waider
Bleykester	•	Mader	Wayder
•	Heuster	Madrer	Woad
Corck	•	Madster	Woadman
Cork	Ledster	•	Woademan
Corke	Lester	Teyntur	Woader
Corker	Lidster	Teynturer	Wodester
Corklittster	Lister	•	
•	Litester	Wademan	

GROUP 63

Cloth Finishers

Calendar	•	•	Teasel
Callander	Drawer	Taselar	Teasleman
Callendar	•	Tasler	Teasler
Callender	Rower	Taycell	Tesler
Callenders	Rowyer	Tazelaar	Tessler
•	•	Tazelar	
Cropper	Shearman	Tazewell	

GROUP 64

Makers of Loom Equipment

Badger	Rucker	Shearsmith	Slemmings
Bagger	•	•	Slemmonds
•	Sach	Slay	Sligh
Cardmaker	Sacher	Slayar	Sliman
•	Sack	Slaymaker	Slimming
Loom	Sacker	Slayman	Slimmon
Loomer	Sackur	Slaywright	Sly
Loomis	Saker	Sleath	Slyman
Loomwright	Sakman	Slee	•
•	Satch	Sleeman	Spindler
Rocker	Secker	Sleigh	Spyndler
Rokker	•	Sleith	
Rooker	Sersmith	Slemming	

GROUP 65

Wool Merchants

Clother	Lainer	Storror	Woolas
Clothier	Laner	Storrow	Woolass
Clothmanger	Leiner	•	Wooler
Clothman	•	Wollas	Woolhouse
•	Packard	Woller	Woolier
Draiper	Packer	Wollester	Woolman
Drape	•	Wollman	Woolpacker
Draper	Storah	Wolman	Woolsorter
Drapper	Storer	Wolmanger	
•	Storrar	Wolmonger	

CHAPTER 12

Linen, Silk, and Other Fabrics

Linen is a product of the flax plant and is probably every bit as ancient as cloth made from wool. The Egyptians seem to have made linen centuries before the rest of the world. The Romans and the Greeks were fond of the material but seemingly were unable to raise the better type of flax to make it, and so they imported large quantities from Egypt.

By the twelfth century, flax was being grown all over Europe, and the art of turning flax plants into linen cloth was well known. With small variations, the English and Norman peoples of the Middle Ages followed the same process. The plants were pulled out of the soil by the roots just before the seedpods were ripe. The seedpods were removed from the plants by dragging bundles of the plants through a metal comb nailed to a table; the seeds would be set aside for crushing into oil later.

Next, the plants were immersed in a pool of water out in the open where the warm sun could beat down on it all day. This was known as "retting" the flax, and one would think that this process could have given us a name, but it did not. Although we do have the name RETTER, it seems to have come from the trade of net-making. At any rate, this soaking in water warmed by the sun brought about a partial rotting of the flax plants, particularly the tougher, woody portions of the stems. After this had advanced to the proper stage, the plants were spread out on the grass to dry and possibly to be bleached slightly.

Then they were ready for the breaker. This was simply a mechanical means of breaking up the woody tissue of the plant and separating it from the precious fibers. It required a lot of beating with the edge of a wooden paddle, and then each bundle of flax had to be pulled through a series of finer and finer combs attached permanently to a table. Waste fibers from this process were not really wasted, since rope could be made from them, and wicks for lamps too. Some of the waste was even woven into very rough cloth that was later used to make bags and sacking. Sackcloth was the name given to this rough material when it was made into wearing apparel. It never became popular, even with the monks who were obliged to wear it now and then as penance for some misdemeanor.

The balance of the material was called "tow." This was the material that would be spun into linen thread and in turn woven into linen cloth. The spinning of tow into thread was not so different from the spinning of wool into yarn. The same distaff and spindle were used, and the loom itself, with a few adjustments, could be changed over from wool to linen.

This must have been convenient for the textile workers of that period, but for nominologists in the twentieth century trying to trace occupational names back to their origin, it is something of a problem. How can one tell whether a weaver worked with wool or flax?

GROUP 66

Linen Makers

BATOUR and BETER referred to a man engaged in making linen, though he might possibly have been involved in the beating of gold leaf or lead instead. COMBER, COMBSTER, KEMBER, and KEMBSTER could also have been in different businesses. The COMB names could have referred to the woolen trade, for instance. FLAXBETER, without a doubt, meant the same thing as BATOUR and BETER, though it does refer *only* to linen making. The name FLAXMONGER tells us that this man was in the business of selling flax. Perhaps he was given that name just at the time he was selling his crop of flax, but this is unlikely. Adding -*monger* or -*manger* to a name ordinarily meant a man who made a business of selling a particular material.

FLAXER, FLAXMAN, FLECKMAN, FLEXER, and FLEXMAN definitely come from the linen industry, but we cannot be sure whether they were linen weavers or linen merchants. They derive from the Old English word *fleax* meaning "flax." HECKLER was definitely engaged in the production of linen. The name derives from the Middle English word *hekel* which meant "a dresser of flax." A William le Hekeler appears in 1229.

TELER and LYNDRAPER were surely linen merchants. I find a William le Teler in 1255 and a Walter le Lyndraper in 1318. LYNER, LYNGER, LYNMAN, and LYNTER all stem from the Old French *linier* or *lingier*. Here again we can't be sure whether they were makers of linen or sellers of linen. The names beginning with LINACRE also derive from *linier* and *lingier,* but in just what capacity they were associated with the linen business is unknown. LINDLEY, LINGLEY, and LINLEY simply tell us that they either owned or lived very close to a field of flax; the remainder may have owned an acre of flax at the time circumstances caused them to be distinguished from their neighbors. All these names are very old. There is a Godwin de Linacra far back in 1086, the year in which William the Conqueror took his Domesday Survey.

GROUP 67

The Silk Business

The business of making and selling silk in medieval England has given us very few names because the silk business was in its infancy during the naming period. Silk had originated in China many centuries before, but its production was a carefully guarded secret. Under the Han Dynasty (202 B.C. to A.D. 220), cloth made of silk began to be exported, but the secret of how it was made remained in China for a very long time after this. Silk was probably completely unknown to the Greeks and Republican Rome. The Spanish seem to have discovered how to produce it in the tenth century, and Italy followed in the twelfth. England and France did not begin to catch up to Italy until early in the fourteenth century.

Of course, silk is a beautiful material with an instant appeal to the ladies as well as the men, but it was unavailable in England except when and if a caravan finally managed to get through the mountains of Asia and Europe. The caravan would have had to pay countless taxes imposed by self-appointed collectors along the way, so when the silk actually arrived, the cost of a yard must have outpriced cloth made of gold thread. It was on sale in London, however, as can be seen from this list.

The three MERCER names were definitely of silk merchants, although they probably sold other high-priced fabrics too.

PALLER and PELLER probably refer to silk, but it is hard to know since the word indicates only a very fine and rich cloth, or something made from it.

SENDALL and SENDELL go back to John Sendal, a London merchant who sold silk. Sendal was a variety of silk cloth. Mr. Sendal registered in 1303. The old records speak of silk cloth selling at from four to seven pounds per yard and if this were translated into modern money, platinum would be comparatively cheap.

SETER comes from the Old French word *saietier,* meaning "a weaver of silk." This was indeed a rare skill at that time.

SILK, SILKMAN, and SILKWOMAN simply tell us these individuals were in the business of making or selling silk.

THROWER and TROWER are interesting in that they almost certainly go back to a man who worked in the actual production of silk, an extreme rarity in those days. In Old English, the verb *thrawan,* which meant "to throw," gave rise to a noun that seems to have been applied to a man who converted raw silk into silk thread. There is recorded a Simon le Thrower in 1293 and a Thomas le Throwere in 1327.

GROUP 68

Rope Makers

Making rope is a very ancient craft; no one has ever been able to identify exactly when or where it was first practiced but probably it was in the Mediterranean ports. Rope-making is a spinning operation just like the making of any thread. The fibers used are very different, however. Hemp is most popular because of its strength. In the Middle Ages, it was spun in exactly the same way as yarn and would continue to be until the machinery of the nineteenth century came in. A "yarn" of hemp was first spun, then two of these were spun together in the opposite direction. This was repeated with three strands, again in the opposite direction.

RAPER meant a maker of rope, as did RAPIER, ROAPER, ROOPE, ROOPER, and the other ROPE names, including RUPP. SIMER derives from the Old English word *simer* meaning a cord or rope of some kind.

GROUP 69

Cord and String Makers

The list of names that have survived from the men who made cords and strings in the Middle Ages numbers thirty-five. This is an astonishing number and indicates a wider use for cords and such things at that time than now.

Any kind of cord had to be a spinning operation, and the kind of cord one would get depended on the material one used. Hemp would produce rope, while wool would result in yarn. Linen could be anything from a fine piece of thread to the heaviest cords, such as archers used for their longbows.

All the BRAID names derive from the Old English word *brezdan* and mean "cordmaker."

CORDER and its seven variants come from the Norman word *cordier* meaning "cord" or "corder." An Osbert le Corder is recorded as early as 1207.

HALTER might have been placed in the Rope Makers list, but a halter for a horse was made from a twisted cord when leather was not used.

The LACE names also refer to a cord maker. In Old French, the origin was *laz,* which gave the Middle English *lace.* The earliest record of the name I have found is Richard Le Lacir in 1278 and William Le Lacer in 1292.

POINTER and POYNTER are slightly different in that they came from an ornamental cord used to fasten a cape under the chin of the wearer. They frequently ended in some kind of metal point.

STRENGER, STRING, and STRINGER meant exactly the same as CORD but they came from the Old English word *streng.* There is a Henry Streng listed as a taxpayer in 1177, and a Walter Stringere in 1194.

TRENDER and TRINDER originate in the Old English word *trendan,* meaning "to turn or twist." Hugo le Trinder appears in the tax records of 1245, while in 1278 a John le Trendar appears. TWINE and TWINER are self-explanatory.

NETMAKER, NETTER, and RETTER are perfectly clear. Nets, whether designed to catch fish or birds, were made of suitable cords just as they are now, and the men who made these were named from their occupation.

THREADGILL, THREADGOLD, THREADGOULD, THREAD-KELL, THRIDGOUL, TREADGOLD, and TREDGOLD all refer to a maker of the finest embroidery. Actual threads of gold might be used to decorate the vestments of the clergy and the garments of the nobility. It is interesting to note that the earliest record of the name I have found is Agnes Tredegold in 1199—we might expect women to have engaged in this sort of artistry.

GROUP 70

Canvas Makers

The men who made the canvas of medieval England could not have been very numerous or they would have left more names. Canvas at that time was woven either from hemp, jute, or the waste material from linen—probably from a mixture of the above materials, depending on their availability. The material would be either dyed or painted in gay colors and would offer some protection from the sun. I suspect it would not be of much help in a heavy rain.

Tents were used mostly by an army at war in those times and then only by the leading nobility. The Old French word *chanevacier,* meaning either a maker or a seller of canvas, gave us the name CANEUACER, which first appeared in a tax record of 1274. The Old French word for tent was *paveillun* and naturally a man who made or sold tents would sooner or later be called a PAVILLONER.

GROUP 71

Makers of Camel-Hair Cloth

Little is known about either CAMPLIN or CAMPLING except that they do exist as family names today. The Old French word from which they come is *camelin,* which was supposed to be a fabric made from the hair of the camel. There were no camels in England at that time, but quite possibly a crusader brought home some camel's hair from the Near East with an idea of making cloth out of it. This is, however, pure speculation.

GROUP 72

Feltmakers

Probably felt was mostly used to make a protective garment to be worn under the armor of a knight, either in battle or in a tournament. As mentioned earlier, nearly all armor in this period was of the chain variety. It was made from many hundreds of tiny iron rings woven together in what amounted to a piece of fabric. All that iron would prevent a sword blow from cutting into a man's flesh, but the force of the blow would tend to drive the iron rings into a man's chest or back. For this reason, a thick covering made from either felt, leather, or some quilted material was a necessity. It must have been terribly hot on a warm day. Felt was made from coarse woolen fibers frequently mixed with either coarse linen or horsehair.

FELTER and FELTMAN need no explanation as *felt* was an Old English word.

GROUP 73

Haircloth Makers

To speak of haircloth today is to speak of Victorian furniture, where it was used so frequently; the second most frequent use was by tailors, for the collars of men's suits. In thirteenth-century England, neither of these uses existed; shirts were made out of it. It's hard to imagine the discomfort of a shirt made out of horsehair—even the horse had enough sense to wear that hair in his tail, where he could control its contact with his skin. However, hair shirts seem to have been worn by some of the monks in the monasteries as penance for some minor infraction of the rules.

HAYREMAKER, HAYRER, and HAYWRIGHT were names applied to the maker of the material, and the last two names on the list, TAILMAN and TAYLMONGER, must have been given to men who made a business of selling horsetails to the makers. Richard le Hayrewritte appeared in 1283 and Thomas Talmongher in 1329.

GROUP 74

Tapestry Makers

Only two names that were first given to artists making tapestry have survived the years. But today's experts on this fine art doubt that any real tapestries were made in the England of that period.

Genuine tapestry is made entirely on a loom, and much of what was carelessly called tapestry was really embroidery. Henry VIII, who reigned well after the naming period, amassed a collection of tapestries that is supposed to have numbered two thousand pieces. Many of these are genuine beyond a doubt, but the earlier pieces probably came from Flanders. One of the most famous of all time is the Bayeux Tapestry, made in the eleventh century. This magnificent piece of work gives us the wonderful history of the Norman Conquest, but the workmanship has to be classed as embroidery, as the designs on it were definitely woven onto a piece of existing material.

TAPICER and TAPSTER derive from the Old French word *tapicer*. Ralph le Tapicer appears in a record of 1282.

GROUP 75

Makers of Curtain Material

About the only proof we have that such things as curtains even existed in medieval times is a single name that has come down to us. COURT-

ENER comes from a Middle English word *courtyn* and definitely means a maker of curtains. Adam Courtainer must have paid his taxes or appeared in some minor court action because we find his name registered in 1345.

GROUP 76
Makers of Clothing

The making of clothing during the whole naming period was very different from modern methods, because the kind of clothes men wore were so very different. Little or none of what we now call tailoring was required. Trousers, in any modern meaning of the word, were unknown. Men wore tunics, and so did the ladies. A tunic was like an inverted cloth bag, open at the hem and with an opening for the head cut in the closed end. One slipped it on over the head. Simple slits could be cut in the sides to allow arms to come out, or short sleeves could be joined to the slit sides. Over this, one would wear another tunic made of heavier material and belted at the waist. Over all this, a long CAPE, COPE, or MANTLE—just a wide piece of material—was draped over one's shoulders and fell down all around, held in place by a string or metal clasp of some kind under the chin.

On one's feet and legs were chauses. A pair of chauses could be put together in a moment. Pieces of leather were wrapped around one's feet and tied with cord around the ankles; then pieces of either leather or heavy woolen material were wrapped around each leg and fastened on by a cord crisscrossed around the leg one or more times and fastened above the knee. That was it—except for the head, on which a hood was worn. The hood might be separated from the tunic or the mantle, or it might be permanently fastened to either one of them.

The only substantial difference between the dress of a wealthy noble and a poor peasant was in the quality of the material and the amount and quality of the embroidery and metal jewelry on the mantle and head covering. The peasant and working craftsman would be inclined to wear shorter tunics than the knights and nobles who had no labor to perform. None of the clothing of the Middle Ages had pockets. If one wanted to carry something with one—and everybody did, just as now— one had to provide oneself with one or more bags that could be leather or cloth, and ornamented or not, according to personal taste and ability. Any necessary keys would be hung from the belt too, and, of course, one had to carry a knife somewhere—even the poorest peasant had to have a knife!

TAYLOR is the first name everyone thinks of when we speak of making clothing. TAYLOR, however, came from the French word *tailleor* or its Anglo-French variation, *taillour,* and originally meant cutter; it was not until the twelfth century that it came to mean a practitioner of the craft of making clothing. There is a William le Taillur listed in 1182, and several others in the years immediately following. All that we can be sure of is that these early *taillours* were in the business of making clothing—the garments they made might include every stitch of clothing a man would wear: linen underthings, various tunics, mantles, and hoods, and even foot and leg coverings. The only thing the TAILOR was not apt to make would be the all-important belt. This would be made by a leatherworker called a girdler, of whom more will be said in Chapter 13, on the leather industry. Shoemakers will also be discussed in a later chapter.

The ten CAPE and COPE names all apply to a man in the trade of either making or selling capes, also known as copes.

CHAUCER and CHAUSER were men who specialized in making chauses, of course. Robert le Chauser is listed in 1256. Chaucer, the author of *The Canterbury Tales,* was fairly well-to-do and spent his leisure time writing beautiful poetry. His father, too, was wealthy, so it is unlikely either of them ever made foot and leg coverings, but we don't know what the business of the poet's grandfather was. It could very well have been that he was a humble maker of leg coverings and thus was at least one of the original holders of this famous name. The Old French source was *chaucier.*

As the leg coverings became a little better fitting, they were called hosiery, and the name HOSIER comes down to us from the French.

The COTE group of names may come from an old word for cottage and thus not belong on this list, but they may also go back to a very old Middle English word *cote,* which meant an outer garment. Modern historians call these garments *surcoats.* The surcoat was simply made from linen that had been bleached as white as possible. It had an opening for the head and each arm (with or without sleeves). Sometimes it was called a JUBE or JUPE (see Group 78, page 161). Its sole purpose, when worn over a suit of complete armor, was to distinguish one fighting man from another by a pictorial design either painted or embroidered on the front and back of the garment. A man dressed in full armor either for a tournament or a real battle could not be readily distinguished from any other man in armor, often with disastrous results.

The surcoat seems to have served its medieval purpose very well, and the pictorial design that was so prominently displayed on it is still with us: we call it a coat of arms.

COWLER, COWLES, COWLMAN, and CULWRIGHT were makers of cowls, the everyday dress of nearly all the great monastic orders of the Middle Ages. They were made from the roughest kind of cloth and were bound at the waist with a piece of rope to act as a constant reminder to the monk of Christ's suffering on the way to the Crucifixion.

CURTLER, KIRTLE, and KIRTLER are interesting in that they all stem from an Old English word meaning anything that was cut shorter than normal (our modern word *curtail* comes from the same source). Some unknown clothing maker, far back in the twelfth century, turned out a short tunic one day. He may have run short on material or he may have had an idea that it was an improvement over the longer kind, but some people liked it and soon he had orders for more. As always, when a new idea is a hit, there are plenty of other tradesmen willing and anxious to make the same thing. They were called CURTLERS and the short jacket was called a KIRTLE. Soon somebody started putting padding or quilting in the KIRTLE, and another name developed for that. These kirtles became very fancy and elaborate, and by the time of the Renaissance they were called DOUBLETS.

HATTRELL means a man who made clothing, and it has no connection with hats. The name comes from the Old English *haeteru,* meaning "clothing."

The MANTLE names come from an Old French word *mantel* and means a maker of that particular item of clothing. Robert Mantell appears in 1176.

PARMENTER, with its variants, comes from another Old French word, *parmentier,* meaning "a man who made clothing."

Late in the naming period (1333), we find the name Richard le Sartour and we happen to know that he was a tailor—not with the skill of a modern tailor, but approaching it. *Sartour* is the Latin word for tailor. William le Coussur, in 1332, was of the same trade.

After Sartour, the next seven names on the list, starting with SEMER and ending with SOUSTER, belonged to people we would call ladies' tailors or even dressmakers today, since each of these names seems to have been given to makers of clothing for women. SHEPPER, particularly, comes from an Old English word *scieppan,* meaning "to shape" or "to design."

SEWER is interesting in that it has several origins, depending on where and when it was used. One of its earliest meanings seems to have been "a man who sewed leather" (he may have been the earliest shoe-maker). In this meaning it came from the Old French word *suor,* but it may also have come from *asseior,* which meant a household official who saw to the proper seating of guests at dinner and who would taste any and every dish to be sure it was not only satisfactory but also not poisoned. *Seieor* is another origin; in this case, it meant a sawyer, a man who sawed wood. And last but by no means least, it could mean a man who was a skilled maker of clothing. The oldest meaning seems to be the Old English stem *seowian,* which meant "to sew."

SLOPER referred to a particularly loose tunic, while a SMOKER— no reference to our word *smoke*—meant "a maker of smocks," which were very short tunics for working men. Geoffrey le Slopere appears in 1279.

There is nothing difficult about the SNIDER names, for the word meant "a cutter of cloth" and thus a man so named was another tailor. The Old English word is *snidan.* John Snyther is listed in 1332.

A STOLLER or a STOLLMAN was a man who made stoles. It comes from the Middle of English word *stole.*

TRYMMER is quite clear and WALSHMAN and WALSMAN came along just a bit later to indicate still another man in the business of making clothing. John Walsheman appears in 1303, and Walter Walcheman in 1327.

GROUP 77

Milliners

The BONNET names derive from the Norman word *bonet* and refer to almost any kind of feminine head covering. There is an Isabella Bonet in 1201 and a John Bonet in 1212. Perhaps John Bonet made the bonnets that Isabella wore.

The CALL names derive from the caul, a hairnet made out of linen thread (rather than hair or nylon, as now). They are definitely feminine. During much of the naming period, women wore veils that covered some of the face and all of the head and headdress. The name VEIL with two variations does exist but does not seem to have originated with any kind of head covering.

The nine CAPP names are fairly obvious. *Caput* meant "head" in Latin, and a man who made head coverings of any kind was almost certain to be dubbed a capper in some form of the name.

COKELER derived from the Old French *coquiller,* another kind of head covering for women.

COYFER definitely did mean a close-fitting cap designed either for a lady or a gentleman. This was most likely a cap designed to hold the hair in place while one was dressing to go out rather than something worn for warmth.

The four HAT names need no explanation except that they derive from the Old English word *haett*. William le Hattere is recorded in 1212.

All nine HOOD names refer to the everyday cold-weather head covering of the medieval man, whether he was a noble or a peasant.

The Norman word meaning the hair on one's head was *hure* and the Middle English word was exactly the same. It seems that, now and then, a hat- or capmaker would be called a HURRER. We have Geoffrey le Hurer in 1288 and William le Hurrer in 1289. At that time, the young fellows wore their hair long. Could it be that some hatmaker developed a headcovering that somehow made him stand out in the crowd of capmakers?

QUAIF and QUAIFE could be listed with COYFER, since they mean a maker of coifs.

WIMPLE and WYMPLER are simply other names for some variety of veil for women. It is still retained in the dress of some nuns.

GROUP 78

Shirt and Underwear Makers

CAMIS to KEEMISH inclusive were shirtmakers. The names derive from the Old French word *chemise* or the Latin word *camisia*. The garment could be worn by either sex. One or more of this group of names was also applied to the maker of the surplice worn by a priest. Stephen de Cameis in 1200 is the earliest holder of this name I have found.

The thirteen names beginning with JOB and ending with JUPP have unusual interest in that they have more than one possible origin. JOB may have come from the biblical Job, meaning someone who has been persecuted. If so, the name is not occupational and does not belong on this list. However, it may have come from the Middle English word, *jubbe* or *jobbe*. A jubbe was a vessel for liquor holding four gallons; hence, a nickname for a man who could drink that much. Or it could easily be a trade name for a man who made a piece of clothing referred to as a jubbe. This garment was usually made from white linen and worn by nobles over their armor in battle or tournaments. (See Group 76, page 160.) Another possible origin was a long woolen garment or the maker of such things. JUBBAH was an oriental word meaning a long garment worn by either sex. It probably reached England by way of the returning crusaders.

GROUP 79
Repairmen

Our worthy ancestors were practical men when it came to clothing; they had no objection to having a mantle patched or a ripped seam sewn up and, that being the case, there were undoubtedly men around to do those things. We met one of them back when we were talking about arms and armor. He was the DUBBER, the fellow who would rub at least some of the rust off one's armor and repair the links if one left the suit with him for a few days. He found he was asked to repair clothing too, to patch and sew and what not. So we have the names DUBBER and PATCHER. If he acquired used clothing or armor and offered them for sale, he would be referred to as a FELIPER. A possible source of the name is the Old English word *fell,* meaning "skin" or "hide." All of the CLOUT names also mean a man who could patch something; clothing was usually implied, but it could be most anything.

Finally, there are two rare names that grew out of those already mentioned. If a Dubber took in a few pieces of furniture that he was willing to sell, he would become known as either an UPHOLDERE or an UPHOLDESTER. These came from an Old English word, *upholden,* which meant to keep in repair.

GROUP 80
Blanket, Quilt, and Mat Makers

Today, a quilt means an old-fashioned bed coverlet fashioned of cuttings from the work of the dressmakers and even the curtain makers. Usually these were sewn together in some design that would cover a big double bed; then a layer of cotton or wool was placed on top of it, and another piece the same size of sewn-together scraps added on top of that; the whole thing was then quilted, which meant sewn through and through to prevent the padding from moving.

In medieval England, a quilt differed only in that a solid piece of heavy woven woolen cloth was used for each side and between these would be a layer of pure wool. They were considerably thicker than our quilts, and warmer, but they had to be at that time.

A QUILTER, obviously, was somebody who made enough quilts to become identified with them.

The five BLANCHET names originally meant a piece of woven woolen cloth, usually undyed, that could be used to make clothing. But this cloth could also be used on a bed at night and came to be called a BLANKET.

The entire CHALLEN group meant the same thing as BLANKET, but it seems that weavers from Châlons-sur-Marne in France were the first to make them popular and some variation of the name of the French town became attached to them permanently. "Chalone of Guilford" became so famous that the royal household used their blankets exclusively for a period.

TAPENER and TAPNER were names given to weavers or dealers who handled CHALONS or burel. Burel was a heavy, rough woolen cloth, as mentioned before, although the name TAPENER seems to have implied a little better quality. There is an Old French word *taponner* meaning a maker of better quality cloth.

The Old English word for a thick pad for a bed, which we would call a mattress, was *matte,* so it is easy to understand where all seven of the names starting with MATT came from. John Matere made such things far back in 1214 and John Mattemaker in 1381.

The three SEGG names refer to a common weed of the time that was gathered and dried and used to stuff mattresses. A SEGGERMAN was also in the pottery business (see Group 1, page 27).

GROUP 81

Makers of Purses, Bags, Pouches, and Sacks

It's easy to understand the large number of names coming down to us from the makers of purses, bags, pouches, and sacks, if we bear in mind that the clothing people wore at that time had no pockets. Today, in a man's trousers, there are at least four large pockets, and in his vest, there are at least four more. In his jacket, there are five and sometimes six sizable pockets. That adds up to more than a dozen pockets and with an overcoat, he has at least four more.

The medieval man had not a single pocket. By his very nature, he wanted to tote many things about with him, and the only practical way he had of doing it was to carry a bag. Sometimes he would carry a bag in his hand, but more often he would need two of them, so he would hook one or both to his belt and, if he had keys, they would be hooked onto that belt too.

This meant a lot of purses, bags, pouches, and sacks that somebody had to make. Perhaps many a lowly peasant might contrive some kind of bag for himself as an everyday bag, but on Sundays and holy days when everyone dressed in his best and went to mass and on from there to the pageant or the archery contest, he would wear his best pouch or sack. And he would have bought it from a man who was in the business of making such things. This man might be known as a POUCHMAKER or by any other name on the POUCH list. Robert Poucher appears in 1275, and Thomas Poche in 1327.

The exact origin of the BAGGER names is not certain, but it is probably the French word *bague*. There is a possibility that one or more of these names could have been applied to a beggar at that time. Here is an old quote that might suggest this: "Hit is beggares rihte uorte beren bagge on bac & burgeises for to beren purses." A liberal translation of this thirteenth century English is: A beggar may be expected to carry a bag while a well-to-do citizen is expected to carry a purse.

BURSER, PURSE, and PURSER hardly need explanation. The word started out as *bursa* in Latin, and by the time it reached England via Norman French, it was *purs*. The purse was smaller than the pouch, and frequently was made to be carried inside the pouch. It may have been made from leather (see Group 88), but whatever its material, it was for carrying something valuable. Both PURSER and BURSER (or bursar) are still occupational names today. Alexander Purcir is listed in 1279.

The POUCH names may come from the Old English word *pohha,* meaning "bag," or from the Norman French word *pouche,* meaning a bag provided with a gathering string or some such means of opening and closing it easily. Such a bag would be used for money and those valuable things that did not need much space. I think it is reasonable to assume that a POUCH would usually be made of better material than an ordinary bag or sack and consequently the POUCHEMAKER, the POGH-WEBBE, and the rest of the names listed were a separate group of craftsmen. Bernard de la Pouche is recorded in 1319 on the Subsidy Rolls of London and there is some reason to think that he may have carried on a pouch-making business with traders in Florence.

The POCKET names derive from the Middle English word *poket,* which was a dimunitive of the Anglo-French word *poque,* which meant "a small pouch." There is a Geoffrey Poket away back in 1210. Then there are three POKE names: *Poke* was an Old English word that meant a bag of almost any kind, so a POKER or a POKEMAN must have made them. Remember the old medieval advice: "Never buy a pig in a poke."

The SACH names derive from the Norman French word *sachier*. The word actually meant a man who makes such things. There is a John le Sachere way back in 1294. But the English had a word for such things too: namely, a *sacc*. A man who made these things might be known by any one of the thirteen names in the group. SAKWEBBE is particularly interesting in that this man was probably a weaver who made material suitable for the sackmakers. In chapter 11 it was mentioned that one name applied to WEAVERS was WEBBE, so a SAKWEBBE must have been a weaver of sacking. SATCH, SATCHEL, and SATCHELL are diminutive forms of the French word *sachel*, which meant a little bag. Thomas Sachel was listed in 1243.

Before leaving the SACK names, mention should be made of another huge market for the product of all the sack makers: the wool business. The wool trade was the biggest industry in England for many centuries, and wool had to be packed in sacks. There was no cheap cotton or paper from which to make sacks so either wool or linen had to be used.

GROUP 66

Linen Makers

Batour	Flaxman	Lindley	Linnekar
Beter	Flaxmonger	Linegar	Lyndraper
•	Fleckman	Lineker	Lyner
Comber	Flexer	Lingley	Lynger
Combster	Flexman	Lineker	Lynman
Kember	•	Liniker	Lynter
Kembster	Heckler	Linley	•
•	•	Linnecar	Teler
Flaxbeter	Linacre	Linnecor	
Flaxer	Linaker	Linnegar	

GROUP 67

The Silk Business

Mercer	Peller	Seter	•
Merchiers	•	•	Thrower
Mercier	Sendall	Silk	Trower
•	Sendell	Silkman	
Paller	•	Silkwoman	

GROUP 68

Rope Makers

Raper	Roope	Roper	Rupp
Rapier	Rooper	Ropes	•
Roaper	Rope	Ropster	Simer

GROUP 69

Cord and String Makers

Brader	Cordon	Pointer	Threadkell
Braid	Cords	Poynter	Thridgould
Braide	•	•	Treadgold
Brayd	Halter	Retter	Tredgold
Brayder	•	•	
•	Lace	Strenger	Trender
Coard	Lacebrayder	String	Trinder
Codner	Lacer	Stringer	•
Corder	•	•	Twine
Cordes	Netmaker	Threadgill	Twiner
Cordier	Netter	Threadgold	
Cordner	•	Threadgould	

GROUP 70

Canvas Makers

Caneuacer   Pavilloner

GROUP 71

Makers of Camel-Hair Cloth

Camplin   Campling

GROUP 72

Feltmakers

Felter   Feltman   Feutrer

GROUP 73

Haircloth Makers

Hayremaker   Haywright   Tailman
Hayrer   •   Taylmonger

GROUP 74

Tapestry Makers

Tapicer   Tapster

GROUP 75

Makers of Curtain Material

Courtener

GROUP 76

Makers of Clothing

Capeman	•	Mantler	Snider
Caper	Cowler	•	Sniderman
Capern	Cowles	Parmenter	Sniders
Capers	Cowlman	Parmeter	Snyder
Capes	Culwright	Parminter	Snyders
Caporn	•	Parmiter	•
Capron	Curtler	•	Stoller
Capuron	Kirtle	Sartour	Stollman
Copeman	Kirtler	•	•
Copes	•	Semer	Taillour
•	Doublet	Semester	Tailor
Chaucer	Doublett	Sewster	Tailyour
Chauser	•	Shepper	Tayler
•	Hattrell	Sheppester	Taylerson
Coat	•	Simister	Taylor
Coate	Hosier	Souster	Taylorson
Coates	•	•	Taylour
Coatman	Jube	Sewer	•
Cote	Jupe	•	Trymmer
Cotes	•	Sloper	•
Cotman	Mantel	•	Walshman
•	Mantell	Smoker	Walsman
Coussur	Mantle	•	

GROUP 77

Milliners

Boneter	Keller	•	Hodes
Bonetta	•	Coyfer	Hood
Bonnet	Caperoner	•	Hoodman
Bonnett	Capiere	Hat	Hoods
Bonnette	Capman	Hatt	•
•	Capp	Hatter	Hurrer
Call	Cappman	Hatts	•
Callear	Capper	•	Quaif
Caller	Capps	Hodd	Quaife
Callier	Chapeler	Hodder	•
Callmaker	Kapper	Hoddes	Wimple
Caules	•	Hoddman	Wympler
Kallmakester	Cokeler	Hodds	

GROUP 78

Shirt and Underwear Makers

Camis	Keemish	Jobes	Jubber
Cammis	•	Jope	Jupe
Cammish	Job	Jopp	Jupp
Camous	Jobar	Jubb	
Camoys	Jobber	Jubbah	
Camus	Jobe	Jube	

GROUP 79

Repairmen

Cloughting	Cloutman	•	•
Clout	Cloutt	Feliper	Upholdere
Clouter	•	•	Upholdester
Clouting	Dubber	Patcher	

GROUP 80

Blanket, Quilt, and Mat Makers

Blanchet	Challens	Mattar	•
Blanchett	Challin	Mattemaker	Segger
Blanket	Challinor	Matter	Seggerman
Blankett	Chalner	Matters	Seggmaker
Branchett	Chalnor	Mattes	•
•	Chaloner	Matts	Tapener
Challen	Channer	•	Tapner
Challender	Chawner	Quilter	
Challendor	•	Quilts	
Challenor	Matt	Quilty	

GROUP 81

Makers of Purses, Bags, Pouches, and Sacks

Badger	Purse	Pocket	Sacker
Bagg	Purser	Pockett	Sackman
Bagge	•	Pocketts	Sackur
Bagger	Pocheler	•	Saker
Baggett	Poghwebbe	Poke	Sakman
Baggot	Pouch		Sakwebbe
Baggott	Pouche	Poker	Satch
Baggs	Pouchemaker	•	Satchel
Bagot	Poucher	Sach	Satchell
•	Pougher	Sacher	Secker
Burser	•	Sack	

CHAPTER **13**

The Leather Industry

Man's use of raw animal skins for clothing and shelter goes back to prehistoric times, and it is not even possible to date when men began to treat raw skins by some process to make them into something that could be called leather. Paleolithic sites the world over never fail to bring to light pieces of shaped and sharpened flint that were used to scrape the hides of animals. This was, and still is, about the first step in changing raw skins into leather: today, the tool is made from steel and is called the CURRIER's knife.

The Egyptians and peoples of the Near East made leather saddles, shields, and bottles; the Romans and the Greeks also produced large amounts of very passable leather. In fact, the Romans probably have to be credited with teaching western Europe the craft of tanning. The soles of old Roman sandals are frequently found in Roman excavations around Britain.

Turning rawhide into leather is a long-drawn-out process even today. Up until late in the nineteenth century, the hides had to be soaked in water for an entire year before tanning could actually begin. While this step has been considerably shortened in modern times, the resulting product is no better.

In medieval England, the craft was well established at the time of the Conquest; one could expect to find at least one leatherworker in the smallest village and as many as four or five in the larger market towns. In Oxford in 1380, there were no less than twelve tanners, twenty skinners, four makers of footwear, and five saddlemakers. In London something like two hundred tanneries were doing business in the fifteenth century.

In medieval times, two processes were employed: Ox-, cow-, and calf-skins were tanned by long immersion in a concoction of tanbark, usually from oak at that time, and the skins of deer, sheep, goats, and horses were tawed with alum, oil, and salt.

Those who used the tanbark method were TANNERS or BARKERS and those who used the alum method were TAWYERS, TEWERS, or TOWERS. The TAWYER ended up with a very light-colored product (almost white), never used for sole leather but highly favored for many items that did not have to stand the wear and tear of sole leather.

In the early part of the naming period, the man who made shoes, or saddles, or what have you, also tanned the leather, just as the early smiths not only made tools or armor from iron but also actually extracted iron from the ore. But in 1351, largely through the increasing influence of the craft guilds, this was stopped; hereafter the TANNER, regardless of which process he used, was to confine his labor to tanning; making useful articles from the leather would be restricted to craftsmen of other trades.

GROUP 82

Producers of Rawhide

SHINNER through SKYNNER were clearly men in the business of selling rawhide to others who would turn them into leather. Though a man could acquire one of these names by simply developing some skill in taking the skin off a carcass, it is far more probable that a man would have to be clearly associated with that process for some time to acquire the name permanently. The animals were usually slaughtered on the farms by a BUTCHER and skinned by a SKINNER; then the hides were sold to the TANNERS, the BARKERS, or the TAWYERS. Over the years, middlemen tried to set themselves up in business, but they never really succeeded.

PELL through PELLY probably meant exactly the same as the SKIN-NER names, *pel* being a Norman word for "skin" or "pelt." PELTER and PILTER can also mean SKINNER but may have been applied as well to a man handling skins with the hair left on them, that is, fur (see Group 93).

All the FELL names, ending with FELPOLLARE, came just a bit later than the PELL and SKINNER names, as they clearly referred to dealers in skins and pelts. We find a Robert le Felur in 1275 and a Mabel Fel-monger in 1332.

GROUP 83

Leather Makers

Though the process of tanning has already been discussed, the TANNER names require further attention. TANNESTER and TANNERESS are distinctly feminine, and while it is hard to imagine a woman doing the hard labor of a TANNER, there they are: Maud le Tannester in 1339, and Margaret la Taneresse still earlier, in 1290.

A BARKER was a tanner who used bark rather than alum, oil, and salt to turn his hides into leather, but the name BERKER could, and definitely did at times, also mean a shepherd. There is no way to distinguish the two names. BARKMAN or BARKNUR could be a supplier of bark.

The TAWYER names usually applied to tanners who handled thinner and lighter types of skins, such as the skin of sheep, goats, and even calves, as well as the thin underbelly skin of a cow. In their tanning process, they used an oil known then as train oil and today as fish or whale oil.

All nine names beginning with WHITEAR and ending with WHITTOWERE stem directly from two very old words: the Old English *hwit,* or "white," and the Anglian *tewian* meaning "to taw." Put them together, and they come out meaning a dresser of white leather. A name such as WHITHAIR could have been given to a man with unusually white or blond hair, but it is far more likely that the name began with a man adept at making white leather. And if some of the spellings in this group seem weird, look at how they used to be: Ralf Wittauuere and William le Wyttawyere in 1285, and Eustace le Wittowere in 1279.

BEAUDERER was simply what some French-speaking Normans called a TANNER when they were unsure of the English word.

COURAOUR, CUNREYOUR, CURRIER, and CURRYER come by a devious route from the tanning industry. The work of the currier was, and to some extent still is, the highly skilled task of a specialist with three different tools—the currier's knife, the stone, and the steel. With successive applications of these tools, an experienced CURRIER could make a piece of tanned hide look and feel as smooth as a piece of satin.

GROUP 84

Belt Makers

At any time during the naming period (1100 to 1350), a date could have been identified by the initials B.T. instead of A.D. B.T. would mean

"Before Trousers." Men did not wear pants at the time, and belts had to serve a function other than the modern one of support for trousers. Men wore tunics and though they might be long or short, they must have felt much more comfortable if gathered in around the middle and held by a belt. Earlier we mentioned the fact that medieval clothing was completely devoid of pockets. Yet men at that time were just as fond of carrying around a wide assortment of paraphernalia as they are now. This meant that what could not be carried in the hands had to be carried in a belt or in a pouch of some kind, supported by a belt. Thus the medieval belt was of much greater importance than its modern counterpart; instead of one function, it had several, and as a result a sizable group of specialized craftsmen in leather developed.

The military man needed a belt that was strong enough not only to bear the weight of his weapons but to ward off the blow of an enemy. Such a belt would be several inches wide and studded with iron rivets or disks that would mark him as a fighting man in any gathering. For formal occasions, he might acquire more distinction if he wore a belt studded with semiprecious stones instead of steel buttons.

The word for belt in Old English was, surprisingly, *belt,* and a man who made belts was called BELTER or some variation of the word. There is a Robert Belt in 1203 and a Benedict le Belter in 1295.

CENTER, CENTURY, CEYNTURER, and SENTER all come from the Old French word *ceinture,* frequently spelled *sainturier,* meaning "belt maker."

The Anglo-Saxons had still another word that meant the same thing as belt—*gyrdel*. In practice, the word was used interchangeably with belt and a man who made *gyrdels* might be called a GIRDLER by some of his customers and a BELTMAN by others. In the records, there is one Luke le Gerdler in 1277 and just two years later a Henry le Girdler. The old Norman article *le* would be dropped in the course of time.

GIRDELESTER is the feminine form of GIRDLER, but whether the name was given to a maker of girdles regardless of sex or whether to someone who made girdles particularly adapted to the clothing of women can't be known. Probably it was the latter.

GROUP 85
Bottle Maker

The idea of a bottle having been made out of anything but glass sounds ridiculous to us today—until recently, with the development of plastics, bottles have been made exclusively from glass for centuries—but glass was quite scarce in medieval times. It was used almost exclusively for church windows and was only made in very small pieces, usually highly colored and leaded together to form a design.

Perhaps some glassworkers of that time may have dreamed of making such things as bottles and drinking vessels from glass, but it was not to happen for three centuries, in the 1500s. On the other hand, making vessels out of leather was a very old craft that had been standard practice long before the Romans and is still being carried on by desert tribes in the Near East. A bottle or jug made from leather is going to be around for a very long time, since it is virtually unbreakable.

If an open dish were to be made, a wooden form of the shape required would be made first, and when the leather was sufficiently tanned but still soft and pliable, it would be molded around the form and left to season and dry out. If a bottle with a narrow neck was wanted, the mold would be made of fine and very hard-packed sand. Frequently the sides of the bottle would have to be sewn together to hold the shape permanently. Recently, I saw a leather bottle made from the whole skin of a young pig. I imagine it was designed to carry a gallon or so of wine, perhaps on horseback, but I was unable to certify whether such ancient skins gave birth to our expression "having a skinful."

A BOTELMAKER was definitely a man who made leather bottles, whether his name was derived from the Middle English word *botel* or the Old French word *bouteille*. BOTTLER, BOTTELL, BOTTLE, and BOTTLES are just variations. The records show many of them—Johan Bottler in 1351 and Sarra le Bottler in 1332, for example. BOUCH, BUCHE, and BUDGE come from a still older Middle English word for a small leather container to hold either food or liquid on a journey. In the twelfth century, the word was sometimes used in the sense *ration* is used today, meaning a daily allowance of food and drink for a man in the service.

GROUP 86

Saddlemakers

In the naming period, riding horses were the prized possession of the nobles and their ladies; a peasant was lucky if he could boast of one poor old draft horse to help him with his plowing. Consequently, the market of the medieval saddlemaker was confined largely to the nobility. These gentlemen needed just two types of saddle, one for the tournament and actual war and another for hunting.

The tournament or war saddle was a huge affair, even larger and heavier than the western saddle of modern times. It was built on a frame of wood called the saddletree, which was covered with leather and to which stirrups were attached. The pommel was high but without the horn of a western saddle; this came along many years later from Spain when roping cattle became part of the cattle business. The cantle of the medieval tournament saddle was its distinctive feature. It was built as much as halfway up the back of the rider to hold him on his horse when his lance struck an opponent. The lance was not thrown like a spear but was held rigidly by the right hand and arm of the rider; the power of the charging horse supplied the thrust. The resulting shock to the body of an attacking knight would easily knock him right off his horse if his back were not amply supported by the high cantle.

The hunting saddle can best be described as simply a smaller and lighter edition of the war and tournament one. The cantle was much lower because its protection was not needed; a knight hunted with a spear and thus needed plenty of room in the saddle for arm action in all directions.

Stirrups and bridles have been covered in an earlier chapter; they were the product of both the leatherworker and the smith. A charging knight with his lance ready to strike would have been unable to control his charge without stirrups in which to brace his feet. Stirrups did not appear until around the sixth century A.D., a very great many years after the horse had been domesticated.

The earliest recording of a family name deriving from saddle-making is Simon le Sadelere in 1288. In 1296 there appears a Peter le Sadelare. The Old English word from which all SADDLER names come was *sadol,* meaning saddle. The last five names derive from this word.

BAISTER and BASTER come from the old French word *bastier,* while CELLIER through ZELLER derive from another old French word, *seiler.* Both mean "saddler."

CODMAN usually meant simply a leatherworker.

FEWSTER, FOISTER, FOYSTER, and FUSTER were probably not saddlemakers in the sense of being leather craftsmen; they made the saddletree. The names come from the Old French *fustier* meaning this. The earliest record of the name seems to be Walter le Fuyster in 1179.

GROUP 87

Glovemakers

Strange about gloves—today a man wears gloves to keep his hands warm while a lady wears them on the hottest day in summer if her costume calls for them. Of course, both sexes wear them to protect their hands when this is needed, and so it was in medieval England. In chapter 6, for example, in discussing the development of a sword hilt, it was pointed out that before there was a hilt, the blade of an enemy could slide down one's sword and do serious injury to one's hand. The glovers came up with a glove of heavy leather to protect the hands; this was passed on to the smiths to supply the armor for it. The glove was a gauntlet, of course, covering not only the hand but half the forearm as well and studded with iron disks. It must have been a heavy, awkward thing to wear but it did protect the sword hand. By the fourteenth century, the sword-making smiths began to develop a practical hilt for the sword that protected the hand and retired the gauntlet. During its long service, however, this had become a symbol of defiance. A knight would "fling down the gauntlet" as a challenge to an enemy.

Very early in the Middle Ages, the glovemakers were presented with another problem: a glove was needed to protect the left hand of a gentleman. The sport of falconry was more than popular, it was a kind of frenzy for centuries. No gentleman could really hold up his head in society if he did not own at least two highly trained falcons that would take off at his command, soar into the air, strike down the bird desired, then return to the wrist of his proud owner. Even after a young falcon had been trained by a professional, it still had to become accustomed to its owner before it would perform. This meant long weeks of carrying the bird around on one's left wrist. The bird would be hooded so that he could not see anything but could become accustomed to his owner's voice.

These birds had long and very sharp claws—in fact, their claws were their main weapon of attack. The new owner would have to choose between having his left hand and wrist lacerated by claws or protected by a suitable glove. It was a real problem in that the owner would have to tote that bird around many hours a day for weeks. For instance, he might even carry the bird to church, and there were sure to be others encumbered in the same manner. Even a king on his throne might have a falcon on his wrist while discussing serious affairs of state. Of course, the glovers did a thriving business. They made a glove of the gauntlet type, but instead of being armored, it would be gaily decorated with embroidery.

It seems that one of the earliest Norman kings induced some Flemish leatherworkers, particularly those skilled in making gloves, to come over to England and set up their shops. To distinguish these foreigners in some way, the native Anglo-Saxons called them ghentmen, GANTMEN, and even GAUNTMEN, after the town from which they came, Ghent. Since all of them were glovemakers at that time, the name stuck. The Old French word for a GLOVER was *gantier,* so the first seven names stem indirectly from this source.

GROUP 88

Leather Bag Makers

In the previous chapter, the bag makers were covered in some detail in the discussion of bags made from woven fabrics such as wool or linen. There can be do doubt that many of the bags and pouches of that time were made from some of the fine leather that the TAWYERS were turning out. Today it is difficult to distinguish the man who made bags from woven fabrics from one who made bags from leather (see Group 81, page 162).

The Normans had a word, *boulge,* meaning "a leather bag," but the native English changed it to *bulge.* At any rate, the man who made leather bags was called a *boulgier,* and from this came the first six names on the list (BELGMAKER through BULGER). One John Bulger appears in the records in Worcestershire in 1300.

BURSER, PURSE, and PURSER, as discussed earlier, came by a roundabout way from the old Latin word *bursa,* meaning a pocket. Adam le Purser is in the records of 1332, and Robert le Pursere came along a few years earlier in 1319.

GROUP 89

Shoemakers

The name SHOEMAKER does not seem to have been applied to anyone before the latter part of the fourteenth century, well *after* most of our names had taken form. Men had been making and wearing foot-coverings for untold centuries, however, and must have been known by other names.

The first three names in this group—BOOT, BOOTE, and BOOT-MAN—were not necessarily given to men who made boots. It seems more likely that they were originally nicknames given to men who appeared with unusual foot-coverings.

The name CHAUSER is from one of the older names for foot-coverings. A pair of chauses covered not only the feet but the legs clear up to the knees. They were not always made from leather or buckskin: any durable material would do.

Then there is the name CORDEN. In Middle English, the word derivers from *corduan* or *cordewan;* in Old French, it was *cordoan.* The word indicated Spanish leather, because originally this very fine leather came from Cordova, Spain. But over the years, the name suffered the usual wear and tear of time and careless use, frequently coming out as CORDON, CORDWENT, or even CORWIN. Now and then it would go down as CORDNER or CODNER or CORRINER or CORD-WANER. A Robert Corduan is listed in 1121.

CORUEYSER comes from the Anglo-French word *corviser* or *corveser* or the Old French word *corveisier,* meaning "shoemaker." CORVEISER has actually survived as a surname itself. It must have been widely used in the thirteenth century, because in 1271 a regulation was enacted in London forbidding the sale of shoes in any area except that district between Corveiserstrete and Soperes Lane, and there only in the morning on ordinary days, though on the eve of a feast day they could be sold in the afternoon too. This district seems to have been the center of the shoe-making craft at that time. One reason for confining sales to morning hours might have been to protect the public from buying shoes made out of inferior leather. The morning light would make bad workmanship a little easier to detect.

COAD, COADE, and CODE come from a very old English word that meant wax, particularly the kind a shoemaker would use to put on his thread. Some form of the word would be applied to the men who used it, and the name stuck. *Code* was the original word in Anglo-Saxon. The earliest use of the name I can find is from an old record in 1275—Nicholas Code.

LAST and LASTER were latecomers, first being recorded in 1385 in the person of William Last. *Last* was Middle English for a wooden form made in the same shape and size as a man's foot and used in shaping shoes for him.

PATTEN, PATTERN, and PATTIN may not sound like shoes to us today, but in medieval England these words indicated shoes that were a cross between a clog and a sandal. Monks in monasteries were probably the first to make and use them. They had a sole and heel made from either wood or leather, with some straps attached to fasten onto the legs. They must have been uncomfortable to walk in, but they did keep the feet off the cold, wet ground. The word origin is the Middle English word *paten,* meaning "a clog." I find a John Patynmaker in 1379.

Then there are three names that point unmistakably to men who made shoes—SCHOEMAKER, SHOEMAKE, and SHOEMAKER—but the earliest record of their use that I have been able to locate is Hugh Schoemake in 1365.

The medieval rolls have plenty of SUTORS. The name derives from the Latin word *sutor* meaning a maker of almost any kind of covering for the feet. It ended up in the several forms listed—SEWTER, SOUTAR, SOUTER, SOUTTAR, SOUTTER, SOWTER, SUETER, SUTER, SUTTER, and SUTTERS.

Then along came Le SUEUR, derived from the Norman French word for a man who sewed things with a needle and thread. Somewhere along the line a man who sewed leather foot-coverings was referred to by that term and it stayed with him and became a name for a shoemaker. SUOUR is a variation. There was a John le Suur in 1255.

There are six other interesting old names: COBBER, COBBLER, COBELER, CLOUTER, SHOUBIGGER, and SPECKER. Early in the fourteenth century, a London regulation attempted to control the trade of shoe-making by specifying that a COBBLER could repair shoes but that he must confine his work to old leather, while a CORDWANER could use only new leather. A SPECKER was the same as a COBBLER, and a still older name for a shoe repair man was a CLOUTER. In Middle English, *spekke* simply meant patch and *cloute* was a verb meaning to patch, so a SPECKER was a CLOUTER, and a CLOUTER was a SPECKER.

A SHOUBIGGER was different. Old English for shoe was *scoh* and the verb to buy was *bycgan.* Put together, they indicated a man who bought shoes. Since everybody had to buy shoes, he must have made a business of buying them and selling them too. There is a Walter Shoubigger in 1333 and a Simon le Shobeggere in 1279.

GROUP 90

Workers in Kidskin

Today kidskin is associated almost solely with kid gloves. In England during the naming period, the association was not quite as specific. Gloves for ladies, particularly when the ladies were invited to go on a hunting party with the men, were probably the biggest outlet for the kidskin craftsmen. There seems to be some reason to think that the enormous cone-shaped hats the ladies wore on certain occasions were also made of kid.

The Old French word for leather made from the skin of a young goat was *cheverel* and it was used interchangeably with *kidskin*. Inevitably, the man who worked with this very fine product found himself named CHEVERELL, or a variant. There was a John Chiverel in 1275, a Simon de Chiverell in 1200, and a Ralph le Cheverelmongere in 1310. This last name does not seem to have survived.

GROUP 91

Bellows Makers

The BELLOWS names commemorate truly important men if one considers the importance of the item they made. Today the only bellows most of us ever see is the one used around the fireplace in the living room—certainly an expendable item. In the medieval period, they were indispensable to a whole group of craftsmen. All the smiths described in earlier chapters and workers in any kind of metal depended on a bellows. Without a means of blowing air into a fire, it was virtually impossible to heat most metals to a point where something could be done with them. The bellows of a smith would, of course, bear little resemblance to today's living-room variety; they were giant affairs fastened to the floor alongside the forge and worked by the strong arm of the smith or his helper.

One of the woodworking craftsmen would make the wooden frame for it, and then the leatherworker would take over. He made the all-important valve and the accordionlike sides that sucked in the air and then forced it into the fire.

There are six names in the group, some of which may have been given to the smith's helper who worked the bellows. It seems more likely, however, that the name would be commonly applied to the man who made and sold the ancient implements. The Old English word *belg* meant "bag" and in Middle English it became *beliman, beli* being the Middle English word for bellows.

GROUP 92

Makers of Odds and Ends

BOSKIN, BUSKENS, and BUSKIN could actually be included in either the SHOEMAKER list or even the TAILOR list. A pair of buskins today might be called a pair of leggings or a pair of breeches. The point is that they were made from *buckskin*. In 1281 a Roger Buckeskyn was recorded and in the very same year a Walter Buskyn.

The BRIDEL and HALTER names need no explanation. To make a bridle would require some iron from a smith for the bit, but the rest would be the work of the leather man.

LEATHER, LEATHERMAN, and LEATHERS were merely convenient names applied to any leatherworker when his specific product was not known.

The LORIMERS were spur-makers. Once again, the help of a smith would be required, but spurs would have to be fastened to the boot with a leather strap.

SKIVER is a little uncommon today, but it seems to have originated with a specially designed knife used by the leather makers to split a hide. These knives are still in use today.

GROUP 93

The Fur Business

The fur business of medieval England was a very small industry even by the standards of that period. This was not owing to any lack of admiration for garments made from fine fur but rather to the lack of skill on the part of craftsmen. The skin of an animal remains just a skin and quickly rots if it is not promptly treated by a skilled furrier.

Although animal life was abundant in the England of that period, not too many animals were suitable for fur, even if the skill had existed. Rabbit was plentiful and so was fox; beaver, martin, and otter were to be had in the northern parts of the island, but this was about the limit of practical fur-bearers. Of course, sheep were everywhere but, at least partly because it was so abundant, the wearing of sheepskin with the wool still attached was scorned by any but the peasants. Even today sheepskin with the wool on it is not considered fur.

Yet the wearing of fur was a status symbol in the Middle Ages even more than it is today. Whole fur garments were practically unknown, at least in part because of the lack of knowledge about "letting out" a piece of fur. This is a process that enables a skilled modern furrier to mold and shape a piece of fur so that it fits an individual and is still soft and clingy.

Wearing ermine did not become the symbol of royal authority until two to three centuries after the naming period. Still later, it became associated with king's judges as well.

But in the twelfth, thirteenth, and fourteenth centuries, things were different. No man from the king on down the social scale through the nobility and even into the gentry would appear in public without at least a bit of fur showing on his clothing. Frequently it was nothing more than a two-inch strip down the front of his mantle. It made no difference how ratty-looking the fur might be; it served as a personal distinction for the wearer. It identified him instantly as a man to contend with in any community.

Women no doubt had the same innate love of fur that they do today, but not much of it ever reached them. At this late date, we do not know how the male gentry managed things, but we do know that the ladies had to be content with very little fur embellishment on their costumes.

As far as I know, not a single sample of the fur of the Middle Ages has survived. Our knowledge of it has come from the statuary and drawings made from more enduring materials.

The medieval fur business cannot be mentioned without saying something about the feltmakers. Felt is frequently made from fur—almost any kind of fur. The fur is shaved off the skin and, by a somewhat complicated process, is made into a thick mat of material with the warmth of fur, yet a longer life.

In the discussion of Feltmakers (Group 72, page 159) the necessity of wearing a garment under armor was mentioned. It had to be thick and soft, something that could absorb and cushion the force of a blow on chain mail armor. Felt was definitely used for this purpose and it must have made the knight supremely uncomfortable on a warm day. Knightly courage and stamina must have been strained to the breaking point.

The brevity of this list is to be expected; even some that I have included have to be classified as doubtful. PELL was a pet form of the first name Peter, as were PELLS and PELLY, but *pel* was also Old French for skin and for a dealer in skins so they might have been furriers in a rudimentary sort of way. PILL is a long shot—it could have been a diminutive of PILCH and PILCHER; both of these names definitely indicated something made from fur. PELLATT and PELLETT are diminutives of the PELL names. They certainly come from the same Old French root word *pel*. There is a William Pelet recorded in 1297. PELTER and PILTER on the other hand, have a much more substantial reason for being connected to the fur business: *peletier* was Old French for either a fellmonger or a furrier. There is a William le Pelter in 1219, an Adam le Peletur in 1296, and a William Pilter in 1332. PELLEW and PILLOW are interesting in that they derive from a French word for a wolf's skin. Perhaps wolfskin was a select fur at that time. FURR comes from the Middle English word *furre*, meaning "something made from fur."

CONEY, CONTIE, CONNING, and CONY have come down to us almost unchanged from medieval days. The word was usually written either *conig* or *cony* and meant "rabbit." As mentioned previously, the lowly rabbit was plentiful. I suspect that the fur of the rabbit was used mostly in making felt and other materials where a soft cushion effect was desired.

GROUP 82

Producers of Rawhide

Fell	•	Pelter	Skinner
Fella	Pell	Pilter	Skinns
Feller	Pellatt	•	Skins
Fells	Pellett	Shinner	Skynner
Felmonger	Pells	Skin	
Felpollare	Pelly	Skinn	

GROUP 83

Leather Makers

Barkas	Barkman	•	Cunreyour
Barker	Barknur	Beauderer	Currier
Barkhouse	Barks	•	Curryer
Barkis	Berker	Couraour	•

Tanner	Tawyer	Whitear	Whittear
Tanneress	Tewer	Whitehair	Whittewere
Tannester	Tewers	Whithair	Whittier
Tanur	Tower	Whithear	Whittowere
•	•	Whittawyer	

GROUP 84

Belt Makers

Belt	Center	•	Gurdler
Belter	Century	Girdeler	Gurtler
Belts	Ceynturer	Girdelester	
•	Senter	Girdler	

GROUP 85

Bottle Makers

Botelmaker	Bottle	Bouch
Botler	Bottles	Buche
Bottell	•	Budge

GROUP 86

Saddlemakers

Baister	Sellars	Codman	Saddler
Baster	Seller	•	Sadeler
•	Sellers	Fewster	Sadleir
Cellier	Sellier	Foister	Sadler
Sealer	Sellors	Foyster	Sadliere
Seler	Zeller	Fuster	
Sellar	•	•	

GROUP 87

Glovemakers

Gant	Gaunt	Gauntman	Clover
Ganter	· Gaunter	•	
Gantman	Gauntlett	Glouer	

GROUP 88

Leather Bag Makers

Belger	Bolger	Bulger	Purse
Belgmaker	Boulger	•	Purser
Bolgar	Bousher	Burser	

GROUP 89

Shoemakers

Boot	Cobeler	Last	Soutar
Boote	•	Laster	Souter
Bootman	Codner	•	Souttar
•	Corden	Patten	Soutter
Chauser	Cordiner	Pattern	Sowter
•	Cordner	Pattin	Sueter
Clouter	Cordon	•	Suter
•	Cordwaner	Schoemaker	Sutter
Coad	Cordwent	Shoemake	Sutters
Coade	Corwin	Shoemaker	•
Code	•	•	Specker
•	Corueyser	Shoubigger	•
Cobber	Corveiser	•	Le Sueur
Cobbler	•	Sewter	Suour

GROUP 90

Workers in Kidskin

Cheverall	Cheverill	Chiverrell
Cheverell	Chiverall	Chivrall

GROUP 91

Bellows Makers

Belger	Bellow	Beloe
Belgmaker	Bellows	Billows

GROUP 92

Makers of Odds and Ends

Boskin	Bridell	•	Lorimer
Buskens	Bridle	Leather	Loriner
Buskin	•	Leatherman	Lorrimar
•	Halter	Leathers	•
Bridel	Halters	•	Skiver

GROUP 93

The Fur Business

Coney	Furr	Pellew	Pilcher
Conie	•	Pells	Pill
Conning	Pell	Pelly	Pillow
Cony	Pellatt	Pelter	Pilter
•	Pellett	Pilch	

CHAPTER 14

The Farming Industry

There are over two hundred family names in this group, and all but four come directly from men who farmed land occupied by feudal tenure or land they owned outright. England's economy in the early part of the twelfth century was almost wholly agrarian. Fully 95 percent of the population lived either in tiny villages or in scattered farmsteads.

The typical village of this period has already been described: the village church surrounded by the rude huts and cottages of peasants and occasionally a house of some quality, and over all, the manor house. This might be a rambling old wooden structure with outbuildings or it might be a great stone castle with tower and battlements frowning down. It made little difference to the peasants: it was the home of the lord who held his power from the king; he was the dispenser of justice and the arbiter of custom for all.

The arable land surrounding the village might be divided into two more or less equal portions; one would be the demesne of the lord, while the other would be cut up into strips for the use of the peasants.

A strip of farmland became a unit for land measurement, in the following way. With the crude plows of the time, eight oxen were required to turn the soil. This was far more oxen than any one peasant would own, so it was customary for them to combine their oxen into teams of eight. Such teams could pull the plow about two hundred and twenty yards through average soil before needing a rest. This established the length of the furrow (later to be called a furlong). The width of the strip was established when, at the end of the furrow, after the animals were rested, they were turned and headed the other way. This turn seems to have averaged about sixteen and a half feet (one rod); four of these strips became known as an acre.

In the very early part of the period, the lord had his demesne of several hundred acres of choice land, and each and every peasant on the manor had to give from a few hours to three full days of labor a week to plowing, planting, cultivating, and harvesting the crops of his lordship. What little time remained could be devoted to the strips of land the peasant held as the tenant of the lord.

At this time, every peasant was a tenant in that he did not own outright any of the land he worked, but over a period of two to three hundred years, this situation slowly changed. A tenant might win the favor of the lord by some extraordinary service to him and, as a reward, find his tenancy changed in any one of many different ways. The labor he owed the landlord might be cut in half or eliminated entirely, leaving no bond between them except that of complete loyalty in case of outside trouble. The tenant might buy either for cash or for excess labor additional strips or acres for himself. The latter was probably the more common way, as cases are on record of such credits being passed down from father to son for several generations until a tenant would find himself a fairly sizable landowner. In such cases, he would almost certainly be called a FRANKLIN or FREEMAN, or one of the dozen or more variations that these names took on over the centuries.

GROUP 94

Peasant-Farmers

The first thirteen names of Group 94 (see page 200), beginning with ACKERMAN, all go back to the Old English *aecermann,* frequently used simply to indicate a peasant-farmer—and not one with much land. He was apt to have from one to ten precious acres. You can be sure Robert le Akerman in 1233 was very proud of his few acres.

The APPLE names clearly indicate a grower or seller of apples. *Aeppel* was the Old English source. One owner of this name was Tomas de Appleton, who lived in the twelfth century.

The three BEAN names may have several possible origins, but bean-growing farmers were certainly part of the medieval scene. The first record of the name I have been able to locate was in Latin—Robertus filius Biene in 1168.

All the BEE names definitely indicate men in the business of bee-keeping. Honey was the only sweetening agent available at that time in England.

The BOND names derive from two distinct sources. Before the Conquest, one was an Old Norse word, *buan,* meaning simply "to dwell somewhere." It was used to indicate a warrior who had given up his habit of wandering from place to place looking for a fight and had settled down on a piece of land permanently. This man would usually be given the name BOND. He was a free man before the Conquest and may well have managed to remain that way even after William imposed his far stricter form of feudalism. On the other hand, the Normans had a word *bonde,* which to them indicated a churl, an unfree tenant, a serf who was bound to the land where he lived. In the course of time, both words became confused, so that it is impossible today to distinguish the ancient freeman from the serf. The name appears on old records as Norman le Bonde in 1180, William Bonde in 1185, and Henry le Bounde in 1297.

The CHERRY names are obvious—undoubtedly they referred to growers of cherries. As early as 1284, I find a Robert Chyry in business.

The COAT names, including DALLICOAT through DELICATE, come down to us from one Old English word—*cot* or *cote,* meaning "a shelter." It certainly did not indicate a castle, but probably a cottage. If a man lived in a cot at that time, he was almost surely a tiller of the soil, so it is safe to call people with this name peasant-farmers in origin. Walter de Cotes lived in the twelfth century. COTTER may have derived from the French word *cotier,* but it meant the same as COTE. William le Coter is mentioned in 1270. The COTTRELL names were simply changes that came about with time—they still hark back to *cottage.* Undoubtedly, human carelessness was responsible for DE LA COTE, DALLICOAT, DALLICOTT, and even DELICATE. There was a Gerard Coterel in 1130. In fairness, the Middle English word *cote,* meaning an outer garment, should also be mentioned. Some of the listed names could have been given to a maker of coats.

DE LA FIELD through VELDEN seem to stem from one Old English word, *feld,* meaning a cultivated field but an open one in the sense of not having a fence around it (fences were uncommon in those times, anyway). It is reasonable to think that these men were FARMERS—tillers of the soil. Geoffrey le Felder lived in the fourteenth century, and Baldwin Felde came along shortly thereafter.

The name DUNGER is an enigma. It comes from the Middle English word *dungen,* meaning "one who manures the soil." There is a Roger Dunger in 1327 and a William Dunger as early as 1221. When the name was first given, it must have seemed that his practice of putting manure on his soil was so uncommon that the name would clearly identify him thereafter, but there is ample evidence that manuring soil was not at all uncommon at that time. We read constantly about manorial lords building a close (an enclosed or fenced-in area) near his house and insisting that all animals be driven into the close every night so that he would benefit from their droppings.

Centuries later, when British colonists were establishing plantations in American coastal areas, the soil became so exhausted in a few years, owing to lack of knowledge of how to maintain fertility, that it was cheaper to abandon the farm, move west, and clear land for a new one. The only conclusion that can be drawn is that the knowledge of using manure to maintain fertility must have been well understood and commonly practiced by individuals here and there but not generally known all over medieval England.

FARMER, with its three variants, is unusually interesting in that the meaning of the word in medieval England was entirely different from the meaning attached to it today. In Anglo-French it derives from *fermer* and in Old French from *fermier,* while in medieval Latin it comes from *firmarius.* They all mean he was a *tax collector.* He was an individual who made a deal with whoever was the tax-collecting authority to "pay a fixed sum for the proceeds." The tax-collecting authority would be sure of his total and the "farmer" would be equally certain of getting his—what chance did the poor taxpayer have? However, the farmer (in the medieval sense of the word) seems to have performed other duties as well. At times he seems to have been assigned to the position of bailiff of a large estate, a granger. Certainly there is no shortage of FARMERS in the old records. William le Fermer appears in 1238 in Essex, then William le Farmere in 1279 in Cambridgeshire, and Richard Fermor in 1293 in Devonshire.

The six names FIFEFEILD through FIFOOT were given to men who possessed a substantial amount of land—600 acres, or nearly a square mile, to be exact.

The FOURACRE names tell us that a man so named owned four acres of ground. This holding was not large, but such a man was a long way from being a churl or a serf. The name goes back to at least 1327, when William Fourake is recorded.

All twenty-eight of the FRANKLIN and FREEMAN names mentioned earlier in this chapter derive on the one hand from the Norman French word *fraunclein* and on the other from the Old English word *freo* and the Middle English *fre*. The only responsibility the FREEMAN or FRANKLIN had was to support himself and his family. Even if he had to relinquish his land for his freedom, he could certainly acquire more of it without too much trouble. He was free to pack up his family and go wherever he desired and engage in any business that might appeal to him. We take such action for granted, but in medieval times one had to earn freedom, and it might take several generations.

The GARDEN names derive from the Norman word *gardinier* meaning "a gardener." Hopefully, William Gardin who lived in Huntingdonshire far back in 1220 was gifted with the proverbial green thumb.

GRAINGE, GRAINGER, and the variants indicate men who had large farms. Just how large cannot be determined, but large enough to require an overseer or a foreman: that is, a GRANGER. The term springs from an Anglo-French word, *graunger,* meaning "a farm bailiff." A BAILIFF was always an executive caretaker of a castle or someone else of real importance, so any man having that name was in a position of genuine responsibility. The fact that the word comes from the Normans shows clearly the policies of the Conquerer in dealing out real estate—the loyal retainers were generally rewarded.

The HARROWER names derive from the Middle English word *harwen*. A Ralph le Harwere appears in 1327.

The HAYMAN names indicate clearly a man who sold hay. It seems unlikely that such a man would own much property, but he must have sold a lot of hay to have that name. He was probably a hay jobber.

A hide of land was 120 acres, and if a man were called HIDE or anyone of the five variations, it meant he was one of the landed aristocracy. Ownership of land was virtually the sole basis of wealth, and 120 acres was a lot of territory. There was a Robert de la Hyde in 1188.

The three HONEYMAN names come from farmers in the business of bee-keeping just as surely as the names in the BEE group do. They had a monopoly on the sweets business at that time. Sugar and the other sweetening agents did not reach England until after the naming period. Everard Huniman was in that business in 1199.

HOSBONS, HUSBAND, and HUSBANDS come from the same general origin as the BOND names. The last syllable of HUSBAND is just BOND. The word *husbonda* meant a tiller of the soil who owned a house: a householder.

The origin of the LATHE names is not too clear. In Old English, *hlava* meant a man who worked in or around a barn, so he may have tended cattle or some other domestic animals. LEATH and LEATHE are dialectal variations from Lancashire. John del Leath lived in the fourteenth century.

The derivation of the LAYTON names is not as clear as that of the GARDEN names, but probably all of them come from an Old English word, *leactun*. This meant "a kitchen garden," and surely Roger de Leyton who lived in the same shire as the GARDENER in 1276 was a kitchen gardener. He may also have been a mechanic around the village—maybe even a smith or a potter—but that kitchen garden of his must have been impressive to have given him a name.

LEAK through LEKER were farmer-peasants without a doubt, but with a specialty—their main crop must have been leeks. Leeks belong to the onion family and their culinary uses are much the same. I think we can assume that they were more generally appreciated in medieval times than they are now—or so it seems from the large number of names from that vegetable that have reached us. *Leac* was the Old English word. There was a Ralph de Lek in 1202 and a William le Leker in 1293.

MAWER and MOWER were names given to men who mowed something. Roger le Mower appeared in 1305.

The PEARCH names could be listed in our chapter on officials, because the PEARCHMAN was, in a small sense, a surveyor. A pearch (or perch) was equal to 16½ feet, or one rod, and the pearcher was the man who measured farmlands.

A PEARMAN was the counterpart of an APPLEMAN.

PEASCOD through PESKETT and including BISGOOD indicate farmers who grew peas. The pea was a popular vegetable then, just as it is now, and doubtless a man could sell his whole crop easily enough. Whether raising peas was his only occupation then is hard to say, but it is doubtful. Perhaps he was a craftsman of some kind and tended his pea garden after hours. The Old English word for pea was *peose* or *pise*. The ending *cod* and its variations simply meant a bag—in this case the pod (or husk) in which the pea grows—thus, John Pesecod in 1317.

The PLANT names clearly indicate a man who loved planting things and watching them grow. Henry le Plaunter flourished in 1281.

PLOWMAN, with its two variants, is self-explanatory. John le Ploghman is recorded in 1275.

REAPER is somewhat of a puzzle. Just about every farmer must have been a reaper some part of each year. Just why one of them should have been singled out to be so named when every farmer the tax man would call on for a week or more would be reaping his grain is unclear. Nevertheless, there is a John Reper recorded in 1327.

SEADER is another obvious name like REAPER, PLOWMAN, and MOWER. The Old English origin was *saedere* meaning a sower of seed. Ralph le Sedere appears in 1221.

TASKER was a term in Old English used to indicate a man expert in threshing grain with a flail. He commonly went from farm to farm as a pieceworker. John le Tasker and Benedict le Tasker are recorded in 1279.

THRASHER and THRESHER meant a man who threshed. They derive from the Old English word *therscan,* meaning "to thresh." Grain is threshed only twice a year and so one might wonder how a man could acquire a name from such an occupation, but indeed he did—Geoffrey le Thressher is registered in 1319.

The TILLER names from TILEY through TYLEY stem back to the Old English word *tilian,* which mean "to till" or to the substantive form of the word, *tilia,* meaning "one who tills the soil." There was a William le Tiller in 1342 and a William le Tylie just ten years before that.

The name VILLAIN and its two variations is rare today for very understandable reasons. This man was just the opposite of the FREEMAN. He was a serf, or bondman, and the land he occupied belonged 100 percent to the lord of the manor. If the lord sold that land, the serf went with it, just like the trees or the buildings. Today the word always means a man of bad character, but the original use of the word had no such connotation. Robert Vilain in 1186 and Roger le Vilain in 1197 were not so named because of their evil characters!

WERKMAN and WORKMAN, from the Old English *weorcmann,* may or may not have been farmers in today's meaning of the word. A quote from a very ancient record says: "Werkemanne that cann werke bothe handys a-lyke." It seems the men given either of the above names must have been ambidextrous.

The five WORT names clearly meant a man who today would be called a truck gardener—he raised and sold vegetables. Old English for "vegetable" was *wyrt,* so WORTMAN simply meant a vegetable man. Simon Wurtman appears on the record in 1297.

The YEOMAN names have an interesting history. Their origin is most likely Germanic. The name probably reached England very early in the Anglo-Saxon period and at that time was usually applied to a trusted servant (we still speak of someone doing yeoman service). As time went on, some of them were rewarded with a rank—something between a sergeant and a groom in one shire, while in another it might be between a squire and a page. Usually some land went with the rank, so the yeoman became a small landowner, a freeholder.

GROUP 95

The Dairy Business

Cheese is easily one of the oldest man-made foods in the world. The Greeks and the Romans enjoyed several kinds, and the entire ancient Near East used it as part of their daily diet. When Caesar's legions invaded Britain, they probably brought some of their cheese-makers with them, but the Britons were already acquainted with the art. No doubt the Britons convincingly demonstrated to the Romans that they could produce their own cheese best because they were necessarily far more familiar with their own native milk and rennet than strangers could be.

When the Romans left Britain in the fourth or fifth century, the Anglo-Saxons began to arrive. They knew how to make cheese, but they do not appear to have developed any new techniques or varieties. In the eleventh century, when the Norman conquerors subdued England, the Anglo-Saxons were still making cheeses that must have greatly resembled what we now call Cheddar, Stilton, and Cheshire.

Cheese-making is quite simple. A small amount of rennet is mixed with a large volume of fresh sweet milk (ten pounds of milk makes one pound of cheese). The rennet coagulates the milk, that is, it turns the protein in the milk into a solid or semisolid mass. This separates more or less completely from the leftover watery liquid, which is called whey. From this point on, the process might be considered mechanical—squeezing and wringing nearly all the whey out of the solid matter. After that, the solid has to age for some time to develop its full flavor.

In the early part of the twelfth century, when the people of Britain were just beginning to discover the convenience and advantages of having a family name, cheese must have been made in a great many of the homes of the peasants. This would be particularly true in the villages and open country where milk was more available. While there might be some exchange of cheese for other items between neighbors, that was to be the limit of commercial production until modern times.

CHEESE

Names from the cheese-making industry of medieval England are remarkably informative. Probably each one of the men originally given a cheese name followed some full-time occupation as well; one might be a potter, another a weaver and still another might be a miller or a baker, but he or his wife found they could considerably enrich their simple daily menu by some after-hours cheese-making. This alone might be enough to cause a tax collector to give them such a name. If the tax man sampled the product, he might even decide to change a man's name from MILLER to CHEESEWRIGHT. Remember the *-wright* on the end of a name always emphasized that the holder was definitely a maker of the item.

The old records are filled to overflowing with names that have come down to us from the early cheese-makers. In the East Anglian dialect of Old English, the word was *cese,* while further west it was *cyse,* and out of these came in 1176 John Chese, later changed to CHEESE, and then, in 1316, a Walter le Cheser. There was an Adam le Chisman in 1327 and Robert le Chesemaker in 1275. (Whenever the definite article *le* appears in front of a last name, it indicates that the tax man was almost surely a French-speaking Norman.) Some of these names have survived the years unchanged, but others have been modernized from time to time. The Old English *cyswyrhte* in modern dress is either CHEESEWRIGHT or CHESEMAKER.

CHESEWRINGER and WRINGER are not very widespread today, but they definitely came from part of the cheese-making process. CHERRETT and CHERRITT are dialectical variations of CHEESEWRIGHT and found mostly in Suffolk.

The whole list of names beginning with FERMINGER and ending with FURMINGER have the same meaning as the CHEESE names above. They come from the Old French word *fromagier,* meaning a CHEESEWRIGHT. There are many of these in the records too—like William le Furmager in 1219.

FENWICK, FINNICK, and VINICK are almost certainly cheese-makers too, but in disguise. They were names given to a man who owned a dairy farm with some land that was swampy—a swamp was known as a *fen.* The dairy farm itself was a *wic* or *wiken,* hence the WICKEN names and the CHESSE through CHISWICK list also. Examples of both groups would be Henry de Wikin in 1279 and John de Cheswyk in 1275. CHISWICK was common in Essex and Middlesex, while in Northumbria they preferred CHESWICK—no matter, both of them meant "cheese-farm."

EWART, YEOWARD, YEOWART, and YOUATT introduce something new. They go back to cheese-makers who started with the milk of ewes instead of the more common milk from cows. The Old English word for ewe is *eowu,* and *hierde* means eweherd. Robert de Ewrth is listed in 1242. This probably became EWART later.

MILK

No names whatever are listed that seem to have come from the basic product of milk. Somewhere, I did locate a modern family with that name, but it is rare. There were a few in medieval times, such as Ailmar Melc back in 1066. This requires some explanation. Milk was not commonly used in medieval times as a beverage or food. It was considered dangerous and, indeed, it was. Milk is the most healthful of drinks if it is fresh and free from contamination, but it can be become dangerously contaminated in a few minutes. And surely this happened again and again in that period. Pasteur would not be born for several hundred years. In the meantime, the medieval peasant had learned from experience that milk had better be left alone or fed to the animals if one didn't make either cheese or butter from it. (Ice cream, the third great product from milk, was still far in the future.)

The origin of the six DAY names is obscure. We know that our word *dairy* comes from the same root and that it was probably first used to indicate a dairymaid. However, there are plenty of examples showing that it was used to indicate a woman who kneaded dough, which would put it properly in the Baker group. Some early records of the name are Aluric Dai in 1196, Ralph Deie in 1211, and Thomas le Deye in 1277.

BUTTER

Butter, like cheese, was not hard to make if one had good fresh milk, and it did not easily become contaminated as untreated milk did. But it was expensive and not as satisfying as cheese, so it became a status symbol for the wealthy in the earlier part of the naming period. Later it became more popular with the peasants, and certainly it must have been a great help in eating that very rough black bread the common folk had on their tables.

The ten names beginning with BUTERER through BUTTRICK hardly need explanation—all that was said of the cheese-makers applies to the butter people. The Old English root for the word was *butere,* and some form of the word was commonly applied to men known to be butter-makers, such as William le Buterar, who lived in Sussex in 1371. BUTTERWORTH refers to a butter farm, since *worth* meant "farm." BUTTRICK—that last syllable is the same word *wick* mentioned above —meant "butter farm," too.

SMEREMONGER is interesting but understandably not too common. *Smeoru* was Old English for anything that was fat, and *monger* meant "a seller." There is a William Smermongere listed in 1296. SMEREMAN meant exactly the same thing. SMEREKERNER indicated a man who churned butter, since *kernere* meant "churn." CHURN and CHURNER are obvious.

GROUP 96

Cattle Tenders

All the names in this group necessarily come from the same general classification detailed in the section on dairy products. Certainly, the dairyman kept cows, but there are so many names relating to cattle with no ostensible connection with the dairy business that a separate group has been created.

The medieval English had very little knowledge of how to raise cattle for beef. Compared to the modern feed-lot where the animals are fed with special foods for many months, prevented from taking any unnecessary exercise, and given all manner of other attention that results in good beef, the cattle of the Middle Ages must have been a scrawny lot. It would be five hundred years before the peasant-cattlemen of Herefordshire, ably assisted by the landed proprietors of the 1700s, would produce the world-famous Hereford breed. And the Aberdeen Angus from Scotland, although its very distant ancestors were probably there in Aberdeen in the thirteenth century, had little resemblance to the Black Angus of today.

From early spring until late fall, cattle were turned out to pasture to eat whatever they could find, but even where the grass was lush and green, the result was a lean and tough beef animal. By the time winter arrived, all of them would have to be butchered, except for those few saved for breeding stock and for oxen. The English of that period simply did not know how to raise sufficiently good fodder to maintain their stock through a winter.

The cattlemen of that period did not even attempt to develop one breed for meat and another for dairy purposes—cattle were just cattle and would remain so for many a year.

There are many interesting names from the cattle business of the Middle Ages.

The first five names beginning with BEST derive from the Old French word *beste,* meaning "beast." Indirectly it meant an animal but hardly a nice, gentle one. BESTMAN is particularly deceiving—it brings to mind weddings.

The BIER group—all thirteen names—derive from the old English word *aetbyrum* meaning "at the cowsheds." After many centuries of hard use and much abuse, these thirteen names are still with us. In 1327 there was a John Buyres recorded, and in 1285 a Richard Byrun.

The names BOOL through BULPIN derive from the Old English word *bula,* meaning "bull." But why so many variations of such a short and simple word? Was it because the bull served so many different functions? Allowed to grow up naturally, he was a bull, but if he was castrated while very young, he became a steer, and if he were not butchered before the age of about three years, he became an ox. Whatever the explanation, there was recorded a Wulfwin Bule in 1170 and William le Bool in 1214. BULLAS, BULLASS, and BULLUS are simply modern contractions or simplifications of the term bull-house. In 1327, a William Bolehouse is listed, and a little later, an Adam Bulluse.

The English of the Middle Ages had still another word referring to a man who worked with cows—it was *bosig* and from that old word came the name BOOSEY. Probably our word bossy, in the sense of "cow," came from the same source.

BOOTH and BOOTHE have an Old Danish origin and mean "a cow-house" or a man who took care of cows.

The CALVERT names are simple. They come from East Anglia, where the word meant "a calf herd." William Calvehird was a cowman in 1297, and so was John Calverde in 1309.

The four names beginning with COWARD obviously originate from the word *cow.* In Old English it was *cuhyrde,* which meant cowherd. There is another possible origin—*cu-weard* meaning "cow guard" (that word *weard* appears frequently in Middle English and always means a guard of some kind). In 1327, I find John Cowherde on a tax roll; in 1255 Thomas le Cuherde, and in 1327 an Adam le Couherd.

DROVER comes from *draf,* meaning "a herd or drove of cattle." A man in charge of a drove would be called a DROVER, and indeed one finds a Henry le Drovere in 1326.

The names FAULDER through FOWLDS stem back to the pens in which cows were kept or at least to the men who kept them there. The Old English word was *fald* and in Middle English it became *fold.* Thus we find John atte Fold in 1327 and Adam de Falde in 1332.

FODOR, from the Middle English word *fodien,* meant "a man who fed cattle." Walter Fodere is recorded in 1334.

The HEARD names need no explanation. The Old English word was *hierde* with the obvious meaning. Of course, one could take care of a herd of sheep as well as a herd of cows, so there is no certainty that all these people were in the cattle business.

All five OX names come from the Old English *oxa*. Thus William le Oxherd is listed in 1332. A Walter de Oxenforde appears in 1319, but is probably a place name rather than an occupational one.

The STEER names refer to those who raised bulls castrated at an early age. The name derives from Old English *stear*, meaning "castrated bull."

GROUP 97

The Meat Business

The greatest single weakness of the meat industry in medieval times was the fact that the farmers did not know how to raise fodder enough to carry their livestock over the winter and, as a result, they had to butcher nearly all their animals every fall, excepting only a few spared for breeding purposes or for draft work.

There must have been complete chaos at the end of each year: the market would be glutted with huge quantities of meat that would spoil if not preserved in some way. Meat had to be salted down and packed in barrels, and certain kinds could be dried or smoked, but these were the only ways known to preserve meat.

Canning was unheard of until the days of Napoleon in the nineteenth century, and freezing by artificial means was still farther away. So they had a Roman holiday of butchering and meat-eating that would last through Christmas. In the Christmas season, the great hall of the castle or manor house would be at its best. Great fires burned in every fireplace and the cooks and kitcheners broiled and roasted huge quantities of meat of every variety. Whereas at all other times of the year the choice pieces would be offered to the lord and his guests and what remained given to the common folk, now there was plenty of good meat for everyone. Furthermore, on Christmas Day itself, even the most humble of peasants was not only invited to the feast but allowed to sit and drink after the meal as long as he cared to. This was indeed a rare privilege— probably the only time in the whole year that the common people could drink wine.

In this group are seven BUTCHERS and three FLESHERS. All the BUTCHER names derive from the Anglo-French word *bocher* or *boucher* or from the old French word *bochier*. Many names from these old words have survived. An Alan le Boucher is recorded in 1327 and a Thomas le

Bochier in 1332. FLESHER meant BUTCHER, but it came from two Old English words—*flaesc,* meaning "flesh" and *heawan* meaning "to cut." John Flesher was a butcher in 1379. FLESHHEWER has the same derivation but is uncommon today. FLESHMONGER meant simply "a man who sold meat"—surely he was a butcher too. KETMONGER has the same meaning, but it derives from a Norse name.

BACKNER and BACON and BAKON refer to a pork butcher. In French the word was *baconnier* and in English it was *backner.*

BUDINER is an interesting name. A man so named was a sausage-maker. It appears in the old records as *marchand de boudin,* meaning a seller of sausage. What combination of spices he used and whether he packed all his sausages in skins or simply sold sausage in bulk is unknown. In any case, it must have been a tasty product to have given him his name.

BUKMARTER and BUKMONGER need some explanation. They were dealers in venison. *Buc* meant "buck"—a male deer—and *mongere* meant a seller of something. Hunting deer, however, was the privilege of the nobles. If one were not a noble and were caught in the forest with a weapon, one would be subject to immediate and very drastic punishment, usually death; so how could a peasant not only kill deer but sell the venison openly? I have no explanation for this, but the names are there on record. In 1275 there was Hugo Bucmonger and Hugo le Bukmarter.

KELLOGG was a nickname, but it was applied only to butchers because it meant "kill hog."

KNATCHBULL was a name given to men who were strong enough to hit a bull on the head with a hammer. They were certainly butchers.

MACECRER, MACEGRE, MASKERY, and MASKREY all come from another Old French word, *maceclier,* meaning "butcher."

SLAGTER, SLAUGHTER, SLAYTER, SLAYTOR, and SLEATOR come from the Middle English word *slahter* and, of course, mean people who kill or slaughter. Some might derive from the Old English word *sleahter* meaning "marshy ground," as in Costwold villages of Upper and Lower Slaughter.

A man named STIKKER was a hog butcher and his method of killing the animal is still followed.

TRENCHARD comes from the Old French word *trenchier,* meaning "to cut." Ralph Trencart had the name in 1086.

GROUP 98

Swineherds

It has been said that the medieval English "ate the pig and wore the sheep," and this is the simple truth. Without sheep wool, the British would have been wearing the raw pelts of wild animals many centuries after this custom passed on, and without the flesh of the humble porker, medieval life would certainly have been very different from what it was.

Everybody had pigs. A pig could forage for himself, so almost every family in medieval England owned at least one or two of the animals. For the most part, they wandered wherever their instincts told them something edible could be found. They were recaptured in the fall and identified by ear markings. They were then butchered to start the annual carnival of meat-eating before the arrival of winter.

The food in what were then deep forests covering much of Britain was more plentiful than within the villages. Acorns were abundant and packed plenty of calories for the pig's diet, but they also imparted a slightly bitter taste to the meat that was undesirable.

The use of the forests for the purpose of grazing pigs, however, was largely restricted to the great landowners. The reigning king had his royal preserves where none but he and his invited friends could hunt, and each and every manorial holder held many thousands of acres surrounding his manor house, which were guarded day and night by his PARKERS lest some churlish peasant take it into his head to shoot one of his lordship's game animals.

The lord of the manor would keep his own great flock of pigs in his forest and, by special arrangement, he might allow the same privilege to a very few others. If one wanted to keep a few pigs to feed a family, one had to find a place for them. It seems not to have occurred to people for quite a while that pigs could live very happily in a small penned area.

Today we think of pigs in terms of two hundred pounds or less "on the hoof"—at that weight, they are ideal for butchering: the proportion of lean to fat is just about right, and if much heavier than that, they will run to fat, causing the price per pound to drop. In medieval times, however, pigs were lucky to reach a weight of seventy-five pounds before being butchered.

ABEAR and A'BEAR both mean "at the swine pasture" and are thus swineherds. The DENN names derive from an Old English word, *denn*, for a swine pasture. A man who had charge of such a place might find himself named after it—like William Denn in 1296.

The FOREMAN names sound as if they might have been given to

someone in a managerial position but that is not so. The name comes from the Old English word *for,* meaning "pig," and *mann,* meaning "man." This adds up to pig-man or swineherd.

FORWARD and FORWOOD have the same origin, only the last syllable is *weard* meaning a guard (the same as *ward*). Strange to say, the only example of the name seems to be the feminine Florence Forewardes in 1327.

All the GRICE names originate from the Middle English word *grise* or *grice* and from an Old Norman French word *griss,* meaning pig, or a man who took care of pigs. The -WOOD of GRISEWOOD was probably a variation of the word *ward.*

The HOGG names all start with the simple Old English word *hogg,* of obvious meaning. It seems strange that there are so many HOGG names, because nearly everybody owned at least a few, and such a name would hardly distinguish one man from another.

I am sure that the great scientist Francis Bacon was not a pork butcher, but one of his ancestors may have been. This seems to be the proper place to interject a brief story about a Connecticut Yankee trader in the post-Revolutionary period. I am deeply grateful to Chard Powers Smith's *The Housatonic* for the story.

The trader of whom I speak shall remain nameless for only a moment. It seems he had lived all his life (he was over sixty now) in the town of Woodbury, Connecticut. He was a trader in an area and in a period that abounded in traders. He would buy *anything*—providing that he could buy enough of it. It was 1783 and the Revolution was just over, so he figured New York City must be hungry for meat—good Connecticut hams and bacon. In a quick trip around the state, he bought every pound of good pork he could find, loaded a small ship with it, and set sail for the big city.

On arrival, he received the shock of his life—every merchant told him that two very large shiploads of pork were due in from Maine that very day and their prices would be lower than his. This was bad news—selling against that kind of competition was not what he had expected.

He rented a saddle-horse and rode up the Manhattan side of the East River, where he could see everything afloat. Arriving opposite Blackwell's Island, he spotted the two heavily laden ships plowing down the river. He got off the horse and into a boat and rowed out to the ships. In ten minutes, he had bought the entire cargo of both ships. He had to pledge his entire fortune to do it, but by the time those ships tied up in lower Manhattan, Jabez BACON owned just about all the pork on the market. Mr. Bacon is said to have netted around $40,000. When he died in 1806, his estate ran close to half a million dollars—an enormous sum at that time.

Who knows if Mr. BACON's unusual vision concerning pork products was inherited? We know nothing of the ancestors who gave him his name.

HOGARTH, HOGGARD, HOGGART, HOGGARTH, and HOG-GETT indicated a herd of pigs—a swineherd, or the man who took care of them. There was a Richard le Hoghird in 1327 and a John Hoggerd as late as 1508.

HUDDART and WOODARD have an Old English derivation—*wudu* and *hierde,* meaning "wood-herd." This would be applied to anyone who took care of animals in the woods, and that would almost certainly mean pigs. Richard le Wodehirde is recorded in 1275.

The two PIGG names were understandably unable to survive modern pride, but there are still a few rugged individualists with the courage to hang on to that ancient and certainly not dishonorable name. There was an Alurious Piga away back in 1066 (probably a nickname), and then a John Pig in 1086, the year of the Domesday Book. And there was a Robert Pigge in 1277. In the late Middle Ages, the word for pig is *pigge*.

The Normans called a man who took care of pigs a PORCHER or sometimes a *porkier,* but both words meant a swineherd.

STYER has an Old English derivation and means the man who either worked at or lived near a pigsty. William Styers is listed in 1674.

The SWAIN names have several possible origins. At some point the Old English word became confused with the Danish and with the Swedish and later even with the Norman French. In Norman it was *sveinn* and in Norse it was *sven;* the English tended to use *swan.* It meant a boy servant, particularly one who looked after the pigs, hence another swine-herd. Many examples exist in the old records, such as Robert Suein in 1166 and Walter Swayn in 1295. In still later times, the name lost its connection with pigs and came to mean simply a young man.

SWINERD and SWINNARD derived from the Old English word *swinhyrde.* SWINYARD came from *swin* and *geard,* meaning "swine yard," or "swine enclosure"; in other words, a pigsty.

GROUP 99

Goat Keepers

Not very much is known about the goat in the economy of medieval England. He was outranked many times over by the sheep, the pig, the cow, and the horse, but we know by looking at the list of family names coming from this animal that he must have been of some significance. The list contains fifteen names including the usual variations: not a large number, but definitely enough to prove the goat must have been a fairly common sight around the villages and small towns in that period.

Milk and meat were the goat's contribution. The milk would be made into cheese and the meat eaten along with the pork and beef in the annual carnival, as I like to call that period in late fall when meat had to be either salted down, dried, or eaten.

The Old Norman French word for goat was *geit* and directly or indirectly all fifteen names on the list stem from this origin, although the Old French word *gaite,* meaning "watchman," may have been responsible for a few of the names through the centuries. In the records are Thomas Gayte in 1297 and Richard Gaites in 1561.

GAITER, GAYTER, GAYTHER, GAYTOR, GEATER, and GEA-- TOR suggest a goatherd. Michael le Geytere in 1279 meant "Michael the goatherd," just as John le Gaythirde, in 1301, was "John the goat- herd."

GROUP 100
Poultry Keepers

Domestic chickens and ducks were unquestionably part of the scene in every medieval village and farm. Geese were also a large factor in the economy because of the very great demand for goose feathers.

Both chickens and ducks had been domesticated many centuries earlier in many countries of the world, and undoubtedly both were in Britain before the arrival of the Romans. We know precious little about them, however. We can be sure they were not commonly fed grain. Like the pigs, they were left to find their own food. Certainly egg production was very much lower than it would be now. Actually, it was only in the present century that the poultry industry made a serious study of poultry-feeding and, as a result, found that hens naturally lay forty to fifty eggs a year (mostly in the spring), but when they are fed certain selected foods, their production of eggs continues through the year and is four to six times greater.

As we look at the names in this group, we find HENNMAN obviously means a man who either keeps hens or sells them—although he might well sell just the eggs. Richard Heneman is registered in 1327. HENN is from the same origin, and a Euorard Henne flourished around 1202.

A man named HENMONGER definitely sold hens and/or their eggs, as did GELYNER. The latter name comes from the Old French word for "hen."

CHICKEN is not a widespread name today and probably never was. It has an Old English source *cicen*, meaning "chicken." POULTER and PULETER go back to the Old French word *pouletier*, meaning "a poultry dealer." The rolls show Richard le Poulter and Osbert le Puleterin in 1230, and Gilbert Le Poletter in 1304.

The DUCK names have the same root and meaning in Middle English —they all meant a bird that could dive under water.

GOSERE and GOSMANGER refer to sellers of geese and their valuable feathers.

GROUP 101

Caretakers of the Horses

In earlier chapters, many family names that have come down to us from the business of raising and caring for horses in the Middle Ages have been covered, but it seems more is necessary.

Anglo-Saxon England had horses long before the Conquest but the Normans brought improved breeds and greater knowledge of the animal, and hence raised the quality somewhat. The Crusades of the twelfth and thirteenth centuries proved the greatest stimulant to horse-breeding in England, however. Large numbers of English nobles were crusaders, going to Eastern countries where the Arabian horse was bred. The speed and agility of these horses so impressed the crusaders that they brought large numbers of them back to England and began a systematic importation of Arabian horseflesh that continues today.

English breeders were to do great things in developing specialized horses in later centuries, but in this period only light, fast animals suitable for hunting and traveling and the great war-horse that the knight could ride into battle were required. The peasant's plowing, of course, was left largely to oxen, although later, draft horses were developed that proved superior to oxen.

An Old English word for a horse was *capul* or *capel*. Naturally enough, a CAPPLEMAN was a man who took care of horses.

The name COLT was probably just a nickname at first. Any young man who seemed to be more frisky than others might be thus tagged because such behavior was associated with a young horse. There is one very early record of the name—Anselm Colt—in 1017, long before the Conquest. COLTER and COLTMAN were probably dealers who sold young male horses. A John le Coltman is registered in 1365. The rest of the COLT names were of people in the business of breeding and selling horses. In Old English, the words were *colt* and *hierde,* meaning "keeper of a herd of colts."

As names CONSTABLE and MARSHALL are very interesting; MARSHALL has been covered in chapter 5, and CONSTABLE in chapters 19 and 23.

A CORSER was a horse trader. Probably the horse trader as a character developed more in nineteenth-century America than any other section of the world. For a man to be compared with a horse trader in the matter of honesty and trustworthiness was the equivalent of being challenged to a duel. COSSAR and COSSER meant the same thing.

The three HACKNEY names come from either the Old French *haquenee* or the Middle English *hakenei,* meaning a horse with an easy gait that might have been considered suitable for ladies at that time. In the nineteenth century, the hackney horse was the most popular coach horse developed in England. Back in the naming period, there was Benedict de Hakeneye in 1275 and Adam Hakenay in 1316.

The PALFREY names have a common origin—the Old French *palefrei,* meaning a saddle-horse. A modification of it might be given to anyone associated with the saddle-horse. But in common usage, it indicated either a horse gentle enough for a lady to ride, or the man in charge of such horses. John Palfreyman is listed in 1279 and John Palframan just a century later, in 1379.

The POTTERELL names are not very widespread today. Their origin was an Old French word, *potrel,* or, in Latin, *pultrellus,* meaning "a colt." It might have been a nickname. The six PULLAN names originate from the Old French word *poulain,* which also meant "colt."

The SIMMER names, plus SUMPTER and SUNTER, indicate men who drove packhorses. A packhorse was, of course, a horse used for carrying goods and merchandise. The driver, or SUMPTER, might ride another horse alongside his packhorse or he might walk. William le Sumeter is mentioned in 1221.

STABELER and STABLER derive from the Old French *establier,* meaning "stable keeper." Laurence le Stabler is recorded in 1196 and Alan le Establer in 1257.

The four STEADMAN names seem to go back to the Old English word *stede,* meaning a caretaker of horses rather than a breeder. Many examples of the name are in the records, such as Roger Stedman in 1275 and Henry le Stedman, or Stedeman, in 1285.

The STODART names derive from the Old English *stod* (meaning "stud") combined with the word for "herd." A man named Stodherda is listed in 1195, Stodhirde in 1286, and Geoffrey Stodhurd in 1219. STOTHARD, STOTHART, STOTHERT, and STUTTARD, according to P. H. Reaney, come from an Old English word *stott* meaning an inferior kind of horse. Quite possibly this is so, but, in any case, they were horse breeders.

GROUP 94

Peasant-Farmers

Ackerman	Beemaster	Coatman	Felders
Ackers	Bees	Coats	Field
Ackley	Beman	Coatts	Fielden
Ackres	Bemister	Cote	Fielder
Acors	•	Cotes	Fielders
Acraman	Bisgood	Cotherill	Fieldhouse
Acreman	(*see* Peascod)	Cotman	Fielding
Acres	•	Cotter	Fields
Akerman	Bond	Cotteral	Fieldsend
Akers	Bondi	Cotterel	•
Akess	Bonds	Cotterell	Dunger
Akkers	Bondy	Cottier	•
Akre	Bound	Cottis	Farmar
•	Bounds	Cottle	Farmer
Apple	Boundy	Cottrell	Fermer
Appleman	Bounday	Cottrill	Fermor
Appleton	Bundey	Dallicoat	•
Appleyard	Bundy	Dallicott	Fifefeild
•	•	De la Cote	Fifefield
Bean	Cherriman	Delicate	Fifehead
Beane	Cherry	•	Fifett
Been	Cherryman	De La Feld	Fifield
•	•	(*see* Velden)	Fifoot
Beaman	Coat	Delafield	•
Bee	Coate	Feild	Fouracre
Beeman	Coates	Feilding	Fouracres

Foweraker

•

Franck

Francke

Francklin

Francklyn

Francom

Francombe

Frank

Frankcombe

Frankham

Franklen

Franklin

Frankling

Franklyn

Frankom

Franks

Frankum

•

Free

Freeberne

Freebody

Freeborn

Freeborne

Freeburn

Freeland

Freeman

Friman

Fry

Frye

Fryman

•

Gairdner

Garden

Gardener

Gardenner

Gardiner

Gardinor

Gardner

Gardyne

•

Grainge

Grainger

Grange

Granger

Graynger

•

Harrowar

Harrower

Harwar

•

Hayman

Heaman

Heyman

Highman

Hyman

•

Hide

Hider

Hides

Hyde

Hyder

Hydes

•

Honeyman

Honneyman

Honyman

•

Hosbons

Husband

Husbands

•

Lathe

Leath

Leathe

•

Layton

Leighton

Leyton

Lighten

Lighton

•

Leak

Leake

Leaker

Leck

Leckman

Leek

Leekman

Leeks

Leker

•

Mawer

Mower

•

Pearch

Pearcher

Pearchman

•

Pearman

•

Peascod

(*see* Bisgood)

Pease

Peasegood

Pescod

Pescodd

Pescott

Pescud

Peskett

•

Plant

Plante

Planter

Plantman

•

Plewman

Ploughman

Plowman

•

Reaper

•

Seader

•

Tasker

•

Thrasher

Thresher

•

Tiley

Tiller

Tilley

Tillie

Tillier

Tillman

Tilly

Tillyer

Tilyer

Tylee

Tyley

•

Velden

(*see* De La Feld)

•

Vilain

Villain

Villin

•

Werkman

Workman

•

Wort

Worter

Wortman

Worts

Wortt

•

Yeaman

Yeman

Yeoman

Yeomans

Youmans

GROUP 95

The Dairy Business

CHEESE

Cheasman
Cheese
Cheeseman
Cheeseright
Cheesewright
Cheesman
Cheeswright
Cherrett
Cherritt
Chesemaker
Cheseman
Chesemonger
Cheser
Chesewright
Chesewringer
(*see* Wringer)
Chesman
Chessman
Chesswright
Cheswright
Chiese
Chieseman
Chisman

Chismon
•
Chessex
(*see* Wheeker)
Cheswick
Chissick
Chiswick
•
Ewart (*see*
Yeoward)
•
Fenwick
Finnick
Vinick
•
Ferminger
Firmage
Firmager
Firminger
Furmage
Furmager
Furmedge
Furmenger
Furminger

•
Wheeker
(*see* Chessex)
Whicker
Whickman
Wicken
Wickens
Wickers
Wickins
Wickman
Wringer
(*see* Chesewringer)
•
Yeoward
(*see* Ewart)
Yeowart
Youatt
•
MILK

Day
Daye
Dayman
D'eye
Dey

Deyes
•
Milk
•
BUTTER

Buterer
Buttar
Butter
Butterer'
Butterfield
Butterman
Buttermilk
Butters
Butterworth
Buttrick
•
Churn
Churner
•
Smerekerner
Smereman
Smeremonger

GROUP 96

Cattle Tenders

Best
Bestar
Beste
Bester
Bestman

•
Bier
Bierrum
Biers
Biram

Buyers
Byars
Byers
Byram
Byran

Byre
Byres
Byrom
Byron
•

Bool	•	Faulds	Hird
Boole	Boosey	Fold	Hord
Bools	•	Folder	Horder
Bull	Booth	Foldes	Hurd
Bullas	Boothe	Folds	Hurdman
Bullass	•	Fould	•
Bulle	Calvard	Fouldes	Oxenford
Bullen	Calver	Foulds	Oxer
Buller	Calverd	Fowlds	Oxford
Bulley	Calvert	•	Oxman
Bullis	•	Fodor	Oxnard
Bullman	Coward	•	•
Bullmer	Cowe	Heard	Stear
Bullock	Cowherd	Hearder	Stears
Bullocke	Cowman	Heardman	Steer
Bullus	•	Herd	Steere
Bully	Drover	Herder	Steers
Bulman	•	Herdman	
Bulpin	Faulder	Herdsman	

GROUP 97

The Meat Business

Backner	•	•	Slaughter
Bacon	Budiner	Ketmonger	Slayter
Bakon	•	•	Slaytor
•	Bukmarter	Knatchbull	Sleator
Boucher	Bukmonger	•	•
Boutcher	•	Macecrer	Stikker
Bowcher	Flesher	Macegre	•
Bowker	Fleshhewer	Maskery	Trenchard
Bucher	Fleshmonger	Maskrey	
Butcher	•	•	
Butchers	Kellogg	Slagter	

GROUP 98

Swineherds

A'Bear	Grice	Hogge	Styer
Abear	Grise	Hogger	•
•	Grisewood	Hoggett	Swain
Denn	Griss	•	Swaine
Denne	Le Grice	Huddart	Swayn
•	Le Grys	Woodard	Swayne
Foreman	•	•	•
Forman	Hogarth	Pigg	Swinerd
Forward	Hogg	Pigge	Swinnard
Forwood	Hoggar	•	Swinyard
Fourman	Hoggard	Porcher	
•	Hoggarth	•	

GROUP 99

Goat Keepers

Gait	Gaitt	Geater	Goater
Gaite	Gayter	Geator	Goatman
Gaiter	Gayther	Goatard	Gothard
Gaites	Gaytor	Goate	

GROUP 100

Poultry Keepers

Chicken	Duckers	Gosere	•
•	Duckes	Gosmanger	Poulter
Doak	Duckhouse	•	Puleter
Dooks	•	Henmonger	
Duck	Gelyner	Henn	
Duckels	•	Hennman	

GROUP 101

Caretakers of the Horses

Cappleman	Marschall	Powdrill	Stedmond
•	Marshall	Putterill	Steedman
Colt	Marskell	Puttrell	•
Coltard	Mascall	•	Stodart
Coltart	Maskall	Pullan	Stoddard
Colter	Maskell	Pullein	Stoddart
Colthard	Maskill	Pulleine	Stodder
Colthart	•	Pullen	Stodhard
Coltman	Palfery	Pulleyn	Stodhart
Coult	Palframan	Pullin	Stothert
Coulthard	Palfreeman	•	Studart
Coulthart	Palfreman	Simmer	Studdard
•	Palfrey	Simmers	Studdeard
Constable	Palfreyman	Sumpter	Studdert
•	Palphreyman	Sunter	Studdy
Corser	Parffrey	Symmers	Studman
Cossar	Parfrement	Symers	Stuttard
Cosser	Parfreyman	•	
•	•	Stabeler	
Hackney	Potterell	Stabler	
Hakeney	Potterill	•	
Hakney	Pottrill	Steadman	
•	Powdrell	Stedmann	

CHAPTER **15**

Millers, Sieve Makers, Bakers, Spicers, and Salters

Grinding wheat into flour is easily one of man's most ancient achievements. Primitive man could obtain meat by killing small game and he could supplement this diet with nuts, berries, and fruits, but bread is something different: it demands some technical skill.

First, man had to learn to recognize the wheat plant when he saw it growing wild; then he had to discover that he could grow a new crop if he planted some of the seeds in the ground. Just this step alone may have taken centuries. But even after reaching this advanced stage, he was still a long way from bread. A way had to be found to grind the wheat into flour and, in the process, to get rid of as much of the husk as possible. Once this was done, flour could be mixed with water and the resulting dough would be edible if it were flattened into a cake and heated on a hot piece of stone. This produced something that could be called bread.

The first millers were probably cave dwellers; their primitive flat stones have been found in many places and always near such a stone is another, rather cone-shaped stone that fits into the hand to do the grinding, like a pestle. A flat stone allowed too much of the wheat to fall over the edges, so a large stone was hollowed out to produce the ancient ancestor of the mortar. Over many centuries, these stones would be enlarged or improved in many ways, but the method would still be essentially that of a mortar and pestle, as it depended on pounding action more than on an ability to grind.

Eventually, along came something that could be called a mill. It consisted of a very heavy disk of stone with a hole bored in the middle, turning on a vertical shaft. Under this, separated by a tiny fraction of an inch, would be another disk of stone, only this one would be firmly fixed so that it could not move. Each stone had a series of grooves cut into their adjacent surfaces. The upper stone would be called the runner and the lower one the bedder. This was the heart of the gristmill. The grain would be funneled through the hole in the runner into the minute space between the stones, where the whirling motion of the runner ground the wheat into flour and caused it to drop out around the perimeter. From here, the flour, still mixed with husk, dropped into some kind of a sifting device designed to remove the husk or the outer covering of the grain.

Needless to say, it took a lot of muscle to turn that runner stone and to keep it turning from sunrise to sunset. Improving this mechanism was to be a problem for the best mechanical brains of Europe for centuries. Horses, mules, or oxen could be used, but they were very slow; the power of either water or air in motion would be much more satisfactory if a way of using it could be devised.

Both waterpower and wind power seem to have been developed at about the same time. The windmill is generally associated with the Netherlands, probably because the Dutch have always made their mills so picturesque that they have tempted generations of artists to reproduce them on canvas and tile, but the fact seems to be that windmills developed simultaneously all over Europe.

One difficulty of working with a windmill is that a constant supply of wind blowing directly into its saillike arms is needed to keep it running. Obviously, wind direction could not be controlled, but one could adjust the mill so that when the wind changed, the mill could be turned around until once again facing directly into it. This meant putting the mill on a huge wooden pivot and manually turning the whole structure every time the wind changed. These mills were common for many years, in England as elsewhere; they became known as "post" mills because of the great heavy timber post that characterized them.

The next development was to attach the sail to the roof of the mill and simply turn the roof around to bring the sail into the wind. This enabled one to build a big solid mill from stone, weighing vastly more than the old post mill since only its top would have to move. This was known as the tower mill.

Then came the water-driven mill. According to Robert S. Hoyt, author of *Europe in the Middle Ages,* no less than five thousand watermills were running in England by the end of the eleventh century.

Watermills had the advantage of always drawing their power from the same direction, but they did need a volume of water running swiftly enough to keep that mill running. This took some good mechanical judgment on the part of the millwright. If the stream was fast-flowing and seemed apt to stay that way, he could put the waterwheel directly in the stream. If the land fell away sharply, he might dig out a pond where he could collect a volume of water that could then be channeled to drop in a steady stream onto the top of the wheel. This was the "overshot" wheel, the most efficient type of waterwheel ever developed.

The life of a community more or less depended on the products of a mill. The Saxon *eorls* had long recognized this and had, accordingly, established the rule that the lord of the manor should own the only mill in his manorial district. This forced every peasant to bring his grain to the lord for grinding and, of course, this allowed his lordship to keep a goodly share of it. When the Normans arrived, this was one of the few Anglo-Saxon customs they immediately approved of. They did change it slightly: they *raised* the lord's share.

This vicious practice died a natural death before the end of the twelfth century. The population was growing so fast and the grain being produced was increasing so rapidly that the Norman lords could not keep up their monopoly.

The miller who had operated the lord's mill may have continued to do so; only now he had competition. It would be nice to report that this competition tended to make the millers honest, but this was definitely not the case. There were just new tricks devised to fleece a peasant of his grain. One trick was to put an extra chute under the mill that terminated in a small bin hidden out of sight. A part of each grind would end up there and no one would be the wiser except the miller. Another trick was to put square housing over the round millstone, which would allow flour to accumulate in the corners of the housing. This would be removed after the day's work was over and the customers were gone.

GROUP 102

Millers

Virtually every one of the fifty-seven names on the list of Group 102 (see page 219) comes from the word *miller*, from the meal produced and sold, or from particular parts of the mill. The amount of names is not large when one considers that there must have been well over five thousand gristmills scattered throughout many hundreds of communities for a period of two hundred and fifty years. The word mill comes from a slightly mixed origin: the Old English word *mylen* means a mill and the Old Norman word *mylnari* means a man who operated a mill—in short, a MILLER.

MELEMAKER, MILLMAKER, and MILLWRIGHT were probably applied to a man who made or designed gristmills, and MELE-MONGER probably belongs to a man who sold meal (though it is doubtful that anyone sold meal he had not made himself).

MILLWARD could be said to mean a mill watchman—the word *ward* has appeared before and always means somebody who watches something. Undoubtedly, the millowner of those times was also the watchman.

GRINDER and GRYNDER almost certainly meant a MILLER, as grinding was his job. William le Grindere is recorded in 1230 and Stephen le Grindar in 1274. He could have been a grinder of tools, but it is unlikely.

BURR, BURRMAN, and BURWRIGHT were probably not millers but they certainly were very much in the milling industry—they made the all-important millstones, sometimes called burrstones. Hugo Burr is listed in 1185.

CORNMONGER simply meant a man who sold grain of any kind.

FARINER was a general name for a man who sold meal of all kinds. Richard le Fariner was in business in 1305.

The origin of FLOWER and FLOWERS is not too clear. Possibly they come down to us from an Old English word *fla*, giving a sense of "arrowmaker" but they were probably used more often as a nickname to describe a miller who sold only the best—the flower of the crop. Robert le Flourmakere appears in 1320.

HAUERMAN specifically tells us that the grain the man worked with was oats. It derives from the Norman French *hafre*. The same applies to OTMONGER: he sold oats, but you can be sure he milled oats too. Thomas le Otmonger carried on his trade in 1300.

QUERNESTER is interesting because a Juliana la Quernestre is listed in 1333. Both the surname and the given name show clearly that this miller was a lady. The name comes from the Old English word *cweorn* which meant a small handmill. This lady may have persisted in its use long after all others in her neighborhood had given their business to the regular mill.

The two WINDMILL names are obvious, and perhaps at least one of them may have been given to the first man in his area to build a mill run on wind power. John atte Wyndmylle is listed in 1360.

GROUP 103

Sieve Makers

In the very early part of the naming period, mere ownership of a practical sieve must have given a lucky individual positive assurance of steady and profitable employment. Sieves that could do even a moderately good job of sifting flour for the miller were extremely hard to acquire. The metalworkers had learned how to draw wire, but the craft was still unable to make wire fine enough for a sieve.

The best sieves at this time had to be imported from the Gallic provinces, where they were made from horsehair, although the Spanish had developed a meal-sifter made from flax and the Egyptians were making sieves from papyrus. All were very coarse by today's standards.

The miller and the baker were helpless without at least reasonably good sifting equipment, and the potter, too, was in desperate straits without any.

The first seventeen names, BOLT through BULTEEL, have a common origin in the Norman word *buleteor,* meaning a sifter of meal. This word seems to have been applied carelessly to almost anyone even remotely connected with sifting and sieves. BONFELLOW, BOUGHT-FLOWER, and BOUTFLOUR are merely variations. We find Roger le Buleter in 1246, Roger Le Boleter in 1261, John Bultell as late as 1524, and many more generally similar in character. Most of them derive from the sieve and its uses or users, although the English had a word *bolt,* meaning a bolt made of iron or the short arrow used by the crossbowmen (see Chapter 8). Then, when the WEAVERS came out with a fairly fine woven piece of linen that could be used for sifting, it was called "bolting cloth," and it still is today. It is unfortunate that we are unable to pinpoint the origin of these old names more exactly, but until more research is done, this will have to suffice.

CREARER, CRERAR, and CRERER first appeared in A.D. 1500, a little late for the naming period, but they have survived regardless. They are Gaelic in origin, from the word *cirathrar,* and meant a sifter or one who made such things. John McAchrerar and William Crerar appear on the tax rolls.

CRIBLUR comes from the Old French word *cribleur,* meaning "a sifter." RIDLER definitely belongs with the sieve names. It comes from the Anglo-Saxon word *ridelen,* meaning "to sift," or from the Middle English word *hriddel,* meaning "a sieve." Andrew le Rydelere registered in 1230.

The remaining names, beginning with SEAVERS, derive from the Old English word *sife* and its verbal form, *siflen*. Those with the *wright* ending mean sieve makers. The other names could have been given to sieve makers too, but the chances are very much against this. It is much more reasonable to think of them either as sieve users or even as owners of sifting equipment that could be leased to millowners. The large variation in the spelling in this group may be an indication of the importance of the sieve and its contribution to the industry of that time. The earliest recorded use of a name from this group seems to be Simon le Siuwricht in 1219, then in 1301, John le Syvewryct. Bearers of these names can be thankful that our spelling has improved since then.

GROUP 104

Bakers

Certainly the Greeks and the Romans baked bread, although it is doubtful that they ever produced any bread that would be called white today. Their milling and sifting of flour fell far short of modern standards. They did have yeast, however, although its action was so little understood that a Roman baker must have been driven to distraction at times. In any case, the bread of the common people throughout Europe for some centuries was apt to be unleavened cakes made by mixing flour with water, adding some salt, making a patty of it, and cooking it as best one could on a slab of hot stone, or by covering it with hot ashes. This produced something edible and nourishing even though it might be lacking in other respects. One could always make one's precious flour go a little farther by adding meal made from dried beans.

The situation in medieval England was not much better than in ancient Rome. The common run of people ate oatcakes cooked on a piece of hot stone. For variety, they might substitute wheat or barley flour along with whatever adulterant they might have. Raised bread, in the early medieval period, was a luxury that could be enjoyed only by the lord of the manor and his noble friends. On a holy day, and fortunately there were many, the peasants might be invited to eat in the castle or manor house, or inside the bailey at least, and then they were given raised bread. It would have only a small resemblance to our bread today, but it was a luxury at that time.

The reason for the scarcity of raised bread was not a shortage of leavening agents—foam skimmed off a vat of beer or ale in the making was used—it was a shortage of ovens.

Oatcakes could be made at home in a few minutes with no such thing as an oven required, but regular bread demanded a substantially built oven in which a hot fire could be built and maintained until the stonework was thoroughly hot. Then one raked out all the fire and ashes, put in one's raised loaves, closed the door, and waited a couple of hours or more. Bear in mind this was long before the day when a proper fireplace could be found in the cottage of a peasant. A fireplace was still something quite new even in the great castle, although it would have an oven and, with the oven, the very necessary mixing and kneading troughs and tables and dough-raising box. Consequently, in the eleventh and early twelfth centuries, raised bread was made only in the castles and monasteries where they would have both the space and the ability to install the equipment.

As time went on and the houses of the people grew larger, some enterprising young BAKER, who may have served an apprenticeship with the baker in the castle, determined to build an oven for himself. With the help of a mason friend, an oven was built, and he was in business. Now he could hire a boy to carry his bread in a basket from door to door. He might have to take his pay in odds and ends, but that was expected in those days. For the record, the establishment of bread-baking as an independent industry by professional bakers met with some stern opposition from the nobility. The lord of the manor had long been accustomed to taking a nice profit from any peasant with the nerve and the cash to buy bread from the manor bakery, and he was not going to allow upstart competition to deprive him of his "rights" without a fight.

But the independent bakers won their fight, although not before they had to accept some very strict rules. A standard loaf of bread had to weigh just so much, and if a baker sold a loaf that weighed less, and was caught, the short-weighted loaf would be tied around his neck and he would be led through the streets of the town, to the delight of the populace. If a baker sold a dozen of some item and it developed that the count was one or two shy, then he had to sell thirteen the next time. Thus, the "baker's dozen" became a fixture everywhere.

Bread was not the only item the baker made, as the very large group of names from the craft of baking indicates.

The nineteen BAKER names come from the Old English *baechus,* meaning "a bakery," or *baecere,* meaning "a man who bakes." BAKER was generally spelled BACKER for many centuries, so a name such as BACKHOUSE did not refer to the position of a man's house, but rather meant BAKE HOUSE and probably referred to a lean-to at the back of a man's house where he did the baking. BACAS, BACCAS, BACCHUS, and so forth are all simple contractions. Early examples of the name would be William le Bakere in 1177 and Walter le Backere in 1280, Walter de Bakhouse in 1306, and Richard Bakhous in 1332.

The Old English word *baccestre* indicated a female baker while *baecere* was for a male BAKESTER was therefore first applied to a female, but in popular usage it soon became BAXTER, and even BACUS, BACAS, and BACKES. BAKEWELL was undoubtedly a complimentary name. Hanne Bakestre is listed in 1260, William le Baxtere in 1333, and Walter Bakman in 1278.

The four BARLEY names hardly need an explanation. They derive from the Old English *barli*, and the holders were bakers of barley bread. John Barlich appears in 1279.

BLAMPHIN and PLAMPIN show little resemblance to *blanc* and *pain*, but those are the Old French words from which they derive, and they referrred to a man who baked white bread.

BOLENGER, BOULANGER, BULLINGER, PILLINGER, and POLLINGER were all bakers. The names derive from the Old French *bolonger*.

CAKE, CAKEBREAD, and CAKES were cakemakers. The Middle English root is *kake*. John le Kakier is in the records of 1292.

DOGHERE, DOWER, and DOWERS come from the Old English word *dah*, meaning "a man who makes dough." A John le Douar appears in 1332 and a William le Dougher in 1333.

FAGG, FAGGE, VAGG, and VAGGS are a little bit out of the ordinary. The root word in Old French meant "clean," and it seems to have been applied to bread. Are we to assume that some bakers were not particularly clean and accordingly those who were clean were singled out in this way?

A FLANNER was a baker who baked FLAWNS or FLANNS. This medieval delicacy must have been the ancestor of the modern coffee-cake. At that time, there was no coffee to name it after. It came from the Old French word *flaunier*. Simon le Flanner is listed in 1262.

FOURNIER and FURNER also refer to bakers, but these men were more interested in selling pies and pastry than bread. The names derive from the Old French word *fornier* meaning "baker." From the tax records come Simon Furner in 1208 and Martin le Forner in 1283.

KETCHELL and KITCHELL, from the Middle English word *kechel*, seem to have originated with a small cake that might occasionally be given in alms. The name of the cake became the name of the man who either made it or gave it away. John Kechel is listed in 1221.

The name KNEDER was given to a man who kneaded the dough.

OVENS, from the Old English word *ofen,* may be another name coming from a baker's equipment. The earliest record of it is a bit hard to recognize—John Attenouene in 1299.

PASTER meant "a maker of pastry." PASTER might easily be mistaken for PASTOR, but they are entirely different both in origin and application. PASTER is from the Old French word *paste,* meaning "dough," particularly the more tender kind that is associated today with pastry. John Pastemakere appears in 1340, and Gilbert Paste in 1210.

PIE, PYBAKER, and PYE did just what their names indicate. The three names came from the Old French word *pye.* Peter Piebakere in 1320, William le Pye in 1296, and John Pyman in 1354 appear on the records. The English have always been particularly fond of pies, above all those made from meat.

The four PEEL names are a problem. Elsdon C. Smith in his new and very fine volume on American surnames indicates that the name comes from an old place-name—Peel Fortress on the Isle of Man. I am not prepared to disagree with this, but there is equally strong evidence that at least some of these names come from a very simple tool used by bakers a thousand years ago and *still* part of their standard equipment, the baker's PEEL. This is a very long, wooden, paddlelike tool that the baker uses to put loaves in the hot oven or take them out. The origin of the baker's PEEL is completely unknown, but we do know that English bakers in this period were using it in every town and village on the island.

WAFER and WAFERER refer to a man who gained at least a local reputation for baking cakes. The Anglo-French word is *wafre,* meaning "small cakes." There was a Simon le Wafre in 1212.

WAISTELL, WASHTELL, WASSALL, WASSELL, WASTALL, WASTELL, and WASTLER, as well as GASTALL, are all examples of inconsistent spelling. They all mean exactly the same thing: a baker who made bread that was so good, it was called a *wastel* instead of just another loaf of bread. The Old French word for it was *wastel,* meaning "bread made of the finest flour," and naturally a man making wastels might be called a WASTLER. John Wasteler is recorded in 1327.

WHITBREAD and WHITEBREAD suggest their source: the Old English word *hwit* and *bread.* They were given to bakers who evidently convinced somebody that they made superior bread, which at that time meant bread that was whiter than the common run. The earliest record of the name seems to be Robert Witbred in 1279.

WIGGER and WIGMAN, WYGGER and WYGGSTER refer to a baker who made wigs. These particular wigs had nothing to do with hair; in Old English, a wig was a cake made in the shape of a wedge.

GROUP 105

The Spice Business

In general, it must be said the food of the medieval English was neither good nor palatable. As has been noted earlier, their beef was grass-fed until the arrival of winter, when all but breeding stock or animals destined for heavy work would be butchered and the meat salted down. Grain-finished cattle and aged beef were unheard of. Under these circumstances, tough, stringy beef was inevitable. Their pork must have been particularly bad, since their pigs fed on acorns and whatever they could find in their wanderings.

In season, there was a fair variety of fruits and vegetables, but they knew of no way to preserve them, so it was feast or famine. They had no tea, coffee, or chocolate, and no sugar whatever—honey was the only sweetening known.

At times, when the hunting was good, game would be plentiful but it was limited strictly to the table of the nobility. The common folk ate soup and black bread for breakfast, and salt fish and vegetables washed down with ale in the evening. Meat, such as it was, might be eaten once a week during most of the year. During the late fall when domestic animals were being butchered, people ate meat to the exlusion of everything else. During this time, the meat would be fresh and very tough and would be roasted or broiled. After a few days of this feasting, the meat that remained had to be covered with a thick coat of salt and packed away in barrels to be eaten during the ensuing months. Heavily salted beef, particularly when the salt used is rank with impurities, does not lend itself to either broiling or roasting; consequently, most beef was boiled, even in the great castles and manor houses. To those who have inadvertently allowed the fiction writers and artists to create an image of medieval banqueting—the roaring fire with cooks serving great portions of meat off smoking hot broiling spits at each table and always a great roasted pig with an apple in its mouth—this may be somewhat disturbing. This sort of thing *did* happen but it was only at Christmastime or on some other big feast day. Day in and day out through most of the year, it would be boiled meat or fish with monotonous regularity.

But something was developing in the Far East that was going to help this situation—not a cure, but certainly an improvement in the drab cooking and eating habits of the people of the Middle Ages. It was the addition of spices to cookery.

It was found that a dash of pepper, a little cinnamon or ginger, when mixed with the coarsest dishes would change them entirely and make them both tasty and nourishing. The demand for spices spread like fire all over Europe. People found that eating became a real pleasure. Pepper was the first, and by the eleventh century, it was in so much demand that it cost as much as pure silver. Many communities kept their accounts in pepper, and taxes were assessed and paid in pepper. Sailors arriving on ships were forbidden shore leave if they insisted on carrying a package ashore, because even a tiny parcel of peppercorns would make them wealthy, at least temporarily.

Cloves added to ham proved sensational; cinnamon mixed with honey and added to bread opened a whole new outlook, and nutmeg—what wonders could be done with it! Mustard now grows in England but at that time it was another wonderful discovery that could make a cook the most popular man in the whole castle. And the man who invented sausage simply by adding pepper, coriander, and a little nutmeg to ground pork must have been a hero of the time.

All this didn't happen overnight, of course; it took a number of years because of the difficulty in transportation. Venice was for several centuries the center of European trade. Ships from the Spice Islands in the East Indies would unload in Venice, where they would be met by merchants from all parts of Europe. Sometimes cargoes would be auctioned off, but more often it was a matter of long and painful haggling between the oriental and the merchant. Once a deal was made, the merchant would either load up his caravan and set off over the mountains or load it into his ship and start west. In either case, he could be certain that he would be stopped numerous times to pay tribute to some local brigand or some pirate on the high seas. It did not matter too much—he could easily cover his losses when he arrived in his market, whether London, Paris, or the Low Countries.

We can get some idea of the terrific amount of spices the English people used back in those days from the following statistic: Edward I (1272–1307) used 1,600 pounds of spices in the year 1301—this, of course, included the royal household.

All five SPICE names definitely come from the Old French word *especier*. This meant a *dealer* in spices. Whether he did a large business or whether he was a small-time peddler cannot be known. Some of the early records of the name are Robert le Spiecer in 1201, Hugo Especer in 1214, and Clement Spice in 1300.

CANNEL, CANNELL, and CANNELMAN point directly back to a merchant who sold cinnamon. The Old French way of saying cinnamon was *canele*. Richard Cannell appears in 1328.

CARKER and CHARKER are quite interesting. They derive from the Middle English word *carke* and the Anglo-French *karke*, and originally meant 300 to 400 pounds. The term seems to have been used only in reference to spices, herbs, and such. Thus, a dealer might buy a kark of pepper or ginger or cinnamon. Such a man must have been a substantial merchant. I have found a Wulgor le Carkere in 1166.

FENNEL, FENNELL, and FENNELMAN derive from the Old English word *fenol* and refer to the herb fennel. Medieval cooks found that the leaves of this plant could be dried and powdered and kept for a long time. When added to a sauce, they made it fit for a king. Christian Fenel was recorded in 1328.

The five names starting with GARLEKMONGER tell their own story, as do GINGER and GINGERMAN. An early example of the former is Gilbert Garlek in 1277. In the case of the latter, the Old English word was *gyngure*. Robert GINGIURE is listed in 1221. He may well have been one of the first dealers to introduce ginger to his community.

LEAK through LEKMAN were names given to men who raised or at least sold leeks, a vegetable belonging to the onion family. Many years ago it became so popular in Britain that it was made the floral emblem of Wales. The fact that there are ten family names that come directly from it is further proof of its appeal. Ralph de Lek in 1202 and Hug le Lekman in 1319 are just a few of the names recorded in the tax records.

The MUSTARD names derive from the Old French word *mostarde*. I found a William MUSTARD in 1191 and a John le Mustarder in 1327.

All the PEEVER through PEPPERS names belonged to dealers in spices, and probably PEPPER was their main item. The word *pepper* comes from an Old English word *pipor*. An Alice Peper is registered in London in 1197.

The Norman French, of course, had their own word for PEPPER—it was *peyvre* and PEEVER, PEEVERS, and PEFFER come from this word. There is William Peyforer in 1293 and Andrew le Peyfrer in 1200.

The PESTELL names also come from the spice business. The Old French word is *pestel*. The mortar and pestle were standard equipment for anyone in the spice trade, as well as for the miller and the baker. A dealer probably had to spend a considerable part of his time reducing large chunks of various spices to a powder for his customers. A tax man who happened in at one of those moments and was impressed with the way the pestle worked in the practiced hands of the dealer might name him accordingly. There was a Mr. Nicholas Pestel in 1221 and a Symon Pystel in 1296.

PORER is an Old French name. William le Porer far back in 1285 raised leeks and other vegetables for the market.

POTHECARY and POTTICARY are very interesting old names. The Normans had a name for a merchant who sold spices, drugs, and preserves—it was *apotecaire*. As the centuries passed, he became a *chemist* in London, while in America he became a *druggist*. The very earliest record of the name I can find is William Apotecarius, in the Latin form, in 1283.

GROUP 106

The Salt Business

The use of salt was already an ancient practice before written history. The Romans probably borrowed the custom from the Greeks and they in turn, from still earlier cultures.

Great underground ledges of salt occur in many places. Today many of these are systematically mined; in fact, most of the salt we use today comes from such operations. In medieval England, this was not the case. At that time, the ocean surrounding England was the most practical source. The water of the ocean offered one advantage and one disadvantage: although the supply of raw material never diminished, her bountiful nature had put fairly large quantities of other chemicals in it. When they were not taken out, the resulting salt contained several percentage points of rather sharp, bitter, and acid chemicals. These chemicals are not deadly to humans, but when they are present, salt is not nearly as agreeable.

In medieval England, evaporating sea water and recovering the mixture of salts was a fairly large business. A number of salt boilers are supposed to have made comfortable fortunes out of the business.

SALT and SALTER usually meant a man in the salt business, and the next seven names through SAWTER meant exactly the same thing. SALTHOUSE would indicate a storehouse for the product, and thus probably a dealer. There are plenty of early examples, like John Saltman in 1327 and Philip le Salter in 1243. However, there was also a harplike musical instrument called a psaltery that may account for some of the SALT names.

Reaney believes that WELLER was a salt boiler too.

GROUP 102

Millers

Burr	Meals	Millman	Molins
Burrman	Melemaker	Milln	Mullard
Burwright	Meleman	Millner	Mullinar
•	Melemonger	Millns	Mullinder
Cornmonger	Mellard	Mills	Mulliner
•	Meller	Millward	Mullinger
Fariner	Mellers	Millwood	Mylne
•	Mileward	Millwright	•
Flower	Miliner	Millyard	Otmonger
Flowers	Millar	Miln	•
•	Millard	Milne	Quernester
Grinder	Miller	Milner	•
Grynder	Milles	Milnes	Windmill
•	Millhouse	Milus	Winmill
Hauerman	Milliard	Milward	
•	Millis	Molin	
Meale	Millmaker	Moliner	

GROUP 103

Sieve Makers

Bolt	Bouttell	Ridelester	Seviour
Bolte	Bouttle	Ridler	Sevyer
Bolter	Bowtell	•	Sievwright
Boltman	Bowtle	Seavers	Siuyer
Bonfellow	Bulteel	Seever	Siversyveman
Boughtflour	•	Seeviour	Siverwright
Boult	Crearer	Seivwright	Siveyer
Boulter	Crerar	Sever	Sivier
Boutall	Crerer	Severs	Sivyer
Boutell	Criblur	Severwright	Syvewright
Boutflour	•	Sevier	
Boutle	Rideler	Sevior	

GROUP 104

Bakers

Bacas	•	Flanner	Pybaker
Baccas	Blamphin	Flawn	Pye
Bacchus	Plampin	•	•
Baccusi	•	Fournier	Wafer
Bachus	Bolenger	Furner	Waferer
Backer	Boulanger	•	•
Backes	Bullinger	Gastall (*see*	Waistell (*see*
Backhouse	Pillinger	Waistell)	Gastall)
Backman	Pollinger	•	Washtell
Backus	•	Ketchell	Wassall
Bacus	Cake	Kitchell	Wassell
Bagster	Cakebread	•	Wastall
Baiker	Cakes	Kneder	Wastell
Bakeman	•	•	Wastler
Bakenhus	Doghere	Ovens	•
Baker	Dower	•	Whitbread
Bakester	Dowers	Paster	Whitebread
Bakewell	•		•
Baxter	Fagg	Peal	Wigger
•	Fagge	Peale	Wigman
Barlee	Vagg	Peel	Wygger
Barley	Vaggs	Peele	Wyggster
Barleycorn	•	•	
Barleyman	Flann	Pie	

GROUP 105

The Spice Business

Cannel	•	Fennelman	Garlickman
Cannell	Especer	•	•
Cannelman	(*see* Spice)	Garlekmonger	Ginger
•	•	Garlic	Gingerman
Carker	Fennel	Garlick	•
Charker	Fennell	Garlicke	Leak

Leake	Mustarder	Pepperman	•
Leaker	Mustardman	Peppers	Pothecary
Leakman	Mustart	•	Potticary
Leck	•	Pestell	•
Leek	Peever	Pester	Spice (*see* Especer)
Leeke	Peevers	Pestur	Spicer
Leekman	Peffer	Pistol	Spyce
Leeks	Peppar	Pistor	Spycer
Lekman	Pepper	Pistur	
•	Peppercorn	•	
Mustard	Peppercorne	Porer	

GROUP 106

The Salt Business

Salt	Salthouse	Sauter	•
Salter	Saltman	Sautter	Weller
Salters	Saulter	Sawter	

CHAPTER 16

Shipping and Merchants

More is known about the ships of the Romans and the galleys of the Norsemen than the ships of medieval England. What is known is that during the centuries of the naming period, the English shipbuilders made giant steps forward. It is doubtful that they were able to contribute anything substantial to the art, but they were quick to adopt the ideas used in a ship from the Mediterranean.

At the time of the Conquest, English shipyards existed on the east coast of the island and among the English Channel ports. There they built galleys with twenty to thirty oars on each side, with a steering oar on the starboard side, and a square sail rigged on a single mast. Little or no decking and virtually no housing existed for either crew or cargo. The single square sail enabled them to sail before the wind but if their course were not downwind, they would have to depend on their galleymen to get them there. Their navigation was of the crudest kind. They could steer by the stars on a clear night or by the sun if the sky was not cloudy, but otherwise they had to follow a coastline.

Pirates infested the seas everywhere. A merchant with a cargo of goods from either a Mediterranean or Adriatic port, and headed for England, carried money or valuables of some kind for the precise purpose of paying tribute. There was nothing particularly medieval in piracy; robbery on the high seas was as ancient as shipping itself and would last almost into modern times.

Over the years, shipbuilding improved. Nobody knows just when or where the sternpost rudder was developed but, by the twelfth century, it had largely displaced the time-honored steering oar. The steerboard, from which our word *starboard* comes and which derives from the Anglo-Saxon *steorbord*, had been steering the ships for uncountable centuries. Then came the lateen sail and two and even three masts, The lateen sail along with the old square sail made the ship of that period much more maneuverable, and faster too. By the latter part of the twelfth century, decks were being built—sometimes more than one—and in both the bow and the stern, high housing was being built (giving us the term forecastle). It was originally intended to give an advantage to the crew in meeting an attack from pirates.

The main use of ships during this period was, of course, to transport goods. Passenger-carrying ships would not even be thought of for centuries yet. In general, if a man owned a ship, he was a merchant, and conversely, if a man were a merchant of any size and importance, he would own and operate one or more ships. Silk and olive oil were brought from Italy and all the Mediterranean ports in exchange for tin from Cornwall, as were wines from Spain and Portugal and precious spices from the Far East, by way of Venice. Wool from England was always tradable; some of the best raw wool and even finished goods were produced in medieval England.

Not a great deal is known about the construction details of the medieval ships. They were built entirely of wood—usually with three layers of planking fastened to oak ribs by both tree-nails (large wooden pegs) and, here and there, an iron bolt running through both planking and ribs. The "bolt" would have a head on one end and a washer slipped over the other end; the bolt would be riveted to the washer to make a tight fit.

GROUP 107

Shipbuilders

Shipbuilders at that time and far into the future, until all-iron ships were developed, were a combination of the carpenter and the smith. Such a man came to be given the special name of BOATRIGHT, or any of the variations listed in this group. SHIPWRIGHT may well have been the earliest name given to the man who plied this trade. A John le Shipwright is recorded as early as 1309. SHIPWRIGHT came directly from the Old English word *scipwyrhta*. BOTWRIGHT came along a little later but it obviously meant the same thing. John Botwright is recorded in 1469.

ANKERSMYTH was discussed in chapter 5 with the smiths. Men so named were specialists in making anchors and other ironwork used in the construction and sailing of ships of that time.

The ASHMAN names seem out of place, but they come from a very old Anglo-Saxon word, *aescmann,* meaning a shipman, a sailor, or even a pirate. This indicates that the line between a sailor and a pirate was sometimes rather shadowy. Roger Asman in 1319 was probably a sailor, since a pirate would hardly find himself on the tax rolls!

BARGE meant a very small sailing vessel. It derives from the Old French word *barga* and was applied to men who sailed such vessels, probably in the numerous bays and rivers of the island. Peter del Barge in 1309 was one such example.

BOATER through BOTTAN derive from the Old English word for boat, *bat* (pronounced *baht*). John Botere is recorded in 1279, Thomas Bootman in 1225, and Thomas Botman in 1371. BOATSWAIN and BOESON appeared in the eleventh century, even before the Conquest. The native English had a word, *batswegen,* meaning a boatman of any kind, so it is easy to see how it developed into BOATSWAIN (which is now pronounced as it was written [BOESON] anyway). The earliest example of the name I have found is Wicing Batswegen in 1050.

The FERRIER names are from the Old English word *feri.* This would mean a man who owned or operated a ferryboat—and there were a great many in a day when bridges were few and far between. Richard le Feriman appears in 1247.

FLOATER and the four names in the same group all come from *flota* which to the early English simply meant "a ship." Any man known to be attached to a *flota* might be called FLOTE or some convenient variation of it. Ralph le Floter is listed in 1219 and Roger Flote in 1215.

All five GALLEY names come from either the Old French word *galie* or the Middle English *galai*—both simply meant a galley type of ship, and if a man were attached to such a ship, he might very well find himself named after it, like Henry Galye in 1218.

GALLIOT and GALLIOTT come from the Old French word *galiot,* meaning "a sailor in a galley." In the course of time, the word came to mean "a pirate." I find only one example, William Galyot, in 1275.

KELMAN and KELMAKER are particularly interesting. The English of that period had a word *kele,* meaning "a ship," and so a KELMAN or KELMAKER could be just another name for a shipbuilder. It is possible, however, that the name could have had a more specific meaning. It could have been given to a man experienced in the making of keels for ships.

This means more than one might think. Ships had been built for centuries without keels. Just where and when the first ship was built with a keel is not known, but the addition of a keel was of enormous importance. It might be that the two keel names from the thirteenth century were given to pioneers in keel-making. A KELMAN or a KELMAKER would certainly be hired by a shipbuilder because of his specialized skill with the new invention. William Kelman worked in 1257 and John Keleman in 1328. KELLAR and KELLER, however, might also be names given to makers of cauls (women's hairnets). The anglian word *keller* means just that.

MARINER and its two variants also meant "sailor." They all derive from the Anglo-French *mariner*. Hugo le Marinier is recorded in 1197.

OREWRIGHT is somewhat unusual today, but its origin is very simple. It meant a man who made oars, and it derives from the Old English word for oar, *ar,* and the familiar *wyrhta* for "maker." Galleys had to have a lot of oars; even a fairly small galley would have to have sixty of them, not counting all the spares that they would have to carry along, and this represented a lot of very exacting workmanship. Today an oar is made on a specially built lathe that turns out one or more oars a minute all day long. But in the naming period, making an oar not only in the correct size but more importantly, in balance, must have been an all-day job for a genuinely skilled woodworker. It is surprising that the craft of oar-making did not leave more names. Richard le Orewrycthe in 1332 is the only example I have found.

PICHER, PITCHER, and PITCHERS were workers in shipyards who caulked seams with pitch. William le Picher appears in 1243 and William Pycher in 1289.

The SAILOR names, regardless of the spelling variations, still mean just what they say. The origin is the Old French word *sailleor*. Robert le Salyour appears in 1275.

The SEAMAN names are not at all mysterious—the Old English word for seaman was *saemann*.

SHIPMAN and SHIPP have two possible origins: the Old English word *scipmann,* meaning "a sailor," or *sceap* and *man,* meaning "a sheep-man" or "a shepherd." There was a Herbert Scipman in 1221 and a William Schepman in 1316.

STEARMAN and STERMAN tell their own story. One of those names would be given to the man who steered the ship or at least set the course. In short, he was the captain of the ship and, in many cases, he was the merchant-owner too. William Stereman operated in 1202 and Simon Sterman in 1296.

GROUP 108

Merchants

We have made numerous references to merchants throughout this volume because of the importance of the trader in the economy of any nation. To begin with, it is difficult to draw the line between a merchant, a small retailer, or a peddler carrying his entire stock in trade on his back. All of them buy goods and sell to the consumer.

The word *merchant* is not widely used today. If a man owns a store, large or small, he is a storekeeper or a retailer. He may own and operate a whole chain of similar stores, but he is still not thought of as a merchant. Even a man who is in the business of importing goods from the far corners of the world, selling them to retail outlets, who in turn sell to the consumer, will not be known as a merchant, but as someone "in the import-export business."

In medieval England, men bought goods from producers and sold them to consumers. The volume of business an individual did seems to have been the most convenient criterion as to whether a man was a merchant. So, in the matter of names, we will have to arbitrarily classify individuals as best we can from their names.

There is no confusion about the BARLEY names. They were given to a man who sold barley, and in large quantities. It was the all-important material that went into the brewing of ale. A BARLEYMAN bought all the barley he could find and sold it to the brewers. One Jordan Barlie appears in 1221 and a John Barlick in 1276.

BARTER as a surname refers to a bargainer in any kind of goods.

The CANDLER names present some problems in that the trade of the original CANDLER has broadened and expanded so much that even before the advent of modern times, it had become something very different from the original. The name itself came from the Old French word *chandelier,* meaning "a man who made candles." But the materials for making candles were not too plentiful in the Middle Ages and so the candler began to make soap from some of the same animal fats. Soon he became a salt-boiler, and then there was no stopping him. As new products were developed, the candlers began to specialize, and so we had ship-chandlers, wax chandlers, and plain tallow chandlers. The ship chandlers began to sell rope and other items a shipowner would buy when preparing for a voyage.

CHAFFER is another name that leaves us somewhat in the dark. In Middle English, *chaffere* simply meant "a man who trafficked in goods."

We fully hope they were honest goods, but we cannot tell for sure. John Chaffar is recorded in 1275.

The CHAPMAN group were merchants beyond any doubt but, once again, it is not known what they sold. The name derived from the Old English word *ceapmann*. Henry le Chapman appears in 1296.

All five COCKERELL names were of dealers in poultry. The name derives from an Old French word meaning "poultry-seller." Adam Cokerell appears in 1200. CONEY, and CONIE, and CONY derive from the Middle English word *conie* meaning "rabbit" and indicate a dealer in rabbit skins.

COPEMAN is a little vague in its origin. It is hard to be sure whether it came from a word meaning *cape* and therefore meant "a maker of capes or copes," or whether it comes from the word that meant a chapman (*ceapmann*). The latter would be a small merchant who might sell anything he could get hold of. John Copeman registered in 1256 and Hugo Coupman in 1230.

The CORSER group were all dealers in horseflesh. The name derives from the Middle English word *cosser*. Peter le Corser is noted in 1227.

The names beginning with ELLERMAN clearly stem back to a man who sold oil, and the oil he handled was mostly olive oil, although perhaps he sold some linseed oil too. ELLERMAN derives from the Old French word *oile* and the Middle English word *mann*. John le Ulemon is listed in 1278.

FAINER and FEINER were dealers in hay. These names derive from the Old French word *fenier*, meaning "hay." Gilbert le Feyner appears in 1299.

All FEDDER names were definitely borne by dealers in feathers. The name derives from the Old English word *feder*. This group dealt in feathers that were used in making pillows and mattresses. Antony Fedder appears in 1296. The PLUME names, discussed later in this section, clearly refer to men who handled feathers used for other purposes.

Geese and ducks were plentiful in those times—almost every peasant would have at least a few in back of his modest house, and if a dealer came along offering him cash for his feathers, he would certainly sell them. The dealer might clean them up and sell them to a maker of bedding and there you were, another merchant—although not on the grand scale of the MERCERS and the SENDALLS. Juliana le Fethere in 1296 was a woman in the business.

FINGARD meant a wholesaler too, but the name gives us no clue as to the type of goods this man sold. It is thought that the original word must have meant "fine goods." Robert Fingood flourished in 1280.

GOSLIN (and we might have added serveral variations like JOCE-LYN) comes from the Middle English word *geslyng* meaning "little goose." This man did not sell geese but may have done a big business in selling goose feathers. Chapter 8 discusses the use of goose fathers on arrows for the longbow.

GRASSMAN is not a well-known name today and it probably never was. It derives from the Old French word *greisse,* meaning "grease," and it refers to a seller of grease, like Walter Graysman in 1297.

GROSER, from the Old French word *grossier,* meant a wholesale dealer in anything. John Grocer appears in 1350. We do not know whether his line was hardware or groceries.

HORSMONGER obviously meant a dealer in horses, just as HEY-MONGER and HAYMAN referred to a dealer in hay.

Let's now look at the nine names beginning with Le MARCHAND and ending with MERCHANT. These names stem directly from the Old French word *marchand,* sometimes spelled *marcheant.* It meant "a trader in goods," without any indication of what kind of goods. It might be applied to a man who imported wines from France and Spain or other Latin countries. He might pay for his wines with English wool or even with finished woolen goods. He would sell his wines to the great castles and manor houses and make a nice profit, as the nobility were fond of good wine and had the money to buy it. He could have owned one or more ships and, after loading them with English goods, he would cruise from port to port, exchanging his English goods for those of the port he was in. This might be olive oil in Naples, silks in Marseille, and cotton goods in Alexandria. It is undoubtedly safe to say that all nine names were given to substantial operators in more than one commodity. Roger Marchaunt is listed in 1219 and Reginald le Marchant in 1247.

MANGER and MONGER were merchants too, but we have no way to tell what product they sold. Richard le Manger appears in 1275 and Robert Monger in 1316.

MERCER, MERCHIERS, and MERCIER are different in that these individuals dealt exclusively in silks, satins, velvets, and other fine materials—they were textile merchants. During the greater part of the naming period, English weavers were unable to produce any of these, since a different raw material was required for silk and satin, as well as an entirely different weaving process. Yet the nobility, including the ladies, loved the looks and feel of a piece of silk or velvet, and so the demand for this type of goods must have been very large. A merchant arriving with a shipload of these materials would have little trouble in selling them. To distinguish this type of merchant from the others, the Normans quickly gave him a Norman-French name—*mercier* or *merchier*. In London, at least, several of these MERCERS opened offices and warehouses where the lords and ladies, and even royalty itself, could go to select the material they wanted. They would buy it in great rolls and take it to their own tailors or seamsters to be made into garments.

An interesting sidelight is the story of one John Mercer, an Englishman who was born in 1791 and died in 1866. Mr. Mercer was in the textile business. He handled calico, a very moderately priced cotton material that seems to have originated in Calcutta, India. He invented a way of treating cotton cloth in alkaline solutions that made it stronger and more receptive to dyes and even gave it a silky look. The process was so successful that it was named after him—mercerized cotton goods are still sold all over the world. The name MERCER, with its variants, was never numerous in medieval times but there is a Richard le Mercer listed in 1298, Hamo le Merchier in 1204, and John le Mercier in 1196.

PARCHMENT and PARCHMENTER are two more rather rare names, probably because parchment was a very difficult thing to make in medieval times. Yet the demand for it was always far greater than the supply. In a country without paper, parchment made from the skin of animals was the only substitute. The Norman root was *parcheminier*. Walter Perchamunt is recorded in 1163.

The people on the PLUME list, as the name indicates, sold plumes to the lords and ladies of the court. There were no ostrich plumes in England, and it is doubtful that any were imported at this time, yet there must have been feathers that were called plumes to distinguish them from the ordinary—otherwise, why should some feather dealers be named PLUMMER and others FEDDERS? Perhaps peacock feathers were called plumes. The birds were quite common throughout the island at that time as were swans. Walter Ploume is recorded in 1275.

REGRATER is a name fairly well known in England but almost nonexistent in America now. It comes from the Old French word *regratier*, meaning a merchant who sold food at retail. There was a Phillip le Regrater in 1220.

SENDALL and SENDELL undoubtedly were names originally given to very special merchants. They came from the French word *cendal*, which came from a Greek word, *sindon*. It meant a very expensive silk material. Among the materials bought for Edward I in 1300 were sindon, or sendal, at 16 shillings a yard; samite, another silk at more than four pounds a yard; cloth of gold at 26 shillings a yard, and finally, a material called turkey at no less than 7 pounds a yard. These prices cannot really be compared with today's equivalent but certainly we could multiply by at least thirty. Imagine *any* fabric costing more than two hundred pounds (or almost $500) a yard. Sendal itself was the cheapest material on the preceding list and the biggest seller on the merchant's list for that reason. Probably this is why the merchant dealing in that item was named after it, like John Sendal in 1303 and John Sendale in 1374.

VENDER, VENDOR, and VENDUR were also merchants, but again, there is no clue from the name that points to any particular line of goods. The origin was the Anglo-French word *vendeor,* which meant a dealer. Peter le Vendier is listed in 1206.

WADEMAN through WODEMAN have been touched on in chapter 11 in the section on textile dyers (see page 131). *Woad* was the name of an extremely popular purple dye. The dyers could never get enough of it, so naturally this presented an opportunity, and many went into the business of supplying it. From these dye merchants came men like Walter le Wadere in 1265.

WARMAN and WARMEN have their origin in the Old English word *waru* meaning merchandise, in the sense of goods for sale. So a WARMAN was a merchant, but we don't know what line of goods he handled. Richard Wareman is listed in 1215.

GROUP 109
Peddlers

In the Middle Ages, the practice of selling goods of all kinds from one house to another was an established part of every local economy. The sellers would not be organized into a guild with regular meetings and stringent regulations as with so many of the merchants but, nevertheless, it was a means of selling a volume of goods.

The nineteenth-century peddler in America drove a two-wheeled cart, if he could afford such luxury, but many were content to carry their merchandise on their back. His medieval forebear was nearly always restricted to travel by foot. This was not always for economic reasons but because a peddler from one village was not allowed to enter the next village and compete with one of his fellow merchants.

BADGER and BADGERS come from the animal of the same name. The verb to badger comes from his habits of teasing or being teased. Somehow this idea was connected to a medieval peddler and it has stayed with us. Adam Badger is listed in 1246.

BROKUR, from the Old French word *borkeor,* is another way of saying *peddler.* BROGOUR is merely a spelling variation.

FAGGETER and FAGGETTER were peddlers who sold kindling wood by the armful. There were millions of acres of virgin forest in England at that time—enough wood to keep all the home fires in the island burning for a century or so—yet twigs and small sticks of wood that could be picked up were hawked through the streets. The root word in Middle English is *fagot,* meaning "a bundle of sticks." Simon le Fagotter is recorded in 1269.

HAWKER today means somebody who offers goods for sale on a public street and in a loud manner. The original meaning of the word was probably a man who sold hawks on the streets. The name stuck and it was not long before any street salesman might find himself being called a hawker even if he had never seen a hawk. In chapter 21, on hunting, a hawker of falcons, Robert le Hauker, is recorded in 1283, but we don't known whether he sold hawks or trained them. JAWKER is just a spelling variation.

The HUCKER names derive from the Middle English word *hucke,* which meant to bargain with someone. A HUCKER or HUXTER was one who could be counted on to drive a hard bargain. John le Hukker did his bargaining back in 1307. A HAGGLER did the same.

KYDIERE seems to be a Middle Dutch word that came into the language from the Low Countries. In Dutch, it was *keder,* meaning one who shouts loudly in the streets to sell an item—still another PEDDLER.

NOTMAN, NUTMAN, and NUTTMAN were street peddlers who sold nuts.

ONIANS and its four variations come from the Old French word for onion, *oignon,* and the word was applied to a man who sold onions. Thomas Onoiun in 1279 was one of them.

PACKMAN and PAKEMAN were men who carried a pack of goods for sale. *Pake* is Middle English for a pack or a bundle. Henry Pacheman carried one in 1165.

The name PANNER indicates a peddler of bread. He may have baked the bread too, but it is more than likely that he simply called at the shop of the baker each morning and packed his huge basket with fresh, hot bread. And, by the way, PANER tells us even more about the man. We know he packed the bread in a *basket,* because in Middle English, *panier* meant a basket and *pan* meant bread. John le Panner sold his bread in 1262.

All PEDDLER names on the list come ultimately from the same origin: the Latin word for foot, meaning a man who works or does something on his feet. Unfortunately, not one of this group gives us any information on precisely what they peddled. William Peddere seems to have been in business in 1243 and Ralph le Pedeler in 1332.

The three TRANTER names were applied to peddlers too. They derive from the Medieval Latin word *travetanus* meaning "A carrier" or "hawker."

TRUCKER comes from the Old French word *troquer* and means "to bargain or barter with someone." So, the TRUCKER was a PEDDLER, a PACKMAN, a HUXTER, or a HAGGLER.

WATERMAN meant a man who carried water about the streets for sale. William Waterladar is recorded in 1197.

GROUP 107

Shipbuilders

Ankersmyth	Bossone	Gally	Seyler
•	Bossons	Galliot	•
Ashman	Bottan	Galliott	Saayman
Ashment	•	•	Seaman
Asman	Ferrey	Kellar	Seamman
•	Ferri	Keller	Seamons
Barge	Ferrie	Kelmaker	Seeman
Bargeman	Ferrier	Kelman	Seman
Barger	Ferriman	•	Semens
•	Ferrior	Mariner	Semmens
Boatright (*see*	Ferry	Marner	Seyman
Shipwright)	Ferryman	Marriner	•
Boatwright	•	•	Shipman
Botwright	Float	Orewright	Shipp
•	Floate	•	Shipwright (*see*
Boater	Floater	Picher	Boatwright)
Boatman	Flodman	Pitcher	Skipwright
Boatswain	Flote	Pitchers	•
Boatte	•	•	Stearman
Boeson	Galey	Sailor	Sterman
Bosence	Galley	Saylor	
Bossom	Gallie	Seiler	
Bosson	Galliman	Seiller	

GROUP 108

Merchants

Barlee	•	•	Parchmenter
Barley	Coney	Goslin	•
Barleyman	Conie	•	Plimmer
•	Cony	Grassman	Plomer
Barter	•	Groser	Plume
•	Copeman	•	Plumer
Candelent	Coopman	Hayman	Plummer
Candle	Coupman	Heymonger	•
Candleman	•	•	Regrater
Candler	Corser	Horsmonger	•
Candles	Coser	•	Sendall
Chandler	Cossar	Le Marchand	Sendell
Chanter	Cosser	Lemarchand	•
Chantler	•	Le Marchant	Vender
Chaundler	Ellerman	Le Marquand	Vendor
•	Elliman	Marchand	Vendur
Chaffer	Elman	Marchant	•
•	Ullman	Marchent	Wademan
Chapman	Ullmman	Marquand	Wader
Chapper	•	Merchant	Wadman
Cheeper	Fainer	•	Waider
Chipman	Feiner	Manger	Weider
Chipper	•	Monger	Wodeman
•	Feather	•	•
Cockarill	Featherman	Mercer	Warman
Cockerell	Fedder	Merchiers	Warmen
Cockerill	Fedders	Mercier	
Cockrell	•	•	
Cockrill	Fingard	Parchment	

GROUP 109

Peddlers

Badger	Huckestere	•	Pedelare
Badgers	Huckster	Packman	Pedlar
•	Huxter	Pakeman	Pedler
Brogour	•	•	Piddler
Brokur	Kydiere	Paner	Pidler
•	•	Panierman	•
Faggeter	Notman	Panner	Tranter
Faggetter	Nutman	Panniers	Trauenter
•	Nuttman	•	Trenter
Haggler	•	Peddar	•
•	Onians	Pedder	Trucker
Hawker	Onion	Peddere	•
Jawker	Onions	Peddlar	Waterman
•	O'nions	Peddler	
Hucker	Onyon	Pedelar	

CHAPTER 17

Innkeepers and Beverage Makers

The inn was an established institution along the main travel routes of the ancient world. In biblical times, the inn played a fairly prominent part in New Testament stories and, while no trace remains, we know the Romans operated inns along the fine roads they built in England. If we can judge by the Romans' well-known love of comfort, these roadside accommodations must have been of quite high standards.

With the disappearance of the Romans in the fourth and fifth centuries, these inns were allowed to fall into ruin and slowly melt back into the landscape. The newly arriving Anglo-Saxons of that early period had no use for such things.

In the centuries that followed, however, conditions gradually changed. Britain became Christian, and that meant pilgrimages to the shrines in England and Europe and even to the far-distant Holy Land. It became the custom for monasteries to invite pilgrims in to have a hot meal and a bed for the night before going on to the next institution. At first, this was highly impromptu: the pilgrim ate the simple fare of the monks and slept on the floor wherever space could be found. But in the course of a few years, it became better organized. Separate dormitories and refectories were added, with certain monks detailed to look after the comfort of the travelers. All of this was done without charge to the traveler and, though one could give a donation to the monastery if one cared to, the whole monastic operation was carried on for the benefit of religion.

This sort of thing made commercially operated inns virtually impossible, a condition largely maintained well into the Middle Ages. When

Henry VIII took over the monasteries and abbeys and handed them over to his friends, the day of the justly famous English inn may be said to have begun.

Building and operating an inn was not something that could be accomplished overnight; one had to undergo years of learning by trial and error. During much of the naming period, the English inn must have been a very crude institution. The traveler was expected to bring his own food and prepare it himself. He had to carry his own bedding with him and find the best spot available for it. The fact seems to be that the English inn of this early period offered little more than a roof over one's head and a fire in the fireplace. However, drinks were available, and in abundance—that was the innkeeper's principal source of income.

As one travels the highways and byways of England today, one can scarcely fail to be impressed with the inns present in almost every town and village. Knowing the tourist's love of the antique, many of them make rather generous claims on antiquity, such as the 1213 date claimed by the Angel at Grantham in Lincolnshire and the 1286 date of the King's Head at Aylesbury, Buckinghamshire.

GROUP 110

The Innkeepers

The inn of the naming period was nothing more than a drinking place where the peasant-farmers and mechanics could gather on holidays and enjoy a tankard of home-brewed ale. The tankard might be made of rough pottery or, in some advanced places, of the great molded leather jacks that were going to be a fixture in English inns on into the nineteenth century. The bar as we know it today was nonexistent. The ale was drawn directly from one of several great casks along the wall and passed by serving girls. The peasants sat on rough benches here and there, but if the crowd was large, many stood or walked about.

The names that originated in these old inns are a genuine aid to the modern researcher in trying to recreate the scenes and atmosphere of medieval England.

ARBER, HARBER, HARBOR, and HARBOUR derive from the Old English word *herebeorg*, meaning a provider of safe lodging in the sense of someone who goes ahead to arrange for that lodging. From that comes our word *harbinger*. It didn't take much time for people to apply the word to a tavern—either the place itself, or the tavern-keeper. And a tavern may well have been a place of security and comfort now and then.

HABERER, HARBERER, and HARBISHER are merely variations. Geoffrey Herbour appears in 1279, John Herbour in 1280, Richard le Erber in 1315, Augustine le Herbere in 1319, Thomas le Harbisher and a William le Herbyiour in 1319. They were all tavern-keepers.

The exact origin of the name GANNOKER is not certain but we do know the original holder was an innkeeper and probably female. Beatrix le Gannoker is recorded in 1330.

The HERBAGE names come from an Old French word, *herberge,* which means "a hostel," and a hostel is another French term for a lodging place.

HORSLER, HORSTLER, HOSLER and OSTLER come from an Old French word *ostelier* or sometimes *hostiler.* The Britons called him an *hostiler* or an *osteler.* All mean someone who receives, lodges, or entertains guests, in other words an inn- or tavern-keeper. Recorded are William Horsler and William Hostiler in 1190, Andrew Hosler, and Robert le Osteler in 1204. HOST, HOSTE, and OST come from an Old French variation of the above, *oste,* meaning "a host," particularly a host who kept an inn. John le Host appears in 1254 and so does Richard le Ost.

INMAN, INN, and INNMAN are obviously names given to an innkeeper. *Inn* was an Old English word that meant a lodging house. William Inman lived in 1379.

The SERVICE names immediately seem to belong very properly in a group of innkeepers because service is what a customer has a right to expect. The real explanation, however, is quite different. The Normans had a word, *cervoise,* which in Old French meant "ale." Thus, when a Norman seated in an inn called out something that sounded like our word *service,* he was actually asking for ale.

TAPPER goes back to an old Anglo-Saxon word *taeppere* or *tapur,* meaning a simple wooden peg that was fitted into a hole in a barrel. It was pulled out when one wanted to draw some of the contents and then replaced. Naturally, the man who controlled the tap would be called the TAPER. One of them is an old tax record of 1279—he was known as Robert le Tapper. TAPSTER was the feminine equivalent. Perhaps she was the wife of the owner. Elisota Tapester seems to have served the thirsty customers of some English inn in 1384.

TIPLER comes almost unchanged from the Middle English *tipeler.* It meant the same as TAPPER. Robert le Tipeler is listed in 1250. TOPLASS, TOPLIS, and TOPLISS, judging as well as one can from this distance, may well have originated just the way one might guess. TIPLADY and TOPLADY may be just another way of referring to a lady tavern-keeper. There appears in the records a John Taplady in 1399, a Johanna Tipelady in 1490, and a John Typlady in 1301. The whole TAVENER group originated in the Anglo-French dialect from the word *taverner*. In Old French, it would be *tavernier*. They both meant a tavern-keeper. Many examples of the name appear in the records, such as William le Taverner in 1268 and John Tavender a bit later.

GROUP 111

The Beverage Makers

Malt beverages have been the national drink of all classes of Englishmen as far back as information is available, and until well into the 1400s, it was ale. Beer was brought in from the Continent in the fifteenth century, but it offered no competition to ale until about the 1700s.

The ale of medieval times was a very different product from the one we know now. It was made from malt, yeast, and water only—no hops whatever. It is hard for modern tastes to imagine any malt drink without the time-honored fragrance and flavor of the hop vine, but so it was.

Andrew Borde, writing about 1525 in his *Dyetary of Helth,* says: "Ale is made of malte and water; and they the which do put any other thynge to ale than is rehersed, except yest, barme or godesgood, doth sofysticat theyr ale. Ale for an Englysshe man is a naturall drynke. Ale must have these propertyes: it muste be fresshe and cleare, it muste not be ropy nor smoky, nor muste it have no weft nor tayle. Ale should not be dronke under V dayes olde. Newe ale is unholsome for all men. And sowre ale, and dead ale the which doth stand a tylt, is good for no man. Barly malte maketh better ale than oten malte or any other corne doth; it doth ingendre grose humoures; but yette it maketh a man stronge."

Note that this defense of ale took place in the early 1500s, when the beer brewers from the Continent must have been doing their best to win the English over to beer.

English ale was thoroughly established by the middle of the twelfth century. It was known as "the people's food in liquid form." The per capita consumption of ale must have been enormous, as the regulations of many monasteries stated that no more than one gallon might be consumed by an individual in any one day. Of course, aside from water and milk (both of which were almost sure to be contaminated), no other beverage was available. Wine was no factor at the time. A thirteenth-century writer, describing the extreme poverty of the Franciscan monks when they were first settling in London in 1224, wrote as follows: "I have seen the brothers drink ale so sour that some would have preferred to drink water."

There seems good reason to believe that women were not only commonly found serving in the taverns but were also involved in the brewing of ale. The term "alewife" may have referred to either situation but it never survived as a family name. One statistic I have found gives some idea of the number of people engaged in the business of brewing ale. In 1520 the little town of Coventry, with a total population of 6600, had sixty public brewers.

Anyone was allowed to brew his own ale at home, but if he attempted to sell it to his neighbors, he ran into a great many rules and regulations. These laws were subject to constant change over the whole period but they all seem to have been aimed at protecting the consumer. The Assize of Ale in the reign of Henry III fixed the maximum price of ale on the basis of the price of malt.

BEER

The BEER names are latecomers compared to the BREWER names, but beer was being made before the end of the naming period, so a few names have come down to us.

ALE

The BREWERE names come from the Old English root *breowan*. From the records come Adam le Browere in 1201 and William Bruwere in 1148. In the early part of the period, BREWSTER, BROSTER, and BRUSTER indicate that these brewers were women. Over the years, however, the custom of having a feminine form of such a word was lost and either form could be used for men or women.

BRACER, BRASHER, BRASSEUR, and LE BRASSEUR meant BREWER too, but they derive from the Old French word *braceor* or *brasseur*. BASUR is a variation of the French while BRACERESSE is the feminine form of the word in Old French.

When a BREWER had a batch of ale ready for the market, he had to call in the official taster, better known as the ale-conner. The CONNER was the law: he tasted a sample, approved it as *good ale,* or if its quality was not up to standard, set a lower price at which the inferior product could be sold.

GOODALE and the three names that follow might be taken as proof of this practice. A brewer might acquire a reputation for always making good ale and consequently, in time, have these words pinned onto him as a name. Recorded are William Gudale in 1379 and John Godhale in 1297.

MALSTER through MALTMAN are rather obviously the names given to men who made the malt that made the brew. Hugh le Malter appears in 1306, as does William Malthouse, and John Maltman is listed in 1332.

CIDER AND PERRY

Very little is known about either of these drinks in the period with which we are concerned. Cider is pressed from apples and perry from pears—each will ferment and produce a strong beverage. From the tax records, we know that both were widely made and consumed. Neither of them was, however, ever a distant competitor to ale.

WINE

The Domesday Book indicates that many of the great Norman lords planted huge vineyards around their newly acquired English estates, similar to what they had had back home in France. William of Malmesbury spoke of the Vale of Gloucester as planted more thickly with vineyards than any other part of the island. Many of the great monasteries brought over their own skilled wine-makers (and they had some of the best in all the world), but English wine-making was never a success. The soil lacked something and there was not enough sun to ripen the grape properly. The best that could be produced was so sour that it had to have honey added to it to make it palatable. Wine continued to be consumed by the English, but during the entire naming period, it was imported, and this restricted its use to the nobility.

The story is told about some nameless wine-maker who made a huge batch of wine, but when he attempted to sell it, the wine was so sour, it could not be swallowed. By moving quickly from place to place, never waiting long enough for a buyer to taste the product, he managed to dispose of most of his stock. But the officials caught up with him. At a public gathering, the vintner was forced to drink a huge draft of the stuff and then stand still while each of his disgusted customers poured the contents of all their jugs and flagons over his head.

The whole group of names starting with VIGNE and ending with WYNYARD obviously came from the business of making wine, and that would include growing the grapes. In Old French, *vigne* meant "vine" and a vinedresser would be a *vigneur*. VINTER probably came more directly from *viniter*, meaning a wine merchant. Richard le Vyntener appears in 1121.

OTHER BEVERAGES

The CAUDELL names have a Latin derivation, *caldellum*, meaning "a hot drink." It was something given to the sick and the invalid. It seems to have been made by mixing a thin soup with wine or ale sweetened with honey and some kind of spice. There are many examples of the name in the records: John Cadel in 1187, William Caudel in 1198, and William Kaldel in 1277.

The three names beginning with MEADER come from the Anglo-Saxon word *meodu*. Mead was a drink made by fermenting a mixture of malt, honey, yeast, and apparently anything else that might be suggested to the maker. There is a John Medemaker in 1332 and Alexander le Meder in 1180.

GROUP 110

The Inkeepers

Arber	Horsler	Innman	Tavenor
Haberer	Horstler	•	Taverner
Harber	Hoster	Sarvis	Tavernor
Harberer	Hossell	Servaes	Taviner
Harbisher	Host	Servais	Tavner
Harbor	Hoste	Service	•
Harbour	Hosteller	Servis	Tiplady
•	Hosteler	•	Tipler
Gannoker	Hustler	Tapper	Toplady
•	Oastler	Tapster	Toplass
Harbach	Ost	•	Toplis
Harbage	Ostler	Tafner	Topliss
Harbidge	•	Tavender	
Herbage	Inman	Tavener	
•	Inn	Tavenner	

GROUP 111

The Beverage Makers

Beer	Brewster	Goodall	Vignes
Beere	Broster	Goddayle	Vine
Beerman	Brouwer	Goodhall	Vinen
Beers	Brower	•	Viner
Beery	Bruster	Malster	Vines
•	•	Maltas	Vinter
Bracer	Caddell	Malter	Vintiner
Braceresse	Cadel	Malthouse	Vintner
Brasher	Cadle	Malthus	Vintor
Brasseur	Caudell	Maltman	Vyner
Brasur	Caudle	•	Le Vine
Le Brasseur	Cawdell	Meader	Wingard
•	•	Medemaker	Winyard
Brewer	Conner	Medur	Wynyard
Brewere	•	•	
Brewers	Goodale	Vigne	

CHAPTER **18**

Coopers, Cabinetmakers, Toolmakers, Molders, and Minters

The craft of the COOPER is an old one and a surprising one. Most ancient crafts required almost as much artistic talent as craftsmanship, but the work of the cooper demanded mechanical accuracy. A piece of cooperage that was not liquid-tight was completely useless. ("Slack" cooperage for keeping grain, fruit, and such is not designed to be tight.)

The medieval cooper preferred white oak because its grain was usually straighter than other woods, and that was important. He first cut a slab of wood to about the length of the barrel he was making, then he split this into conveniently sized staves. Next, with an inside draw knife he hollowed out each stave to form the inner surface of the barrel and then with an outside draw knife he trimmed the outside of each stave. Now the really fine work began. He boiled the staves in a huge kettle until they had become as soft as possible; then, quickly taking them out of the water, he fitted them around a circular piece of oak designed for the bottom of the barrel, slipped one or two temporary hoops around them, and placed as heavy a weight as he could on the whole assembly in order to bend each stave to form a uniform bulge. This done, he had to plane *each* edge of *each* stave to the exact radius of the barrel intended. After that it was a matter of putting the hoops on and fitting a head into the barrel.

The medieval English drank a lot of wine when they could get it, but most of it had to be imported from France in tuns or pipes, butts or hogsheads, and now and then, in barrels. A tun of wine was the equal of two pipes or four hogsheads.

243

The English brewers made vast quantities of ale for it was then the national drink, and that required a lot of cooperage. But they used the work of the cooper for many other products as well, such as herring and other salt fish, olive oil (imported), and salted meat.

GROUP 112

Coopers

The name BARREL is quite obvious, but BUSS and BUSSE are more obscure. *Buss* was an Old French word for "cask." A man named BUTT made a container, but the name could also refer to the man in charge of the butts (longbow) practice. CASKER is self-explanatory, and CADMAN was from the Anglo-Saxon word *caedmon*, also meaning a maker of casks. The CHURN names referred to men who made the special vessel in which butter was made.

COOPER and the nine names following derive rather obviously from the same word. *Couper* seems to have been the earliest Middle English spelling. There is a Robert le Couper recorded in 1181.

COVER and CUVER derive from the Norman-French word for COOPER, *cuvier*. KEUER was Middle English for a tub-maker.

The four names beginning with HOOPER need no explanation—a hoop was a very essential part of the COOPER's activity. Many variations of the name can be found, such as, for example, Philip le Hoper in 1228.

The three KITTER names were given to men who made tubs, milk pails, and so forth.

LARDER referred to the small barrel used to keep bacon.

A man named MEYSEMAKER was a barrel-maker but the barrel had to be for herring to get that name. *Meise* was an old French word meaning "barrel for herrings." There is a Vyncent Meysemakere listed in 1332.

The three PALER names are obvious—their bearers made pails.

The PIGGIN was a small pail with one stave extended for a handle. It was made in America until less than a century ago.

STAVELY and STAVER were names given to men who supplied the various COOPERS with good oaken staves. However, the men who supplied staves to the longbow makers were also called STAVERS, and it is impossible to distinguish the two.

The TUB names meant just that and TANKARDER meant a tub too, although later it meant a drinking mug.

The TUN names indicate a COOPER who made huge wine containers.

A VATTMAN made vats for the tanners and the brewers. They were made of cooperage, but did not require a top like a barrel.

GROUP 113

Basket Makers

Unlike most of the other useful arts about whose origin something is known, basket-making and the people who first made baskets are mysteries. During the nineteenth century, civilized men penetrated to just about every corner of the world, from one pole to another. Their collected explorations uncovered a vast amount of new information on the peoples of the world but not a single tribe, even in the most remote areas, that was not already skilled in making baskets from native vegetation. It is amazing that a small tribe from Central Africa could have learned how to make essentially the same basket that the Eskimos make.

The English of the medieval period made baskets and apparently made them in considerable quantity, judging by the number of names they have passed down to us. In this group there are thirty-five names, and every one of them comes directly from the basket-making business.

The three BANISTER names that head our group came from the Old French word *banastre,* which meant "basket" or by metonymy a basket maker. A Richard Banastre is recorded in 1149. BASKETT and BASKETTER were also basket makers.

The nine BUSHELL names refer to bushel baskets—either an official who owned one and as part of his duties went about town checking other baskets to see if they measured up to his, or a basket maker who had developed skill in making containers of exact capacity. There are many in the records: Robert le Busselar appeared in 1243.

CORBELL, CORBILLER, and CORBLE all mean either a basket or a maker of baskets. The root word is *corbeillier.* Richard Corbeille is recorded in 1180.

FANNER, VANNAH, and VANNER probably came from the Old English word *fann,* which meant "a maker of fans or winnowing baskets."

HOTT and HOTTER were from the Old French word *hotte,* meaning "basket." John le Hottere seems to have been in the basket-making business back in 1275.

LEAPER and LEEPER are a little confusing in that they have two possible meanings. They might have applied to a dancer or leaper (see chapter 20, page 285), but also might have come from the Old English word *leap,* which meant "basket." LEPMAKER probably came from the same word and, if so, it would mean "basket maker" too.

Next comes PANIERMAKER, which still refers to a basket, but a big basket designed to carry bread either on the back of a man or a horse. It was somewhat oval in shape, and two of them could be strapped onto a horse.

The three PECK names probably all mean a maker of peck baskets.

RIPPER sounds like something fierce and wild. but it isn't. It was just one of the Old English ways of saying "basket." It derives from *hrip.*

SKEPPER, SKIPP, and SKIPPER come from an Old Norman word *skeppa,* meaning "basket" or "basket maker." There are a John Skep and a William le Skippere listed in the late twelfth century.

WILLER and WILLERS are from an Old English word, *wilige,* meaning "basket."

GROUP 114
Cabinetmakers

The woodworking crafts of medieval England had progressed just beyond the stage of rough carpentry and into the finer trade of joinery by the middle of the naming period. But the English craftsman was still centuries behind his counterpart in the Mediterranean countries. Italy, in particular, perhaps because of the lingering influence of ancient Roman civilization, was far ahead of any nation in northern Europe at that time. The Italian furniture makers were using the dovetail joint and the mortise and tenon as standard practice long before the rest of Europe had even heard about them.

Very little of the furniture made before A.D. 1000 has survived, but we do have numerous reproductions of it in sketches, paintings, and sculpture. One piece in the Vatican was definitely made in the eighth century, and its dovetail joints are still a joy to look at.

Another feature that we take for granted today but that was unknown in England until well into the sixteenth century is the drawer. Paneling was just beginning in England, and this was largely confined to what we call wainscoting today. It is probably fair to say that wainscoting was the first actual step taken by the British workmen to get beyond the rough saw, the ax, and the adz. This initial effort was probably designed more for protection from the cold and dampness than for beauty. The tongue and groove joint was used for the first time in this wainscoting and it was a vast improvement over the old butted joints.

But the furniture was still very crude. Virtually nothing that could be called a chair today was made in England at that time. The only exception seems to have been what is called the "X" chair. It consisted of two X's fastened together rigidly, with either leather or fabric bands forming the seat. These were used largely by royalty. The few other chairs made at that time were all of rigid right angles, utterly overlooking the fact that the body does not recline at that angle. They did make three-legged stools in some quantity, and the legs were fastened in holes in the solid seat with the same wedge that is used today.

Furniture light enough to be easily moved about the house was rare. Tables, for example, were nearly always of the trestle type—a long stretcher joining footed uprights that served as legs with a top sliced out of a log from end to end and something like two inches thick. The seats for the diners would be long heavy benches.

The walls of the house, if it was the home of a prosperous merchant, were usually filled with cupboards. These were then simply shelves attached to the walls on which the proud owner could display his dishes. Many years later these cupboards would be removed from the walls and made into a cabinet, and then it would be a cupboard as we know it; but this did not happen for another two hundred years. A similar cabinet, designed for keeping food rather than dishes, appeared in the sixteenth century and was called an ambry.

Settles were built-in benches near the fireplace and were common in the thirteenth century. They too were built with much heavier wood than one would use today. The tools of the medieval carpenter had changed very little in a thousand years. He used the saw, the chisel, the adz, the ax, the square, the plane, and the auger. As the new and more delicate craft of joinery developed, the tools didn't change except to be made smaller.

The slow but constant development from carpentry to joinery and, later, to cabinetmaking is reflected in the names that have survived from that period. One of the very first pieces of movable furniture a man would have built for his house was a great, roughly built chest that would store surplus food. Frequently these chests were made from riven boards; that is, boards that had been split from a log without benefit of either saw or plane. They would be nailed together, and a top would be hinged to the body of the chest and provided with some kind of lock.

This was known as an *arc,* and it was soon considered a necessity by everybody—or at least everybody with surplus food. The men who made

these great chests were naturally ARKWRIGHTS and the four variations are simply the result of centuries of carelessness.

Strictly speaking, COFFER referred to a chest and COFFRER to the
man in charge of its safekeeping. In the early part of the period, the
COFFER was what must be called a trunk today—one carried one's
clothing in it when traveling. As the years slipped by, it began to be
used for carrying valuables. Money at that time meant coin—great piles
of it if one was lucky—so, since there was no paper money, it took a
strong box to carry it. The COFFER was usually covered entirely with
leather and studded with brass tacks in an ornamental design. It would
have iron bands around it and protective pieces at all the corners. In
time the COFFER became synonymous with money, and it still is to
some extent today. Thomas le Coffer is in an old tax record of 1298.

ESCRINER comes from an Old French word meaning "a small box"
or "a small COFFER."

C'ests are interesting in that the very early chests were made low
enough for people to sit on. They must have been a blessing in a period
when chairs were almost unknown. Once the English woodworkers
learned how to make drawers and put one or two in a chest, the chest
would be too high to sit on. When three drawers were made, one had
what is now called a lowboy. More drawers made it a highboy—and at
this point it would have a mirror on top of it.

HUCHER means "a maker of chests," but the word derives from an
Old French word, *huchier.* A John le Huchere is listed in 1327.

KYSTEWRIGHT stems from the Middle English word *kyste,* meaning
"a small chest." Wright is that familiar name suffix meaning "a maker of
something."

TABLETTER was the name given to a man who made chessboards.
A Peter le Tableter is recorded far back in 1281, which tells us something
of the entertainments available at that time.

WHICCHER and the four names that follow are not quite as clearly
defined as the ARK and COFFER names. They were all chest makers, but
one can't be sure just what type of chest they made. The Old English root
of the name is *hwicce,* meaning "a chest." In the 1300s, Mr. Robert le
Wicchere and Mr. Richard Le Wycher were living in London and in the
business of making chests.

This completes the chest makers, but there were some who had a talent
for woodcarving and, judging from the illustrations left to us, they had
genuine ability. They would cover the entire lid of a chest with an intricate design, and then the front and either end. Sometimes the owner's

name would be incorporated into the design and, now and then, the date. The artists doing this sort of thing left two names to us—CARVER, meaning "to cut," and KERUERE, with the same meaning.

TURNER, TURNOR, and TURNOUR were names given to woodworkers who could turn a piece of wood on a lathe into a round chair leg or whatever piece of furniture was called for. The lathe is an extremely old piece of machinery and probably had a common origin with the potter's wheel. Round turnings must not have been in great demand during the medieval period—they would be too fancy—but as time went on, they increased in popularity until straight lines became rare. Many examples of the name are in the records, such as Warner le Turnur in 1180.

DISHER was a name sometimes given to a TURNER. He turned dishes on his lathe, using good white oak when he could get it. Not just any size and shape would do: the wood had to have certain capacities. He had to put his mark on each dish and have it passed on by local officials. Richard Dysser was doing this work in 1304.

MASER, MASLEN, and MASLIN were also TURNERS or DISHERS. They made maple bowls. The Middle English word for a maple bowl was *maselin*.

GROUP 115
Wheel and Wagon Makers

Even before the Conquest, the horse and cart were something of a factor in the economy of an English community. Lumber and stone had to be moved to where they were needed, and traveling merchants going from one market town to another had to transport their goods. But at some point in the twelfth century, an idea reached the British that greatly increased the use of the horse and wagon—they learned how to harness the animal. This may sound strange today, but from somewhere in the Near East had come the idea that a horse could pull a much heavier load if one did not put a strap around his neck that would choke him. If a padded collar were used instead, the collar would take all the pressure off his neck and he could do more. No one knows exactly where this idea originated, but it worked, and worked so well that it is still being used all over the world.

Wagons, as they were made in England at this time, were fairly simple. There were no springs, of course, and the floor would usually be made of solid planks with wicker woven in and out of stakes set into the planks.

At some point, it occurred to someone that the tongue or shafts did not have to be stiff extensions of the wagon floor—this was hard on the horse when going over bumps or depressions—but could be hinged so each shaft could react independently. Then the idea developed that the front wheels could be pivoted. All this applied particularly to the four-wheeled wagon, but actually the two-wheeled cart was very much more common at that time. It could get over roads that the four-wheeled vehicles would not even attempt. By the latter part of the thirteenth century it could be said that the English people had a fairly practical cart or wagon.

The wheel was the crucial part. If the vehicle did not have wheels that would turn and hold weight, nothing else mattered. The wheel is easily one of man's most glorious achievements. Probably the use of fire and the invention of the wheel did more to raise mankind from savagery than any other material development he has accomplished. The Romans and the Greeks and even the earlier Egyptians had developed wheels, but they were far from being the smooth-running dependable things they are today. The Roman wheels had spokes, but it is doubtful if either the Greek or Egyptian ones did. They never seem to have got beyond the idea that once the wheel had an established hub of some kind, one merely had to brace it here and there to the rim. This was very much weaker than having spokes radiate out to the rim from the hub.

The English did have these radiating spokes from the thirteenth century on, but undoubtedly there were a great many peasant carts with wheels made of solid planks nailed together and sawed off in a circle, with a hole in the center to slip onto the axle.

CARTWRIGHT and its variant, KORTWRIGHT, were names given to individuals who in some manner became identified with the building of carts.

The names WAGNER through WHENMAN all come from the same Old English word for wagon, *waegn*. It can't be proven that all were wagon *makers* as some of them must have been *owners* of a wagon. Certainly wagon owners were rare enough to call attention to themselves and thus be named for this envied possession. The four WAINE-WRIGHT names come from the Old English word *waegnwyrhta* meaning "a wagon maker." There was Ailmar Wanwrecthe who made wagons in 1237, and by 1332 the name had become modernized to le Wayne-wright.

The entire list of sixteen names beginning with WAILER and ending with WILESMITH obviously comes from the highly skilled craft of making wheels. The spokes had to be let into the felloe with round holes, but in the hub it had to be a square mortise. If one could find some way of putting a metal bearing in the hub, one would have a vastly better wheel. Nineteenth-century samples of this have recently been found in Britain. NAWRIGHT was a wheel maker too, from a different Old English source. ROWER and ROYER derive from a Norman word, *roier,* also meaning "a wheelwright."

GROUP 116

Toolmakers

Man has been called "a toolmaking animal." Many animals are bigger and stronger and faster on their feet than man, but none of them has ever made a tool. In saying this, I am aware of the habit some birds have of dropping shellfish on rocky shores, apparently to break the shells open and make the creature inside the shell available for food, but this is hardly toolmaking in any realistic sense.

The basic hand tools available today are not very different from the hand tools ancient mankind developed. We have saws, hammers, axes and hatchets—so did men in prehistoric times. We have tools that bore holes and planes that smooth boards, but these are not modern inventions. We have improved upon these tools wonderfully, but prehistoric men invented them.

Men were making and using the hoe, the rake, the shovel, the plow, and even the needle when they were living in caves.

When one looks at the tools of the medieval English, it is expected that all the basic hand tools existed. And in fact, they did. The steel men had was certainly not the dependable quality we have today, but the English were keenly aware of this and were making almost superhuman efforts to improve it. (See chapter 5.)

Let us look at some of the family names that indicate by their spelling, their derivation, or even their sounds that they may first have been given to some hard-working man who had either acquired unusual skill in making a tool or extraordinary ability in using it.

The three BEC names probably come from the Old English word *becca,* which meant a maker of mattocks, tools that were a combination adz, ax, and pick.

A BESMER was a broom maker, and there is recorded a John le Besmere in 1263. The broom used to be an item commonly associated with the housewife, mostly as a tool but on occasion as a weapon. The

BROMERE was a maker of brooms, too. The name derives from the Old English word *brom.* John Bromer is recorded in 1466.

BRAYER referred to a man who made pestles, and a BURSTLERE was a maker of brushes from bristles.

A CUILLERER was a man who made spoons. Spoons were undoubtedly a welcome product since table forks were unknown.

The name FILER derives from the Middle English word *filen,* meaning a man who used a file or a man who made them. John le Filur registered the name in 1275.

HACKER is interesting in that it was first applied to anyone who made hacks (garden tools), such as mattocks and hoes. Adam le Hakkere in 1262 might have used such tools, but so did almost everybody else, so it would seem that this man *made* them to come by his name.

HAFTER is an Old English term used to designate the handle of a tool, particularly of a hammer.

The name HAMMER is not too common today, but the tool was so widely used in the Middle Ages that the name was almost as prevalent as SMITH.

The four HARDY names are not too clear. They may be just descriptive terms from the old French word *hardi,* meaning one who was bold and courageous; but there is also a tool with this name that every blacksmith has used for centuries, so I like to think that the modern name may have started with the first user or even inventor of that tool. The blacksmith's hardy is a tool shaped to fit into the square hole in an anvil. The projecting end is either sharpened to allow a piece of hot iron to be cut off or given some new shape. William le Hardy is recorded in 1206, and there are many others.

HORNERE made combs from horn.

HUDGHEL and its two variants come from the trade of the Smith. A hudghel was another tool that fit into an opening provided in the anvil.

A LADELER was obviously a maker or user of ladles like Robert le Ladelere back in 1286.

MALLET names have an extremely mixed origin. One of the sure sources is the Old French word *maillet,* meaning "hammer." It could have been applied to a man who made hammers. One very early example of the name is Gilbert Malet. This particular Mr. Malet was given that name in 1086, in the Domesday Book.

PEAL, PEALE, and PEEL have been mentioned earlier in chapter 15 on bakers, as the PEEL was, and still is, a tool in constant use by that craft. It is a long wooden paddle used to take hot bread from the oven.

A PENIUR made combs.

PIGACHE meant a pickax, or the man who could either make one or use one.

The whole PINCHEN list of seven names is a little unclear. Professor Ekwall, one of the great authorities on nominology, believes that these names originated with either of the Old French words *pincon* or *pinchon*, both of which meant "pincers" or "forceps."

PLOWRIGHT, of course, refers to the man who made plows.

RASOR definitely comes from the Old French word *rasur*, metonymic for a maker of such things. A Thomas Rasur is listed in 1159.

RASTALL comes from the Old French word *rastel*, meaning "a rake." Thus, Walter Rastell, who lived late in the twelfth century, must have been a smith who made rakes, though he may have merely been so proficient in their use that he acquired the name.

The SHOVEL names all stem from the Middle English word *schovelyn*. Again, it could mean either a man who made shovels or a man who used them.

SICKLES is not so common today, but its ancient origin is certainly that long-established garden tool.

SPADE and SPADER come very directly from the Old English word *spadu*, which was used to distinguish a man who made spades. There is a John le Spadere in 1336 and a John Spadier in 1332.

GROUP 117

Molders and Bellfounders

The craft of the MOLDER in the medieval period when names were first being created had not progressed much beyond the days of classical history. Useful items of brass and bronze and even iron were made (though to a very small extent as there was only a very sketchy knowledge of cast iron at that time).

Probably what retarded the trade most was the mold itself—the idea of molding in sand with linked molding boxes was totally unknown, and baked clay was still being used.

The casting of bells for churches and monasteries was just beginning in this period and would not reach its peak until about the seventeenth century, when most of the great bells of Europe were produced.

As a consequence, the craft of the molders has left us very few names. BELLER, BELLEYETER, and BILLITER are among the best known.

These names have an Old English origin in the words *belle* and *geotere,* together meaning "bellfounder." A William le Belyotar is listed in 1247 and an Alexander le Belleyeter in 1377.

FOUNDOUR seems to have appeared in 1275 with William le Fondur. William Founder came along a century later. These two gentlemen must have cast both bells and some of the very early cannon (at that time, called, among other things, bombard).

MOLDEMAKER and MOLDER appeared in the fourteenth century at the very end of the naming period. The Old English root of both was *molde.* There was a Gilbert le Moldemaker in 1335.

PANNEGETTER and PANNER are names given to molders who cast pans in the fourteenth century.

GROUP 118

Minters

The story of the COINERS, the MINTERS, and the MONNYERS of medieval England is a long and complicated one. It is said that during the reigns of the Conqueror and the Norman kings immediately following there were periods during which no less than one hundred widely separated mints were in operation throughout the island, and this does not include counterfeiters. This seems hard to believe—so unlike the very businesslike William I—but for a time, not only could every shire produce its own coinage but so could every sizable castle or manor.

Gold, silver, and copper were the metals used, but the exact proportions were changed so frequently that it must have been impossible to keep up with them. In general, early coins were molded and then stamped with a die, but later the metal or alloy was pounded into sheets and the coin stamped out of this. The milled edge was, of course, unknown, so coins could be shaved with ease. Most early coinage was stamped on one side only.

A Mr. John le Conyare is listed in 1327 and a Mr. John le Meneter in 1310.

SEELER and SEINTER were names applied to men who made seals. They may well have been silversmiths.

GROUP 112

Coopers

Barrel	Cooper	•	Staver
•	Cooperman	Keuer	•
Buss	Coopersmith	•	Tankarder
Busse	Coopper	Kitter	•
•	Copper	Kittermaster	Tub
Butt	Couper	Kittewright	Tubb
Butts	Coupere	•	Tubby
Buttman	Cowper	Larder	Tubman
•	Cupper	•	•
Cadman	Cuppester	Meysemaker	Tun
•	•	•	Tuneler
Casker	Cover	Paler	Tunn
•	Cuver	Payler	Tunnah
Churn	•	Paylor	Tunner
Churner	Hooper	•	Tunwright
Churnman	Hoops	Piggins	•
Churnwright	Hoper	•	Vattman
•	Hopper	Stavely	

GROUP 113

Basket Makers

Banister	Bushill	Hott	•
Bannester	Busseler	Hotter	Ripper
Bannister	Bussell	•	•
•	•	Leaper	Skepper
Baskett	Corbell	Leeper	Skipp
Basketter	Corbiller	Lepmaker	Skipper
Bishell	Corble	•	•
Bissell	•	Paniermaker	Willer
Bissill	Fanner	•	Willers
Boshell	Vannah	Peck	
Bossel	Vanner	Peckar	
Bushell	•	Pecker	

GROUP 114

Cabinetmakers

Arkwright	Coffrer	•	Turner
Artrick	•	Kystewright	Turnor
Hartrick	Disher	•	Turnour
Hartwright	•	Maser	•
Hattrick	Escriner	Maslen	Whiccher
•	•	Maslin	Whicchewright
Carver	Hucher	•	Whicher
•	•	Tabletter	Whitcher
Coffer	Keruere	•	Witcher

GROUP 115

Wheel and Wagon Makers

Cartwright	Waine	Wennman	Wheeller
Kortwright	Wainer	Weyman	Wheelwright
•	Waines	Whenman	Wheler
Nawright	Wainewright	•	Whelmonger
•	Wainman	Wailer	Whelsmyth
Rower	Wainright	Wayler	Whelster
Royer	Wainwright	Weldsmith	Whelwright
•	Wayne	Whaler	Whilesmith
Wagner	Waynwright	Whealler	Wildsmith
Wain	Wenman	Wheeler	Wilesmith

GROUP 116

Toolmakers

Bec	•	Brayer	•
Beck	Besmer	•	Burstlere
Becke	•	Bromer	•

Cuillerer	Hornere	Peel	•
•	•	•	Rasor
Filer	Hudgel	Peniur	•
•	Hudghel	•	Rastall
Hacker	Hugel	Pigache	•
•	•	•	Shouler
Hafter	Ladeler	Pinchen	Shovel
•	•	Pinchin	Shoveller
Hammer	Malet	Pinching	Shovels
•	Mallet	Pinchon	Showler
Hardee	Mallett	Pinsent	•
Hardey	Mallette	Pinshon	Sickles
Hardie	•	Pinson	•
Hardy	Peal	•	Spade
•	Peale	Plowright	Spader

GROUP 117

Molders and Bellfounders

Beller	•	Moldemaker	Pannegetter
Belleyeter	Foundour	Molder	Panner
Billiter	•	•	

GROUP 118

Minters

Coiner	Minter	Monnyer	Seeler
•	•	•	Seinter

CHAPTER 19

Castles and Manor Houses

An amazing number of our most familiar names seem to have originated in those big, gloomy old structures called castles that dotted the whole face of England from the twelfth century on. Many are still there but fallen into picturesque decay, while others exist as tourist attractions.

For a full three hundred years after the death of the Conqueror in 1087, England went on a castle-building spree. No matter where one went, one was within sight or sound of masons chipping away at great blocks of granite or other workmen digging away at a moat.

A few details about the construction and form of castles in general is necessary if one is to understand how and why so many names came out of them.

It will serve convenience better to describe a composite castle; one that will contain the crudities of eleventh-century buildings along with the improvements and changes that succeeding generations installed.

Such a castle will have an enormous staff of retainers in all sections of the building, with duplication on top of duplication, because our composite castle is to contemplate some three hundred years and the whole of medieval England. Thus, the people of a castle in Kent in the twelfth century might refer to their cook as the kitchman, while a generation or so later the family in the very same castle might call their cook the hastler or the gilliver. There were a great many names for cooks, and just as many for each different job.

A castle was primarily a fortress, built to withstand either a sudden attack or a prolonged siege by an army. It was also the home of the lord

258

of the manor and his family, along with a constantly changing but never-ending stream of guests who had to be fed, bedded, and entertained. Castles were always built on top of a hill if that were possible, and at the fork of a river as well. A deep and wide moat with flowing water was considered necessary at least around the greater part of the structure, in order to discourage the enemy. A drawbridge connected the outside world with the main gate of the castle. This gate was usually placed between two towers well provided with quarters for the gatekeepers who looked over the credentials of any stranger seeking entrance.

Once inside, one would be impressed with several things simultaneously. A castle was not just one huge building: it was a whole complex of structures enclosed by a stone wall. Around the inside of the wall would be many buildings of various sizes and shapes, and in the center of the enclosed area would be a huge stone building known as the keep. This building was the last resort in case of attack; to it all retainers as well as peasants from the village would retreat. It contained its own well and a huge supply of food in its lower portion. Somewhere below would also be a place reserved for prisoners. Sometimes this was called by the Middle English term donjon, although the entire tower was properly called by the same name. The name is spelled *dumjon* once or twice in the records.

Up in the castle is a great hall that might measure a hundred feet long by more than half that in width. It would have two or three huge fireplaces, and its walls would be hung with tapestries that were in turn the background for old hunting and warring weapons. At one end of the hall, raised well above the level of the floor, would be a gallery for musicians and in front of the gallery would be a raised dais running across the hall. On this would be the great table where the lord of the manor and his distinguished guests would dine. All the rest of the company would sit at trestle tables running at right angles to the dais.

A narrow stairway, right up against one of the walls, led to a long corridor with numerous doors. At the largest door might be a liveried servant called a chamberlain (spelled several different ways), who was the personal servant of the lord of the manor.

GROUP 119

Nobility

The lord of the manor may have had any one of the titles shown in Group 119 (see page 273). If he were a PRINCE, he was the son of the king, but if he were merely a DUKE or an EARL, a COUNT or a BARON, he would still be known as the LORD of the manor (in Scotland, LAIRD). Many of the names in this group represent misspellings of the period, as well as errors of later years. Understandably, it must have been difficult for a man of the period to recognize a proper way of spelling his own name when he could not write it himself!

Before leaving this group of names, it should be noted that all these titles were frequently used as nicknames by the common people of the time (see page 14). The nobles had tournaments that were restricted to the gentry, but the peasants had pageants for their own entertainment. In these affairs, the most humble of peasants might dress himself in any fantastic semblance of royalty he might care to imitate, and if it made a hit with his friends, he might be called on for the same impersonation time after time and so become known as the EARL or the HURLL.

GROUP 120

Deputies

The names in this group number almost a hundred, and every one of them has something in common. They are all deputies. Unlike the previous group, who held their land directly from the crown, these men were deputized by the direct holder to operate the castle for the holder's benefit. These deputies managed every detail of the estate, including collecting taxes and holding court.

Acting for an absentee landlord was not at all uncommon in those days. Earlier it was mentioned how liberal the Conqueror was with the Normans who had served him well in his conquest of the English, and how he handed out huge estates with a lavish hand. Just how lavish he was can be judged by a few statistics. William's brother Robert must have been of enormous help, because William gave him no less than 793 manorial estates. These consisted of anything from a small farm of a few acres to huge manors covering many square miles, including dozens of villages and thousands of peasants and craftsmen. William's other brother, Odo, received only 439 manorial estates. There was Alan of Brittany as well—his share of the spoils came to 539 manors, mostly in Cornwall (and, I might say, most of Cornwall).

Nobody could possibly occupy more than two or three big manors even if he moved from one to another every day; yet, as the original holder from the king, he had the first responsibility for each manor. Deputies, men whom the lord could trust to operate each estate, had to be the answer.

Now look again at these names. There are no less than thirty names all starting with BA. In Old French there was the word *bail,* which meant "to deliver something," so the word already seems to fit the duties of a man entrusted with the care of a big institution. What was apparently the same word (though it derived this time from a word meaning "to enclose") was applied to the stone wall that surrounded the castle and, before long, it was used to indicate the huge area between the bail and the keep too. This was an extremely important sector of the castle and the man placed in charge of it had to be highly responsible, so he came to be called the BAIL or even BAILEY or any one of the numerous variations. (I know of no record to prove it, but I am sure that in numerous instances such men were put in complete charge of the castle when an attack occurred that called for a new appointee.) BAILIFFS became legal officers throughout England and some of the variants listed still remain in the legal system.

The CASTELLAN names are easy because they all come directly from either of the Old French words *castelain* or *chastelain,* which meant "governor of a castle." There is one William de Castellon in the old Domesday Book of 1086.

CONSTABLE is particularly interesting in that it developed from humble beginnings. Forget the CON and one is left with STABLE—exactly where the word originated. A constable started out in charge of the horses in the stables of a great lord, and he seems to have served so well that he was pushed up the ladder until in numerous cases he was placed in charge of a complete estate. There is no known relationship between the MARSHALL names and the CONSTABLE names, except that they both had their origin in the stables of medieval castles and by hard work and whatever else, they climbed the social ladder with giant steps. CONSTABLES were commonly appointed as governors of important castles throughout the entire Middle Ages.

The GRANGER names were given to overseers of large farms. The names are discussed more fully in chapter 14 (see page 184).

Both the PRATER and the REAVES names mean essentially the same thing in that they belonged to men of authority. They may not always have been the top man in a manor, but they were certainly close to it. The Latin word *praetor* meant "an assistant," while *reeve* meant "a trusted servant."

The PROCKTER names come from the Latin word *procurator,* meaning simply a manager or an agent for an absentee owner. And the PROVEST names, although from a different origin, mean the very same thing. Later these names came to be associated with medieval universities (see chapter 25, page 352).

In Norman French, *seignour* meant "lord." If a man were given an estate to manage by one of the Conqueror's beneficiaries, he might well end up with any one of the thirteen names beginning with SAINER.

There are at least four ways of spelling STEWART, but all have the same meaning and similar origin. In Old English, it was spelled *stiwerd* and for a long time, it was thought that the word referred either to a man who kept pigs or to the place where he kept them, but modern scholarship is of a different mind. They regard it as meaning "the keeper of the house." The Normans had a French word, *seneschal*, that definitely meant the officer in charge of a very large household, so if a man were placed in charge of a castle or large manor house, he would be known by one of the STEWARD names or any of the SENESCHAL names.

The SHERIFF names refer to the chief law-enforcement officers of a shire or county. They could be of noble birth, but this was not usually the case. They were frequently directly appointed by the king and were answerable only to him. Any man with that kind of authority would live in at least a fortified manor or small castle.

This finishes the very top ranking men in the castles; from here, the list moves more or less down the line of command—I say more or less because we are looking at a time interval of some two hundred and fifty years, and in such a long time a great many changes took place in the practical meaning of the words that developed into names.

GROUP 121

Gentry

Every name in this group might be referred to as gentry. The BACHE-LOR names come from the Norman word *bachelor,* meaning nothing more than "a young man." He might be a knight, but more often he was in training for the honor of knighthood.

The CHILD names are interesting even if their earliest meaning isn't clear. During the thirteenth century and later, the name CHILD or one of its variations was applied to a young man of good family—even perhaps noble—who was training to become a KNIGHT.

The SQUIRE list, as well as ARMIGER and ARMINGER, is of names almost invariably given to lads training for knighthood. In fact, the ARMINGER type of name tells us definitely of one who carried some of the knight's arms and armor as part of his training.

KNIGHT, KNIGHTS, RIDER, and RYDER, in practice, meant about the same. Knights did most of the riding, so the terms were virtually synonymous.

This gives us six basic names with their variants, all of which indicated knights or men in preparation for knighthood—ARMIGER, BACHELOR, CHILD, KNIGHT, RIDER, and SQUIRE.

The seven names beginning with GENT were given to young men of good family and frequently of noble descent. Probably none of them aspired to knighthood or they would have been tagged with one of the six preceding names, but they would be at home in the castle.

HENSMAN and HINCKESMAN changed their meaning so much in the Middle Ages that it is impossible to pin them down. In Old English the word came from *hengest,* meaning "stallion," and *mann,* meaning "a groom," but before that could crystallize into a real surname, it began to be applied to a young squire training to be a knight and, in at least one case, a HENSMAN was a page of honor.

JEWSTER, JOESTER, and JUSTER seem to have been applied to knights who made a business of entering tournaments. The Normans were fond of the tournament, and in the twelfth century it was a rough affair. One group of young knights would ride against another group, each trying to unhorse his opponent or even wound him enough so that he was out of the fight. If one knight knocked his opponent off, he was entitled to the other's armor, weapons, and even his horse. The winner could also demand a ransom. In the course of a century or more, at least a few men seem to have made a business out of this.

A young boy of good family, placed in the house of a lord to train for knighthood, would first serve for seven years as a PAGE or PAIGE.

CLARK and SCRIVENOR and many similar names will be treated in some detail in chapter 25, but they were of such importance and interest that the composite castle simply had to have at least one of each. They were men who could write. Aside from the clergy, almost nobody could write at that time; in fact, a nobleman would be insulted if one were to ask him to write even one or two words.

GROUP 122

Sergeants

The Normans seem to have introduced the term SERGEANT into English medieval history. In Old French, *sergent* or *serjant* generally meant a servant, but it is impossible to find a single one by that name or any of its variations who was in any literal sense a servant. Far from it —they held important jobs.

Men to whom this name was given were definitely not nobles, but they were a long way from being peasants too. They were not knights, and there seems to be reason to think that the name may have been given when knighthood was out of the question because of age. They may have won favor with the lord of the manor and his way of rewarding them was to give them a rank that would set them well above the yeoman but still short of knighthood. Cases are known where they were empowered to arrest offenders and bring them before the court of the manor as well as deliver the guilty into the hands of the keeper. There are also cases where the lord of the manor made no secret of his desire simply to have his friend in the comfort of the castle where he could live in relative luxury, and, we may suppose, brighten up the day of his lordship. At least one case is known where a sergeant's sole duty in the castle was to replace the chessmen in their regular receptacle when a game was over.

The spelling variations are innumerable.

GROUP 123

Tax Assessors

There can be no doubt about the location of this office and the group of men who held forth there. They were definitely quartered permanently in the castle of the lord where he could keep a daily check on them if he cared to. As was detailed earlier, the medieval tax man assessed property and collected the tax all at the same time. This put enormous power into his hands, as, generally speaking, there was no appeal from his assessment.

These are names tax men were called publicly; many of them certainly reflect the hatred of the population for them in general, but if we could have listened to what they were called privately we would have a still more accurate description.

The CATCHPOLE names derive from the Old Norman-French word *cachepol,* which means "to chase fowl." In 1086, in the Domesday Book are listed Aluricus Chacepol and Robert le Chachpol. It is not hard to visualize a tax man chasing chickens, ducks, and geese to put in the cagelike cart waiting to take them back to the castle.

CATCHER and KETCHER are clearly involved in a similar chase.

COUNTER refers to the auditor who checked up on the collectors as they came back to the castle each evening.

The FARMER names in the list have no relation whatever to today's agriculturists. The word came from an Old Latin word, *firmarius,* which meant a man who undertook the hateful job of collecting taxes.

GABLER and GABLEOR are at least honest names. They don't pretend to be anything else but what they were—tax collectors. The names come from the Old French word *gabelier,* and GABLEOR actually meant a usurer. The name still persists in England but always in its French form.

The GARNER names were given to the man who was to gather and store grain. The GARNER got the grain from the GABLERS and the FARMARS and stored it away for the lord of the manor.

GATHERER is self-explanatory.

HORDER was another name given to a man who saw to the storage of all the livestock and food that came in.

The LARDER and the LARDNER were the men who stored the food brought in that wasn't on the hoof or in the form of grain.

The LANGSTAFF names are probably nicknames for tax collectors who carried staffs of unusual length. It is a common name in Westmorland today. Richard Langstaff is registered in 1210.

The TOLLER group gives us a glimpse into the life of that period. No lord of a manor ever overlooked an opportunity to obtain money or goods. If a merchant on the way to a fair with a string of pack animals loaded with goods had to pass over some of the land of the lord, there would be toll men out there to make him stand and deliver. Even a tiny footbridge across a brook could be made profitable. Richard le Toller appears in 1214.

GROUP 124

Guards

The names given to the men charged with the responsibility of guarding a great castle were many and varied. The man called a WARD in one castle would have been called a YEOMAN in another, and a generation later the WARD might be known as a TOTMAN or a WAITMAN and the YEOMAN as a SPIER. Early records of the names are Robert Toteman in 1202, William le Spiour in 1379, and Roger le Wate in 1251.

ALABASTAR and ARBLASTER were names given to men skilled in the use of the crossbow (see chapter 8). Richard le Arbelaster appears

in 1198. BOWMAN usually meant a user of the longbow. The ARBLAS-
TERS were key men in the defense of a castle. The crossbow was a very
deadly weapon within a range of a hundred yards or so. The walls of a
castle and particularly the tower were always crenellated (crenellation is
the familiar notches and spaces always associated with castles, and also
called battlements). The crossbowmen stood behind a merlon to wind
up his weapon and stepped over to an embrasure or open space when
he was all set to shoot. These merlons and embrasures look picturesque
to us today, but they were not built just to look nice.

The BRIDGEMAN group tell their own story, and TOTMAN and
TOTTMAN differ only in that they were usually assigned to high lookout spots on the battlements where they could see some distance.

The DARWOOD group were doorkeepers and the entire group of
WAIT names meant "watchman," more or less, and were interchangeable
with any of the already mentioned names. The name comes from the Old
French word *guaite*. A William Doreward is listed in 1230.

GARD, GARRISON, and GUARD need no explanation. John le
Garde is listed in 1275.

GARTH and GARTHMAN refer to the inner wall surrounding the
castle tower. At times the word meant the wall itself but more frequently
referred to the space inside the wall and finally to the particular guard
charged with the defense of this area. John del Garth appears in 1297.

GATWARD is just a combination of "gate" and "watch." Richard le
Gateward is in the tax records of 1255.

In the PONT names, it is possible to be a little more specific, as they
must have been watchers at the great drawbridge, the main entrance to
the castle. William Punt is listed in 1316.

The PORTER names belonged to men who were not baggage carriers
as they are today, but gate-watchers. And so were the WATCHERS.
Andrew Portour is recorded in 1356.

The SPIER names were given to the watchmen, sentinels, guards, and
so on.

The name WARD with all its variations appears constantly in medieval history and is still with us today. It comes from an Old English word,
weard, meaning "one who watches or guards something." The something he was called upon to guard might be small and unimportant, but
it could also be something as important as the whole castle.

YEOMAN, with its variations, was a very common word in the Middle
Ages. It was used loosely to indicate a man in almost any capacity. He
might rank between a sergeant and a groom or between a squire and
a page.

GROUP 125

Messengers

It seems that young men who carried messages were quite important and so numerous that they left us many names. We are so accustomed to modern means of communication that we seldom even have to think of messengers. The Norman word was *messagier,* and a Hugh le Messager is recorded in 1211.

The BODE names were given to messengers who acted as heralds, or carriers of official messages. Walter Bode appears in 1220.

The COURIER names derive from the Old French word *coreor,* meaning "a runner used to carry messages." Thomas Corour is in the 1331 records.

The GALLATLEY and GOLIGHTLY names were probably first used as nicknames, as was LIGHTFOOT. GALPEN, GALPIN, and GAL-PYN are related to the word *gallop.* I am not sure how a man would go about galloping, but perhaps it referrred to a messenger who was especially speedy. Henry Gellatty is listed in 1291, and William Galpin in 1279.

PASSANT and PASSAVANT meant a messenger who went ahead of somebody—maybe to warn the people or to announce something. Andrew Passeavant appears in 1212. The whole PIRKIS group had nothing to do with purchasing but meant messengers also.

RENNER comes from the Middle English word *renner* meaning "runner" and referred to a runner of messages.

SHERWEN and SHERWIN meant a messenger who could cut the wind with his speed. The name derives from the Old English word *sceran,* meaning "to cut wind." John Sherwyn is listed in 1524.

The TROTTER names derive from the Old French word *trotier.* Robert Trotar appears in 1148.

GROUP 126

Cooks

The kitchen of our composite castle was just off the great hall. It was connected to the hall by two doors: one for entering and one for exiting. The kitchen itself was very large, as it might have a staff of a dozen or more men. It would have two very large fireplaces with cranes and spits large enough to broil a quarter of beef and a couple of porkers at the same time. The pigs would not weigh more than a hundred pounds each, and they would be almost split down the middle. The English of that period, and for centuries after, loved to serve pigs whole with the head in place and an apple held in the jaws.

This listing indicates a great many cooks in the kitchen, but over the ten or more generations of the naming period, the names of occupations were constantly changing. COOK would change to COOKSON and a generation later might be CUXON or even COKE.

A BREWITT had nothing to do with brewing: the BREWITTS and BORWETTS made soup. The name comes from the Old French word *brouet*. John Brouet appears in 1268.

COLLOP derived from a combination of Anglo-Saxon words meaning either ham or bacon fried with eggs. John Collop is listed in 1280.

The CURREY names mean kitchen as, indeed, do the KITCHEN names. CURREY derives from the Old French word *curie*. Philip le Curry is recorded in 1162.

The name CUSYNER is Old French for "cook" and the KEW names are also from Old French words made to do service in England. Hugh le Kew is recorded in 1246.

If a cook learned how to make a fair dish of custard, he might find himself being called a FLAONER or any of the other FLANN names. Richard le Flauner was one in 1211.

The GILLIVER was a sauce-maker. The Old French word was *gilofre*, while in Middle English it became *gilliver*; in both languages, it meant the spice clove. Evidently some inventive cook developed a new sauce with a clove flavor that was very popular. Sauces were more important in medieval times than they are now; they had to be strongly flavored to disguise many foods that were more or less tainted. The old records have numerous examples of the name, such as William Girofre in 1210.

A HASTLER roasted meat. The Old French word was *haste* meaning "meat roasted on a spit" or *hasteler*, meaning an expert user of a spit. The HASTLER frequently took charge of the whole kitchen. Henry le Hasteler appears back in 1190.

KETCHEN through KITCHMAN come from the Old English word *cycene* which simply meant a room where food was prepared. Naturally some variation of the word might be used on the spur of the moment to designate an employee in that room. I find Henry atte Kychene in 1311 and Thomas Kytchener a little later.

The two POT names come from the Old French word *potagier,* meaning a maker of soup. Walter le Potagier is listed in 1300.

SAUSER referred to someone who made sauces.

GROUP 127

Household Executives

In our hypothetical castle, a vast amount of help would certainly be required, and this would necessitate some departmentalizing. The cook, by whatever name he was known, would run the kitchen, but he would not have charge of the bread supplies. Another man took care of this and he picked up the name of PANTER, PANTHER, PANTREY, PANTRY, or even PA, PANS, or PANNIERS. All of the PAN names have a slightly mixed origin. The derivation is either from the English word *panne,* which meant "a pan" or "a man who made pans," or from the French word *pan,* which meant "bread." One example is Reginald le Paneter in 1200.

The BUTLER names (for example, Hugo Buteiller in 1055, and Baldwin le Buteilier in 1200) indicate men who not only bought wine for the castle but carried the keys to the wine cellar. These men ruled the wine cellar with an iron hand. The three BURLE names were variations. The Old English word was *byrele,* meaning "cupboard."

The five names starting with CATER refer to the man in charge of buying food supplies; this is somewhat puzzling because a huge estate raised just about every foodstuff necessary. Spices and wine and olive oil would have to be imported and consequently bought, but it would hardly seem a full-time job. There was a William Katerer in 1260.

Then there was SPENCE. This name might be spelled five different ways, but it meant a man who was in charge of dispensing all the food. He was evidently an official of some stature; a bit later, he was known as the SPENDER, or the STEART (see Group 120) of the food.

The HALL names leave no room for doubt. The hall was the castle; that is, the showroom, the room on which visitors were going to form their opinion of the host and his whole institution. The man who bore this name had to have the right combination of taste and ability to get things done. He was in total charge of the hall and could hire and fire at will. He might even prepare the menu and tell the musicians what to play. Warin de Halla is listed in 1178.

The WARDROBE names are complicated in that we know what they had to do but not how far their duties may have extended. They were definitely in charge of the wardrobe of the whole castle. The name derives from the Old French words *warderobe* and *garderobe* meaning "to watch the clothes." It seems reasonable to think that the duty of a WARDROBE was something like a modern protocol officer—he made it his business to know all the rules of courtesy to visiting nobility and issued the proper garments to his own castle's staff for special occasions. I find a William Warderober in 1275, and a Thomas Garderober in 1351.

GROUP 128

Personal Staff

Next come the members of the staff whose duties to the lord, his family, his noble guests, and to all invited gentry as well as resident gentry, was more personal.

Some of these names indicate clearly the exact duties of an individual, at least at the time fate decided to tag that individual with a name. EWER, for example, with its several variations definitely meant a person who brought water around to each guest at the table just before dinner was served so that each guest could wash his hands. Hand-washing was not considered a prime necessity at that time, even among the upper classes, and the job must have been an easy one, but it gave us at least seven names that are still with us. The Middle English word was *ewery*, and it meant a room where water and linen were kept. John del Ewry is listed in 1370.

The CHAMBERLAIN names indicate men who serviced chamber pots (in Scotland they called them CHALMERS). This useful item became a fixture all over the civilized world in an age when modern plumbing was still undreamed of. Probably the custom of having a CHAMBERLAIN started with royalty, but during the naming period, it was extended far and wide until by the sixteenth century the better-class inns employed the service of such persons.

In the case of the king's chamberlain, it can easily be understood how his duties would grow more numerous and varied from day to day. He would comb the royal hair and trim it now and then, clean the king's boots, and help him to dress. The king, being human, might very well chatter about his problems of the day, and in the course of a generation or two, the lowly servant of royalty found himself advising and counseling the king and being taken seriously. Eventually, the chamberlain might be rewarded with a far more dignified status. Chamberlain is the earliest French spelling. Robert le Chamberleyn is recorded in 1232.

The BOWER names were similar to the CHAMBERLAIN group originally, the only difference being that usually the bower was a room reserved for the ladies. This did not mean a ladies' room in today's sense of that term, but rather a room in the castle where ladies unaccompanied by a man might not only sleep but spend the whole day, if they cared to, in spinning, sewing, or any other entertainment they might wish.

The nine names beginning with DUMJOHN and ending with KEEPER referred to men who were jailers. They were certainly resident in the castle of the manor because that was the location of the only jail. It was usually in the lowest part of the tower or KEEP of the castle. And the man with the keys to it would naturally be called the KEEP or the KEEPER or some other variation.

Then there was NAPER, NAPIER, and NAPPER. All clearly indicated a man or woman in charge of the table linen. The Old French word was *napier,* meaning "table cloth." Ralph le Naper is recorded in 1130. The USHER names meant men who would wait at the door to the hall and escort guests to their proper seats at the table or to their room if they were just arriving at the castle. The Old French word is *ussier.*

The PAGE names could have been placed in the list of MESSENGERS earlier in this chapter, because a page was definitely that. However, a PAGE might now and then be given the additional duty of handing the first cup of wine to his lordship at dinner. This was considered something of an honor, and since it served to bring the young man to the attention of the lord at a favorable moment, being a page had its advantages. William le Page is listed in 1229.

The HERALD names are somewhat unusual in that the duties of their owner varied from place to place and from time to time. In one area, he might be the official who formally declares peace between contenders. He could not be in command of either faction, but because of his impressive appearance and his loud voice, he would be selected to read the peace treaty to the assembled populace. Again, there was the HERALD who carried messages between monarchs—messages considered too important to be carried by an ordinary messenger. In the tournaments, he was always called on to issue challenges between important nobles. A noble might very well feel that his own prestige would mount in the eyes of his opponent as well as the whole assembly if he sent a challenge by means of an imposing HERALD. After the naming period, the HERALD became associated with heraldry, but this did not come about until after our names were fairly well fixed. John Heraud is listed in 1296.

Then there was the BANNERMAN. He was the chap chosen to carry the banner in tournaments or whatever events might call for a banner. Donald Banerman appears in 1368.

The historians of the period are somewhat divided on the character, particularly the professional character, of the JESTER and the MIN-STRELL. Some would make the JESTER a probable halfwit, so witless that the lord of the manor could take any amount of abuse from him and laugh at the whole tirade because he, and everybody else within hearing, knew that the man didn't realize what he had been saying. While this may have been true in some cases, I am inclined to believe that most JESTERS were simply natural comedians with an extraordinary supply of ready wit that could be depended upon to brighten up a situation that might otherwise get too serious. John Gestour lived in 1380.

The MINSTRELLS, on the other hand, were artists. Like all artists, they varied greatly in quality; some were probably geniuses while others were mediocre. They were singers, musicians, and storytellers. A MIN-STRELL might be all of these things or none, but he could and would hold the eager attention of an audience for long periods. For the most part, they traveled about from one castle to another—staying a few days in each as a welcome guest. They would carry the news and quite possibly the gossip of neighboring manors, and this alone made them more than welcome. Now and then, one would appear on the scene with obviously superior talents and he would be asked to remain permanently. He might even be made a SARGENT.

GROUP 129

Servants

All of these names refer to servants. Unlike most of the other names in this chapter, they do not tell us what kind of work such men did. Of course, in any real sense of the word, everyone in the Middle Ages had to be the servant of somebody, excepting only the king himself who owed allegiance only to God. The king owned everything and everybody owed him either money, service, or property—that was the whole basis of feudalism. Nevertheless, these men were undoubtedly servants of lords with much the same stature as chamberlains and bowers and ewers.

It is interesting to note the name LADYMAN in this group, for there are a very great number of names in English that end in -*man*. This type of name was usually applied to an assistant or, in a broad sense, a servant

—a LADYMAN would be the servant of the lady of the manor, a RICH-MAN the servant of RICH or RICHARD.

GROUP 130

The Chaplain and His Chapel

The castle would always contain a chapel, with a resident chaplain, where all residents of the castle could attend mass every morning. The peasants living in the village might also hear mass or attend vespers in the chapel if it happened to be more convenient.

There seems to be no logical reason for so many different spellings of the two names as both CHAPLAIN and CHAPEL come from the same Latin root *cappela,* meaning a short cloak. The Old French word is *capele.* We find a William Capelain listed in 1203, a Thomas le Chape-lyn in 1241, and a John Chapel in 1202.

GROUP 131

Miscellaneous

By no means are all the occupations of residents of the castle ex-hausted. Those remaining, however, are so important that they were not confined to the castle. BAKERS and MILLERS, BREWERS and AR-MOURERS could be found far and wide and they are each treated in some detail in other chapters. One more of these, the FALCONER, was located *only* in the castle, but he is discussed in chapter 21.

GROUP 119

Nobility			
Baron	•	Hearl	•
Barron	Duke	Hearle	Laird
•	•	Hurl	Lord
Count	Earl	Hurle	•
Le Count	Earle	Hurll	Prince
Lecount	Harle	Hurles	

GROUP 120

Deputies

Bail	Baylor	Provost	Senskell
Bailar	Bayly	•	•
Baile	Baylyff	Reaves	Sheriff
Baileff	•	Reeve	Sheriffs
Bailes	Castellan	Reeves	Sherriff
Bailey	Castellain	•	Sherriffs
Bailie	Castelein	Sainer	Shireff
Bailif	Castling	Sayner	Shiriff
Bailiff	Chatelain	Saynor	Shirman
Bailis	•	Seanor	Shirra
Bailiss	Constable	Seener	Shirreff
Baillie	•	Seignior	Shirreffs
Bailly	Grainge	Senier	Shirrefs
Bailor	Grainger	Senior	Shreeve
Bails	Grange	Seniour	Shreeves
Bailward	Granger	Senyard	Shreve
Baily	Graunger	Seyner	Shrieve
Bale	•	Sinyard	Shrieves
Bales	Prater	Synyer	Shrive
Baly	Preater	•	Shrives
Baylay	Pretor	Senchell	•
Bayle	•	Senecal	Steuart
Bayles	Prockter	Senescall	Steward
Bayley	Procter	Seneschal	Stewart
Baylie	Proctor	Seneschall	Stuart
Bayliff	Provest	Sensicall	
Baylis	Provis	Sensicle	

GROUP 121

Gentry

Armiger	•	Bachelor	Batchelder
Arminger	Bachellier	Batchelar	Batcheldor

Batcheler	•	•	•
Batchellor	Clark	Jewster	Scrivenor
Batchelor	•	Joester	•
Batchelour	Gent	Juster	Squier
Batchlor	Gentile	•	Squiers
•	Gentle	Knight	Squire
Cheeld	Gentleman	Knights	Squires
Child	Gentles	•	Swiers
Childe	Gentry	Page	Swire
Childs	Jent	Paige	Swires
Chiles	•	•	Swyer
Chill	Hensman	Rider	
Chilles	Hinckesman	Ryder	

GROUP 122

Sergeants

Sargaison	Sarginson	Seargeant	Serginson
Sargant	Sargint	Searjeant	Sergison
Sargeant	Sargison	Sergant	Serjeant
Sargeantson	Sargisson	Sergean	Serjeantson
Sargeaunt	Sarjant	Sergeant	Serjent
Sargent	Sarjantson	Sergeaunt	Surgison
Sargentson	Sarjeant	Sergenson	
Sargeson	Sarjent	Sergent	

GROUP 123

Tax Assessors

Catcher	Catchpoole	Farmar	Gableor
Ketcher	Catchpoule	Farmer	Gabler
Catchpole	•	Fermer	•
Catchpoll	Counter	Fermor	Garnar
Catchpool	•	•	Garner

(Tax Assessors, continued)

Garnier	Horder	Langstaff	Toler
Gerner	•	Longstaff	Toller
•	Larder	Longstaffe	Tolman
Gatherer	Lardner	•	Tolmon
•	•	Toleman	Towler

GROUP 124

Guards

Alabaster	Garthman	•	Whait
Arblaster	•	Totman	Whaite
•	Gatward	Tottman	Whaites
Bowman	•	•	Whaits
•	Pont	Wacher	Whate
Bridgeman	Ponte	Watcher	•
Bridger	Ponter	Watchman	Ward
Bridgman	Punt	•	Warde
Brugger	Punter	Waight	Warden
•	•	Waighte	Warder
Darwood	Port	Wait	Wardsman
Dorrad	Porte	Waite	Wards
Dorrett	Porter	Waites	Wordman
Dorward	Porters	Waits	•
Dorwood	•	Wakeman	Yeaman
Durward	Speir	Wates	Yeman
•	Speirs	Wayt	Yeoman
Gard	Spier	Wayte	Yeomans
Garrison	Spiers	Waytes	
Guard	Spyer	Weait	
Garth	Spyers	Weight	

GROUP 125

Messengers

Bode	Golightly	Passant	Purkis
Boder	•	Passavant	Purkiss
Bodman	Galpen	•	•
•	Galpin	Pirkis	Renner
Courier	Galpyn	Pirkiss	•
Courror	•	Porcas	Sherwen
•	Lightfoot	Porkiss	Sherwin
Gallatley	•	Purchas	•
Gallatly	Massinger	Purchase	Trotman
Galletly	Messenger	Purches	Trott
Gellatly	Messinger	Purchese	Trotter
Gelletly	•	Purkess	

GROUP 126

Cooks

Brewitt	Currey	•	Kitchen
Browett	Currie	Gilliver	Kitchener
•	Curry	•	Kitchin
Coke	•	Hastler	Kitchiner
Cook	Cusyner	•	Kitching
Cooke	•	Kew	Kitchingman
Cookes	Flann	Le Keux	Kitchman
Cooksey	Flanner	Lequeux	•
Cookson	Flanning	•	Potager
Cuckson	Flaoner	Ketchen	Pottinger
•	Flawn	Ketchin	•
Collop	•	Kichin	Sauser
•	Flawner	Kitcheman	

GROUP 127

Household Executives

Burle	Chater	Panniers	Spenser
Burles	Chaytor	Pans	•
Burls	•	Panter	Wardrobe
Butler	Hall	Panther	Wardrop
Buttery	Hallard	Pantrey	Wardrope
Buttler	Halle	Pantry	Wardroper
Buttrey	Haller	•	Wardropper
•	Halls	Spence	Wardrupp
Cater	Hallward	Spencer	Waredraper
Caterer	•	Spend	
Cator	Pan	Spens	

GROUP 128

Personal Staff

Bannerman	Champerlen	Jailer	•
•	•	Keep	Jester
Boorman	Delhuary	Keeper	•
Borman	Ewer	•	Minstrell
Bour	Ewers	Herald	•
Bower	Lewer	Heraud	Naper
Bowerman	Lower	Herod	Napier
Bowers	Lurey	Herold	Napper
Burman	Lurie	Herrald	•
•	•	Herrod	Padgett
Chalmers	Dumjohn	Herrold	Page
Chamberlain	Dunjohn	•	Paget
Chamberlaine	Dunjon	Husher	Pagett
Chamberlayne	Galer	Lusher	Paige
Chamberlen	Gayler	Usher	
Chambers	Gaylor	Ussher	

GROUP 129

Servants

Hine	Ladd	Sarvant	Swain
Hines	Ladds	Sarver	Swaine
Hyne	Ladyman	Servant	Swayn
Hynes	•	Servante	Swayne
•	Mann	Servent	
Lackey	•	•	

GROUP 130

The Chaplain and His Chapel

Capelen	Caplen	Chaplain	Kaplan
Capelin	Caplin	Chaplin	Kaplin
Capeling	Chaperlin	Chapline	
Caplan	Chaperling	Chapling	

GROUP 131

Miscellaneous

Armour	Coward	Gossard	Poulter
•	•	•	•
Baker	Doctor	Marshall	Swinyard
•	•	•	•
Brewer	Falconer	Miller	Vintor

Entertainers

Today when one speaks of entertainers, one usually means professionals, but in the historical period we call the Middle Ages a great majority of the entertainers were amateurs with no intention whatever of making a business out of their particular skills. They performed on demand and accepted the plaudits of the crowd as sufficient reward, although if something more substantial were offered, it would be accepted.

People looking back at these middle centuries of history have referred to Merry England. Modern writers scoff at the expression, pointing to the undoubted crudities of the age, but in spite of all the cruel laws, barberous customs, ridiculous restrictions on the peasants, and the almost unbelievable gap between the common man and the lordly noble, the English people as a nation were a fun-loving, boisterous, bawdy crowd, anxious to squeeze every tiny bit of enjoyment they could from every situation. The age of the puritan, when anything that was fun must necessarily be sinful, was still far in the future.

There were wars, of course, and Englishmen lost their lives, but wars were not at all the continuous things they are today. A whole generation might pass where a sizable portion of the population would have no knowledge of war. A young fellow could be born, be raised to manhood, and even grow into middle age, without even hearing about a war.

The peasant-farmers worked from sunrise to sunset on their tiny fields. This usually meant three days on the land belonging to the lord and then three days on their own tiny strips. Then, there would be a blessed Sunday when no man worked. Also, interspersed throughout the year were numerous religious holy days on which no one was allowed to work unless the task was declared essential.

With the peasant-craftsman, the situation was about the same; he worked on the domain of the lord for part of the week, and the balance he spent in his own shop at home. By the early part of the twelfth century, the craft guilds began to exert a very healthy pressure on the labor hours. The guilds were so effective that for most of the crafts, the actual working hours were considerably less than they were to be in the early part of the nineteenth century. Although the guilds deservedly take much of the credit for this, the lack of good artificial lighting also played a part.

The names this period produced tell us something about the amusements of the people. A man would not be called a DANCER and have the name stay with him the rest of his life unless he did enough dancing to become known for that skill. To be called a HARPER or a PIPER or a HORNBLOWER would say nothing of one's ability to raise crops, but surely did indicate that one played one of those instruments at least well enough to make that name serve as ready identification. The mere fact that the list of names coming down to us from the amusements of the common people of that period is so large (170) does seem to indicate that there was indeed a "Merry England."

GROUP 132

Stringed-Instrument Players

These men are mostly fiddlers. The violin was certainly not the beautifully made instrument produced in Italy centuries after the naming period, but the English version must not have been too bad in the hands of a patient and determined person. In the northern part of England, the Old English word was *fideler,* while in Kent and Cornwall, it was *vidler.* The CROWTHER names go back to the Middle English word *crowdere,* which also meant "a fiddler."

What has been said about the fiddlers could also be said about the HARPERS, except that some form of the harp was much more widely used than any other musical instrument. Some harps were so small they could readily be carried under the arm. Perhaps a young man working with a POTTER or a SMITH or a WEAVER and well on the way to being permanently tagged with one of these names brings his HARP to the tavern one holy day, with some idea of showing off his skill with the instrument. His music may not be the best, but it may impress his friends enough for them to tag him with one of the harp names from that time on. In Anglo-French, the word was *harpeor* or *harpour*. It is in an old record of 1275 as Reginald le Harper.

The LUTE names mean players of another stringed instrument called the lute, although they may be confused with an old name for otter (see chapter 21, page 298).

The SALTER group is more complicated, because those names were given either to men in the business of making salt (and they usually made a lot of money) or to men who played a stringed instrument known as the *psalter*. John le Sautreor in 1276 was definitely a saltmaker while William le Sautreour not only played the instrument but did it so well that in 1304 Lady Margaret, who became queen of England in that year, engaged him as her regular minstrel.

GROUP 133

Horn Blowers

The Latin word for "horn" is *cornu,* but the Normans changed that to *cornet,* meaning any kind of horn that could be blown to produce music. BEAMER and BEEMER refer to a blower of a trumpet. It comes from the Old English word *biemere.*

All eight HORN names have added interest in that some of the original holders may have blown a horn for reasons not even remotely connected with musical entertainment. An old record indicates that, at Caernarvon Castle in Wales in 1320, one Adam Horneblawer had the duty of blowing his horn when it was time for certain workmen to lay down their tools for the day. The chances are, however, that most HORN names were given to men able and willing to give a few toots whenever called upon. In Old English a horn blower was called a *hornblawere.* The Old English word for the instrument itself was *horn* so this word could be applied to a man who made horns or even to a man who made things out of horn (see chapter 9, page 92). I find an Adam le Horner in 1297, and sometime later he is referred to as Adam le Harpour.

The FLUTE names go back to the Middle English word *floute,* meaning a man who could play such an instrument. William le Floutere in 1268 seems to have been able to.

For some reason, the PIPERS are today associated almost exclusively with the Scottish Highlanders—so much so that a man in a kilt without his bagpipe is incomplete. The instrument goes far back in history. In fact, one story about it is that the Irish really invented it but gave it to the Scots as a joke, and the Scots took it seriously. We do know that to-day in Tyrone, and some other sections of Ireland, the native Irish not only still wear kilts but also play the pipes. As I suggested, if one goes back far enough, they were all the same people. And there must have been a fair number of pipers in medieval England to have given us six family names. All six PIPE names come unchanged from the Old English word *pipe*. The Norman word with the same meaning was *pepin* or *pipin*. PIPE, or one of its variants, usually referred to a man who played a pipe, but it might also refer to a man who made pipes. William le Piper is on the records for 1202.

The two TRUMP names come directly from the Old French word *trompeor*, meaning "trumpeter." There was an Adam Trumpur in 1253.

WAGHORN, with or without the final *e*, referred to a blower of any kind of horn. One such was Roger Waggenorn in 1332, and another was Peter Waghorn in 1327.

GROUP 134

Drummers

Then come the drummers. The drum has been around for a very long time. Thousands of years before the Middle Ages, men seem to have been fascinated by the rhythm one could beat out on a drum. Primitive men were probably able to beat out rhythmic sounds that met with an instant response from all those within hearing distance. The response would be rhythmically dictated by the drummer's cadence; it might be a measured step forward, a dignified moment of expectant waiting, or a wild stimulation to dance.

During the naming period, drums were pretty much the same as those of ancient man: a sheet of animal skin stretched over the ends of a hollow cylinder, tapped with one or two hardwood sticks.

The word *drum* itself is very ancient. Indications are that it may be Gaelic, but we know the Normans had the word *tabur*, and variations of that word, some of which are rather obscure, account for many of the names on our list.

There are many examples of names, such as Adam Tabur in 1204, Benedict Taberner in 1274, Robert le Taburur in 1301, and Bernard le Taborer in 1280.

The Normans also had another name for a drum or for a man who played the instrument. In Old French, it was *tympan* (in Latin, *tym-*

panum). Examples of names deriving from these words are Nicholas Tympanye in 1402, and Henry Tynnepanne in 1274.

GROUP 135
Poets and Orators

This is a very interesting group in that they made names for themselves without making use of any instrument whatever except their own speaking voices and nimble wits.

It was a universal custom in the Middle Ages to invite entertainers of many varieties to dinner every day in the castle of the lord. Some would stay on for many days and even permanently, while others would pass on from castle to castle, welcome wherever they went. These entertainers had another function that is probably not as well known: they carried the news with them. In a day when no news media existed, these men served a very useful purpose.

BARD and BARDMAN were speakers who told their own stories in the form of poetry. While the others may also have used the poetic form, we can be sure the BARDS did.

MUTER, MUTTER, and MUTTERS, from the Old English word *motere,* indicated a man with the ability to speak on his feet. We know little else about the name. There is nothing to indicate that he was an entertainer, so we must assume that men with this name were chosen to present petitions to the lord of the manor. One William le Mouter is recorded in 1327.

PREACHER and the three SERMIN names are in all probability nicknames originally given to entertainers who might try to moralize now and then. The Norman word was *precheor.* In the records are William le Precher early in the thirteenth century and Hugh Precheour in 1297.

SERMAN, SERMIN, and SERMON all come from the Middle English word *sermoner* and the French-speaking Normans changed that into *sermounier.* There was a Richard le Sermoner as early as 1212.

The nine names starting with SPELLAR refer to speakers, that is, their talents ran from storytelling to poetry recitation. SPELL names had nothing to do with spelling, but rather referred to a speaker's ability to cast a spell over an audience. A very early record shows a William Spileman in 1167 and a Robert Speller in 1202. Then there was an Edmund Spelyng in 1337 and a John Speleman in 1273.

SPEAKMAN and SPACKMAN, from the Middle English *spekeman,*

were definitely to be classed as advocates or spokesmen. Probably they were men with no special training but with natural ability. We find a Nigel Spakeman in 1195, and a William Speakman in 1340.

TAGUE, TIGHE, McTIGUE, KEGG, and KEIG were poets. If I may quote Elsdon G. Smith in his recent scholarly book, *American Surnames:* "The word for poet was *tadhg* and tadhg became a personal name which originated the family name TIGHE, TAGUE and McTIGUE. Descent from the royal post, Rioghbhardan, produced the family names REARDON and RIORDAN."

GROUP 136

Jugglers

Juggling a number of balls or what have you in the air is probably a very ancient entertainment. One can easily imagine a Stone Age man amusing himself and perhaps some friends by juggling some bones that had just been licked clean of meat. I don't know for a certainty that juggling was practiced in classical Rome or Greece, but by the Middle Ages juggling was an established entertainment that came as a welcome relief to dinner guests. The Old French root of JUGGLER was *jougelour*. The earliest record of the name I have found is William le Gugelour in 1250.

The three TREDGETT names indicate a juggler too, but there is an implication in the Middle English root of the word that the items juggled may not have been material objects—they might have been words. The Middle English word was *treget* or *trigit* and meant jugglery or trickery. Robert le Tregettur in 1203 and Symon le Tregetor in 1279 appear in the records.

GROUP 137

Dancers

DANCE and DANCER need little explanation. Undoubtedly they were talented performers, perhaps even professionals. For once, both the Old French and the Middle English root word are the same—*dance*. Robert de la Daunce is recorded on a tax roll in 1305, while a Robert Daunce appears in 1247. A Godwin Dancere is listed in 1130 and a Ralph le Dancere in 1240. In 1203, we find an Edric le Hoppere. HOPPER comes directly from the Old English word *hoppian,* which meant to hop or to leap, which is to say, to dance. LEAPER and LEEPER were probably dancers too, but the Old English word *hleapere* that gave them their names did not have quite such a specific meaning and could also have been given to a courier. There is still another possibility. In chapter 18 we noted that the Old English word for a basket was *leap,* so a LEAPER could also have been a man who made baskets. Henry Leper in 1200 probably was a dancer, and so was William le Leapere in 1295. John le Lepmaker probably was a basket maker.

All five SAILOR names were dancers. The Old French word was *sailleor, salleor,* or even *sailleur* and indicated clearly a man who could dance. It had no reference to the modern seagoing sailor. There are many on the old tax rolls, such as Herbert le Sayllur in 1191 and John Sayller in 1327.

SPRINGER comes from the Old English word *springan,* meaning to jump. However, I have chosen to put the name among the dancers as being the more likely activity. Simeon Springer is recorded in 1185. TRIPP and TRIPPER were dancers beyond a doubt. *Trippere* was another word in Middle English indicating a dancer. William le Trippere appears in 1293. One more name for a dancer was TUMBER. This comes from the Old French word *tombeor* or *tumbeur,* which probably developed into our word tumbler. In any event, he was a dancer of some ability to have received that name. John Tumber is listed in 1276.

GROUP 138

Singers

Here we touch on a talent that frequently was of a more serious nature than juggling or dancing. There was certainly plenty of suitable after-dinner singing, but the Church had learned over the years how to make use of the singing voice in her most solemn religious services too.

Long before the naming period, Pope Gregory I (540–604) is credited with the initial development of Gregorian chant, but this was confined to the monasteries and cathedrals all over the Christian world. The man in charge of the singing in a monastery, either a priest or a monk, would be distinguished by one of the names beginning with CANTOR. In a cathedral the leader of the choir would usually be a layman, but he would bear one of the same names given his counterpart in a monastery.

Psalms and canticles were the order of the day and, at least in the early part of the naming period, very nearly all music was vocal. Instrumental accompaniment was still of such primitive character that it must have been more of a hindrance than a help.

The names in this group start with CANT. They come from the very Old Norman-French word *cant,* which was later changed to *chant.* Both words simply meant a song, or just the act of singing. But people began to apply the word to the singer and in a few years the CANTER (including KANTER) and CHANTER names were being used in various parts of the country to mean a singer of sacred music. We find a Richard Cante in 1327 and a Walter le Canter in 1230. CANTRELL, CANTRILL, CHANTRELL, and CHANTRILL are not quite so definite in their origin. The Normans had the word *chanterelle,* which seems to have had several loosely related meanings. It might mean a small bell with a high sound, the treble in singing, or a diminutive of any of the CANTER names. There was a Philip Canterel in 1203, a Robert Chanterel in 1221, and a John Cantrel in 1297.

All five DIXEY names may cause one to smile, because the medieval meaning of the word is far removed from the well-known Civil War song. The first three words of Psalm 39 are: "I have spoken." In Latin, that thought was expressed by the short word *dixi.* But the French had a word *dixi* that was used to indicate a man who sang in a chorus. There was a Robert Dysci in 1301 and a Roger Dixi in 1379, both of whom were definitely singers.

The GLEA names are easy because they are familiar. The word was the Anglo-Saxon *gleo,* meaning music, particularly of a lighter kind, the type that would be sung as much for the entertainment of the singers themselves as for their audience. In the Middle Ages, a GLEEMAN might even use his privilege to make unkind remarks about an individual.

The SANGAR group were church singers. I find a John le Songere in 1296 and a Richard le Sangere in 1337. SINGER, SINGERS, and SONGER were certainly singers—the name is derived directly from the Old English word *singan* which meant "to sing." An old tax roll brings to light a Lucas le Syngere in 1296 and a William Syngur in 1297.

GROUP 139

Whistlers

To speak of WHISTLER is to bring to mind the picture of a little old lady sitting in a rocking chair. But this was the work of the nineteenth-century artist Whistler.

The source of WHISTLER is the Old English word *hwistle.* It meant a pipe or a flute. (One who played these instruments was a hwistlere.) By metonymy (using one word for what it suggests rather than what it says), it meant a sound more or less like that made by one of those instruments, a whistle. An entertainer with perhaps nothing better to offer than a whistle was given it for a name. William Wystle appears in 1247, and just a few years before him was a John Whiseller.

GROUP 132

Stringed-Instrument Players

Crewther	Fidler	Harper	Lutter
Crother	Viddler	Harpin	•
Crowder	Vidler	Harpour	Salter
Crowther	Vieler	Harpur	Saulter
•	Viola	•	Sauter
Fiddle	•	Lute	Sautter
Fiddler	Harp	Luter	Sawter

GROUP 133

Horn Blowers

Beamer	Flute	Hornor	•
Beemer	Flutter	Orneblow	Trump
•	•	•	Trumper
Corner	Horn	Pipe	•
Cornet	Hornblow	Piper	Waghorn
Cornett	Hornblower	Pipes	Waghorne
Coriner	Horne	Pype	
•	Horner	Pypes	
Flauter	Horniblow	Pyper	

GROUP 134

Drummers

Drum	Tabberer	Tabern	Tabrar
Drumm	Tabberner	Taberner	•
Dummer	Tabboroh	Tabiner	Tempany
•	Taber	Tabner	Tempener
Tabah	Taberer	Tabor	Tempenor

GROUP 135

Poets and Orators

Bard	Mutter	Surman	Spelman
Bardman	Mutters	•	Spiller
•	•	Spackman	Spillman
Kegg	Preacher	Speackman	Spilman
Keig	•	•	•
•	Reardon	Spellar	Tague (see
Mc Tigue	Riordan	Spellen	Mc Tigue)
(*see* Tague)	•	Speller	Tighe
•	Sermin	Spelling	
Muter	Sermon	Spellman	

GROUP 136

Jugglers

Juggler	Tredgett	Trudgett
•	Tredjett	

GROUP 137

Dancers

Dance	Leaper	Seiler	Tripp
Dancer	Leeper	Seiller	Tripper
•	•	Seyler	•
Hopper	Sailer	•	Tumber
•	Saylor	Springer	

GROUP 138

Singers

Cant (*see*	Chant	Dixie	•
Kanter)	Chanter	•	Sangar
Canter	Chantrell	Glea	Sanger
Cantor	Chantrill	Glee	Sangster
Cantour	•	Gleeman	Singer
Cantrell	Dicksee	Gleigh	Singers
Cantrill	Dixcee	•	Songer
Caunt	Dixcey	Kanter (*see*	
Caunter	Dixey	Cant)	

GROUP 139

Whistlers

Whissell	Whissler	Whistler	Wissler

CHAPTER **21**

Hunting, Fishing, and Other Sports Names

Hunting was easily the most popular sport in England at this time. Much of the island was covered with forests, teeming with deer and all kinds of wildlife. One could expect to find a boar rooting for acorns almost anywhere, and wildfowl were so plentiful that the supply must have seemed inexhaustible.

But all this did not mean that English peasants could have venison or roast pork whenever they wished; that was a privilege reserved for the king and the nobility.

The ancient Anglo-Saxon nobles had done a lot of hunting, but with the coming of the Normans the sport really came into its own. One of William the Conqueror's first acts was to set aside a huge tract of land (17,000 acres) in Hampshire for his private use, destroying in the process some twenty villages and many churches. This area came to be known as the New Forest. Then he brought over fallow deer from France, which multiplied and prospered along with the larger native red deer.

GROUP 140
Watchmen

To guard against poachers, William engaged a small army of men to patrol the New Forest day and night, the year round. They became known as FORESTERS or WARRENDERS (with many variations, as can be seen from Group 140). Their authority was almost absolute. Though William had done away with the death penalty, he had replaced it with a mutilation penalty too horrible to detail here. In Middle English, the root word is *forester*. Richard le Forester is listed in 1240.

Of course, nobles in the great castles and manor houses followed his lead by setting aside large areas on their vast estates for their own use. They called these areas parks and, as one might expect, the watchmen they employed were called PARKERS or one of the variants listed. The lord and his friends could hunt any and every day of the year with no such thing as a bag limit. These names derive from the Old French word *parquier*, meaning "one in charge at a park." Anschetil Parcher appears in 1086.

VARDER and VERDIER were also forest watchmen. They derive from the Old French word *verdier* or *verdeur* meaning just that. Walter le Verder appears in 1279 and Richard le Verdour in 1327. WARBOY, WARBOYS, and WORBOY are a bit unusual in that they resulted from the Old French words *garder, warder,* and *bois,* used interchangeably to mean "to guard wood." Thus we find William Wardebois in 1207, and John Gardeboy as well as William de Wardeboys in 1280. WARNER and the five variants that follow derive from the Old French word *warrennier*, meaning a forest guard. This leaves only WOODWARD. Here we see wood, meaning forest, and ward, meaning watchman. In Old English the word was *wuduweara*.

GROUP 141
Guides

The GROSVENOR group of names is quite interesting. The Normans seem to have brought this name over, although it may not have been a full-fledged family name in the eleventh century. It meant simply "big hunter." Today we would call such men guides. Like hunting guides today, they were skilled in finding game and leading the inexperienced hunter to it. Kings and nobles used to employ many guides, and those who were genuinely skillful in locating game would soon find themselves rewarded and recognized by this name. The name derives from the French words *gros* and *veneor*, meaning literally "large hunter." Robert le gros venour is listed in 1200, while Waine le Grovenur served in 1259.

GROUP 142

Hunters

The type of hunting one did depended, naturally, on the game one was after that day. Coursing, the old Anglo-Saxon method of deer-hunting, was not favored by the Normans in the earlier years of their dominance but did become very popular some years later. Coursing required dogs. Almost any kind of dog would do, as the dog followed the game by sight rather than by scent. Hunters followed the dogs on horseback, and when the game was exhausted or cornered by the dogs, the hunters dispatched it with sword or spear.

The names in this group all simply mean "hunter" and give no indication of what kind of hunting. Obviously, a man so named must have been serious about his hunting to have been tagged with the name. *Hunta* was an Old English word applied to a hunter. There was a Humphrey le Hunte back in 1203, a Ralph Hunte in 1219, a John Hunteman in 1219, a Simon Huntere in 1220, and a Geoffrey Hunthing in 1209. The FEN and VEN names derive from the Old French words for hunter, *venear* and *fenn*.

The CHACE names derive from the Old French *chaceur,* also meaning "hunter." Walter Chacere appears in 1327.

CURRANT comes from the present participle of the Old French word *courir,* meaning "to run." Since running was so important to a hunter, it was sometimes applied to him and in at least a few instances became a name. William Curaunt appears in 1180 and John Corant in 1260.

HUNTINGFORD, HUNTINGTON, and HUNTLEY are really place-names or, as I prefer to call them, address names. I have already spoken of those names given to men because of where they lived: WELLMAN was a man who lived near the well, and GATES someone who lived near a gate. HUNTINGDON in Old English meant "a huntsman's hill" and HUNTINGFORD referred to a ford in a river handy for hunters. HUNTINGTON was a farm (because of the *ton* ending), while HUNT-LEA or HUNTLEY meant a clearing or a field for hunting. LEA, LEE, LEY, or LEIGH all mean a field, clearing in the woods, or a meadow.

The TRAIN and TRAPP names come from the sport of hunting, too, but the original holders of these names did their hunting by means of traps or snares of some kind. The Middle English derivation was the *trayne;* Old French was *traine*. Both meant guile or trickery. Walter Traine appears in 1181. *Traeppe* was the Old English word for a snare. Henry Trappe is recorded in 1230.

GROUP 143

Deer Hunters

Stag-hunting, unlike coursing, was very popular after the Conquest. It was this type of hunting the Normans had done back in France, and it required large numbers of well-trained hounds. It is said that Edward III was so fond of his hounds that even in the midst of war, when he went over to France, he insisted on taking his entire kennel of 120 hounds.

What came to be known as staghounds were trained to hunt red deer, and buckhounds to follow the fallow deer. Both types depended on their keen noses to follow the game. The noblemen followed the baying hounds on horseback. This may sound almost like modern fox-hunting, but not so; the fox at that time was a despised animal. He was a stealer of poultry and quite beneath the dignity of the gentry.

BROCKET or BROCKETT was the name given to a two-year-old stag just showing his first antlers. John Broket appears in 1327. PRICKETT was a nickname for a two-year-old deer. The Middle English root is *priket*. Laurence Priket is listed in 1296.

ROBACK and ROEBUCK come from a variety of small deer once common in England. Adam Robuck is on the tax rolls of 1245. TRIST and TRISTER are particularly interesting names to deer hunters of today. Tryst is an unusual word in modern English; it means an appointment or a waiting place where one might have an appointment. The Middle English word is *triste*. A deer hunter usually stands more or less hidden while the rest of the hunting party drives the game in his direction. He is keeping the TRIST, which makes him a TRISTER. William Trystour is listed in 1394.

GROUP 144

Boar Hunters

Another favorite target was the boar. The boar was a dangerous animal and completely unpredictable. One might pass by without his appearing to notice, but on another occasion he might take after one without any provocation and his long, sharp tusks could make short work of a hunter. There seems to have been no established method of hunting this much-prized animal—one used whatever weapon one liked. But the nobility despised the bow and arrow for fighting, and while it would have been well adapted for boar-hunting, there is no record of its use for this purpose. The spear seems to have been the favored weapon against the boar. And it was a risky one: if not hit in a vital spot the first time, the boar was on the hunter in a flash. In fact, the boar had so much strength and ferocity that he could be stabbed clear through by a spear and yet have enough power left to turn on the hunter and rip open his whole side with one slash of his sharp teeth. Some unknown smith invented a spear designed to be run through a boar, but long enough to keep the hunter out of reach of his teeth. It was a simple device. The spear had a longer staff than normal, and some eighteen inches behind the spearhead a crosspiece was welded onto the shaft. This must have acted like the guard on the hilt of a knife—when the spear was thrust clear into the animal, the hiltlike bar kept that raging boar at a safe distance.

The BOAR names hardly need an explanation. The Old English word was *bar*. One good-sized boar would provide more than a hundred pounds of very fine eating when broiled over an open fire and if a hunter came home once or twice with something like that, he might very easily pick up the name of BOARMAN. There was a Walter Bor in 1255, and a Robert le Bor in 1287.

GROUP 145

Boar Watchers

These names might well have been combined with those of Group 144, as they also come from the sport of hunting. The ERRICKER names, however, are not boar hunters, but boar watchers. Thus they were not of the nobility or even the gentry, who were the established hunters of the boar, but presumably peasants who wandered through the haunts of the boar and were rewarded if they routed out someone at the manor house to go out and "bring home the bacon." The Old English root was *eoforwacer* meaning "boar watchman." Richard Herewaker appears in 1247, John Euerwaker in 1237, and Edmundus Erwak in 1230. [The English of that time pronounced it Erricker no matter how it was spelled.]

GROUP 146

Falconers

Then there was the very ancient art of falconry. Centuries before the Normans existed, men in the Near East were training certain birds to hunt small game for them. This particular sport does not seem to have been very popular before the Middle Ages; in Europe, in fact, it has been suggested that it was an art picked up by the crusaders and brought to England on their return. No matter; it took England by storm. It was a type of hunting that could be indulged in by the more timid who might not like the rough-and-tumble business of stag or boar pursuit. Even a lady from the castle or manor house might now and then be tempted to carry a little sparrowhawk on her wrist for some hunting.

Hunting with a falcon required the right bird. By no means would every hawk do, even if big and powerful. The bird had to be very carefully trained for many weeks by someone with real experience. After that, the man who planned to use the hawk would have to carry him, hooded, on a gloved hand for many days, stroking him gently with a feather and whispering reassurances to him, before the bird would be considered ready for an actual field test. This seems to have been largely a matter of the bird's getting used to the sound of his owner's voice.

Let us take a closer look at the training of these birds. Those to be trained would be housed in an outbuilding near the castle or manor house under the particular care of an experienced trainer. Such trainers would invariably find themselves being addressed by one of the listed names. Though these names could refer to a man who hunted with falcons, more commonly they were applied to a trainer because with him it was an all-day, everyday association. A falcon was a hawk by the way, and in daily use the terms were interchangeable.

The building where the birds were kept was called a mews, or some variation of the Old French word *mue,* meaning "a cage for hawks," and several names deriving from these words and referring to a trainer have come down to us. The word *mews* has additional interest today. In modern London, it is applied to rows of very fashionable dwellings once used to stable horses. Many do not know that the style of the mews for falcons was adapted for the use of horses.

When captured, the bird was provided with a bell and leg straps and fed freshly killed small animals or birds fastened to a board several feet away. They were always put in the same spot. Soon the hawk's eyes were covered with a hood that was taken on and off many times a day until the bird appeared indifferent to it. He was then made to fly some distance to his food, and when he had learned to do this and return to the trainer, he was considered ready for an actual field trial.

Full-grown falcons were difficult to capture and exceedingly hard to train because by that time they were set in their ways. They were called

HAGARDS, HAGGARDS, or HAGGARTS. The most popular of the sixty-odd varieties of falcon was the peregrine, particularly the female. She was commonly about one-third larger than the male of the same species. The MUSKETT was a small variety of falcon, the name coming from the Old French word *mouchet,* and an OSTRIDGE, from the Old French word *ostrice,* was a hawk.

BUSZARD and BUZZARD were names given to members of the hawk family that could not be trained to do anything at all. The Middle English word was *busard.* William Bozard lived in 1258.

The method the falcon uses to kill another bird in the air has been likened to dive-bombing. Having gained altitude, the falcon flies directly at his victim, and when close to him, he folds his wings, clenches his claws like two fists, and literally knocks the other bird out of the air —dead almost instantly. Falcons have been known to reach a speed of 180 miles an hour on that dive, so it is not surprising that the victim is usually killed upon impact.

The goshawk kills in a different way. He grasps the victim in his powerful claws, driving his sharp points into the vitals of the other bird, then drops to the ground with him.

None of the falcon family has ever been taught to retrieve. A pair of well-trained falcons given as a gift from one nobleman to another, or even to a king, was considered the height of courtesy.

GROUP 147

Fox Hunters

These are the fox hunters. Nothing could be clearer. TOD was the Middle English word for fox. In the medieval period, the fox was not at all the objective of large gatherings of pink-coated gentlemen out for a day's sport in the woods and fields. In fact, fox hunting was not a sport at all; foxes were hunted down because they killed poultry.

I find a Hugo Tod in 1168, a Richard Todd in 1231, a Thomas Tod-hunter in 1332, and a Juliana Todman in 1275.

GROUP 148

Bird Hunters

The FOWLER group, as you might suspect, were the bird hunters. Geese, ducks, pheasants, and many other game birds were plentiful, and while they could not be had for the taking, an arrangement could be made with the lord of a manor allowing a certain number to be taken. Undoubtedly, his lordship made a handsome profit out of the work of the FOWLERS.

The Old English root of most of these names was *fugol,* which meant simply "a bird" or "a fowl." There are many examples in the old tax records: Robert le Fugel in 1186, William le Foul in 1271, Nicholas Vogel in 1327, and Roger le Fugler in 1227. These men were unquestionably at least part-time professional bird hunters. The names beginning with V seem to have originated in Sussex.

HOSLER, OSLAR, and OSLER came from a Norman word *ostelier,* meaning a bird hunter too.

GROUP 149

Otter Hunters

At that time the otter was recognized as a worthwhile fur-bearing animal, but it never became as popular in modern times because of the primitive methods the furriers of that period employed. As noted in chapter 13, fur was a status symbol, something that instantly marked its wearer as a noble—regardless of how ratty the fur.

LUTER and LUTTER come directly from the Old French word *loutre,* meaning otter, or a man who made a business of hunting them for their fur. An example is John le Leuter in 1304. In 1130, one found he had acquired the name Lelutre, and it stayed that way. Some authorities feel that the name may also have indicated a lute player, since the Old English word for the musical instrument was *lute.*

The family name OTTER came from the Middle English root *oter.* The oldest recording of the name I have located is Adam Oterhunter in 1246.

GROUP 150

Miscellaneous Hunters

CATCHLOVE is an interesting name. The root of the name is given in Group 123—tax assessors. CATCHPOLE and its several variations referred to men who chased and sometimes caught poultry as tax payment in lieu of money. *Cachelove* or *Cacheleu* in Old Norman French meant "chase wolf" or a "wolf hunter." That animal was common in medieval England and he was truly a scourge to the all-important flocks of sheep that were the lifeblood of the wool trade.

Bernard Cachelu was one in 1189 and William Cacheluve was another in 1208.

FERRETER is familiar to those of us who hunted rabbits in our youth—before we were allowed to use a gun. We had a ferret, an animal with a long neck and an astonishing ability to crawl into a rabbit warren and drive the rabbits out into the open. The word ferret comes from the Middle English word *feret* or the Old French word *fuiret* and was applied to young men who seemed to be fond of this type of hunting. Rabbit flesh was good, clean food that could be found everywhere, and the coney fur was of some value too, but it took some doing to catch them. William le Feret appears back in 1296 and Walter le Furettour in 1318.

OWLER and OWLES are rather obvious—they were men who hunted the owl. The word comes from the Old English word *ule*. Thomas Owles did so in 1176 and Stephen Owle a little later.

GROUP 151

Dog Trainers

In Norman French the word *berner* or *bernier* meant a man who trained and maintained a kennel for hunting dogs. BRACKNER from another Old French source, *bracenier,* meant almost exactly the same thing. BRACK comes from the same root word, although there is reason to feel that it was generally used to indicate a dog trained to hunt by scent. BRENNER is a variant of BERNER. A John le Brenner is recorded in 1280, a William Brak in 1275, and Walter le Brakener in 1309.

GROUP 152

Fishermen

In the medieval period, fishing was just another occupation. A man could feed his family with his catch or he could exchange any surplus with other craftsmen for their goods and services. It was strictly a business and had always been. One recalls that in Biblical times Peter and many of the apostles were commercial fishermen.

Apparently it was Izaak Walton in the seventeenth century with his *Compleat Angler* who showed the civilized world the enormous fun of fishing. The joy of dropping a fly into a cold mountain stream and watching it float down the current till some hungry trout could no longer resist it or of sitting quietly by some favorite pool waiting for the big one to make up his mind and grab the hook—these were things many men knew nothing about until Walton demonstrated the art to his companions.

Since our interest is in the origin of names, it is fascinating to reread *The Compleat Angler* because we suddenly realize that Walton's two companions were hunters. He was trying to make fishermen out of hunters. We know they were hunters because of the names he gave them: Venator and Auceps. Neither name ever became a family name because Walton's classic would not be written until 1653, some three centuries after the naming period, but Venator meant "a hunter" and Auceps was a name given to a falconer.

When one thinks of fishing today, one thinks of hooks and all the modern paraphernalia that goes with them, but hooks in the sense of a hook on the end of a line were almost certainly unknown in medieval times. Hooks from that period are preserved in some museums, but they were permanently attached to a stick of wood. Fish were caught with them, but as any fisherman knows, this is called snagging. So while the name HOOK and HOOKS and HOOKER are widely known today, their origin did not come from fishing. Rather, they are place or address names. A man would be called Hook because he was known to live near a sharp bend in the river or perhaps because he had a hooked nose.

BAISS, BASE, and BASS may or may not have come down to us from fishing. *Bass* and *bace* were Middle English words generally applied to a fish. There was, however, the Middle French word *basset* as well which referred to a dog with short legs, and which may be responsible for these names.

BODFISH was a name given to flounder, flatfish, sole, and several fish. A man with that name was definitely a fisherman. John Botefyshe is recorded in 1333 and Alice Bootefishe a bit later. CODLIN through QUODLING derive from the Middle English word for a small codfish, *codling*. Thus we find a George Codlyng in the twelfth century and an Emma Codelingg in 1297. The other variations were merely due to scribal whim.

Historically the names FISH, FISHER, FISHERMAN, and even FISK are not too interesting as their origin is so obvious. FISHERTON might well be given to a man who lived on or near a farm with a pond or stream where fish were plentiful (the *-ton* ending indicates this). FISH-LOCK seems to be another example of careless spelling down through the years; if it were FISHLAKE, the origin would be clearer because that is exactly what the name means. The earliest record of the name seems to be Simon de Fislake in 1204 and William Fysshlak in 1274.

FISHMAN strongly indicates a man who sold fish, probably a dealer. We have a Randolph Fissheman in 1474. FISHMONGER would indicate a fellow seller of fish. And FISHWICK is easy to trace back to a dairy farm or farmer who had a lake or stream on his place where fish could be readily caught. The *-wick* ending on that or any name indicates a dairy farm. FISK and FISKE are either variations of FISH or perhaps shortened forms of FISHWICK. Robert Fisk is listed in 1330.

The three HERRING names indicate fishermen who did a solid business with them. Herring were very plentiful in the waters off East Anglia and as a consequence, they were a drug on the market in that area. It was soon found that they could be sold farther afield at a nice profit. For many generations this operation was standard practice, and a barrel of herring became as negotiable as a gold piece. Ralph Hereng did business in 1166, Roger Hering in 1279, and Theobald le Heryngmongere in 1212.

With KIDDLE and KIDDELL we begin to get some detail on how men of that period caught their fish for market. The WEIR names are similar in that the same method and equipment produced both types of name. A definition from a medieval work goes as follows: "A wicker engine whereby fish is caught—a dam, weir, or barrier in a river with an opening fitted with nets, etc., for catching fish." Commercial fishermen of that period could usually sell all the fish they could catch, and consequently they tried any method that promised to increase their volume. A vast assortment of devices was developed. The simplest might be a low fence strung across a stream. It would be built by thrusting short sticks about an inch or so apart into the river bottom. Instead of going straight across the river, they might be built in the shape of a horseshoe with the open end upstream. The fish would wander into the trap, and before they could find the exit the attendant was there with his basket to scoop them up. The same thing could be done on the seashore. A weir would be built on the beach at low tide; when the tide came in and went out, it was sure to leave some fish stranded in the sand.

The Anglo-French word for this kind of fish trap was *kidel*. Simon Kidel was given the name in 1219 and Katherine Kydelman carried on a prosperous business in 1327.

The WEIR names derive from the Old English root *wer,* meaning a trap for catching fish. John atte Wer appears in 1332.

LAX and LAXMAN come from the Old French word for salmon and

were given to fishermen who appeared to sell more salmon than their competitors.

NETTER and NETTMAN come from the Old English word *net,* meaning "a maker of fish nets." John le Nettere is listed in 1298 and John le Netmaker in 1336. RETTER means the same, only its origin was the Old French word *retier.*

PEACHER and PETCHER come from an Old French word *pescheor,* meaning a fisherman. PIKE and PIKEMAN have a mixed origin. In chapter 6, dealing with weapons (see page 57), the word meant a man who carried a pike or was skilled in making pikes. The Middle English, however, had a word *pike* that indicated a particular kind of fish. We know that in 1292 one Alexander le Pic was a fishmonger in London and that in the same period London was served by at least three other fishmongers, all of whom were given the family name of PIKE.

GROUP 153

Miscellaneous Sports

COXETER and COXETTER were names given to men who arranged cockfights; we would call them promoters today. Adam le Cocsetere is recorded in 1260. DRAGON was a name given to a man who carried the banner at the head of a parade. Such a man was Walter Dragun in 1166.

The FURLONG names come from the word *furlong,* meaning "one-eighth of a mile." This was the length of one furrow, or the distance a team of oxen were supposed to be able to pull a plow without resting. The distance was also used for foot races, so a FURLONGER was a runner who trained for that distance. Robert Furlang is listed in 1242.

All the GAME names refer in some manner to men who were skilled at playing various games. It may have been chess or checkers or most any kind of game, and it may well be that the name was not always meant to be complimentary. The name derives from the Old English word *gamen* and was originally a nickname.

HURLBATT and its variations were nicknames for a rough and dangerous game played between two men armed with swords and bucklers. An early record of the name was John Hurbatt in 1327.

KEMP and KEMPE seem to have been names applied to strong, husky fellows who might have been wrestlers or doing some such rough sport. They derive from the Old English word *cempa,* meaning "warrior." Edmund Kempe appears circa 1100.

The Old Norman word for a parrot was *papegai* and the six names headed by **PAPIGAY** spring from it. It was the name of a game in which a real parrot, if one could be had, or else a dummy made out of wood, was set on top of a pole or up in a tree and all the young bloods in the village would try to hit it with an arrow. The prizes were many and varied, but were mostly releases from duties that otherwise would have to be performed. Robert Papejay is recorded in 1321.

PLAYER is more interesting. There is a William le Player in the records of 1276. The man seems to have acquired distinction in some unspecified outdoor sport on the public playgrounds of London. Like every other dub golfer all over the world, I know the famous South African golfer, Gary Player. I began wondering: could there be any connection, however vague, between the modern-day Gary Player and his namesake of so long ago? I was intrigued enough to write to Mr. Player in South Africa. He was away on tour but his sister, Ian, did reply, saying that their great-grandfather had come from England in 1850 and that every generation since had excelled in some outdoor sport. She said that exact knowledge of the family before 1850 was too fragmentary to be catalogued, but there was a family tradition that in the 1600s one of the Players had been lord mayor of London.

RESTLER and its variant **RESSLER** indicate an athlete that today would be called a wrestler. The Old English word was *wraestlere*. A William le Wrastler is listed in 1317.

GROUP 140

Watchmen

Du Parcq	•	•	Warren
Dupark	Forest	Varder	Warrender
Park	Forester	Verdier	Warrener
Parke	Forestier	•	Warriner
Parker	Forrester	Warboy	Warrinor
Parkers	Forrestor	Warboys	•
Parkes	Forster	Worboys	Woodward
Parkman	Foster	•	
Parks	•	Warner	

GROUP 141

Guides

Gravener   Gravenor   Grosvenor

GROUP 142

Hunters

Chace	Venner	Huntingford	Trainer
Chase	Vennor	Huntington	Trainor
•	Venour	Huntlea	Trapp
Currant	•	Huntley	Trappe
•	Hunt	Huntman	Trapper
Fenner	Hunter	Huntsman	Trayner
Fenners	Hunting	•	Traynor
Venn	Huntingdon	Train	Treanor

GROUP 143

Deer Hunters

Brocket	•	Roback	Trist
Brockett	Prickett	Roebuck	Trister

GROUP 144

Boar Hunters

Boar	Boor	Bore
Boarman	Bor	Boreman

GROUP 145

Boar Watchers

Earwaker	Earwicker	Erricker

GROUP 146

Falconers

Buszard	Faulkner	Hawkes	Mewitt
Buzzard	Faulknor	Hawkett	Mews
.	Fawckner	Hawkin	Muer
Facon	Fawkner	Hawking	Muers
Valcon	.	Hawkings	Muir
Falconar	Hagard	Hawkins	Mure
Falconer	Haggard	Hawkitts	Mushet
Falconnier	Haggart	Hawks	Muskett
Falkiner	.	.	.
Falkner	Hauke	Meur	Ostridge
Falknor	Hawk	Meurs	.
Faucon	Hawke	Mew	Sparhawk
Faulconer	Hawken	Mewer	Sparrowhawk
Faulkener	Hawker	Mewett	

GROUP 147

Fox Hunters

Tod	Todd	Todhunter	Todman

GROUP 148

Bird Hunters

Fowell	Fowls	Vowell	•
Fowells	Fuggle	Vowells	Hosler
Fowle	Fuggles	Vowels	Oslar
Fowler	Fugler	Vowler	Osler
Fowles	Voules	Vowles	

GROUP 149

Otter Hunters

Luter	Lutter	Lutterer	Otter

GROUP 150

Miscellaneous Hunters

Catchlove	Ferreter	Owler
•	•	Owles

GROUP 151

Dog Trainers

Berner	Brack
Brenner	Brackner
•	

GROUP 152

Fishermen

Baiss	Fisher	Heryngmonger	Petcher
Base	Fisherman	•	•
Bass	Fisherton	Kiddell	Pike
•	Fishlock	Kiddle	Pikeman
Bodfish	Fishman	•	•
•	Fishmonger	Lax	Wear
Codlin	Fishwick	Laxman	Weare
Codling	Fisk	•	Wears
Girling	Fiske	Netter	Weir
Quadling	Fysh	Nettman	Weirmaker
Quodling	•	Retter	Were
•	Harenc	•	Where
Fish	Herring	Peacher	

GROUP 153

Miscellaneous Sports

Coxeter	Gaman	Hurlbatt	Pobjoy
Coxetter	Game	Hurlbut	Popejoy
•	Games	Hurlbutt	Popjoy
Dragon	Gamman	•	•
•	Gammans	Kemp	Player
Forlong	Gammon	Kempe	•
Furlong	Gammond	•	Ressler
Furlonge	Gammons	Papigay	Restler
Furlonger	Gamon	Pebjoy	
•	•	Pobgee	

CHAPTER **22**

Messengers, Guards, and Porters

To the modern reader it must be difficult to see any connection between a messenger, a guard, and a porter. One thinks of a messenger as the boy who delivers a telegram, a guard as the uniformed man standing in the bank who directs one to the proper window, and a porter as the man one calls when checking out of a hotel to carry one's bags. In medieval times life was a bit different; there was need at times for all three of these services, but they were not nearly so distinct and specialized as they are today.

GROUP 154

Messengers

It is almost impossible for modern man to envisage a life without means of communication—no postal service, no telegraph, no telephone; in fact, no way of getting a message to or from a person without the use of a personal messenger. In the naming period, less than 10 percent of the people could manage a written note, and the chances of the other fellow being able to read it were close to zero. Everyday communication between friends and relatives living anywhere near each other had to be either in person or carried verbally by a messenger who would return with a verbal answer if it was required.

These messengers were undoubtedly a motley collection of individuals, probably composed of small boys and grown men—some of whom might make a business of running errands. A study of the names in this group provides a little insight into this phase of medieval life.

The first three names in this group—BODE, BODER, and BODMAN —are unusual and somewhat confusing. In 1066, *bode* was an Old English word meaning a herald or a messenger. An old record shows a Hugo filius Bode (meaning "Hugo, son of the messenger") in 1086. In the following century, the word became BODER, and it might mean a messenger, an announcer, or even a town crier. The earliest record of BODER is Andrew le Bodere in 1296.

COURIER and CURROR were professional messengers, but they did not take ordinary messages between friends in the same general area. They were called upon to carry important messages between great nobles who might be long distances apart. The message might even be written, as the noble would surely have somebody in residence who could read it, either the chaplain in the castle or the parish priest. The Old French word was *corero*, which meant, literally, "a runner." COURIER should not be confused with CURRIER or CURRYER, which were names for leatherworkers. We find one example of a messenger in the records: Thomas Corour in 1331.

The meanings of the GALPEN names became mixed up at some point, so it is impossible to know whether a GALPEN was a messenger who took off at a gallop, a young page in a castle, or a turnspit in a monastery! There was a William Galpyn in 1279 and another William Galopin in 1195.

GALLATLY through GOLIGHTLY were originally nicknames for a messenger, and complimentary ones at that. A small boy might fit the description more accurately than a grown man. Howe Golichtly received his name in 1221.

HARFOOT was another nickname for a swift runner. The Old English roots are *hara* and *fot* meaning "hare's foot." A quote from a record in 1170 uses the nickname: "Harald, Godwyne sone he was ycleped harefot."

LIGHTFOOT is still another complimentary nickname for a messenger who could run fast. It comes from the old English words *leoht* and *fot*. John Lyghtfot appears in 1296.

MASSINGER and MESSENGER come directly from the Old French word *messagier* or *messager,* and meant messenger in the sense that we might use the word today. Either name would be given to a man in the business of carrying messages. The records show Lucas le Mesagier in 1193, Hugh le Messager in 1211, and William le Messinger in 1293.

PASSANT and Passavant introduce something new. In Old French, *passe avant* meant somebody who went in front of something or somebody else. Since both words became family names in time, we have to assume that they were given either to messengers who commonly went ahead of a delegation to prepare the audience for what was coming or to a regular herald who might have either blown a horn to get the attention of a crowd or given the message through a kind of megaphone. William Passavant appears in 1198.

All eleven names beginning with PIRKIS ₁nd ending with PURKISS have an obscure Old French origin. The word was *purchas* in Old French, and it meant "pursuit." There was a William Purchaz in 1190 and William Purkas in 1327.

A RENNER was a runner, and undoubtedly the reason he ran was because it was his business to carry messages speedily. The origin of RENNER is the Old English word *rennan,* meaning "to run." There are plenty of examples: Aluuinus Rennere in 1134 and Richard Renner two centuries later in 1319.

SHERWEN and SHERWIN come from the Old English words *sceran,* meaning "to cut," and *wind.* It must have taken centuries of rough handling to end up with SHERWIN, but there it is. One name in the records is William Scherewind in 1187, and many years later (in 1479) I find a John Shirwyn. Anyway, the common application of the term was to a messenger who could cut the wind.

The last three names, TROTMAN, TROTT, and TROTTER, derive from the Norman word *trotier,* meaning "messenger." Adam le Troter appears in 1219.

GROUP 155

Guards

In chapter 19 on castles and chapter 23 on lawmen and officials, guards are discussed in some detail. There were guards of all kinds in a castle, and certainly many of them were officials in the loose meaning of the word at that time, but there are still more names that were not included in the early chapters.

The WARD names have been mentioned throughout the book simply because WARDS were to be seen almost everywhere. The origin was the Old English word *weard,* meaning a watchman or a guard of some kind. Simon le Warde appears in 1194 and John le Wardeyn in 1289.

The four WATCHER names begin with a form of the Old English

word *waecce,* meaning to watch. Anyone so employed might very easily be called a WATCHER. John Wachere is listed in 1237.

The WAIGHT through WHATE names—seventeen in all—come from the early Norman word *waite,* meaning "a watchman." When the Normans made a man a *waite,* it meant that he was to function as a watchman of a fortified place or a town, so the WAITES came close to being policemen. There must have been many of them to have resulted in such a variety of spellings.

WAKEMAN comes from the Middle English word *wake,* meaning "watch." When *-men* was added to it, one had "watchman." WAKEMAN was the title of the chief magistrate of Ripon until 1604, when it was changed to mayor. He was the active head of a body of WAKEMEN whose duty was to blow a cow's horn every night at nine o'clock. If between then and sunrise any burglary took place, it would be *made good* at the public charge. WALKMAN is actually just a variant of WAKEMAN. An old quotation of 1398 says:

> Angels ben called walkmen and wardeyns
> for they warne men of perylles that may
> fall.

The whole group of BRIDGE names are obvious. They clearly indicate a man who did his watching and his guarding at a bridge. The Old English for "bridge" was *brycg.* Early recordings of the name are Alexander Brugeyn in 1260 and John Brygemean in 1296.

The five names beginning with PONT need very little explanation. In both Middle English and Old French, the root word was *pont,* meaning "bridge," so a PONTER was a bridge watchman or guard. Walter Pont had that duty in 1327 and so did Richard Ponter in 1255.

The three PORT names come from the Latin word *porta,* meaning "gate." The English called it *port* and the Normans called it *porte,* but that was no matter; it meant gate-keeper, gate watchman, or even door-keeper. There is some confusion with the Italian verb *porto,* meaning "carry" (see Group 156). Adam de la Port in 1243 certainly watched a gate.

The SPEIR names come from the Middle English word *espyen* and the Old French word *espier,* meaning "to spy on" somebody or something. This man was a guard or a watchman. It seems doubtful that he did his watching from the *spire* of a church, as has been suggested by some. William le Spiour appears in 1302.

TOTMAN and TOTTMAN, from the Old English words *tot* and *man,* mean "lookout," that is, "watchman." Robert Toteman lived in 1202.

FLADGATE and FLOODGATE were names given to men who took care of a gate that controlled the flow of water into a canal or basin of some kind. The earliest example of the name is Walter atte Flodgate and the date is 1327, almost at the end of the naming period.

GARD and GUARD come from the Old French *garde,* meaning "a watchman." John le Gard was one in 1275.

BARGATE, BARR, BARRS, LE BARR go back to a Middle English word, *barre,* meaning a barrier of some kind. A barrier had to have an entrance or a gate somewhere, and this necessitated a watchman or a guard—someone who could bar one's entrance, or let one pass.

GROUP 156

Porters

I have purposely placed the PORTERS in the same chapter with the MESSENGERS and the GUARDS because there must have been many instances in which one substituted for the other. A gate-keeper might be asked to carry a package a short distance for a lady, and during those few minutes he would be acting as a porter; or he might have picked up the name PORTER anyway as a gate-keeper because of the confusion between the Latin word *porta,* meaning "gate," and the Italian verb *porto,* meaning "carry." Milo Portarius far back in 1086 performed porter service at Winchester Castle and David le Portur carried packages in 1263. The definite article soon became unnecessary, and we find an Andrew Portour early in the fourteenth century.

CARRIER and CARRYER are definitely PORTERS, if we are to believe the root word of the name, which was *carier* in early Norman French. Robert de Carier is recorded in 1332.

The four names from HALER through HAYLOR go back to the Middle English word *halien,* which meant to haul or to drag something, or the Norman word *haler,* meaning to pull something. Whichever the origin, they both mean PORTER. John Haler was a porter in 1375 and William le Haliere was a porter in 1279.

HEAVER and HEUER come from the old Anglo-Saxon *hebban,* meaning "to lift." The people of medieval England changed *hebban* to *heve,* but it still meant to lift and to carry. So also did HALER and just as surely PORTER, too.

DRAY and DRAYMAN derive from the Old English word *dragan*, meaning to drag something, presumably something heavy. It might be heavy enough to require a cart, so this man could have become a CARTER, CARRIER, or CARRYER or, not having a cart, the man may have hitched his oxen to the thing itself and dragged it to a given destination, thus becoming a DRAY or a DRAYMAN.

DRAWER is interesting in that it might stem back to several occupations. Its nominal origin was the same Old English word *dragan* that gave us the DRAY names above. Its owner might have been a wool-drawer—a carrier of sacks of raw wool—or a carrier of manure. That he was a carrier of something is all we know. The name appears in 1327 as Draghere and as John le Drawere in 1332.

The JAGGAR names are, again, unspecific. They derive from the Middle English word *jagger*. A man so named was a carrier, a carter, a peddler, or a hawker. The name is common still in the West Riding.

The LOADER group of names stem from the Middle English word *lode*, meaning "to carry." Simon le Loder is recorded in 1332.

TRUSS and TRUSSMAN were porters too. John Trusseman is in the old tax records of 1327. These men probably carried baggage. The names come from the Old French word *trousse*, meaning "a bundle." The CAMEL names were probably complimentary nicknames given to porters because they could carry so much more than one might expect. I find a Walter Camel in 1200 and a Richard le Cammel in 1319.

GROUP 154

Messengers

Bode	Galletley	•	Purkess
Boder	Galletly	Passant	Purkis
Bodman	Gillatly	Passavant	Purkiss
•	Gilletly	•	•
Courier	Golightly	Pirkis	Renner
Curror	•	Pirkiss	•
•	Harfoot	Porcas	Sherwen
Galpen	•	Porkiss	Sherwin
Galpin	Lightfoot	Purchas	•
Galpyn	•	Purchase	Trotman
•	Massinger	Purches	Trott
Gallatly	Messenger	Purchese	Trotter

GROUP 155

Guards

Bargate	Gard	•	Weait
Barr	Guard	Totman	Weight
Barrs	•	Tottman	Whait
Le Barr	Pont	•	Whaite
•	Ponte	Wacher	Whaites
Bridge	Ponter	Wachman	Whaits
Bridgeman	Punt	Watcher	Whate
Bridger	Punter	Watchman	•
Bridgers	•	•	Wakeman
Bridges	Port	Waight	Walkman
Bridgman	Portal	Waighte	Waker
Brugger	Porte	Wait	•
Dealbridge	•	Waite	Ward
Delbridge	Speir	Waites	Warde
Dellbridge	Speirs	Waits	Warden
•	Spier	Wates	Warder
Fladgate	Spiers	Wayt	Wardman
Floodgate	Spyer	Wayte	Wards
•	Spyers	Waytes	Wordman

GROUP 156

Porters

Camel	Drayman	Heaver	Loadman
Camell	•	Heuer	Loadsman
Cammell	Drawer	•	Loder
•	•	Jaggar	•
Carrier	Haler	Jaggars	Porter
Carryer	Hayler	Jagger	Porters
Carter	Hayllar	Jaggers	•
•	Haylor	•	Truss
Dray	•	Loader	Trussman

CHAPTER 23

Lawmen and Officials

The names that derive from the lawmen and officials of the Middle Ages are particularly rich in their variety because, during the entire naming period, the laws themselves were undergoing constant changes, and not only the laws but the local customs that eventually became laws. Thus, in the eleventh century, a "bail" was the outer wall of a castle and the man in charge of it would frequently be called the "baily." Soon, the space enclosed by the wall began to be called the bailey and on pleasant days the court might move out of the damp, gloomy old castle into the bright warm sun. The court might be presided over by an official called a BAILIFF and if the prisoner was lucky, he might have his BAIL set at a reasonable figure.

GROUP 157

Bailiffs

There are twenty-four names that have come down to us from the Old French word for an outer wall, *bail* (which also meant "to deliver something").

Some form of the word would be applied to the deputy manager of a castle, the temporary man placed in charge during the owner's absence. He would preside in the local court as a regular part of his duties.

The records are full of the name. There is, for example, a Eudo del Bail in 1301, a John Bayl in 1332, and a Thomas Bale a bit later. Then there was Richard le Baillif in 1242. The name, under several spellings,

some of which have since been dropped, came to mean the public admin-
istrator of a district, the chief officer of a Hundred, an officer of justice
under a sheriff, a warrant officer, a pursuivant, or even a CATCHPOLE
(see Group 160). This represents quite a range in importance and responsibility, but this is easy to understand if we keep in mind that the
title sprang up naturally in a great many different localities at widely different times.

BAILIE is almost unheard of today in England, but in Scotland it is
still commonly used to mean the chief magistrate of a barony or even a
sheriff. An early record of the name was John ata Baylie in 1317. The
"ata" is used in this case to indicate a magistrate who was at or near the
bail or wall.

BAILWARD is a little different: it is the same word *bail* plus the
Anglo-Saxon word *ward,* meaning "a wall guard."

The long history of these names and their almost infinite variety today indicate clearly their age-long importance.

GROUP 158
Sergeants

There are no less than sixteen variations of the name SERGEANT. It
is apparent at once that the name was used over a wide geographical
area and over a long period. A man might have been called a SARGANT
in Kent, while in Sussex or Essex he might have been called a SERGENT
or a SARJEANT, and the official duties of each might be quite different
or they might be identical. A man with *any* of these sixteen titles would
almost certainly have been one of the gentry, meaning that he was not a
member of the nobility but he was many steps higher on the social scale
than a peasant. To receive this title, he had to be officially and publicly
so designated by the lord of the manor. And from then on, his duties
would consist of exactly what his lordship might require of him. He
could not be knighted because this required years of training, but his
lordship wanted to make something of him, so he named him *Servientes
Regis,* or king's sergeant. A small estate might or might not be included
with the sergeanty; several including estates are to be found in the
Domesday Book.

The duties of the SERGEANT covered an extremely broad range (see
chapter 19). He might be given military duties, such as bearing the
royal standard on formal occasions, or he might be made an officer of the
court with power to issue a summons, arrest an offender, or carry out

the judgment of the tribunal. Clearly what the title entailed depended entirely on the whim of his lordship.

Frequently the reward of a holder of this title was to be companion to the lord on his hunting trips. In Oxfordshire alone, as far back as 1086, we have records of SEARGEANTS being made dispensers, naperers, herb gatherers, larderers, ushers, falconers, and foresters. One naperer on record had to present his lordship with a new tablecloth every Michaelmas, worth at least three shillings. Then there were SERGEANTS with such onerous duties as giving his lordship a live goose or a dozen eggs every year at Christmastime. And if it appeared that a SARGANT could sing or recite poetry, he might be made a permanent minstrel.

The title in its medieval meaning has long since disappeared from the English scene, but many of its former holders must have been blessed with winning personalities. Edric le Sergant was given the name in 1190 and Robert le Serjaunt in 1221.

GROUP 159

Sheriffs

The office of sheriff goes far back into Anglo-Saxon England but, unlike the sergeant's, it has always been taken seriously, and still is, in all English-speaking countries. In the ninth century, the Anglo-Saxon shire or county was ruled by an *eorl,* or earl, who presided over its court jointly with a bishop and the king's reeve. Put *shire* and *reeve* together and you have SHERIFF.

One of the Conqueror's reforms was to make the sheriff supreme in his own shire. (The bishop could hold his own court for ecclesiastical offenses.) The sheriff was empowered to muster the entire military strength of the shire, execute all writs, and preside over all civil and criminal cases in the shire. His power and influence steadily grew for more than a century, until Henry II established the *curia regis,* or the King's Court, in which ministers of the king traveled from place to place all over the country to hold court. This proved to be only a temporary curb on the power of the sheriffs, however, for by the twelfth century, they had regained most of their old prerogatives and added some new ones. The office threatened to become hereditary, but by 1300 a statute was passed that attempted to make the office elective. This was discarded in 1315, and from that time on, the sheriffs of England were appointed by the vote of various officers of state.

So many of our medieval surnames are of Norman origin that it is interesting to know that SHERIFF derives from an Anglo-Saxon word *scirgerefa,* meaning "shire reeve." That complicated spelling may account in some small way for the very large variety of modern spellings. An Aethelwine Sciregerefa was recorded in 1016, long before the Conquest, and Hugo le Sirreve appears in 1212. The latter rendering must have been the work of a Norman as he put that French *le* in.

Then in 1219, an Alan Sciriue appeared and the very next year, a Walter Sherrev. In 1273 followed a John Schiref and by 1457 there was Thomas Shreeve.

REEVE, REEVES, and REAVES are what happened to the Anglo-Saxon word *gerefa.* They mean sheriff, without a doubt. SHIRMAN comes from another Old English word, *scirmann.* Usually it meant a sheriff, but there was some confusion in the thirteenth century when the same word was occasionally used for a bailiff or even a steward. SHIRRA was the name used in Scotland for a sheriff.

PRATER, PREATER, and PRETOR have a Latin root *praetor.* In 1150, there was a Willelmus Pretor. He was known as either a reeve or a sheriff, because that is the job he held, but PRETER, or one of its variations, was the name given to him and his family.

LACKMAN seems to have been a colloquial term used for sheriff in some of the Channel Islands.

GROUP 160

Tax Collectors

In earlier chapters, we have referred many times to tax collectors. As individuals, they were thoroughly hated by just about everyone in England.

From the standpoint of the origin of names, particularly names stemming from the occupation of an individual, the tax collectors are very interesting.

CATCH through CATCHPOULE (and including KETCHER) derive from the medieval English word *caccepol* or the Old French word *cachepol* and are listed earlier (see chapter 19, Group 123).

Surely the collector would not saddle himself with that name. Perhaps it was the head tax man back at the manor house. He sat in his office all day and checked the goods—poultry, produce, pottery, and paraphernalia—that each collector brought in. He might have been so impressed with the abnormal number of squawking ducks and scrawny chickens in the cart of one of his men that he called him CATCHPOLE and the name stuck.

Some of the early examples of this name are Aluricus Chacepol in 1086 and Hugo le Cachepol in 1221.

In fairness, CATCHPOLES were by no means all tax collectors. Some of them were petty officers of justice, sheriff's deputies, warrant officers, and even sergeants.

CATCH comes from an Anglo-French word *cachier,* meaning "to catch or chase." CATCHER and KETCHER are not necessarily CATCHPOLES; they might have been hunters who chased game, but chances are they were used in the same sense as the diminutive CACHEREL, which was a common tax collector's name in Norfolk in 1275 or thereabouts. The Cacherels were also bailiffs of the Hundred and as a group they gained a bad reputation of extortion and oppression in general. Jordan Cachere is listed in 1221 and Alexander le Catcherel and William Kacchehare are both from the twelfth century.

All four FARMAR names (also covered earlier in chapter 19) are difficult to pin down to one origin. In Old French, there was *fermier,* which simply meant tax collector. Richard Fermor is listed in 1293. On the other hand, the word might be translated to mean a man who cultivates land for someone else. This would make him a steward. Probably, the same term had these different meanings in different areas.

GABLER is just another Norman word for tax collector (see chapter 19, page 265).

GATHERER tells its own story. It was from the English word *gaderian,* meaning "to gather." He may not have been a tax collector, however, as the word was also used for a collector of dues for a guild.

The TOLLERS (see chapter 19, p. 265) did not have to go to the peasants to make their collections. Toll collection became a really fine art in the Middle Ages. Since there was a more or less constant flow of packmen or peddlers on the road, there was unlimited opportunity for collection. When an important merchant came along with a whole train of pack animals carrying great stocks of fancy goods from the Near East and the Continent, en route to one of the fairs in a market town, his toll might be a whole bolt of fine cloth or a flagon of perfume from the Orient.

Medieval landowners, from the largest down to the smallest, never overlooked an opportunity to shake down the traveler unfortunate enough to have to pass over their property. It was not considered dishonest by the collector, and probably most of the victims knew only too well that they would do the same thing if circumstances were reversed. Richard Towler is listed in 1255 and John le Tollere in 1251.

The three LONGSTAFF names (see chapter 19, page 265) were probably nicknames given to catchpoles and even to minor bailiffs.

The TRAVERS names derive from the Old French word *travers,* meaning the act of crossing over something like a river or even passing through a gate. So the man who stood at the river or by the gate with his hand out to collect a toll was called TRAVERS. The earliest example I have found is Walter Travers in 1172.

GROUP 161
Marshals

We have treated the MARSHALS at some length in chapter 5 (page 35). Originally a MARSHALL was a shoeing blacksmith, but as the importance of horses grew in both the economic and the social life of the age, the importance of men expert in their care and selection grew too. The earliest record of the name I have found is one Goisfridus Marescal in 1204.

GROUP 162
Seneschals

The SENESCHALS were very important people in France all during the Middle Ages, and when the Normans took over England, they introduced the title there, but for some reason it never became permanent in Britain. For centuries, a seneschal was the second in command in a great castle or royal palace. He was in direct charge of all domestic arrangements and frequently even presided over the local court. When a great noble went on a long journey, it was the seneschal who planned every detail of the trip. The title seems to have slowly changed over to either STEWARD or BAILIFF. Ralph le Seneschall held forth in 1222.

GROUP 163
Officers of the Court

A CRIER or CRYER, from the Old French word *criere,* was an officer of the court who made announcements in the streets to the public. Robert le Crieur appears in 1221.

DEAM through DOOMAN meant "doom man." The Old English word was *demere,* meaning one who pronounced the verdict of doom; that is, a judge.

DITER and DYTER are curious old names. They seem to have been given to men who did very different things. In Old French, an author might be known as *ditour,* but the same word was used to indicate a composer, a public crier, a summoner, and an indicter. I find a Helewisa Ditur in 1327.

JESTICE, JUDGE, JUDGES, and JUSTICE were all names of medieval judges. A JUDGE during those days had *more* power than he would have today, a fact clearly indicated by the DEAM and DOOMAN names above. This was long before the day of trials by jury and much of the formality that goes with a modern court of law.

MAIR was a term used mostly in Scotland. It is from a Gaelic word, *maor,* meaning an officer. This man's duty was to issue summonses and other legal writs, but on occasion he could be called on for various other duties such as those of head forester.

The PROCKTERS were attorneys, particularly in an ecclesiastical court. The name came in directly from the Latin word *procurator,* which in Roman days simply meant "a manager." Johannes le Proketour worked in 1301.

The last six names on the list, SIMNER through SUMPNER, were given to an officer whose duties included warning persons to appear in court. The origin is the Anglo-French word *somenour.*

GROUP 164

Overseers

The six names in this group, starting with GREEFF, have a slightly mixed origin. In northern England there was an Old English word *graefa,* which meant much the same as REEVE did in southern counties, but it was frequently applied to the overseer of a large farm. In some areas, it was used interchangeably with STEWARD. Johan Greve registered in 1199.

GROUP 165

Weighers and Measurers

These names come from the Old Norman word *peseor,* meaning a man who weighed things. Today, he would be the Sealer of Weights and

Measures for a county or a whole state. Simon le Peser appears in 1198 and John Poser in 1275.

GROUP 166

Animal Impounders

The names listed here were applied to medieval officers who had the duty of catching stray animals and impounding them until the owner could be located and prove his claim. Today we might call him a dog-catcher, but in the naming period he had to catch a much greater variety of animals and certainly a vastly greater number of them. The medieval peasant put up no fences, so it is not hard to imagine that this man was kept very busy. All the names derive from the Old English word *pyndan,* meaning "to catch and impound." William le Pendere is listed in 1231.

GROUP 167

Men Who Punished the Guilty

The centuries of the Middle Ages were violent. Many offenses that would be classified as minor today were capital crimes at that time. In all fairness, this situation was to grow much worse in the sixteenth and seventeenth centuries, when about two hundred and fifty "crimes" in England were punishable by death. William the Conqueror actually did away with capital punishment, but he substituted such horrible mutilation in its place that a quick death might frequently be preferred. Rufus and the Norman kings who followed reinstated capital punishment and also continued much of the mutilation.

Beheading and hanging were the old reliable methods, although these varied in popularity from century to century. A nobleman might insist on hanging while one of lesser rank could choose the ax, but even this changed over the years. I am reminded of the story of Sir Thomas More, who was sentenced by Henry VIII to be beheaded. As he approached the scaffold, one of his guards offered to help him up the steps; his reply was, "No thank you, I can get up there alone but you will have to help me down."

BAILHACHE comes from the two Old French words, *baille* and *hache,* which may be translated as "give ax." Understandably it never became a popular name. One John Baillehache is recorded in 1418.

The names BRENNAN through BURNAND look innocent enough,

but in truth they were nicknames given to the officials who carried out some of the mutilations ordered by the courts, particularly burning the hands of a prisoner.

CRAKEBONE means just what it sounds like—an official who could and did crack the bones of some poor prisoner. This too was originally a nickname. I have a quotation from an ancient document: "Quikliche cam a cacchepol and craked a-two here legges."

A HANGER was just what the name implies. Executions were daily events in those turbulent times, but in spite of the enormous quantity and widespread frequency of capital punishment, the number of family names that stemmed from the titles of these officials is very small.

GROUP 168

Stewards

This fine old name is quite properly spelled in any of the four ways shown on the list. It has had a checkered history up and down the whole island of Great Britain, but it has always indicated a person of authority in a large household. When the Normans tried to substitute their SENESCHAL for the English STEWARD, they failed to make it stick. The Lord High STEWARD of Scotland was the first officer of the Scottish king in medieval times. STUART seems to be the French way of spelling the name; this spelling is supposed to have been adopted by Mary, Queen of Scots. The spelling STEWART is more common in Scotland.

The name has climbed the social ladder over the centuries but it no longer has its one-time royal association.

GROUP 169

Fee Collectors

This is a name that seems to have come along after the naming period. The earliest example I have located was Alexander Feemaister in 1458. He was a collector of fees from the peasants and small landowners when an arrangement had been made with the lord of a big manor to use some of his pasture land.

GROUP 170
Chancellors and Constables

In the early days the CANCELLOR or CHANCELLOR was the usher of a law court, and later, the custodian of its records. Then the title was adopted by the universities and a CHANCELLOR became the equivalent of a modern university president. Back in 1214, there is a record of Richard le Chaunceler and in 1066, a Reinbald Canceler.

CONSTABLE has had its ups and downs as discussed in chapter 19 (see page 261). The name derives from the Latin *comes stabuli,* meaning "an officer of the stable." As early as 1279, however, we find a CONSTA-BLE listed as the chief officer of a whole house and again, later, as governor of a royal fortress. By the 1300s the CONSTABLE was the equal of the bailiff or the steward of a great castle. He probably was more apt to be the deputy of the real owner, but the real owner might never get around to visiting this castle and so the CONSTABLE in charge would be, in effect, the lord of the manor. Richard Conestabl appears in 1130 and Alice la Konestabl in 1200.

GROUP 171
Special Officers of the King

In feudal England, when a king granted land to one of his vassals, he could, and frequently did, put a stipulation in the agreement that would return the land to the crown if no *acceptable* heirs appeared. A special officer was appointed to protect the interests of the crown in this respect. He was called either a CHEATER or a CHETTER. Although no one knows just who first applied these names to such officers, it does seem clear that they were not meant to be flattering. There seems to be a record of only one: John Chetour in 1327.

CHECKER and CHEQUER relate to both the games of checkers and chess, as well as to the checkerboard on which the games are played. It seems that when the nobles and the representatives of the crown met to settle their financial differences each year, someone devised a huge table with its top marked off into squares like a checkerboard. In some manner, this checker tabletop was supposed to simplify the accounting— just how this worked, I may never know, but apparently it did, because from it came the Court of Exchequer. The surnames CHECKER and CHEQUER were no doubt given to officials in charge of this operation. Gilbert le Cheker is listed in 1316.

STRIKE and STRIKER are interesting because they show how predictable human nature is, even through the centuries. One clause in the Magna Carta (1215) provided that when grain was sold, it had to be measured in the London quarter (a measuring container). But local custom called for heaped bushels, and eight heaped bushels were equal to nine striked bushels. Of course, all this called for a special officer to do the striking, and hence the name originated. He carried a straight flat stick with him, which was passed over every quarter measure of grain. Many names came from this office, such as Nicholas Stryke in 1296 and Reginald le Striker in 1297.

GROUP 172

Officials in Charge of Land Allotment

All five names in this group refer to the officials who measured off the land allotted to each peasant and in general supervised its use, at least trying to keep destructive animals off it. Each peasant had a strip of land that was supposed to be permanently marked off from that of his neighbor by a deep furrow made with the plow. But, with the crude plows of that day, it must have been very difficult to make even a very shallow furrow, so the frequent presence of an official to recheck the strips was necessary. The constant repetition of *hay* and *hey* in those names probably indicates that at least some of these officials bought or sold hay, perhaps as a legitimate sideline. The Old English word *heze-weard* meant "an enclosure protector." MESSER comes from the Old French word *messier,* but means the same thing.

GROUP 173

Wards and Wardrobers

The fine old name WARD has been mentioned many times in foregoing chapters, and listed in chapter 22. It comes from the Old English word *weard,* meaning "watchman" or "guard." In a broad sense, that is still its meaning. A WARDEN in a modern prison may have numerous guards or watchmen under him, but he is still the chief watchman.

The WARDROBE names come from the Old French word *garderobe,* a combination of *warder* or *garder* and *robe,* meaning "to watch the clothes." Actually, ward and guard are from the same word, since Norman French replaces the French *gu* with a *w*. In a very large manor house or castle, with a huge staff of vassals running from the lowest to the highest, it is easy to imagine that occasions would arise when his lordship would be most anxious to impress someone (perhaps the king) with the perfection of his whole staff. At such a time, he would assign someone to superintend the dressing of everybody. As such, this man would be called a WARDROBE or some variation of it (see also chapter 19, page 269).

GROUP 174

Tiddemen

These six names are of very obscure origin. They have to do with tithing. The earliest example of the name is that of William Tedingman in 1193.

GROUP 175

Keepers of the Granary

The man who was first given one of the names in this group may or may not have been an appointed officer, but nevertheless he did carry a lot of authority and responsibility. His job was to check incoming and outgoing grain in the grain storehouse of the village. GARNER and its variants come from the Old French word *gerner* or *garnier,* which meant "a keeper of the granary." Two examples of the name are Geoffrey Gerner in 1272 and William del Gerner in 1372. Another Old French source was *warinot.* It had the same meaning and gave us the name WARNETT.

GROUP 176

Provosts

PROVOST was a common title in medieval times (see chapter 25). The deputized manager of a manor house or a castle might be called a PROVOST in one area, while in another shire he would be called a STEWARD, a SENESCHAL, a BAYLIE or a SERGEANT. One Geoffrey le Provost was recorded in 1206 and a William le Pruvost in 1219.

GROUP 177

The Sealer of Writs

This is an uncommon name today but there are a few around. The name itself goes far back, into the twelfth century, to Walter Spigernel in 1192. The name has an Old English origin. A SPICKERNELL was a court officer whose primary duty was the sealing of writs.

GROUP 178
Mayors

The MAYER type of name is usually considered either Jewish or German today, but in twelfth-century England it was English. Bartholomew le Meyre lived in 1275 and David le Meir in 1243. A MAYOR did preside over a portion of a town of some size and he was given the Old French name of *maire*. The extent of his authority is uncertain. There is inevitable confusion over this name, since the Normans had a word *mire* that meant a doctor.

LAMMOND, LAMOND, and LAMONT, with all three of the LAW names, simply mean "a lawman." With the large number and variety of officials listed in this chapter, it would seem inevitable that there be a general term by which these men could be addressed. The names derive from the Old French word *logmaor*, meaning a lawman.

GROUP 179
Miscellaneous Officials

A HORDER was the keeper of the hoard, or the treasurer—exactly what the word meant in Old French. There is one Simon le Horder listed in 1225.

COUNTER meant the same as HORDER, although it comes from another Norman word, *conteor*. One John le Counter registered somewhere in 1289.

LARDNER and LARDER were names given to castle officials in some areas. They were in charge of the food supplies, particularly the meat. A Thomas le Lardiner is recorded in 1193.

Originally, PEARCH was a measure of land but later the word was applied to a man equipped to measure land, a surveyor of record. Adam de Perche is listed in 1221.

PONTER and PUNTER were men placed in charge of bridges. We presume they were not TOLLMEN, but we can't be certain of this. Stephen le Ponter appears first in 1214.

A PORTMAN or PORTMANN was the name given to individuals chosen to help govern a section of a city. Today we would know him as a commissioner. The name derives from the Old English word *portmann*. One example is Thomas le Portman in 1275.

A TRUNCHION was a club comparable to one carried by a policeman today. All three names were probably first used as nicknames to indicate an officer who carried a club. *Trucun*, meaning "club," is the Norman root. I have found a William Trunchun recorded in 1209. *Trouncer* means the same thing.

VARDER, VERDER, and VERDIER were officers of the royal forest. Walter le Verder is listed in 1279.

The Jailers

The power to arrest and detain a person in prison was a frightening thing in medieval times. Almost any of the officials listed in this chapter could arrest somebody, if he were not of high rank, and put him in prison for an indefinite period. A prisoner's right to a speedy trial did not exist—he could be allowed to rot in jail indefinitely if the lord of the manor was so minded. If the prisoner had money or friends willing and able, they could get him out of custody by paying the sums stipulated for each offense.

In the period of the Norman kings, the jail was a portion of the castle's *donjon*. This was always in the base of the castle's keep and naturally the jailer would frequently be called the KEEP, the KEEPER, the DUMJOHN, or the DUNJOHN. Ralph Dungun is listed in 1255. Recently I read a local history of Lock Haven, Pennsylvania, in which the author named all the early citizens of the town who had acquired reputations for their contributions to the community in the eighteenth century; I was pleased to read that one Joshua KEEP had been the town jailer for many of those early years.

The Norman-French word for the man in charge of the prison was *gayolierre,* but even in the early years of the period this changed to *gaioler* and still later, to *jaioleur* or *gaoler*. The GALE names come from one of these early words and indicate the man with the keys. Robert le Gaoler in 1255 was one of them, and let us hope he had a heart as well as a bunch of those enormous keys.

CAGE and CADGE were probably metonymic for JAIL. A cage is, after all, a place of confinement. I find a Richard Cagge in 1275.

GROUP 157

Bailiffs

Bail	Bailie	Bale	Baylie
Baile	Baliff	Bales	**Bayliff**
Baileff	Baillie	Baly	Bayliffe
Bailes	Bails	Baylay	Baylis
Bailess	Bailward	Bayles	Bayly
Bailey	Baily	Bayley	Baylyff

GROUP 158

Sergeants (See Group 122)

Sargant	Sargint	Seàrjeant	Sergeaunt
Sargeant	Sarjant	Sergant	Sergent
Sargeaunt	Sarjeant	Sergean	Serjeant
Sargent	Sarjent	Sergeant	Serjent

GROUP 159

Sheriffs

Lackman	Reeve	Shireff	Shreeves
•	Reeves	Shiriff	Shreevs
Prater	•	Shirman	Shrieve
Preater	Sheriff	Shirra	Shrieves
Pretor	Sheriffs	Shirreff	Shrive
•	Sherriff	Shirreffs	Shrives
Reaves	Sherriffs	Shirrefs	

GROUP 160

Tax Collectors

Catch	•	Gatherer	Tolman
Catcher	Farmar	•	Towler
Cacheral	Farmer	Langstaff	•
Catchpole	Fermer	Longstaff	Travers
Catchpoll	Fernor	Longstaffe	Traves
Catchpool	•	•	Travis
Catchpoole	Gabler	Toler	Traviss
Catchpoule	Gableor	Toller	
Ketcher	•	Tollman	

GROUP 161

Marshals

Marschall	Marskell	Maskall	Maskill
Marshall	Mascall	Maskell	

GROUP 162

Seneschals

Senchell	Senesccall	Seneschall	Sensicle
Senecal	Seneschal	Sensicall	Senskell

GROUP 163

Officers of the Court

Crier	Deem	Demings	•
Cryer	Deemer	Dempster	Diter
•	Deeming	Doman	Dyter
Deam	Demer	Dome	•
Deamer	Demers	Dooman	Jestice

Judge	Mair	Proctor	Somner
Judges	•	•	Sumner
Justice	Prockter	Simner	Sumners
•	Procter	Simnor	Sumpner

GROUP 164

Overseers

Greeff	Grief	Grieve
Greif	Grieff	Grieves

GROUP 165

Weighers and Measurers

Peiser	Piser	Poyser	Pyser
Peizer	Poser	Poyzer	Pyzer

GROUP 166

Animal Impounders

Pender	Pindar	Pindor	Ponder
Penfold	Pinder	Pinfold	Pound
			Pounder

GROUP 167

Men Who Punished the Guilty

Bailhache	Brennand	Burnand	•
•	Brennans	•	Hanger
Brennan	Brennen	Crakebone	

GROUP 168

Stewards

Steuart	Steward	Stewart	Stuart

GROUP 169

Fee Collectors

Femister	Phemister
Fimister	Phimester
	Phimister

GROUP 170

Chancellors and Constables

Cancellor	Constable
Chancellor	

GROUP 171

Special Officers of the King

Cheater	•	Chequer	Strike
Chetter	Checker	•	Striker

GROUP 172

Officials in Charge of Land Allotment

Hayward	Heyward	•
Haywood	Heywood	Messer

GROUP 173

Wards and Wardrobers

Wardrobe	Wardrope	Wardropper	Waredraper
Wardrop	Wardroper	Wardrupp	Whatrup

GROUP 174

Tiddemen

Tiddeman	Tidman	Tittman
Tidiman	Titman	Tydeman

GROUP 175

Keepers of the Granary

Garnar	Garnet	Garnier	•
Garner	Garnett	Gerner	Warnett

GROUP 176

Provosts

Provest	Provis	Provost

GROUP 177

The Sealer of Writs

Pickernell	Spickernall	Spickernell	Spicknell

GROUP 178

Mayors

Lammond	Lawman	Mayers	Meyers
Lamond	Lawyer	Mayor	
Lamont	•	Meier	
Law	Mayer	Meyer	

GROUP 179

Miscellaneous Officials

Cadge	Gayle	Larder	•
Cage	Gayler	Lardner	Tronson
•	Gaylor	•	Trounson
Counter	Jailler	Pearch	Trunchion
•	•	•	•
Dumjohn	Horder	Ponter	Varder
Dunjohn	•	Punter	Verder
•	Keep		Verdier
Gale	Keeper	Portman	
Galer	•	Portmann	

CHAPTER **24**

The Church

Christianity was the dominating influence in the daily lives of the English people of the period, and a brief word about it seems essential to understanding the origin of many names.

During the naming period, the entire island was solidly Roman Catholic, as was the whole of western Europe. It was a time of great conflict between the authority of the church in the person of the pope and the authority of the king and his civil courts.

English kings, like all other European monarchs, ruled their own kingdoms, but the confrontation of popes and kings over ecclesiastical rights and prerogatives usually resulted in the church's power being maintained. Henry II in the Becket affair submitted to a public lashing and walked barefooted to a designated shrine as penance.

The first Christians in England were almost certainly Romans in the third century; their number was not large, as can be determined by the few Christian artifacts found in Roman excavations. The legend of the martyrdom of Saint Alban places that event at the beginning of the fifth century, but bishops of London and York are known to have attended a church council in Gaul in 314. With the fall of the Roman Empire and the consequent removal of her legions to the Continent, the Britons slid back into the state of semibarbarism they had occupied before the Roman conquest. The work of civilization had to be started all over again, and it began with the reintroduction of Christianity. In A.D. 597, Pope Gregory sent the Italian missionary Augustine, at the head of some forty monks, from Rome to Kent in southeast England. Augustine was a

335

monk following the rule of Saint Benedict, the founder of the **Benedictine Order**, a congregation of men both clerical and lay banded together to advance the cause of Christianity. These monks supported themselves by their own labor and built their own communities called monasteries. They spent part of each day in manual labor and the rest in study and contemplation, or preaching in the surrounding towns and villages.

The arrival of Augustine in Kent was fortuitous because the people of Kent had had far more contact with the Continent than had any of the more distant parts of England. The wife of the Kentish king, Ethelbert, was a daughter of the Frankish king who reigned in Paris. She was already a Christian and privately worshiped at an old, dismantled Roman church on the outskirts of Canterbury. In spite of his wife's feelings, King Ethelbert was suspicious, so when Augustine sent word to him asking that a meeting be arranged, the king agreed, but only if it were held out in the open air where there would be less likelihood of these strangers working some kind of evil magic.

The scene has often been painted: Augustine leading his band of brown-clad monks, carrying a silver cross and a picture of Christ painted on a board, and the whole group singing a litany. The king and his attendants listened to the words of the saint and gave him and his monks permission to preach throughout the Kingdom of Kent; sometime later, he became a Christian himself.

Later, Augustine returned to the Continent, where the pope appointed him archbishop of Canterbury, the first in what was to become a very long line of notable churchmen. On his return to Canterbury, he organized and systematized the work of his missionaries. At first, the monks used Queen Bertha's chapel of Saint Martin as a church, and then another old Roman church was discovered. This was rebuilt and became the predecessor of today's magnificent Canterbury cathedral. Other buildings and lands were given to them, and their missionary efforts were steadily extended, as far in every direction as the influence of the king went.

Thirty years after the arrival of Augustine in Kent, a priest named Paulinus, possibly a convert and pupil of Augustine, was consecrated bishop and sent from Kent far up into Northumbria to convert the people of that kingdom. He succeeded temporarily, baptizing the king and the leading men of the area and building a fine stone church, which later became York Minster. But when the Northumbrian King Edwin was slain by the pagans of Mercia, who took over his kingdom, Paulinus fled back to Kent with the widow and children of the dead king. Not much later a group of Scottish monks under Aidan, a bishop trained by the Irish in Iona, came to Northumbria, and they stemmed the tide of paganism. They did so well that they were granted Lindisfarne, or Holy Island, just off the coast. On this they built a monastery that was to be the center of all missionary efforts in the north for many centuries and that is today one of the most picturesque monastic ruins in all England. Missionaries from Lindisfarne spread all over the north, winning converts from the lowliest peasants to royalty itself.

In the meantime, still other devoted monks came from the Continent into East Anglia to continue the work of bringing civilization and Christianity to the island. By A.D. 650, hardly fifty years after the landing of Augustine and only twenty years after Aidan, all of England with the exception of Sussex had become Christian.

However, there was a division between the Celtic Christianity left over from the Romans and that brought by Saint Augustine from Rome. The Britons in the western part of the island had retained more of the old faith they had received under the Roman occupation than might have been expected. When the Romans left, Christianity was carried from there over into Ireland by Saint Patrick and those who followed him. In the meantime, the Scots who occupied parts of northern Ireland began to settle the western coast of what is now Scotland. Here the monastery of Iona was founded by Saint Columba, a saint almost as dear to the Irish as Saint Patrick. All this Christianity, running from Wales into northern England over into Ireland, was Celtic in influence. Celtic Christianity had all the natural enthusiasm that has always seemed to be part of the Celtic temperament, and her priests and monks resisted being told to confine their missionary efforts to prescribed places and regulated times. They went about saying mass, baptizing, and performing all of the church rites without the close direction of a superior. The clergy from the Continent, on the other hand, were strongly organized. A bishop was definitely in charge of all the priests under his care. He could and did spread his clergy around according to the needs of each community. There were also disciplinary differences, such as the form of baptism and the proper calculation of the date for Easter. These differences were resolved at the Council of Whitby in 664. The old Celtic customs were given up, and within a short time after the Council, all Scotland, Wales, and Ireland were in harmony with the Roman church. The church thus took shape as one united body with the same customs, teachings, and organization all over Europe and Britain, with Rome as the center. At this time, Theodore of Tarsus was archbishop of Canterbury; he had been trained in Rome and, accordingly, had the Roman love for organization. When he took over, England had but seven bishops; each district corresponding roughly with one of the old kingdoms. Theodore divided the larger bishoprics into smaller ones, following to a large extent the ancient tribal lines, so that now there were fifteen dioceses. Each and every village had its own church and its own resident priest, and each PASTOR or RECTOR was answerable only to his own Bishop. In 672, a synod was held at Hertford at which all fifteen bishops were present and the regulations were finalized. It is truly remarkable that England was organized into a single body for religious purposes at a time when it was still divided politically into a number of independent kingdoms.

MONASTERIES

For nearly a thousand years, the monasteries of various religious orders were to be prominent features of the English landscape. They would be centers of learning and culture and industry in an age when mere survival seemed to be uppermost in the minds of men.

The monastery was a community of men voluntarily living together under the direction of a superior, known as an abbot or a prior. The monastic orders were open to any man of good character who was willing to take the vows of poverty, chastity, and obedience and live by the Rule of Saint Benedict. This rule was altered slightly from time to time in the various other orders that grew out of the Benedictines, such as the Dominicans, the Franciscans, the Carmelites, and the Augustinians, but it never changed substantially.

If a man applying for membership was accepted, he would be designated a NOVICE for a period of several months; if he continued to show that he was fitted for the life of a monk, he would be admitted to full membership. He might be ordained a priest or he might continue as a lay brother. He could advance from one responsibility to another and even become an abbot or prior. At various times during the thousand-year period, an abbot or prior was actually elected by the monks who would serve under him, an astonishing bit of democracy at a time when feudalism was the accepted civil government.

The day of the monk was a long one: he would get up at daybreak, hear mass in the chapel, eat a breakfast of soup and coarse bread, and then go to his assigned duties. These would be as varied as the knowledge of the time permitted. Nearly every monk in the monastery would be called on for a period of labor each day, but once that was over, each one would proceed to his particular assignment. This might be in the extensive cultivated acres surrounding the monastery where all the fruits, grains, and vegetables for the whole institution and its visitors were planted and harvested. Or, if a man seemed to have a liking for animals, he might be assigned to care for the sheep, cattle, and poultry. A man of a scholarly bent would be assigned to the scriptorium. This was a very special room. All the books of the monastery were kept here, but it was far more than a library. Here it was that the incredibly patient, painstaking monks copied books. Today, we take books for granted; everyone owns at least a few, and more are easily available in bookstores and public libraries. But in England, things were very different then. Printing by movable type was not even dreamed of, and consequently the production of a book had to be by the unbelievably long process of hand lettering with either a quill pen or a brush. Furthermore, paper was still almost unknown and wholly unavailable—one used parchment or vellum, and either of these was extremely expensive. In one corner of the room might be a tall, thin monk working over a high desk. To his left would be a huge volume, held open by some kind of paperweight. The monk would glance at the open volume now and then before applying himself to the single sheet of vellum in front of him. Clearly, he was copying a page from that book. A closer glance would clearly show that the book was the Bible and it was open to Paul's Epistle to the Romans. He had written it while he was in Carthage although it would be some years yet before Paul would be in Rome himself. At any rate, this monk would be known about the monastery as a SCRIVENOR or sometimes as Brother SCRIPTURE. His work was copying each and every word of the Bible. Without the kindly old monk and others like him, the Bible would have been completely lost to us today.

To make just one copy of the Bible required many hours of patient labor every day for a whole lifetime. In practice, whenever a monastery had more than one man qualified for such exacting work, the monk in charge might sit with the volume open and slowly, word by word, dictate its contents to several SCRIVENORS. This was mass production for that period. Understandably, they might be able to produce three, or even four Bibles in a single lifetime. The most famous English monk of this period is undoubtedly the Venerable Bede. He was born in A.D. 673, almost four centuries before the naming period began. His parents died when he was a child, and he was adopted by a nobleman who had recently become a monk. The monk's name was Benedict and, as fate would have it, he was very much of a scholar and an artist. Under the tutelage of Benedict, Bede entered Benedict's first monastery at Wear-mouth and, when the neighboring monastery at Jarrow was completed in 682, Bede moved there. For the rest of Bede's long life, Jarrow with its altar and choir, its library and scriptorium, was to be his entire world. Bede died in 735, having written some of the greatest books of the period. His *Ecclesiastical History of the English Nation* is still con-sidered a model for modern historians. It was written in Latin, as was everything else at that time, but King Alfred the Great, two centuries later, thought so much of it that he had it translated into the English of his day. Hardly less important were the works of Caedmon (circa 670) and Cynewulf (circa 750). Both these monks, along with the later Aelfric (?955–?1022), lived before the naming period so they still have their Saxon names.

Every monastic institution in the whole of Britain contained a hos-pital. Based on the crude standards of medical knowledge of the time, they were good. Probably the very earliest of them were intended pri-marily as infirmaries for the sick and ailing monks themselves, but soon the beds were open to all outsiders too. Knights wounded in a tourna-ment or real battle might spend months in a monastery bed. Even royalty was treated by the monks.

That word *hospital* is very interesting. Today, its meaning is much narrower than it was centuries ago. At that time, it included the whole concept of hospitality. The monks opened their doors to every traveler, young and old, of both sexes. The stranger had but to ring the bell at the main gate to be admitted to the best in food and lodging the place might have.[1]

The Cistercian order of monks did not open monasteries in England until some time in the thirteenth century. In addition to all the normal monastic activities, they seem to have given great attention to the de-velopment of better sheep and, consequently, better wool. Scattered about the grounds of every monastery would be the shops of craftsmen: a blacksmith to make and repair tools; a woodworker's shop and a COOP-ER'S shop to make the kegs and barrels the VINTNERS would need;

---

[1] The writer recalls a personal experience in this connection. Traveling in Austria some years ago, I rang the bell at the door of an old monastery, having in mind looking around the old place like any other sightseer. The door was opened by a brown-clad monk in the traditional habit of the Cistercian order (founded in 1098). My question was, "Is the monastery open to visitors today?" His reply, given in soft-spoken German was, "Mein Herr, this door has been open every day for more than 812 years—come in, please."

a TANNERY to make leather, and certainly a PARCHMENTER to make parchment and vellum out of goat- and lambskins for the SCRIVE-NORS. There would be a cloth-making shop where WEAVERS and DYERS would produce the coarse cloth required for the robes of all the MONKS or FRIARS in the institution. The colors would vary with the order. The Franciscans used dark brown, while the Dominicans preferred black and white, and some of the others used gray. These shops were operated by the lay BROTHERS of the monastery whenever possible, but craftsmen from the outside were employed when necessary.

GROUP 180

Secular Clergy

This whole group presents some practical problems to the researcher. An ordained PRIEST, from a POPE all the way down, either in the secular clergy or in the monastic, was not supposed to marry. Consequently a name given to one of the clergy would normally pass out of existence with his death.

Also, many were originally nicknames that came out of pageants, perhaps the most popular type of communal entertainment in every village, town, and city. The church encouraged observance of holy days and they served a double purpose: they centered attention on an event in the Christian calendar that might be overlooked otherwise; in addition, they gave the common people a chance to drop their hoes and hammers, leave their looms and forges, and enjoy a day of rest and recreation. At a time when the working day started at sunrise and ended at sunset six days a week, holidays must have been exceedingly welcome. A holiday meant the peasant could, in a small way, imitate the nobility by doing something that represented pure fun to him.

Pageants and miracle plays were largely the product of the holidays. Plans would be made far ahead of time. Costumes were enormously popular. In the pageant, the parade would start with a boy or young man dressed to represent the POPE, and he was the pope all that day. If he did well, he might be drafted for the same part again and again until he began to be called POPE. Following him might be a dignified CARDINAL or BISHOP and an ABBOT and a whole string of monks and lesser churchmen. Even the KING and QUEEN were included.

This sort of thing went on in every community in England for centuries. The nobility and their families were interested onlookers and so were some of the real clergy. A feast would follow and prizes would be awarded. A great deal of ale would be consumed and everybody would go home happy and relieved from at least one day of the monotonous grind that was their normal existence.

Throughout the year, similar nicknames were created. A man might be a blacksmith or a baker, a butcher, or a shepherd, but if there seemed to be something in his looks or behavior that might suggest a CHAPLAIN or a RECTOR or even a dignified CANON attached to the cathedral, the name his actions suggested might be applied to him in fun and it might stick.

There is an additional possible source. As indicated many times, the tax collector more than any other individual may have been the most frequent initial source of new surnames. With that exceedingly common situation, it seems reasonable that an encounter like the following might come up:

The collector enters a cottage for the usual purpose of taking a few of the peasant's chickens, but before he has a chance to open his mouth, the long-suffering taxpayer greets him, saying, "Good morning, sir. Tell me, how is the good bishop [or whatever clerical title he might choose] this morning? He is an uncle of mine, you know." The collector couldn't possibly know that the poor peasant was *not* the relative he claimed to be. Of course, the collector could get an interview with the bishop and ultimately determine the truth of the claim, but all this would be extra work, and no matter how it turned out, a little embarrassing to the bishop and to him too. It was a lot easier and safer to take only one of the citizen's pigs instead of two. Then he could enter him on the tax roll as "John (bishop)—paid 1 pig." That word *bishop* (or whatever) would act as a warning to himself if he happened to be assigned the same tax route next time.

There is no proof that incidents like the above ever happened, but it is not unreasonable to think that some variation of this scene could have happened a great many times all over England.

POPE, as a surname, is particularly interesting. England has produced only one POPE in all the centuries: Adrian IV, who occupied the chair of Peter from 1154 to 1159. Before being elected, his name was Nicholas Breakspeare. The records show at least three others of this name in the same general time period, such as Alexander Brekespere in 1199, Geoffrey Brekespere in 1206, and Thomas Brekaspere in 1227. These are probably namesakes, but they might have been actual relatives of Adrian IV. Others might well have adopted his new title as a name.

VECK, VICAR, VICK, and VIKER come from the Old French word meaning "bishop," *le eveske,* and later, *vikere.* Stephen le Vyker is recorded in 1313. A PRIEST was an ordained minister and doubtless some of them married and had families in spite of the strict rule against it; many of the names, however, came by way of more distant relationship. And CHAPLAIN names may fall into the same class.

All three CARDINAL names were undoubtedly nicknames. The traditional color of a cardinal's vestments is red, so one can imagine that youngsters preparing for a parade would suddenly decide to dress up as a cardinal with some red material found in the family's scrap bag. There was a Geoffrey Cardinell in 1208.

The origin of CANON, PASTOR, RECTOR, and VICAR is somewhat unsure. Ordinarily a priest would be well along in years before receiving any of these offices and unlikely to have any ideas of taking a wife. PASTOR, not to be confused with PASTER meaning "a baker of pastry," comes from the Anglo-French word *pastour,* meaning "a shepherd" or "herdsman." A priest was in charge of a flock and the image of him as a shepherd comes from the New Testament.

CHANTREY was the name of both an altar or chapel and the priest who said mass there. The SERMIN names simply refer to men more or less noted for their ability to speak.

The Old English word for priest was *preost.* In the early part of the naming period, the word seems to have indicated the office, but soon it became a nickname that might be given to anyone who had the appearance or behavior that might be expected of a priest. No doubt it was also given to individuals whose character was just the opposite. To quote a few early records, we find a Walter Prestes in 1332 and Hugh Prust and Paul Prest in the same year.

All of the DEACON names go back to the Old English word *diacon,* which changed to the Middle English *deakne* and still later to the Norman *diacne*—all meant a deacon, a minor official in the church whose duties would change many times in the centuries. William le Dekon is on the tax roll of 1330. In Old English, the word *arceercediacon* meant the chief deacon. The Normans changed this to *arc(h)ediacne* but its meaning remained the same. ARCHBISHOP simply meant the chief bishop. SHRIVER goes back to the Anglo-Saxon word *scrifan,* which meant the act of a priest hearing a man's confession, particularly if the man considered himself in danger of imminent death.

GROUP 181

Church Laymen

SEXTEN, with all its variations, was the name given to a man in charge of the sacred vessels and vestments in a church or cathedral, and not a grave-digger as he sometimes is now. Every church had at least one so the name is fairly common; William Sexstain is listed in 1299.

The CROSIER names were given to laymen or even boys who carried either the bishop's crozier or a large cross in a religious procession. They were responsible for the care of the crozier at all times. William le Croyser appears in 1264.

KERMAN through KIRMAN were church custodians, the laymen in charge of the church property. John Kirkus is listed in 1219.

A VERGER had more than one meaning: at times, he was the man in charge of the church property, and more frequently, as above, called a KIRMAN or KIRKMAN; while in other places, his duties were the same as those of the CROSIER.

The name CHURCHARD is not very exact in that its sphere frequently conflicts with those of both the CROSIER and the VERGER, men who were in charge of at least some part of a church's property.

The CANTER lead the singing and the SANGARS were simply other singers in the church choir.

FETTIPLACE comes from an Anglo-French word meaning "to make a place for someone." Today, he would be called an usher. The word was used particularly in Oxford and was the name of a fourteenth-century mayor of Oxford.

An USHER was primarily a doorkeeper in a church.

BELLMAN and the two TOLLER names are obvious. GRAVER may have dug the graves, or he may have been an engraver of gold and silver.

VESTRY and VESTRYMAN could be the names given to the man in charge of the VESTRY room of a cathedral.

GROUP 182

Monastic Institutions

All nine ABBATT names are simply variations of the name given the superior in charge of a great monastery or a group of several such institutions. Peter le Abbot appears in 1227.

ALMONER—a rare name—refers to the monk designated by the AB-

BOT or PRIOR to be in charge of dispensing food and clothing to the poor of the area. The monasteries, as a whole, did become wealthy over the centuries, owing to both the unceasing labor of the monks and the gifts of deceased nobles, but historians are in agreement that they handed out life's necessities to the poor at their doors without fear or favor.

FRATER through FRYOR simply meant "brother," a term used to designate a man in a monastery who had taken minor orders. Usually he was not an ordained priest. Richard del Fraytour appears in 1301 and Roger le Frier in 1243.

PRIOR was the usual term indicating the man in charge of a priory (such as Nicholas Prior in 1317) and MONK was the general term applied to all members of a monastery. At least twelve names have come down to us from the word MONK. One of the most famous is Charles Moncke, who was a London blacksmith in the early part of the nineteenth century. Mr. Moncke invented a wrench that was so useful that it is still a standard tool with many mechanics. Naturally, it was called a "MONCKE wrench." The very earliest recording of names from this source is Aylric Munec in the early part of the eleventh century. MONK names were probably occupational in the early part of the period but, like so many church names, became nicknames. William Munc is listed in 1222 and Walter le Monec in 1243. The names MONKHOUSE, MONKMAN, and MUNKMAN were probably first applied to certain lay assistants to the monks. Thus they could be address names as well as occupational ones. Thomas Munkas was definitely employed as a servant in a monastery in the fifteenth century and John Munkman is listed in the thirteenth century.

All six DEAN names were applied to men in somewhat varied positions, but the name has always been associated with dignity and learning. Ralph le Dean is recorded in 1006. Together with STEWARD and PROVOST, DEAN was frequently given to the monk or layman who was second in command at a large monastic institution. Martin Stenhard appears in 1275. All eight SCRIBNER names indicate writers. Unfortunately, these terms do not enable us to distinguish between those who wrote their own material, and those who patiently reproduced classical writers and the Scriptures. The contribution these monks made to modern civilization is beyond computation. The LIMMERS and LUMNERS were artists; they were the monks who, with their pens and brushes and a large selection of colored inks and paints, illustrated the pages the SCRIVENERS had written. The often-seen black-and-white reproductions of their initial letters are beautiful, but the originals, in color, are spectacular. The name comes from the Old French word *enlumineor,* meaning an artist who illuminates manuscripts. Ralph le Liminar appears in 1230 and Richard Lemner in 1275.

GROUP 183

Monastic Laymen

The ABBA names are probably Scottish in origin. Each of them indicated an ABBOT, but in parts of Scotland an ABBOT might be a layman. In such cases, he seems to have been distinguished by one of the name variations listed here. There is a Ralph le Abbe in 1177 and a Geoffrey Labbe in 1199. Then there was a John Abby in 1297. They all supposedly were lay abbots.

The CELLARER was something like the steward of a modern club. He was in charge of the food, drinks, and dishes of the monastery, but he also had some control over the funds, so in that respect he might be compared to the bursar of a university today. He probably lived in separate quarters and he was excused from some of the duties of the other MONKS. In some of the old illustrated records, the CELLARER is shown with a purse in one hand and a bundle of huge keys in the other. There is at least one instance in which we know that a CELLARER was buried in the section reserved only for ABBOTS and PRIORS, a high honor.

CONVERSE was the name applied to a convert from the secular world to the monastic life; he had to be middle-aged or older. He was never ordained but remained a layman. The Cistercian and Augustinian *conversi* were almost entirely illiterate laborers and, at most, semiskilled mechanics living under a rule very much less strict than that for the other members of the institution. They occupied separate quarters in or near the monastery.

KITCHNER, with its variations, has been treated in chapter 19 (see page 268). He might have been a cook or an assistant of some kind. The food served in a monastery was of the simplest kind.

PARCHMENT and PARCHMENTER are not common names today, but the skill and craftsmanship of the first bearers of either of these names gives them an importance that can hardly be exaggerated. They made parchment, the one and only substance that could be used for written records at a time in which paper of any kind was practically nonexistent. Without the work of the parchment makers our knowledge of medieval and earlier history would be limited to what we could obtain from such things as statuary, brasses, and actual masonry.

All honor to Walter Perchamunt in 1200 and Gille Parcheminer in 1180.

The four PATTEN names come from an Old French word meaning "clogs." In Middle English, the words were *pateyne* or *tymbyre* or *yron*. They were made from either wood or iron and were put on the feet with leather straps. They must have been uncomfortable to wear, but the stone floors of an ancient monastery would have been much more so to walk on without their help. The name was probably first given to a man who made this sort of footwear, like John Patynmaker in 1379.

PATERNOSTER, of course, means "Our Father": the first words of the Lord's Prayer. With the passage of time, they came to mean first the prayer itself and then, since a PATERNOSTER was so prominent in the rosary, a rosary. Since beads were and are commonly used in saying a rosary, and since they require some skill to make, the man who made them became a PATERNOSTERER. This was naturally shortened to PATERNOSTER, and there it remains. Plenty of them appear in the old records, like William le Paternostrer in 1280. And the name is still found in modern English streets, such as Paternoster Row near Saint Paul's Cathedral in London and another one near Carlisle Cathedral. Doubtless these streets contained the shops of the bead-makers in medieval times.

PORTERS were doorkeepers and package carriers, as discussed in chapters 19 and 22 (see pages 266 and 312).

SENESCHAL has also been discussed earlier (see chapter 19, page 262) but when the word applies to a monastery, it takes on a separate meaning. In a large monastery with many thousands of acres of land, which might include one or two whole villages and even a couple of castles, a lay nobleman was sometimes put in charge of the purely business transactions. This man would be called a SENESCHAL. A William Seneschel was listed as such in 1243.

All eight SPITTELER names come from the same root as our word *hospital* and have no connection with "spit." A SPITTLEHOUSE was a hospital, and if your nominal ancestor was employed in a hospital in almost any capacity, he might have been given one of these names. Since the only hospitals in existence in those times were the infirmaries of the monasteries, a SPITTLER must have been a lay brother of some kind. Adam Spitelman appears in 1176.

GROUP 180

Secular Clergy

Archbishop	Caplin	•	Prestt
•	Chaperlin	Deacon	Priest
Archdeacon	Chaperling	Deakan	Prust
•	Chaplain	Deakin	•
Bishop	Chaplin	Deakins	Rector
•	Chapline	•	•
Cannon	Chapling	Pape	Sermin
Cannons	Kaplan	Pope	Sermon
Canon	Kaplin	•	Surman
Channon	•	Parson	•
•	Cardinal	•	Shriver
Capelen	Cardinall	Pastor	•
Capelin	Cardnell	•	Veck
Capeling	•	Preist	Vicar
Caplan	Chantrey	Press	Vick
Caplen	Chantry	Prest	Viker

GROUP 181

Church Laymen

Bellman	Churchward	Ussher	Sexton
•	Churchyard	•	•
Canter	•	Kerman	Sangar
Cantor	Croser	Kirkhouse	Sanger
Caunter	Crosier	Kirkman	Songer
Kanter	Crozier	Kirkus	•
•	•	Kirman	Toller
Church	Fettiplace	•	Tollman
Churchard	•	Sacristan	•
Churchers	Graver	Seckerson	Verger
Churches	•	Secretan	•
Churchman	Husher	Sexon	Vestry
Churchouse	Le Usher	Sexstone	Vestryman
Churchus	Usher	Sexten	

GROUP 182

Monastic Institutions

Abbatt	Deans	Lumner	Prier
Abbett	Deen	•	Prior
Abbitt	Dene	Monck	Pryer
Abbot	•	Moncke	Pryor
Abbots	Frater	Monk	•
Abbott	Frear	Monke	Provost
Abbotts	Freear	Monkhouse	•
Labbet	Freer	Monkman	Scribner
Le Abbot	Frere	Monks	Scripture
•	Friar	Monnick	Scriven
Almoner	Frier	Munck	Scrivener
•	Fryer	Munk	Scrivenor
Dean	Fryor	Munkman	Scrivens
Deane	•	Munks	Scrivings
Deanes	Limmer	•	Scrivins

GROUP 183

Monastic Laymen

Abba	Kitchiner	•	•
Abbay	Kitchner	Porter	Spital
Abbey	•	Porters	Spittall
Abble	Parchment	•	Spittel
Abby	Parchmenter	Seneschal	Spitteler
Labey	•	Seneschall	Spittle
Le Abbey	Patten	Senchell	Spittlehouse
•	Pattern	Senecal	Spittler
Cellarer	Pattin	Senescall	Spittles
•	Patton	Sensicall	
Converse	•	Sensicle	
•	Paternoster	Senskell	

CHAPTER 25

Other Medieval Occupations

In this chapter an effort will be made to pick up various small groups of medieval occupations, not so much for their size but for the importance of their contribution to our modern family names.

GROUP 184
Men Who Could Read and Write

The number of men living in medieval England who could read and write was pitifully small—perhaps no more than two or three out of every hundred individuals seen in a day's walk about any village, and these would include the higher clergy. The clergy were literate to a man —some of them scholars whose writings are influential even to this day— but they were small in number and mostly sequestered in the great monasteries. The man on the street, the peasant on his farm, the craftsman in his shop, and even many of the petty officials who swarmed over the landscape were not only unable to read or write but, for the most part, had no desire to. This attitude was probably influenced by that of the nobility, who, with rare exceptions, considered the ability "to make hens' tracks on paper" unmanly, and something unworthy. Men were supposed to fight; the pen was a mark of servility—the sword the weapon of the man.

Slowly, almost imperceptibly at times, a new attitude toward learning became apparent. A young fellow might decide that the life of a monk in a nearby monastery had certain attractions. He could fulfill his religious

duties, live in a clean and orderly community along with others of similar tastes, and in general receive the respectful attention that clerics were
usually accorded. He would apply for admission to the venerable old
abbot, and he might be accepted for a period of probation that would
last a year or more before final vows could be taken. At the monastery
he would have to spend a few hours each day doing what he was assigned
to do; the balance of the day was divided between the chapel and the
scriptorium.

In the scriptorium he would see older members of the order copying
from huge books with quill pens on sheets of parchment; at the far end
of the room other monks with a large assortment of colored paints and
brushes would be decorating the finished pages. His initial duties in this
unfamiliar atmosphere of learning might consist of nothing more than
holding down the page for one of the copyists or, now and then, one of
the limners. In the course of a few weeks, he would find an opportunity,
when Brother John had to leave the room for a few minutes, to pick up
the quill and do some experimenting with it. It was quite easy—one just
dipped that feather in the jar of black liquid and rubbed its point over
the parchment, and, sure enough, it made a line. Thus might have been
born a CLARK. In a year or two, he might have learned how to copy
the simpler lettering and, with the encouragement of Brother John, even
a few words of his own. Parchment was extremely hard to come by. It
was made right in the monastery and every available piece was needed
by the monks in their lifelong labors to reproduce the Scriptures. He
might somehow acquire a small piece, however, that, if bleached, could
be used over and over again.

This young man might go on with his training for the full period of
his novitiate and become an ordained priest and even ultimately an abbot
or a prior; on the other hand, he might decide the life was not for him
and so, before it was time to take his final vows, he would leave the
austerities of the monastery for the world outside. He would take with
him, however, a knowledge of writing that he could use for the rest of his
life.

As far as names are concerned, the Latin word *clericus* seems to be the
root. The word originally meant "priest," and since priests had long
been associated with reading and writing, it is easy to see how people got
into the habit of calling any man who could write a cleric. This was
soon shortened to clerc, and before long it was clerk and eventually clark.
For a great many years, the people of England learned to distinguish a
CLARK by the tiny leather bottle of ink that he carried in his belt along

with his quill. The very earliest record of the name I have found was still dressed in its original Latin form, Richerius -clericus. This was in 1086. A little later, in 1205, I find a Reginald Clerc and in 1272, a John le Clerk. BUNCLARKE, from the Old French words *bon* and *clerc,* meant "good clerk."

GRAFF was the Norman word for a public SCRIBE or SCRIVENER. The root was *grafer,* meaning "to write." Robert Graf appears in 1279.

The LATIMER names were almost certainly of clerks too. The names indicate the ability to either speak or read Latin. Remember, Latin was the language of learning at that time. People talked Norman French around the castle or the court, but if one were a baker or a blacksmith, one would speak English. Legal documents of all kinds were carefully drawn up in sonorous Latin, and if a man could write in Latin, he would probably find his name proclaiming that fact to the whole community. Ralph Latimarus carried that proud name around in 1086 and Richard Latoner somewhat later.

MARKER, from the Old English *mearcere,* means "notary" or "writer."

NUTTER might sound like a man in the business of selling nuts, but this was not so. NUTTER came from the Old English word *notere,* meaning a "scribe" or "secretary." There was an Adam le Notyere in 1293.

PENMAN is obvious and, along with the SCRIBBLER through SCRIUEYN names, tells us that the man so named was a writer. He may have written many different things, but at some time or other he was probably associated in some way with the copying of parts of the Bible. Ricardus Scriptor did this in 1158. The root word was *scribo,* Latin for "write." ESCRIUEYN and SCRIUEYN come directly from the Old French word *escrivain,* meaning "a copier of manuscripts."

TEACHER is from an Anglo-Saxon word, *taecean,* meaning to teach. Surely that must have required the ability to read and write, so we have another CLARK, except that he was called a TEACHER.

WRITER and WRYTERE mean just what they say. They derive from the Old English word *writere.* There was an Adam le Wrytar in 1275.

GROUP 185

University Personnel

The English people look back with justifiable pride at their two oldest universities, Oxford and Cambridge, founded in the twelfth century. They were probably located on sites that had already served the cause of education for some years. In a sense, both universities may be considered outgrowths of the University of Paris. Robert Pullen, the theologian, arrived from Paris in 1133, and shortly after, four of the great monastic orders, the Dominicans, the Carmelites, the Franciscans, and the Benedictines, arrived. They set up a system of lectures that has not changed greatly in all the years since.

From the beginning, these universities operated on a plan of separate colleges, each complete in itself and presided over by an elected official from its own faculty. Presiding over the entire university was the chancellor.

It cannot be claimed that the name CHANCELLOR or CANCELLOR originated with either of these universities. The name had been in use for centuries, not only in England but all over Europe. Its origin seems to have been the French word *cancelli,* which meant a system of lattices surrounding the seat of judgment. Not only has it been used in the university but in departments of government as well.

The many BEDEL names derive from the Old English *bydel.* Perhaps the very earliest meaning of the word was "a town-crier," the man who went through the streets of a town making announcements; then later, we see him as an attendant to a BAILIFF or a SHERIFF. Still later, he appears as an apparitor, an officer prepared to execute the order of a magistrate. Always he seems to have carried something in his hand—a staff, a club, a mace, some symbol of authority. It is not known just when the universities adopted this official to precede their dignitaries in academic processions, but that seems to be his sole function nowadays. Oddly enough, even in modern times, the spellings vary: at Oxford it is Bedel and at Cambridge it is Bedell. The earliest record of the name I can find is in 1066: Brictmarus Bedel; then, in 1148, there is Richard Budel. In 1327, there was Robert le Budel; in 1541, Richard Bedle; in 1655, John Biddle, and in 1664, William Beadle.

A famous BEADLE of the present time is Doctor George W. Beadle, Nobel Prize winner in genetics, lecturer at Oxford University, and one-time president of the University of Chicago.

BURSAR nearly always means the treasurer of the university. The name derives from *bursa,* meaning a purse for keeping money.

FELLOW, FELLOWES, or FELLOWS were members of the faculty or at least graduate students. The Old English root is *feolaga.* Walter Felagh is listed in 1256.

MACE was a name given occasionally to a BEDEL, as he always carried a mace as a symbol of his authority.

MARSTERS, MASTER, and MASTERS derive from the Old French word *maistre,* meaning "master." The name is used in many nonacademic activities too. John Maister appears in 1225 and John Mastere in 1379.

MENTOR comes from a Greek word meaning "counselor." It is still used in universities to mean an instructor.

TUTOR comes from another Old French origin, *tutour,* meaning a university official who supervises the study of a group of students.

VERGER and VIRGER come from the Old French word *verge,* meaning a rod that was carried as a symbol of office in front of a dean, a bishop or a justice.

WARDEN was always a guard of some kind and, at Oxford at least, one of the Colleges has a WARDEN as its head. Other colleges there call their heads PROVOSTS, DEANS, or PROCTORS.

GROUP 186

Bookbinders

Books were precious in the Middle Ages. They had to be hand-made operations from start to finish. Every word had to be either written or hand-lettered with quill pens and brushes. When this was done, the pages of vellum would be gathered together in the indicated order, sewed with waxed cord, and placed between fine leather covers—to last for centuries if given reasonable care.

The names that come from the ancient craft of bookbinding are not numerous, because very few men followed that craft. There was a William le Bokbynder in 1333 and a Huge le Binder in 1219.

GROUP 187

Doctors

If a doctor from ancient Greece or Rome could have suddenly found himself transported from the Tiber to the Thames in the twelfth century, it would not be suspected that he was centuries out of date. There were no doctors in the modern sense of the word. Anybody could prescribe for illness if the patient were willing; no training at all was required, just the desire to diagnose and prescribe.

The anatomy of the human, aside from what could be observed from the outside, was virtually unknown. Surgery was, by custom, largely confined to the BARBERS. Therapy was based on bloodletting, cupping, baths, emetics, purgatives, and an incredible and ever-increasing conglomeration of organic and inorganic mixtures, practically none of which was understood by even the most skilled practitioner of the time.

This, then, was the practice of medicine in medieval England. But before bemoaning the so-called Dark Ages, it should be remembered that medical knowledge was only very slightly advanced in either England or America as recently as the early nineteenth century—fully five hundred years after the medieval doctor had passed from the scene. Nineteenth-century doctors were still cupping and bleeding and purging, and virtually anybody could call himself a doctor.

The names in this group do not tell us much that we don't already know. The BARBER names, from the Old French word *barbier*, refer to men who could give you a shave or cut off a sore finger that didn't seem to get better by itself. John le Barbur is in the records of London in 1221, and Robert le Barbier appears in 1213.

The BLOOD, BLEDER, and BLODLETER names are quite obvious. A doctor would know his exact treatment before he saw the patient, and the patient would know just what his prescription would be before the doctor arrived. *Blodlaeters* is the Old English origin. William Bledere is listed in 1293 and Adam le Blodeleter a bit later.

Both of the CUPPER names and VENTOSER were also names of bloodletters, only they did it by means of a suction cup. The origin of VENTOSER is the Old French word *ventouseur*, which meant a man skilled in the use of the suction cup. One example of the name is Richard le Ventoser in 1279.

FISICIEN, PHYSICK, and VISICK are Middle English terms that meant "doctor." These men prescribed cathartics for just about everything. John le Fisicien appears in 1269.

The name PHYSICK brings to mind an interesting man. Some *twenty generations* after the naming period, a man with the name appears in Philadelphia. And he is not just another doctor, but so famous for his magnificent work in medicine that he is known as the father of American surgery. I refer to Dr. Philip S. Physick, born in Philadelphia in 1768 and died in 1837. It is well known that when the future Dr. Physick was a young man, he wanted to be a goldsmith, to follow in the footsteps of his grandfather, but his own father induced him to study medicine, which he did to the everlasting benefit of today's surgical practice.

The LECHE names come from the Anglo-Saxon word *laece,* meaning "doctor." Later the term was to be applied to the bloodsucking worm that the doctors used on patients. There is a John Lache and an Edmund le Leche in 1227.

The entire MAYER group is hard to pin down to one origin because of the confusion between the Old French words *maire,* a town official, and *mire,* one who treats the sick. We can't be sure whether William le Maier in 1243 was mayor of his town or a doctor, and we must entertain the same doubts about Henry Meyer in 1275.

NORREYS, NORRIS, and NORRISS might seem to have no connection with medicine, but in fact there is an Old French word *norrice* or *nourrice* meaning "nurse." In the course of years, the name settled down to our modern Norris. It is interesting to note that even back in the fourteenth century, the word was feminine. Alice la Norrise is recorded in 1310 and Agnes le Norice in 1374.

A SOUKER's or SUCKER's method of treating a patient is obvious from the name. I find a William le Soukere in 1325.

The SURGEN group of four names indicates a medical man, but not a surgeon in the modern sense. The names derive from the Anglo-French *surgien.* There was a Thomas le Surigien in 1255.

GROUP 188

Champions or Mercenaries

Before the day of jury trials, there were many methods of trying to ascertain the guilt or innocence of a prisoner. One of these was the trial by battle. The accused man was forced to stand up and fight against either the man who was supposed to have been injured or damaged in the affair or some substitute engaged for the purpose. The accused man might also engage a proxy. The winner of the fight won the case.

In criminal cases the accused and the injured usually appeared personally, but in disputes over land and property proxies were more usual.

Such proxies became more or less professional fighters and were called CHAMPIONS from a French word *champiun,* meaning "a fighter." There was a Geoffrey Champiun in 1154. A BEATER or a FENDER was in the same business. FENDER meant a defender like Thomas le Fender in 1301.

BATTELL, BATTLE, and BATTYLL, as well as POYNER, POYNOR, and PUNYER, were also men who fought for money. They come from an Old French word *poigneor* meaning "fighter."

GROUP 189

Military Engineers

There are only a small number of names on this list because only a small number of men could qualify as engineers in medieval times. A man had to be a combination master stonemason, woodworker, blacksmith, and architect—a big order. And such a man would be priceless to any king or prince fortunate enough to have his services.

Before the arrival of the Conqueror in 1066, Anglo-Saxon England was dotted with wooden manor houses surrounded by wooden palisades, but in the following century very large numbers of these were replaced with great stone fortresses built on strategic sites that could withstand the siege of an army many times the size of the garrison.

These great stone castles changed the whole procedure of medieval warfare from a disorganized rabble made up of nobles on horses accompanied by a swarm of poorly armed peasants meeting an exactly similar army on an open field. Hand-to-hand fighting was the result, and the side with the greater manpower would be the winner.

With a castle, things were very different. Here, one sat in a strongly fortified building stocked with enough food and water to last all hands for months. The livestock from all the surrounding area were pulled into an enclosure provided, and the only way an enemy could win was either to batter down the walls of the castle or to surround it with a huge army and maintain a state of siege for months until the castle food supplies eventually gave out.

In the meantime, the garrison would not be idle—the engineers would develop missile weapons. They would hardly compare with modern missiles, of course, but for a distance of three hundred or more yards from the outer walls of the castle, they could make things decidedly uncomfortable for the enemy.

We have already covered the crossbow in chapter 8 (page 79). This was not original with the medieval engineers, but it was greatly improved by them. Instead of a bow made from wood, they developed one made of steel with a great deal more power than a wooden bow could ever give. Pulling the string of the steel bow back to where it would be held by the lock required so much muscle that a mechanical contrivance had to be invented to accomplish this. And, indeed, a huge siege crossbow was developed. It had a steel bow that might be fifteen feet long, mounted horizontally on a permanent base atop the castle keep. A large windlass was required to pull the cord back, but when that was done, the machine could be loaded with a stone weighing as much as a man, and fired at the machine. of the enemy a considerable distance away.

In at least one respect, things were no different than they are today— a new weapon always produces a new defense against it. The besieging enemy had to take its engineers along. Once before the castle, where they could test out the garrison's equipment, they had to devise and build, on the spot, equipment to open a breach in the castle wall that would enable their own army to enter. This was a normal situation in medieval warfare. An attacking army could not transport heavy equipment any distance so, once it was determined on the spot what equipment was necessary, field shops and forges had to be set up to make it. This must have taken extraordinary skill and resourcefulness.

A battering ram, for example, might consist of nothing but a log thirty or more feet long. It could be carried right up to the wall by a force of strong men, and holding it with short pieces of sapling at waist height, they could eventually knock a hole in the wall. But in the meantime the defenders would be dropping big stones down on their heads, making any prolonged stand out of the question. The engineers countered that by building a portable roof completely covering the ram and its crew.

Then there were the great portable towers built of wood and mounted on wooden wheels. The whole tower could be rolled up to the castle wall with a dozen archers in it protected from the arrows of the defenders by the wooden walls. Inside would be ladders so the archers could climb to the top of the tower, where they could shoot down at the defenders.

The mangonel was a machine designed to throw sizable stones over the wall and directly at the castle keep, where the defending noble and his family might be hit. The ballista was another piece designed for the same purpose but depending for its power like the crossbow on the elasticity of wooden planks.

Mining was a favorite scheme for attacking any place with a stone wall around it. It must have taken many weeks of very hard labor but it would succeed if done carefully and if luck were with the attackers. In a spot hidden by trees or brush, men would be set to work digging a tunnel toward the castle wall. As they went forward, they would shore up the earth overhead with timbers. If undiscovered, they would drive this tunnel clear under the castle wall, taking care to shore up the section actually under the wall and bearing its weight. When all this was done, providing the enemy still had not discovered what was going on, a fire would be started in the tunnel under the wall. The men would with-draw and wait for the fire to do its work. This might take many hours or even days, but the fire would eventually burn the supporting timbers and the wall protecting the castle would come tumbling down.

But let us look at some of the descriptive names given to these re-sourceful men. In Middle English times, there was a habit of dropping off first syllables from many words. For example, with the Old French *engin,* which meant "clever," "skillful," or "ingenious," the English dropped the *en* and just used *gin;* as time went on, it became GINN, or GINNER, or GYNN. Thus we find a man named Roger Gin in 1191 and a Walter Gynn in 1275.

The French-speaking Normans had a word *engigneor* or sometimes *enginior* (still with the *gin*) that they used when they wanted to refer to a man with real skill in building military things. And so we have our modern English word *engineer.* I find a Walter Jenour in 1327, a Robert le Ginnur in 1230, a Ralph Gynnour in 1301, and even a William le Engynnur in 1255. There is also a Richard Lenginnur in 1191. To get Lenginnur, the French article *le* was put back in.

MANGNALL and its two variants come from the old French word *mangonelle,* and refers to the machine for throwing huge stones men-tioned before. The name of the machine would sooner or later be associated with the inventor of it, or at least a favorite operator, and the name would far outlast the machine. There was a Geoffrey Mangwinel in 1204 and a Stephen Manguinel in 1212.

GROUP 184

Men Who Could Read and Write

Bunclarke	Latner	•	Scrivens
Clark	Lattimer	Scribbler	Scrivin
Clarke	Lattimore	Scribe	Scrivings
Cleric	Lattiner	Scribner	Scriueyn
Clerk	•	Scripter	Escriueyn
Clerke	Marker	Scriptor	•
•	•	Scripture	Teacher
Graff	Nutter	Scriven	•
•	•	Scrivener	Writer
Latimer	Penman	Scrivenor	Wryter

GROUP 185

University Personnel

Beadel	Biddles	Fellow	Prockter
Beadell	Buddell	Fellowes	Procter
Beadle	Buddle	Fellows	Proctor
Beadles	Buddles	•	•
Beddall	•	Mace	Provost
Bedel	Bursar	•	•
Bedell	•	Marsters	Tutor
Bedells	Cancellor	Master	•
Bedle	Chancellor	Masters	Verger
Beedell	•	•	Virger
Beedle	Dean	Mentor	•
Biddell	•	•	Warden
Biddle			

GROUP 186

Bookbinders

Binder	Block	Bookbinder
Binders	Blocker	Buckman

GROUP 187

Doctors

Barber	Cuppman	Lecher	Meier
Barbour	•	Leech	Meyer
•	Fisicien	Leetch	Meyers
Bleder	Physick	Leitch	•
Blodleter	Visick	•	Norreys
Blood	•	Mayer	
•	Leach	Mayers	
Cupper	Leche	Mayor	

Norris	Souker	Surgen	Surgeoner
Norriss	Sucker	Surgenor	•
•	•	Surgeon	Ventoser

GROUP 188

Champions or Mercenaries

Battell	Beater	Campion	•
Battle	Better	Champion	Poyner
Battyll	Bettor	•	Poynor
•	•	Fender	Punyer

GROUP 189

Military Engineers

Engynour	Ginner	Jenoure	Manknell
Genner	Gynn	•	
Genower	Gynour	Mangnall	
Ginn	Jenner	Mangold	

Selected Bibliography

AIRNE, C. W. *The Story of Medieval Britain*. Manchester, England: Sankey Hudson & Co., 1930.

———. *The Story of Saxon and Norman Britain*. Manchester, England: Sankey Hudson & Co., 1930.

AMERICAN SPICE TRADE ASSOCIATION. *Treasury of Spices*. Baltimore: Pridemark Press, 1956.

APPLEBY, JOHN T. *England without Richard, 1189 to 1199*. Ithaca, N.Y.: Cornell University Press, 1965.

BARDSLEY, CHARLES WAREING. *A Dictionary of English Surnames*. Baltimore: Genealogical Publishing Co., 1967.

———. *English Surnames*. Rutland, Vt.: Charles E. Tuttle Co., Inc., 1968.

BARING-GOULD, S. *Family Names and Their Story*. 1910. Reprint. Detroit: Gale Research Co., 1969.

BRAGG, SIR WILLIAM. *Old Trades and New Knowledge*. London: G. Bell & Sons Ltd., 1945.

BRANCH, NEWTON. *This Britain*. New York: Harper & Row, Publishers, 1951.

BRANTL, RUTH. *Medieval Culture*. New York: George Braziller, Inc., 1966.

CHEYNEY, EDWARD P. *A Short History of England*. Boston: Ginn and Company, 1945.

———. *The Dawn of a New Era: 1250 to 1453*. New York: G. P. Putnam's Sons, 1936.

Collier's Cyclopedia of Commercial and Social Information. Compiled by Nugent Robinson. New York: Peter Fenelon Collier, Publisher, 1882.

COTTLE, BASIL. *Penguin Dictionary of Surnames*. Baltimore: Penguin Books, Inc., 1967.

CUTTS, EDWARD LEWS. *Scenes and Characters of the Middle Ages*. London: Virtue and Co., 1872.

DAVIS, WILLIAM STEARNS. *Life on a Medieval Barony*. 13th ed. New York: Harper & Bros., 1936.

EHRLICH, BLAKE. *London on the Thames*. Boston: Little, Brown and Co., 1966.

Encyclopaedia Britannica. All volumes 1968 ed. Chicago: Encyclopaedia Britannica, Inc.

Encyclopaedia Britannica. Facsimile of the 1766 ed. Chicago: Encyclopaedia Britannica, Inc., 1966.

FEATHERSTONE, DONALD. *The Bowmen of England*. New York: Clarkson N. Potter, Inc., 1968.

FRANSSON, GUSTAV. *Middle English Surnames of Occupation*. 1935 reprint. Nendeln Lichtenstein: Kraus Reprint Ltd., 1967.

FREY, ALBERT R. *Sobriquets and Nicknames*. Boston: Ticknor & Co., 1888.

GEOFFREY OF MONMOUTH. *History of the Kings of Britain*. London: J. M. Dent & Sons, Ltd., 1944.

HANSON, MICHAEL. *Two Thousand Years of London*. London: Country Life Ltd., 1967.

HILL, THOMAS E. *Hill's Album of Biography and Art.* New York: Banks & Co., 1890.

HISSEY, JAMES JOHN. *The Road and the Inn.* London: Macmillan & Co. Ltd., 1917.

HOYT, ROBERT S. *Europe in the Middle Ages.* New York: Harcourt, Brace & Co., Inc., 1957.

HUGHES, PHILIP. *A Popular History of the Catholic Church.* Garden City, N.Y.: Doubleday & Co., 1953.

JAMESON, STORM. *The Decline of Merry England.* Indianapolis: The Bobbs–Merrill Co., Inc., 1930.

KOLATCH, ALFRED J. *The Name Dictionary.* New York: Jonathan David Publishers, Inc., 1967.

LACROIX, PAUL. *Military and Religious Life in the Middle Ages.* New York: Frederick Ungar Publishing Co., Inc., 1964.

LATHAM, EDWARD. *A Dictionary of Names, Nicknames and Surnames.* 1904. Reprint. Detroit: Gale Research Co., 1968.

LLOYD, ALAN. *The Making of the King, 1066.* New York: Holt, Rinehart & Winston, Inc., 1966.

LOW, ARCHIBALD MONTGOMERY. *The Past Presented.* London: P. Davies, 1952.

LUNT, W. E. *History of England,* New York: Harper & Bros. Publishers, 1938.

MARTI-IBAÑEZ, FELIX, M.D. *The Epic of Medicine.* New York: Clarkson N. Potter, Inc., 1962.

MATEAUX, C. L. *The Wonderland of Work.* London: Cassell & Company, Ltd. Undated but clearly written about 1890.

MATTHEWS, C. M. *English Surnames.* New York: Charles Scribner's Sons, 1967.

MENCKEN, HENRY LOUIS. *American Language.* New York: Alfred A. Knopf, Inc., 1936.

MONCREIFFE OF THAT ILK AND HICKS, DAVID. *The Highland Clans.* New York: Clarkson N. Potter, Inc., 1967.

NATIONAL GEOGRAPHIC SOCIETY. *This England.* Washington, D.C.: National Geographic, 1965.

O'DONNELL, BERNARD. *Cavalcade of Justice.* New York: The Macmillan Co., 1952.

QUENNELL, MARJORIE. *A History of Everyday Things in England.* London: B. T. Batsford Ltd., 1963.

——. *Everyday Life in Roman and Anglo-Saxon Times.* New York: G. P. Putnam's Sons, 1959.

REANEY, P. H. *Dictionary of British Surnames.* 3rd ed. London: Routledge and Kegan Paul, Ltd., 1966.

——. *The Origin of English Surnames.* London: Routledge and Kegan Paul, Ltd., 1967.

RUSSELL, CARL. *Firearms, Traps, and Tools of the Mountain Men.* New York: Alfred A. Knopf, Inc., 1967.

SALZMANN, L. F. *English Industries of the Middle Ages.* Boston: Houghton Mifflin Co., 1913.

SHOOK, JOHN. *The Book of Weaving.* London: John Day & Co., 1928.

SINGER, CHARLES. *History of Technology.* 5 vols. New York: Oxford University Press, Inc., 1915.

SMITH, CHARD POWERS. *The Housatonic.* New York: Holt, Rinehart & Winston, Inc., 1946.

SMITH, ELSDON C. *American Surnames.* Philadelphia: Chilton Book Co., 1969.

SULLIVAN, RT. REV. MSGR. JOHN F. *The Externals of the Catholic Church.* New York: P. J. Kenedy & Sons, 1951.

SWANK, JAMES H. *History of the Manufacture of Iron in All Ages.* New York: Burt Franklin, 1965.

THATCHER, OLIVER J. *A Short History of Medieval Europe.* Meadville, Pa.: Flood & Vincent, 1897.

TOZIER, JOSEPHINE. *Among English Inns.* Boston: L. C. Page & Co., 1904.

TUNIS, EDWIN. *Colonial Craftsmen.* Cleveland: World Publishing Co., 1965.

VALENTINE, L. *Picturesque England, Its Landmarks and Historic Haunts.* London: Frederick Warne & Co., 1891.

WOODS, GEORGE B.; WATT, HOMER A.; and ANDERSON, GEORGE K. *The Literature of England.* Chicago: Scott, Foresman and Company, 1941.

INDEX OF SURNAMES